ESSAYS IN MUSICOLOGY

Dragan Plamenac

essays in musicology

IN HONOR OF DRAGAN PLAMENAC
ON HIS 70th BIRTHDAY

Edited by
Gustave Reese and
Robert J. Snow

UNIVERSITY · OF · PITTSBURGH · · · PRESS

SBN 8229-1098-5
Library of Congress Catalog Card Number: 68-12731

Manufactured in the United States of America

Editors' Preface

THE plan to publish a collection of musicological essays as a tribute to Dragan Plamenac on his seventieth birthday originated in 1961. At that time the editors hoped—much too optimistically, as it later proved—that they would be able to have the volume issued by the appropriate day. Several circumstances prevented this, and on Professor Plamenac's seventieth birthday it was possible to present to him no more than an incomplete list of the proposed contents. In due course, however, the complete manuscript was assembled and submitted to the publishers, but other unavoidable delays ensued. The editors wish to express their regrets for the lateness of the volume and to present their apologies to all concerned.

The editors also wish to express their gratitude to those at the University of Pittsburgh Press who aided in the production of the book, especially Miss Bonnie Harrington, who removed many burdens from the shoulders of the editors, to Dr. Norris Stephens, Music Librarian of the University of Pittsburgh, who assisted in many ways, and to Mrs. Allen Cooper, who helped with the music examples.

GUSTAVE REESE

ROBERT J. SNOW

Autour de Plamenac

THE mind of Dragan Plamenac has the many-sidedness that Enobarbus found in the charms of the fabulous Egyptian. Its variety has at one time led him to pursue the study of law. At other times, that versatility has virtually turned him into a full-fledged philologist, notably in the field of French poetry of the Renaissance. After studying composition with Franz Schreker (1912–13) and with others, he showed accomplished craftsmanship as a composer, though he has produced little in this capacity. In 1925–26, he functioned as coach and assistant conductor under Bruno Walter at the Berlin Städtische Oper. During World War II, he served the Office of War Information, a zealous American broadcasting messages to his native Yugoslavia. As a teacher, he is one of the most distinguished and effective of those who have been instructing a new generation and have thereby been developing American musicology into the vigorous young Hercules that it is. But he has certainly made his largest and most enduring contribution in the role of a practicing musicologist.

Just as Dragan Plamenac will be able to function as his own philologist in dealing with the texts of Ockeghem's chansons, if and when he gets around to completing the third, final volume of his collected edition of that composer, so, if he had become a lawyer and if the need had arisen, would he have been able to be his own professional investigator in hunting down evidence. What member of the bar could evolve a brief more ingeniously than he has within the article in which he identifies the Seigneur Léon addressed in an anonymous fifteenth-century chanson as a person almost certainly known to Dufay and argues that the piece is a work by that composer? He has made his case so convincingly that Heinrich Besseler has included the chanson in his collected edition of Dufay—and not as an *opus dubium*. His discovery of the *L'Homme armé* text in 1925 and of new facts about the composer of his quondam preoccupation in *Autour d'Ockeghem* (1928); his more recent casting of "New Light" on the last years of C.P.E. Bach; his rescue of an unknown violin tablature of the early seventeenth century from oblivion and of the "Second" Chansonnier of the Biblioteca Riccardiana from undeserved neglect; his unearthing of buried information while pretending to browse through a little-known manuscript of the Strahov Monastery in Prague; his ascertaining that the folios pasted to the binding boards and to the blank leaf at the end of a codex at Padua preserve vocal polyphony of the second half of the fourteenth century; his outstandingly important finds: that a section of the manuscript, Nouv. acquis. franç. 4379 at the Bibliothèque Nationale in Paris, actually consists of missing portions of the French chansonnier at the Biblioteca Colombina in Seville, and that some music preserved in a manuscript at Faenza, music whose existence was already known but whose nature had been seriously misjudged, is in fact a highly significant repertory of late medieval keyboard compositions and arrangements—all this reveals the alert, knowledgeable, and inspired musical scholar. A survey of the complete list of his works—which includes also valuable articles on Yugoslav music and editions of it—reveals, besides, a linguist able to write for publication in at least four languages without the help of any translator.

Admittedly, the elements that go into the making of a "detective" like Plamenac are to be found in other musicologists too. It is in the very nature of things that these elements should be present to some extent in any scholar who advances from the stage of learning to that of doing. In Plamenac, however, they combine into a flair that is uncommonly powerful and conspicuously successful. Nevertheless, there are times when one looks upon this flair with something less than utter rapture and wishes it were present in greater moderation. Perhaps he would then settle down long enough to finish his edition of Ockeghem. It is characteristic of the man that the music that formed the subject of his Ph.D. dissertation, *J. Ockeghem als Motetten- und Chansonkomponist* (1925), is the very portion of the composer's output that he has not yet included in the edition. To the extent that Plamenac has worked on this magnum opus for direct publication, he has felt driven to concern himself primarily with those compositions he had not yet, in his dissertation, studied in the minutest detail.

Whatever reservations we may have about our friend's persistent flair, we can take comfort in the indisputable fact that custom has not staled the warmth and spontaneity of his character. One little anecdote will perhaps suffice to illustrate his capacity for generosity and tact. Ordinarily uncomplicated, frank, and outgoing, he can nevertheless bring considerable subtlety to bear upon the doing of a kind deed. As the summer of 1948 approached, I was getting ready to go back to a portion of the uncompleted *Music in the Renaissance* that I had skipped and to write the section on Ockeghem. At the same time, Plamenac was preparing for one of his many trips to Europe. As the time for his departure drew near, he paid my wife and me one of his ever-welcome visits. Something seemed to disturb him. He said that he was greatly worried about sailing away and leaving his large and invaluable file on Ockeghem unguarded in his apartment. Suppose there should be a fire! Would we be kind enough, he pleaded, to take the file under our roof and protect it? If I wished to refer to it while writing my section on Ockeghem, it was entirely at my disposal for any use I chose to make of it. And he added, in an apologetic tone, that he did not think the file would really take too much room. So convincing an actor was he that a long time elapsed before I realized that, after all, this file had often been left unguarded before (as it has been since) and that this was simply his delicate, unpatronizing way of making the finest existing body of material on Ockeghem available to a friend whom it could profit.

The many who hold Dragan Plamenac in esteem and affection may rejoice not only that his mind reveals infinite variety, but also that age shows little sign of withering the man himself. This happy circumstance is no doubt due in large part to an excellent constitution inherited from his unforgettable mother. That elegant and lovable lady retained her fluency in four languages and her skill in handling the painter's brush and palette until well after her ninetieth birthday. No tribute to Dragan would be complete that did not include also a tribute to her. The prospects are highly favorable that her son will prove equally durable—and that he will even last long enough to complete Ockeghem Volume III and many other works after it!

GUSTAVE REESE

Contents

Plates

ESSAYS IN MUSICOLOGY

1 / Josquin and "La belle Tricotée"

ALAN CURTIS
University of California, Berkeley

Je me complains de mon amy
Qui me souloit tant venir veoir
La freische matinée.
Or est il prime et s'est midi
Et si n'oy nouvelle de luy
S'aproche la vesprée.
La tricoton, la tricoton,
La belle tricotée.

ONE of the most problematical, and one of the best, of Josquin's chansons is the five-part lament, *Je me complains.*[1] That it is indeed a lament one assumes from the first glance. Certainly one cannot doubt the composer's intent in setting the doleful opening line to a descending tetrachord, that harbinger of grief which was to become, during the two and a half centuries that separate (or rather connect) Josquin and Mozart, the very stereotype of sorrow. Yet if we look more closely, and particularly if we examine the setting of the curious final line, we find rapid repeated notes, and, for tenor and bass, virtuoso scalar runs utterly unbefitting a solemn plaint. To reconcile beginning and end, in this short piece, requires a probe into the possible meanings of the poem. From the more practical standpoint of performance, it also necessitates a compromise in choice

1. Published in Tylman Susato's famed *Septiesme livre* (Antwerp, 1545), fol. 7; modern edition by A. Smijers, nr. 11 of Josquin, *Wereldlijke Werken* (Amsterdam, 1925). Our text follows Susato.

of tempo, so that both extremes may live within the same piece, subject to the same basic pulse.

Of the two principal recordings which have been made of *Je me complains,* neither represents such a compromise but they serve to illustrate the extremes. Safford Cape chooses a very rapid tempo, which he attempts to justify in asserting that "one of the artifices of late mediaeval and Renaissance literature was to express sorrowful or terrible things in a light and carefree manner. This artifice continued to be applied in the seventeenth- and eighteenth-century French popular ditty, and is akin to a certain spirit found in the Nursery Rhymes. Josquin expresses in an off-hand and carefree way a girl's regret that her lover did not appear when expected. This bravura piece might well be entitled 'fire-works' for it calls for uncommon virtuosity, especially in the tenor parts."[2]

It is true that the tenor part is not easy, and both tenor and contratenor must sing the range of a thirteenth. Yet of "virtuosity" or "fireworks" there is none in the rendition conducted by Marcel Couraud, who chooses a most lugubrious pace. Though he clearly takes the piece as a serious lament, he cannot help remarking, in reference to the last line, that "la coda, haute en couleur, fortement scandée, semble là pour créer une opposition nette, presque brutale, avec tout ce qui précède."[3]

Let us examine the "opposition" which the last line presents. Cape translates the poem as follows: "I am sad because of my lover,/ Who often came to see me/ In the fresh morning-time/ But now it's Prime and on to noon/ And so I have no news of him/ As evening comes on./ Knit Knit, Fine knitting."[4] In this interpretation, we see the girl as a kind of Renaissance "Gretchen am Spinnrade," who sits not at her wheel but with her knitting basket, mourning her love; but although the agitation of a spinning wheel may call forth a musical portrayal of adolescent passion, the clatter of knitting needles could hardly be expected to summon deep feelings of any sort. Does Josquin's music have anything to do with knitting? Helmuth Reiffenstein considers it one of the six outstanding examples of

2. Safford Cape, "Josquin des Prez Secular Works," recording by Pro Musica Antiqua (E.M.S., #213).

3. Marcel Couraud, "13 Chansons françaises," recording by Marcel Couraud Ensemble (Les Discophiles français, #2379).

4. See note 2.

"tonmalerisches Erfassen einzelner Textworte in Josquins weltlichem Werk . . . " and finds that "la tricoton, la belle tricotée" is "durch eine langsam aufsteigende, federnde Viertelnotenbewegung mit plappernder Syllabik nachgezeichnet."[5]

French etymologists assure us, however, that "tricoter" did not acquire its modern sense until the late sixteenth century.[6] In the fifteenth and sixteenth centuries the word did not lack for use, but with meanings related to song and dance, not knitting. According to Godefroy's *Lexique*, "tricot" is a very old word for a stick, and "faire tricoter quelqu'un" meant to make someone dance by beating him with a stick. Another meaning was "faire l'amour." The original "belle tricotée" was probably "The Beaten One" in the latter sense; in any event, we find her often associated with "diableries" (*cf.* Godefroy), and the term "tricotée" or "tricotet" has a long low-life, lasting even into the eighteenth century, as we shall presently see. First, however, let us begin by noting the earliest musical sources to preserve a reference to "la belle tricotée."

In the tenor of a simple, light, three-voice chanson[7] from the mid-fifteenth century we find, as has already been pointed out by Howard Brown,[8] that the words are associated with essentially the same tune Josquin uses. Heinrich Besseler, speaking of the melody as found in this source, says, "Sein durchlaufender 6/8–Rhythmus mit Tanzcharakter war schon im 13. Jahrhundert so üblich. Offenbar handelt es sich um ein Spielmannslied im 1. Modus, dessen Entstehungszeit wir nicht kennen."[9] Unknown to Besseler was its appearance in duple meter not only in the chanson of Josquin, but in at least two settings of similar or earlier date: as contratenor for a three-voice quodlibet,[10] and as upper voice in *La tricotea Samàrtin la vea,* a

5. H. Reiffenstein, *Die weltlichen Werke des Josquin des Prez* (Inaugural dissertation, Frankfurt a. M., 1952), p. 51.

6. See, for instance, O. Bloch and W. von Wartburg, *Dictionnaire étymologique de la langue française* (Paris, 1960).

7. Bologna, Liceo Musicale, Q.15 (olim 37). Modern ed. in B. Disertori, *La Frottola* (Cremona, 1954), pp. xxxiv f.

8. H. Brown, *Music in the French Secular Theater,* 1400–1500 (Cambridge, Mass., 1963), pp. 251 f. See also A. Curtis, *Dutch Keyboard Music of the 16th and 17th Centuries,* Monumenta musica Neerlandica, III (Amsterdam, 1961), xxx f.

9. H. Besseler, *Bourdon und Fauxbourdon* (Leipzig, 1950), pp. 211 f.

10. Escorial, IV.a.24 (Cited by Besseler); modern ed. in H. Brown, *Theatrical Chansons* (Cambridge, 1963), pp. 170 f., and P. Gülke, "Das Volkslied in der burgundischen Polyphonie des 15. Jahrhunderts," *Festschrift Heinrich Besseler* (Leipzig, 1961), pp. 198 f.

Spanish reworking of the tune, set by "Alonso." The latter incidentally forms an interesting example of the penetration of the popular French idiom into the repertory represented by the famed Cancionero de Palacio.[11]

Apart from the word "tricotea," the Spanish text seems to bear no resemblance to that of the fifteenth-century French chansons. They, in turn, are far from being in total concordance with each other. Both share, however, amid corruptions, nonsense, and either unintelligible or illegible words, the one clear statement that "la tricotée fut par matin levée." Not much to go on, to be sure, yet do we not sense here a possible connection with "la freische matinée"? More to the point, if we solemnly reread the little poem (or sing it again at a mournful pace), does the lady's expectance of her lover, regularly, at an early morning hour, ring totally true, pure, and touchingly innocent? No, Josquin must have meant the piece as a satire—warm-hearted and sympathetic, perhaps, but nonetheless a mock-lament, ending with the ridiculing laughter of a vulgar ditty. Whether the poem had more verses, clarifying the satirical intent, whether they all ended with the refrain "La tricoton, etc.", or whether Josquin added it himself, we may never know. A peek into the past history of "la belle tricotée" at least helps explain some part of the enigma of Josquin's music.

It would be pleasant if we could now demonstrate an unbroken line of descent from the fifteenth-century (or even earlier?) *tricotée* tune, through the *tricotet* dances of the seventeenth century, to Rameau's well-known *Les Tricotets* (*Nouvelles Suites*, c. 1728): an unknown underworld link between Josquin and Rameau! Unfortunately, no amount of effort in reducing Rameau's charming *rondeau* to its *Urlinie* could possibly prove any such melodic connection. Yet somewhere a remote link does exist. That the *tricotée* tune was taken over into instrumental music, its words forgotten, and its melodic shape drastically altered, is proved by the appearance in a peripheral source of a piece titled *Almande trycottee.*[12] It was copied among simple psalm settings, Lassus' *Susanne un jour*, and popular dances,

11. Madrid, Cancionero de Palacio; modern ed. in H. Anglés, *Monumentos de la música española,* X (Barcelona, 1951), 20 f.

12. London, British Museum, Add. 29485. The entire manuscript has been edited, with commentary, by the author (see note 8 above). For the *Almande Trycottee,* see p. 37 and the illustration p. xlvi.

in the keyboard book used by a young Dutch girl in London at the very end of the sixteenth century. Without the title, one would certainly never, even on repeated hearings, find any connection between this piece and Josquin's *Je me complains.* But since there the title is, we cannot help noticing that whereas Josquin stresses one salient feature of the tune—the repeated strokes of the fifth to the third degrees—the little keyboard dance stresses another: the opening 1–7–6–(7)–1–5. If we simplify this still further to 1–7–1–5,[13] we can accept the hypothesis of Daniel Heartz that "la belle tricotée" is behind the tune *Je suis Cassandre,* which in turn begets the famous *Vive Henri IV*—both deeply involved in the history of France from Ronsard through the nineteenth century.[14] In defense of this conjecture, we might add that it would be strange were it only coincidence that in Benserade's *Ballet de Cassandre* (February 26, 1651),[15] which naturally makes use of *Je suis Cassandre,* there is danced the *tricotets poitevins* (by none other than Louis himself). Scarron mentions the *tricotets* together with "la Cassandre, le trémoussement et le saut" as being "danses de sabbat."[16] However, the further we try to follow the instrumental history of the tune, the more pointless it becomes to attempt to trace melodic connections. A tune implies a harmonic progression, a phrase length, or a rhythmic pattern, which becomes associated with a dance step, to which, for the sake of variety, ultimately a new tune is added.

Unfortunately, none of the early books on dancing which we have been able to consult contains any description of the *tricotet.* However, Curt Sachs, without quoting any source, gives the following account: "Tricoté. On the first count the right foot moves out of the fifth position behind the heel of the left foot; on the second count the left heel is lifted and the foot glides into the first position beside the right foot; on the third count the right foot glides into the fifth

13. If, in turn, we reduce it to 1–7–6–5, we find it not totally out of the question that the strange word "Trigalore," opening the tenor part of a triple chanson in the French Chansonnier at the Biblioteca Colombina, Seville, might be a corruption or variant of "tricoton" or "tricotée" and the first few notes of this tenor part a reference to the tricotée tune. See Dragan Plamenac, "A Reconstruction of the French Chansonnier in the Biblioteca Colombina, Seville," *Musical Quarterly,* XXXVII (1951), 521–22 and 534–35.

14. Article "Vaudeville" in *Die Musik in Geschichte und Gegenwart.*

15. For an extensive bibliography, see P. Bjurström, *Giacomo Torelli and Baroque Stage Design* (Stockholm, 1962), p. 127.

16. *Oeuvres,* VIII, 378.

position in front of the left foot; on the fourth count the left foot is lifted slightly off the floor. Both feet are always kept close together."[17]

The quoted description accords ill with the standard late seventeenth- and early eighteenth-century dictionary definition: "sorte de danse élevée et en ronde." Whatever the dance steps may have been, it seems they were often associated, from the mid-seventeenth until the early eighteenth centuries at least, with three-bar phrases. This would suggest a connection between the *tricotets poitevins*, cited above, and the *branles de Poitou*, as well as the earliest *menuets (de Poitou)*. Yet two examples copied (by Matthias Weckmann?) in the Yale Hintze manuscript[18] are ascribed to other parts of France. They are given here as an appendix not only because they are hitherto unpublished, but also because they well illustrate the two *tricotet* tunes most frequent in the seventeenth and eighteenth centuries. That marked "de Paris" was commonly called *vieux tricotets*, and those termed *nouveaux* are usually variants of the tune here marked "de Blois." An English version, likewise published here for the first time, from a late seventeenth-century manuscript containing mainly keyboard works of John Blow,[19] is also given, to illustrate the kinds of variant that circulated, and to show what happened to the three-bar phrase when it crossed the Channel. It must have crossed back again, to judge from the following Low German or Dutch corruption of an English-French *tricotet:* "Letriquotets gloterre fransch." The title occurs on page 247 of a keyboard manuscript of 1662 in the Bomann-Museum, Celle. Earlier in the same source, on page 163, is "Los Tricotets Fransch."

In France, the *tricotet* as a dance seems to have enjoyed a brief but truly upper-class vogue around 1650: not only was it danced by Louis in 1651, but according to J. Loret in the *Muze historique* for June 5 of the same year, at Bois-le-Vicomte:

> . . . Tout son divertissement
> N'est que d'avoir bien quoy frire,
> Que de courir, cauzer et rire,
> Que de prendre de bons bouillons,
> Que d'exercer des violons,

17. C. Sachs, *World History of the Dance* (New York, 1937), p. 404.
18. New Haven, Conn., Library of the Yale Music School, MS. 21.H.59, p. 11.
19. Oxford, Christ Church, MS. 1179, p. 18.

Danser un peu de chaque danse,
Et les Tricotets d'importance.[20]

References to the dance in England, however, seem to indicate a less than noble standing: "A Monkey dancing his Trick-a-tee on a rope" (1659); "poor Dido . . . tho' oppressed with Woe and Care, cut Capers, and Tricotee'd it barefoot" (1664); "The dancing Bears shall dance the Tricotees with him for a wager" (1667).[21] The 1752 edition of Boyer's popular French-English dictionary translates *Tricotet* as "a Cheshire Round," but this was probably only a vague approximation meant to indicate that just as the Cheshire Round was a type of country dance, so the *tricotet* was an "espèce de contredanse." By then both were likely regarded as somewhat vulgar and antiquated.

It was in a context of dances both bawdy and outmoded that Diderot referred to *les tricotets* in Chapitre 45 of his licentious little book, *Les bijoux indiscrets* (1748): ". . . l'un s'écriait d'une voix aigre: Violons, *le Carillon de Dunkerque,* s'il vous plaît; l'autre, d'une voix rauque: Et moi je veux les *Sautriots;* et moi *les Tricotets,* disait un troisième; et une multitude à la fois: Des contredanses usées, comme *la Bourrée, les Quatre Faces, la Calotine, la Chaîne, le Pistolet, la Mariée, le Pistolet, le Pistolet.* Tous ces cris étaient lardés d'un million d'extravagances."[22]

This may well be the most appropriate place to take leave of *la belle tricotée,* "lardée d'un million d'extravagances." Her double life as vulgar bawd (sung and danced in the streets and who knows where?) and polished courtesan (acquainted with such as Josquin, Rameau, and Louis XIV) comes to a gradual end with the fall of the *ancien régime.*

There remains only to correct a confusion of long standing. It is a curious coincidence, but nothing more, that Rameau's *Les Tricotets* (c. 1728), which has no connection at all with knitting, was written at about the same time as Couperin's *Les Tricoteuses* (*23e Ordre,* 1730), which has nothing whatever to do with the *tricotets.*

20. Quoted by A. Pirro in his article, "Louis Couperin," *La Revue Musicale,* I (Nov. 1920), 15. Cf. also p. 13 for a reference in 1465 to *la tricotée.*

21. All three references are taken from Murray and Craigie, *A New English Dictionary* (Oxford, 1926).

22. I wish to thank my colleague D. Heartz for calling this reference to my attention.

Triscottes de Paris (New Haven, Yale Univ., Hintz MS. Ma. 21. H59, p. 11).

Tricottes de Blois (New Haven, Yale Univ., Hintz MS. Ma. 21. H59, p. 11).

Trickatees (Oxford, Christ Church College, MS. 1179, p. 18).

2 / Jakob Zupan: The Last Master of the Slovenian Baroque

DRAGOTIN CVETKO
University of Ljubljana

THE first intimations of a change from the Baroque to the Classical style in Slovenian music appeared as early as the middle of the eighteenth century, and from that time onward the new stylistic concepts gradually established themselves there. The new style was introduced into the area by various individuals, and above all by German theatrical troupes, whose repertories at that time already consisted, at least in part, of works with a Classical orientation. The first Slovenian composer to utilize the new style in a definitive manner was J. B. Novak, who in 1790 set to music A. T. Linhart's comedy, *That Merry Day, or Matiček's Wedding* under the title *Figaro.*[1] Both Novak's use of this play and the music he wrote for it testify to a marked change in stylistic outlook, for the music proves to be closely related to the first period of Mozartian classicism.

However, the transition to the new stylistic concept was neither rapid nor smooth, for there were many factors at work which tended to preserve or at least prolong the domination of the Baroque style. On the one hand, visits by Italian opera singers continued without interruption during the first decades of the second half of the

1. See D. Cvetko, "J. B. Novak—ein slowenischer Anhänger Mozarts," *Bericht über den internationalen musikwissenschaftlichen Kongress, Wien, Mozart-Jahr 1956* (Graz-Köln, 1958), pp. 99–103; also "Mozarts Einfluss auf die slowenische Tonkunst zur Zeit der Klassik," *Mozart-Jahrbuch 1956* (Salzburg, 1957), pp. 200–01.

century.[2] The programs they presented consisted almost exclusively of Baroque works, and this tended to keep the older style in favor in the city of Ljubljana, which at that time was the capital of the duchy of Carniolia, and whose influence extended over the entire territory that was ethnically Slovene.

The activities of the Italian opera singers were supported mainly by the Carniolian aristocracy, who were opposed to all the social changes then taking place. The leading figure in the struggle to maintain the status quo was Baron Sigismund Zois.[3] This highly urbane and cultivated aristocrat was the initiator and director of the efforts that were being made at that time to revive Slovenian literary activity, and here he revealed himself to be a progressive person who was fully in touch with the spirit of his age. His musical tastes, however, were reactionary. He was a resolute supporter of Italian Baroque opera, and willingly played the roles of adviser and Maecenas in an effort to maintain it in favor. As a result of his influence, Italian opera troupes continued to visit Ljubljana at least sporadically; and the considerable success enjoyed by these troupes in the last two decades of the century prevented the German singspiel from attaining any great degree of popularity.

Nor did Zois stand alone. He was surrounded by a rather large circle of sympathizers who also preferred Italian opera to German singspiel, either for purely artistic reasons or as an expression of resentment against the increasingly pressing politico-cultural encroachments of Joseph II. This preference for Italian Baroque opera could be explained in various other ways; but for whatever reason, it was perpetuated long beyond its natural life span, thus greatly hindering the natural development of the new classical style in Slovenia.

On the other hand, the efforts to preserve the Academia Philharmonicorum also obstructed the development of classicism.[4] During

2. See D. Ludvik, *Nemško gledališče v Ljubljani do leta 1790* (Ljubljana, 1957); S. Škerlj, *Italijanske predstave v Ljubljani od XVII. do XIX. stoletja* (Ljubljana, 1936); D. Cvetko, *Zgodovina glasbene umetnosti na Slovenskem* (History of Music in Slovenia), I (Ljubljana, 1958), 265 ff.

3. See D. Cvetko, *Zgodovina . . .*, I, 270–73; J. Mantuani, "Razvoj slovenske glasbe," *Cerkveni glasbenik*, LVII (Ljubljana, 1934), 130–31; A. Trstenjak, *Slovensko gledališče* (Ljubljana, 1892), pp. 25 ff.

4. See the Slovenian State Archives, LIT, A. N° 1.

the years 1767 and 1768 Carl Seyfried Perirhoffer v. Perizhoff, both in his own name and in that of the other members of this institution,[5] exerted all his influence in an effort to stem the march of time and to revivify an institution which had been engendered by the Baroque and which had supported the art of that period in Slovenia. It was, of course, quite natural that such an attempt was made because the Academia was, among other things, a typically aristocratic institution. The attempt was, however, a failure. The Academia was of a former age and incapable of adjusting to the new stylistic concepts of classicism. Nevertheless, the attitudes of Perizhoffer, even though they did not prevail, were extremely characteristic of Slovenian musical life in the first half of the eighteenth century. They were, in fact, essentially the same as those that dominated the field of opera at that time and were supported by the activities of Zois and his circle, as mentioned above.

Given such an atmosphere, it is not surprising that music in the Baroque style continued to enjoy great favor—especially in the theatre where the influence of the Baron Zois was considerable. In particular, he was interested in having the Slovenian language introduced into the theatre. With this goal in mind, he himself translated the texts of Italian operatic arias that Italian singers had used in performances at the Theatre of the Estates (or Theatre of the Nobility) in Ljubljana. There is documentary evidence that the translations of Zois were extremely successful, and that the Italian singers themselves found the Slovenian language "cantabilissima" and much easier to sing than German.[6]

The influence of Zois and the impetus of the Slovenian resurgence served to stimulate the activity of Jurij Japelj. In about 1780 this writer and philologist translated Metastasio's *Artaxerxes* into Slovenian, probably for a performance in that language.[7] It is still not known whether the translation was destined for use by Slovenian or Italian singers. In all probability, however, it was intended to be sung by Slovenians—even though at that moment conditions were still not favorable to the success of a Slovenian opera repertory and

5. In the document he signs himself "Carl Seyfried v. Perizhof/Director und übrige HH. Academici Philharmonicorum Labacensium."

6. See I. Prijatelj, *Duševni profili slovenskih preporoditeljev* (Ljubljana, 1935), pp. 44–45.

7. Cvetko, *Zgodovina . . .*, I, 274.

did not, in fact, even offer much hope for the eventual evolution of Slovenian opera.

That Japelj favored the art of the Baroque no less than Zois may be seen from the libretto he chose to translate. His work, however, made no real contribution toward maintaining the Baroque style of music, which was already rapidly disappearing by that time. Nevertheless, his translation of *Artaxerxes* was a literary success simply because he, along with Zois, was primarily interested in seeing the Slovenian language firmly established in the theatre.

These factors had at least an indirect effect on the musical taste of the time and upon the atmosphere in which Slovenian music was to evolve. The principal personality in this final phase of the Baroque in Slovenia was Jakob Zupan (Suppan), who was born July 27, 1734, at Schrötten, a town not far from Hengsberg, in the district of Wildon in Upper Styria.[8] His name indicates that he may have been of Slovenian origin; quite probably he came from that element of the population which some years earlier had emigrated to the more prosperous regions of Upper Styria.

No one has yet succeeded in determining where Zupan received his basic musical training or the degree of perfection that his compositions reveal. In 1758 he took up residence at Kamnik, a small provincial city not far from Ljubljana which had a rich musical tradition and where, about 1620, was born Janez (Joannes) Baptist Dolar (Dollar),[9] a Jesuit and a prolific composer of sonatas and ballets in a very advanced style. During his four years in Kamnik he made his living as a private music teacher. There he also married Jožefa Goetzl, the mayor's daughter.

In 1762 he moved to Komenda, a town not far from Kamnik. Here he taught music and directed the choir and orchestra at a seminary under the direction of Peter Pavel Glavar, a learned and highly cultivated priest who bore the title of Apostolic Prothonotary. Very little material has been preserved concerning Zupan's activity here. Nevertheless, we know that during his stay at Komenda he wrote a large number of works that undoubtedly were intended for performance by the choir and orchestra of the school there and that

8. See the baptismal registers of the parish of Hengsberg, VII, 15.

9. See J. Gr. Thalnitscher (Dolničar), *Bibliotheca Labacensis publica collegii Carolini Nobilium,* MS., Library of the Seminary, Ljubljana.

were probably religious. On the other hand, no definite information is available about the nature of the other compositions he may have performed. We can, however, form a general idea about the nature of his repertory from the few compositions still preserved in the archives of the seminary. These include, among other things, the *Octo Missae* of the Benedictine Lambert Kraus, which are dated 1762, the year in which Zupan entered the service of Peter Pavel Glavar. It is very probable that he performed these instrumentally accompanied Masses, and it may have been he who procured them for the seminary.

Zupan stayed at Komenda until 1765, when he again took up residence in Kamnik. He remained there until his death on April 11, 1810. This last period of his life was spent, once again, in the private teaching of music. In addition he held the position of "regens chori" at the parish church of Kamnik, for which he assembled the best vocalists and instrumentalists he could find. His efforts to sustain the creation of an intensive musical activity were not, however, limited by any means to the performance of religious music. He also was instrumental in founding the Akademische Confoederation Sanctae Caeciliae, an organization that probably was a last echo of the former Academia Philharmonicorum, as can be seen from its title and organization. By this time, however, such an organization lacked a proper *raison d'être*, and the conditions that had made its predecessor a success were no longer present. It was probably designed primarily to assist the church with its musical needs. Its activities as a performing group were in accord with the ideals of its founder; that is to say, despite the fact that it was founded in the last third of the eighteenth century, it was committed to the spirit and ideals of the Baroque.[10]

The posts Zupan held at both Komenda and Kamnik obliged him to compose. His compositions indicate that he must have been a prolific composer, and one of great power within the Baroque style. Take, for example, his Te Deum, which according to the frontispiece, was written for "Canto/Alto/Tenore/Basso/Violino Primo/Violino

10. For the biographical facts see also L. Stiasny, *Kamnik* (1894), pp. 161–70, 121–22; D. Cvetko, *Zgodovina . . .*, I, 274–75; A. Dimitz, *Geschichte Krains* (Laibach, 1876), IV, 192; P. v. Radics, *Frau Musica in Krain* (Laibach, 1877), p. 31; Fr. Rakuša, *Slovensko petje v preteklih dobah* (Ljubljana, 1890), p. 26.

Secondo/Clarino Primo—Clarino Secondo (ad libitum) Tympano con Organo."[11] The organ part is conceived as a basso continuo. Fioriture in the Baroque style abound in the vocal parts and are even more plentiful in the instrumental parts. The limited resources at his disposal in the small towns where he worked undoubtedly account for the restricted instrumentation cited above; but the vocal and instrumental elements in the Te Deum combine to form a well integrated and picturesque whole. Stylistically, the Te Deum of Zupan reflects the influence of both Bach and Handel. Technically, it is the work of a craftsman who knew how to shape both vocal and instrumental lines. Thanks to his masterly craftsmanship Zupan was able, within the limits of the framework and character of the work, to give free rein to his musical imagination, and he stands revealed as a composer of originality and character.

We have no information on when the Te Deum was composed. It was probably written well before the end of the century, however, because by about 1800 the activity of the composer had declined considerably and he was rapidly retiring into the background.

Zupan composed many settings of the Te Deum, the Ordinary of the Mass, and other religious texts. These compositions are written in a style identical with or similar to that of the preserved composition discussed above. Zupan's art was firmly rooted in that of the Baroque, and this is as true of his secular as of his sacred music.

Many of Zupan's secular works are lost. Nevertheless we have much information about the most famous of them all, his opera *Belin*.[12] The libretto he chose for this opera was by the priest Janez Damascen Dev (1732–1786) and was the first such libretto to be written in the Slovenian language. Published in 1780, it was based on material from classical mythology and from the works of the Italian poet Pietro Metastasio.[13] The very complicated symbolism that pervades the whole work may be interpreted in two ways. According to the first, Belin is the personification of the Carniolian Apollo, the ruler of the Muses, who in turn stimulate and encourage Carniolian poetry. According to the plot of the book, the Muses are

11. The original is found in the musical archives of the cathedral of Ljubljana.

12. For the text see *Pisanice*, 1780.

13. See F. Kidrič, *Zgodovina slovenskega slovstva* (Ljubljana, 1929–1938), pp. 714 ff.

deprived of the guidance of Apollo; he has left them and gone to Italy. With yearning they wait for their sister Muses in Italy to send him back; they pledge him their love and promise to inspire the Carniolians to write songs in his honor as a sign of their gratitude for the golden age his presence will call forth.

According to the second interpretation Belin symbolizes a historic person—possibly Franz Adam, count of Lamberg, who was appointed governor of Carniola in 1780. It seems that the various editors of the Slovenian almanac *Pisanice*, in which *Belin* was published, wished to gain the favor of the new governor; for immediately after the text of *Belin* there is found, along with the chronogram 1780, a laudatory statement celebrating "the joyous arrival of His Excellency, the new governor of the province of Carniola, count Franz Lamberg."[14] This second interpretation seems the more probable.

The protagonists of *Belin*—the librettist emphasizes that they are to be singers ("pojozhe pershone")—are Belin (the Sun or the God of Day), Burja (the "Bora," the North Wind), and the nymphs Sejvina (Ceres), Rožnecvitarca (Flora) and Sadjanka (Pomona), whom the author calls "teh bogov gospodizhne," the maidens of the gods. The action is spread out over three acts, each of which has a distinctive structure. In the first act each of the nymphs has in turn an aria, a recitative, an aria, and a recitative. In the second act Burja joins the nymphs, and all the characters again sing in turn, this time a recitative, an aria, a recitative and again a recitative. The act concludes with a chorus in the form of an arioso ("ariosnu chor"). In the third and final act Belin joins the nymphs and Burja. Again, each performer sings in succession a recitative, an aria, and an aria. The result is most effective. It should also be noted that the librettist has given rather detailed instructions concerning the scenery and stage action.

The manner in which the libretto is conceived proves that the author intended *Belin* to be set to music. This raises the question of whether Dev himself had sufficient knowledge and understanding of the musical aspect of opera to cast it in the form in which we know it. It seems that this question must be answered in the affirmative. Dev, along with the majority of the Slovenian intellectuals of the

14. See L. Pirnat, " 'Pisanice,' prvi slovenski pesniški almanah," *Ljubljanski Zvon*, XXVI (Ljubljana, 1906), 569.

time, had an encyclopedic knowledge. He was also a member of the Academia Operosorum, a society originally founded in 1693 and reactivated for a brief time in 1781. Above all, however, Dev was intimately acquainted with the works of Metastasio, and in these were to be found suggestions and models for the construction of his work. Without doubt he also knew Italian opera, even from the practical side, since at that time he would have had numerous opportunities to attend operatic performances in Ljubljana. However, although the facts favor the thesis that Dev alone gave *Belin* its specific form, he seems to have consulted the composer Zupan in regard to its structure. Zupan's musical knowledge was much more profound than Dev's, and he would have been able to give the librettist many useful suggestions. Consultation with Zupan may in fact have been necessary because of an author's obligation to take account of the technical aspects of staging. At any rate, the supposition that Zupan had at least some influence upon the structure of *Belin* as we know it is fully justified.

It has not yet been possible to determine exactly when Zupan set Dev's libretto to music. Some documents suggest that the music was finished in 1780, others suggest 1782.[15] In any event, the opera must date from between these two years—that is to say, the time immediately following the publication of the libretto.

It is evident that in the composition of the music Zupan was obliged to adhere to the libretto.[16] As we have said, the exact structure of the opera is not known. Nevertheless, on the basis of the evidence available, we are justified in concluding that Zupan used a vocal and instrumental ensemble. Although we do not know exactly which instruments were called for, we may safely conclude that at least those which figured in the Te Deum mentioned above were used. It is also probable, given the character of the work, that he

15. M. Pohlin wrote concerning him: "Ludi et Chori Magister Kamnecensis, egregius Compositor et Musicus, composuit melodias et modos musicos pro theatrali opera Carniolica: Belin, ena opera, quam composuit et 1780, in 8. evulgavit P. Joan Damascenus et sub. Lit. J. invenies. Musices Ms. 1782 extabit Kamnecii." (*Bibliotheca Carniolica,* appended to *Mittheilungen des Historischen Vereins für Krain,* Ljubljana, 1862.)

16. The text of Dev calls *Belin* an operetta. It is obvious that this designation is not to be taken literally, since the entire text was sung, and since despite its brevity it has the character of an opera.

added others. It goes without saying that the instrumental ensemble was limited by the resources at his command. Although design was modest, its structure and content offered Zupan considerably greater possibilities for displaying his imaginative powers and compositional talents than such a text as that of the Te Deum.

That the music of *Belin* was typically Baroque can be deduced from the libretto whose content and manner of treatment are both typically Baroque. In order to maintain an equilibrium between the libretto and his music, Zupan was forced to adjust himself to its specific requirements; but he did not have to struggle to express himself in the Baroque style since that was perfectly familiar to him—as can be seen from his Te Deum and other compositions. Musically, Zupan's entire orientation was completely Baroque, and this determined his musical conception of *Belin*. Also, it should not be overlooked that the libretto offered him a wide range of expressive possibilities and gave him an opportunity to express his preference for Italian opera, whose style was far more familiar and congenial to him than that of German opera. The Te Deum itself very clearly revealed this stylistic preference. The literary style of the libretto is similar to that of Metastasio, and could not but influence Zupan's music.

There is no evidence as to whether or not *Belin* was ever performed.[17] It may be argued that the composer would not have set Dev's text to music unless there was a reasonable certainty that it would be staged either at Kamnik or at Ljubljana. There was no lack of instrumentalists or singers, of course, and certainly adequate theatrical facilities were available; at that time both Italian and German opera troupes regularly performed at Ljubljana with the greatest success. Since, however, there is no concrete evidence that *Belin* was ever performed, the question remains open.

Another question to be asked is what prompted Zupan to set Dev's text to music. It is quite probable that the suggestion came from Dev himself, but it is equally possible that Zupan suggested the idea of the libretto to Dev. It is also possible that Zupan was influ-

17. See J. Jireček, *Paul J. Šafařík's "Geschichte der südslawischen Literatur,"* I (Prague, 1864), 85; A. Trstenjak, p. 27; P. v. Radics, p. 31; D. Cvetko, *Zgodovina . . .*, I, 276.

enced, either directly or indirectly, by Baron Zois, to whose circle Dev and perhaps Zupan himself belonged.[18] The three men all had a decided propensity for the Baroque, and each in his own way manifested that propensity in all that he did. The uniformity in the esthetic outlook of these three representatives of Slovenian cultural life at that time is incontestable. Given this fact, one must probably accept the hypothesis that reciprocal influences were at work in the writing of the libretto and the composing of the music. Again, the evidence necessary to allow one to reach a definitive conclusion is lacking.

The importance and value of *Belin* resides both in its literary and musical aspects. It is not only the first example of an original opera libretto in the Slovenian language but also the first example of an original Slovenian opera in Baroque style. Therefore, despite the reactionary character of its style, the work occupies an important place in the history of Slovenian music. Previous to the appearance of *Belin,* Italian opera had dominated the Slovenian musical theatre. Zupan's opera, however, both because of its quality and because it was the original product of a Slovenian composer, gave a great impetus to the development of the Slovenian musical theatre, even though it was but the first effort of its kind.[19] At the same time it constituted a peculiar success for all those who wished to see a revival of Slovenian arts and letters, since it embraced both music and literature. Without doubt, this success had been the desire and ambition of the Slovenian adherents to the doctrines of the Enlightenment. From the esthetic outlook that united Zois, Dev, and Zupan, it would appear that one of the aspirations of the Slovenian resurgence in the last decades of the eighteenth century was to create a Slovenian music as well as a literature. Thus, it well could have been

18. See J. Mantuani, pp. 131–32; F. Kidrič, *Dev Feliks (p. Johannes Damascenus a nomine Mariae),* in *Slovenski biografski leksikon,* I (Ljubljana, 1925), 130–31.

19. According to Dimitz, Zupan must have been prompted to write a work for the stage by the activity of the German theatrical troupes (see Dimitz, p. 192: "Die Thätigkeit der deutschen Bühne wirkte anregend auf dem Gebiete der musikalischen Composition . . ."). This is not correct, for it was only after 1780 that the German troupes began to perform regularly in Ljubljana. Before that date, mainly Italian operas were performed. Far more probable is that Zupan was stimulated by them, which is suggested by the nature of his total musical activity as described in the text above.

Zois who, in order to attain this end, urged Zupan to set to music the libretto of Dev.[20]

After Zupan, Baroque tendencies reasserted themselves here and there in Slovenia, as they did throughout Europe. It was in this direction, for example, that the much later activity of the composer Gregor Rihar evolved.[21] Nevertheless, neither in his work nor in that of any later Slovenian composer did the Baroque style manifest itself as clearly, decidedly, and consistently as in the work of Zupan. It was hardly ten years after the composition of *Belin* that Novak wrote his *Figaro*. In the brief intervening period, two diametrically opposed styles appeared in Slovenian music. The conflict between them was resolved when Slovenian music became committed to the new styles characteristic of West and Central European music in the second half of the eighteenth century. Zupan himself, despite the positive qualities of his art, was unable to prolong the life of the Baroque style in Slovenia. The line of Slovenian composers who wrote in the Baroque style terminated with him.

(Translated by Robert J. Snow)

20. See also D. Cvetko, *Zgodovina . . .*, I, 276; also "Slowenien," "Kunstmusik," in the article "Jugoslawien," *Die Musik in Geschichte und Gegenwart,* VII (1958), col. 310, and "Yougoslavie," in *Encyclopédie de la musique,* III (Paris: Fasquelle éditeurs, 1961), 1001; also *Histoire de la musique slovène* (1967), pp. 141–43.

21. See the details in D. Cvetko, *Zgodovina glasbene umetnosti na Slovenskem,* II (1959), 244–58, and III (1960), 73–76, 88–92; also *Histoire de la musique slovène,* pp. 207–10.

3 / A Group of English Manuscript Volumes at the University of Pittsburgh

THEODORE M. FINNEY
University of Pittsburgh

THE volumes described here form part of a private collection deposited in the music library of the University of Pittsburgh. The music represented is almost altogether that of English composers or of foreign composers living in England. The first volume listed will not be described since that has been done elsewhere.

Manuscript Fi 1. A Collection of English Restoration Anthems, c. 1695, from the library of William Gostling. It has been described in "Studies and Abstracts," *Journal of the American Musicological Society*, Vol. XV, No. 2. Because it belongs in this group, however, its contents will be indexed at the end of this article.

Manuscript Fi 2. A Collection of English Anthems. 23.7 x 28.5. The volume carries the bookplate of Sir John Dolben, Bart. of Finedon in Northamptonshire (1684–1756). This Dolben was the grandson of the John Dolben who was Dean of Westminster from 1662 and later, from 1683, Archbishop of York. By means of an advantageous marriage, the archbishop's son, Gilbert Dolben, settled in Finedon and became first baronet in 1704. Sir Gilbert's son, the owner of this book, was subdean of the Chapel Royal during the reign of Queen Anne. He became Vicar of Finedon in 1719 and inherited his father's title in 1722. His interest in music is indicated by his taking the organist James Kent from the Chapel to Finedon.

Except for the table, the writing throughout is in the same hand, that of an expert copyist. That it is not the hand of James Kent can be seen from a comparison with MS. Barber 5003, Barber Institute Library, University of Birmingham, which is described as being in Kent's hand. The modern G clef is used throughout, the proportional "tripla" time signatures that are seen in late seventeenth-century manuscripts are not used, and consequently bar lines appear with modern regularity.

The paper in the body of the volume, on the basis of watermarks, dates from between 1720 and 1730. Some slight loss by trimming indicates that the book was bound after it was written. Endpapers carrying mid-century watermarks confirm this.

On the evidence, then, of ownership as indicated by bookplate, of notation, and of paper, the manuscript comes certainly from the first half of the eighteenth century, c. 1730.

The contents are as follows:

		Page
Clarke, Jeremiah	Praise the Lord O Jerusalem	132
Croft, William	Give the King thy judgments	88
———	I will give thanks	61
Purcell, Henry	Behold I bring you glad tidings	30
———	Be merciful unto me O God	15
———	Blessed is he that considereth	50
———	I was glad when they said	41
———	O give thanks unto the Lord	1

Manuscript Fi 3. Services by William Croft. This is a companion volume to Fi 2: size, bookplate, handwriting, paper, and binding are the same. It can, therefore, be assigned the same date, c. 1730.

The contents are as follows:

		Page
Croft, William	Service in B minor	1
	Te Deum	1
	Jubilate	29
	Sanctus	41
	Gloria	42
———	Service in E-flat	48
	Te Deum	48
	Jubilate	76

Pages 80 and 81 in the second Jubilate have been left blank, confirming the tradition that Croft composed no music to the verse "O go your way . . . speak good of his name."

Manuscript Fi 4. A Collection of English Anthems. 23.4 x 29.5. This volume carries the handwritten name of J. H. Cotton in both front and back inside covers, with the date 1820 at the back in the same hand. This Cotton has not been identified. On page 17 the name D. Evans has been stamped twice in block letters. If this refers to the Welsh composer (1843–1913), it represents later ownership than Cotton's. The first anthem in the book—"I am well pleased," by Aldrich—shows carefully made corrections. At the end, on page 18, is the annotation in a quite different hand, "Examined and Corrected, J. P." One may guess that this is John Page (d. 1812), who in 1800 edited and published a three-volume collection of anthems with the title *Harmonia Sacra.*

The music seems to be the work of the same copyist throughout, and there are certain notational mannerisms, such as the double-looped sixteenth-notes, which tended to disappear as music engraving became more common later in the eighteenth century.

The paper in the body of the book carries watermarks which indicate that it was manufactured between 1730 and 1740. The index, in a later hand, is on an endpaper which dates c. 1760. Outside endpapers and pastedowns carry a clear watermark date, 1818. Trimmed titles and page numbers—with no real loss of text—indicate that the book was bound after it was written. One might guess that it has been bound twice—once when the endpapers carrying the index were inserted, and again about 1820 for J. H. Cotton. In any event, the music is the oldest part of the book, and its copying can be dated c. 1740.

The contents are as follows:

		Page
Aldrich, Henry	I am well pleased	1
Clarke, Jeremiah	I will love Thee O Lord	114
Croft, William	Burial Service	86
———	I will sing unto the Lord	48
———	The earth is the Lords	126
———	We will rejoice in thy salvation	71

		Page
Goldwin, John	O praise God in his holiness	169
Greene, Maurice	My soul truly waiteth still	190
Hawkins, James	O sing unto the Lord a new song	179
Jackson, John	The Lord said unto my Lord	148
Purcell, Henry	Be merciful unto me O God	19
———	I was glad when they said	137
———	My song shall be alway	102
———	They that go down to the sea	36
———	Thou knowest Lord (*in* Croft's Burial Service)	96
Tudway, Thomas	Sing we merrily unto God	154
Wise, Michael	I will sing a new song	62

Manuscript Fi 5. A Collection of Anthems by Maurice Greene. 30.3 x 24.5. This volume carries the bookplate of Charles John Bird, "AM & FAS Mag. Coll. Cambridge." A Julia Purton has written her name above the Bird bookplate, with the date 1855. A Charles John Bird got his M.A. at Cambridge in 1802. It is not likely that he was the first owner of the book.

The manuscript, including the table, is in the same not very expert hand throughout, with no indication of who the copyist might have been. The paper carries watermarks that indicate English manufacture c. 1770. The book appears to have originated as a bound volume of blank music paper. It can be dated c. 1780.

The contents, all anthems by Maurice Greene, are the following:

	Page
Acquaint thyself with God	98
Hear O Lord and consider my complaint	130
Lord how are they increased	115
Lord let me know mine end	123
My God my God look upon me	105
My soul truly waiteth	55
O God of my righteousness	33
O God thou art my God	65
O Lord give ear	1
O Lord grant the king a long life	74
O sing unto God sing praises	14
O sing unto the Lord with thanksgiving	89

	Page
Sing unto the Lord a new song	41
Thou O God art praised in Sion	25

Manuscript Fi 6. A Collection of English Anthems, Psalms, and Hymns. 32.4 x 22. The front endpaper of this volume carries, with some decorative flourishes, the inscription "S. Woolly his Book June 30 1795." The following sheet, f1, carries a large partly colored circular figure with the following: "Samuel Woollys Book a companion to Harmonia Sacra. Anno Dom. 1753." Dates are given throughout: from these, it appears that Woolly spent a great deal of time over the copying during 1753 and in the summer of 1754. He finished the Purcell Te Deum on July 10, 1754, and the Jubilate on July 18. The anthems that follow immediately are almost all dated: i.e., July 31, August 2, August 4, August 16, and September 1, 1754. Those copied later are not dated consecutively, although throughout the book other dates appear: 1777, 1781, 1784. The writing is done on various kinds of paper, variously paged. The material must finally have been brought together and bound, as is indicated also by some loss by trimming, and the 1795 date in the front must approximate the time the book came back from the binder. Because of the nature of the compilation, and also because some leaves have been removed, a new numbering of the folios has been made.

For present purposes no attention will be given to the psalms and hymns that are among the contents of the book; only choral works, in the sense that a trained body of singers is called for, will be listed.

One attribution in this volume should be noted. Both in the table and with the music, the anthem "I am well pleased" is ascribed to Henry Purcell, with the clear date August 2, 1754 for the completion of the copying. This anthem apparently was well known and widely used during the eighteenth century. But everywhere else it is attributed to Henry Aldrich or Carissimi-Aldrich. Hawkins mentions it;[1] a copy of it is to be found in another volume in this group (Fi. 4, p. 1); manuscript copies are to be found in many libraries in England, including Aldrich's own library at Christ Church in Oxford; and Arnold printed it in his *Cathedral Music*, Vol. III, p. 48, as "Anthem for three voices, in the key of B (i.e., B-flat), with the greater third

1. Hawkins, John, *A General History of the Science and Practice of Music* (London, 1776), V, 10.

as altered from Carissimi by Henry Aldrich . . ." Probably the only reason for noting this ascription is that it adds another item to Dr. Zimmerman's list of "Spurious Ascriptions to Purcell."[2]

The John Smith who is represented by four anthems is identified here, as he is in the British Union Catalogue, as being "of Market Lavington."

The contents are as follows:

		Folio
Aldrich, Henry (attr. Purcell)	I am well pleased	97
Bond, Capel	Blessed be the Lord	196v
Boyce, William	The Lord liveth	199v
———	Te Deum in A major	9v
Broderip, John	Awake up my glory	147v
Brydle, William	How long wilt thou forget me	143
———	Let God arise	119v
Clarke, Jeremiah	I will love thee O Lord	103v
———	The Lord is full of compassion	116
Croft, William	Blessed is the people O Lord	110v
———	Praise the Lord O my soul	93v
Handel, G. F.	As pants the hart	88v
Hine, William	I will magnifie thee	190
Kent, James	All thy works praise thee	153v
———	Blessed be thou Lord	162v
———	In the beginning was the word	184
———	Lord what love have I	168v
———	Sing O heavens	149v
———	The Lord hath prepared his seat	158
———	When the son of man	180v
———	Who is this that cometh	174
———	Why do the heathen	171
Knapp, William	Hear ye heavens	135v
———	I said I will take heed	178v
———	I will sing unto the Lord	126v
Purcell, Henry *(spurious)*	I am well pleased	97

2. Zimmerman, Franklin B., *Henry Purcell 1659–1695* (London, 1963).

		Folio
Purcell, Henry	Blessed is he that considereth	114
———	I was glad when they said	128
———	Jubilate for Voices and Instruments (Full score—D major)	78v
———	My song shall be always	124v
———	O give thanks unto the Lord	106
———	Te Deum for Voices & Instruments (Full score—D major)	64
Smith, John	Bring unto the Lord	139
———	Lord let me know my end	137v
———	Lord thou art become gracious	141v
———	O how amiable are thy dwellings	130v
Townsend, Roger	I will magnifie thee	143v
———	O praise God in his holiness	100
Unidentified	Anthem for Christmas day (There were shepherds abiding)	17v
———	Behold I bring you glad tidings *(incomplete)*	2
———[3]	Except the Lord build the house	133v
———	Favorite Ode, A (From heav'n the land the angelic song)	14
———	God be merciful unto us	145v

Manuscript Fi 7. Service, Responses, and Litany. 29.4 x 23.6. This volume has been signed, both on the front pastedown and on the verso of the first endpaper, by J. Mapletoft, with the date 1719 on the pastedown. One John Mapletoft (1631–1721) appears in the *Alumni Oxoniensis*, in the *Dictionary of National Biography*, and as a Fellow of the Royal Society. For a long period he was Vicar of St. Lawrence Jewry in London, and he spent the last ten years of his life between Oxford and Westminster. He could very well have known Goodson, who was organist at Christ Church and Professor of Music at the University during those years. On this basis, the manuscript is contemporary with the composer of the Service contained in it—as

3. "One of the greatest masters in Europe."

is confirmed by the paper, which carries watermarks dating c. 1690.

The contents are as follows:

		Page
Goodson, Richard	Morning Service in C	1
	Te Deum	1
	Jubilate	15
Tallis, Thomas	Responses	26
	Litany	27

Manuscript Fi 8. A Collection of Secular Songs. 33.6 x 20. This manuscript consists of once-folded sheets totaling thirty-six pages, piled one on top of the other and sewed by stabbing through the sides. It is unbound, and shows no evidence of ever having been in a binding. It has been folded halfway from top to bottom with a resulting heavy crease. The first folio is badly torn, with about one-fourth missing. What appears to be a hot-coal burn extends from the front through eight folios with, fortunately, very little loss of text. Rough corners have been trimmed, also with no loss of text. The four watermarks visible in the paper fall between 1725 and 1765. The Boyce Trio in *The Winter's Tale*, composed in 1757, appears to be the latest in date. Thus one can surmise that the manuscript was probably finished c. 1770. Attributions made in the manuscript are indicated by an asterisk.

The contents are as follows:

		Page
Boyce, William	Get you hence for I must go: Trio in *The Winter's Tale*	26
Clark, N.	*O Praise our God	35
Eccles, John	*Let us revel and roar	22
Handel, G. F. [?]	When Phoebus the tops of the hills	30
Isham, John	*As Celia was learning	16
Ives, Simon	*Thus saith the preacher	4
Oswald, James	*The Dust Cart Cantata:* As tinkring Tom	12
Purcell, Henry	**Bess of Bedlam:* From silent shades	5
———	Fair Cloe my breast so alarms	17

		Page
Purcell, Henry	*Jack thour't a toper	11
———	Julia your unjust disdain	9
———	*Once, twice, thrice	21
———	When Myra sings	1
———[?]	Fie nay prithee John	21
Travers, John	When Bibo thought fit	33
Unidentified	Of battles or sieges	24
———	The watery God *(fragment)*	36

Manuscripts Fi 9, 10, 11, 12. A Set of Four Instrumental Part Books. 22.3 x 29.3. These books contain no bookplates or other certain indication of former ownership. The full-leather, gold-decorated bindings are labeled, front and back, "Violino: I^{mo}"; "Violino: II^{do}"; "Tenor"; "Basso cont:." Each volume has, written with a wide pen on the leather of the outside front, the identification of the set: "Quator by Banister." The first violin book carries, above this identification, a pasted paper label upon which has been written "Suittes d'airs et ouvertures du Sieur Banister a. 4 parties."

The paper on which the music is written carries watermarks that may be dated c. 1690—the same marks that appear in MS. Fi 7. Endpapers are a little later, c. 1711. Slight losses by trimming indicate that the books were put into the present bindings after they were written. One is tempted to suggest that this set matches the description (in Item 9) that John Hawkins printed when he copied the sale catalogue of Thomas Britton's library.[4] In Volume V, page 80, Item 8 is "Two sets of books, by Mr. Paisible, Grabu, etc.," and Item 9 is "Three ditto, two by Mr. Courtevil and one by Mr. Banister." British Museum Add. MS. 24889 contains a handwritten note indicating that it was in Britton's library. It consists of a set of parts, similar in content to these, but bound together in one volume. At least ten hands were involved in the copying. One, on folios 73 and 74, is so strikingly like that of the copyist of the four books under discussion that the assumption of a close relationship to Britton seems to be justified.

The contents tend to confirm a possible connection with Thomas Britton and his concerts. The suites are made up of theater music.

4. *General History.*

Most of the Purcell music may be identified by collation with the 1697 *A collection of ayres, composed for the theatre . . .*, although the choice of pieces for each suite is quite different.

There are no tables of contents in these volumes. The following tabulation is given with no changes from the titles as they appear with each of the pieces. Page numbers are given only for the first violin book, since the copyist has taken care to have the suites begin on the same page in all books. Movements are generally designated in the books by number, and are so indicated here. The names given in square brackets—e.g., [Purcell]—do not appear in the books, but derive from identifications made by the present writer. Certain variants from book to book in the way names and movements are written also appear in the tabulation.

Page	*Composer and Movements (Violino Imo)*	*Variants in other parts*		
		V. II	*T*	*B-C*
1	Mr. John Bannister 1 Overtur, 2, 3, 4, 5, 6, 7, 8, 9, 10, 11, 12	By	Set by	
8	Set by Mr. John Bannister 1 Overtur, 2, 3, 4, 5, 6, 7, 8, 9, 10, 11, 12		Mr.	Mr.
12	By Mr. Morgan 1 Overtur, 2, 3, 4, 5, 6, 7, 8, [9]			, 9.
18	Mr. Morgan 1 Overtur, 2, 3, 4, 5, 6, 7, 8, 9, 10, 11, 12			Mr organ
24	Mr. Morgan 1 Overtur, 2, 3, 4, 5, 6, 7, 8, 9			
30	Mr. Pasebell 1 Overtur, 2, 3, 4, 5, 6, 7, 8, 9, 10	Pasibell	Pasibell	Pasibell
38	Mr. Finger Overtur, 2, 3, 4, 5, 6, 7, 8, 9			
43	Mr. Finger 1 Overture, 2, 3, 4, 5, 6, 7, 8, 9			
49	Mr. Purcell 1 Overtur, 2, 3, 4, 5, 6, 7, 8, 9, 10, 11, 12			
54	Mr. Finger 1 Overtur, 2, 3, 4, 5, 6, 7, 8, 9			
62	Mr. Clarke Symphony, 2 Gavotte, 3 Air, 4 Hornpipe, 5 Boreè, 6 Prelude, 7 Minuett, 8 Symphony, 9 Air			

Page	Composer and Movements (Violino Imo)	Variants in other parts V. II	T	B-C
68	Mr. Pesible 1 Overture, 2, 3, Roundo 4, 5 Mr. Keller, 6 Roundo, 7, 8, 9, Chacone		*No music*	10 Chacone
74	[Purcell] 1 Overture, 2, 3, 4, 5, Roundo 6, 7, 8, 9 Roundo			
79	[Purcell] Overture, 2, 3, 4, 5, 6, 7, 8, 9, 10			
83	[Purcell] Overture, 2, 3, 4, 5, 6, 7, 8, 9 Chacone			
88	Mr. Banister 1 Overture, 2, 3, 4, 5, 6 Roundo, 7, 8 Chacone			
94	Mr. Barrett 1 Overture, 2, 3, 4, 5, 6, 7, 8		*No music*	
98	Mr. King 1 Overture, 2, 3, 4 Roundo, 5 Jigg, 6 Mr. Barrett Allemanda, 7, 8, 9, 10		*No music*	6 Mr. Barrett Allmain
103	Mr. Purcell 1 Overture, 2, 3, 4, 5, 6, 7, 8, 9			
108	——— 1 Overture, 2, 3, 4, 5, 6, 7, 8, 9		*Inserted extra page 113;* "For a Hoboy"	
114	Mr. Finger Overture, 2, 3, 4, 5, 6, 7, 8, 9			
118	Mr. Purcell 1 Overture, 2, 3, 4, 5, 6, 7, 8, 9, 10			
124	——— Overture, 2, 3, 4, 5, 6, 7, 8, 9			Mr. Finger

Three suites are attributed in the books to Purcell. Three others, with no identification of the composer, have also been put together from Purcell's music. There are no indications in the manuscripts of the sources of any of this music. Those sources are given in the following table. Pieces that appear in the 1697 *A Collection of ayres* have been tabulated under *Ayres*. For those not to be found in that collection the reference—Z followed by a number—is to Zimmerman's thematic index.

(1) The suite beginning on page 49

				Ayres
1	Overture	Indian Queen	Overture	1
2		Indian Queen	Trumpet Tune	2
3		Bonduca	Aire	4
4		Bonduca	Aire	6
5		Bonduca	Hornpipe	7
6		Bonduca	Song Tune	3
7		Indian Queen	I came to sing	3
8		Bonduca	Song Tune	2
9		Indian Queen	First music	4
10		Indian Queen	Hornpipe	5
11		Indian Queen	Second Aire	6
12		Indian Queen	Second music	7

(2) The suite beginning on page 74

				Ayres
1	Overture	Gordian Knot	Overture	1
2		Fairy Queen	Preludes	6
3		King Arthur	Hornpipe	5
4		Gordian Knot	Aire	2
5		Gordian Knot	Rondeau-Minuett	3
6		Abelazar	Aire	9
7		Bonduca	Minuett	9
8		Abelazar	Aire	6
9	Roundo	Distressed Innocence	Rondo	6

(3) The suite beginning on page 79

				Ayres
1	Overture	Married Beau	Overture	1
2		Married Beau	Slow Aire	2
3		King Arthur	Aire	2
4		Amphitryon	Minuett	6
5		Amphitryon	Aire	5
6		Amphitryon	[Hornpipe]*	7
7		Fairy Queen	Aire	3
8		Fairy Queen	Hornpipe	2
9		Virtuous Wife	Minuett	7
10		Double Dealer	Minuett	6

*So named in a manuscript insertion into a copy of the 1697 *A Collection* . . . , once belonging to the Musical Society at Oxford.

(4) The suite beginning on page 83

				Ayres
1	Overture	Bonduca	Overture	1
2		Fairy Queen	Aire	14
3		Old Bachelor	March	8
4		King Arthur	Trumpet Tune	11
5		Fairy Queen	Aire	15
6		Virtuous Wife	Preludio	5
7		Virtuous Wife	Hornpipe	6

				Ayres
8		Old Bachelor	Boreè	7
9	Chacone	Fairy Queen	Air	18

(5) The suite beginning on page 103

				Ayres
1	Overture	The Virtuous Wife	Overture	1
2		Fairy Queen	Dance for Furies [sic]	11
3		King Arthur	Aire	6
4		Distressed Innocence	Aire	7
5		Abelazor	Aire	4
6		Abelazor	Minuett	5
7		Dioclesian	Z 37d	—
8		Gordian Knot	Jigg	5
†9		Dioclesian	Country Dance	5

†Also in suite beginning on page 114.

(6) The suite beginning on page 118

				Ayres
1	Overture	Dioclesian	Overture	1
2		Dioclesian	Dance Z 36	—
*3		Dioclesian	Country Dance	5
4		Dioclesian	Dance of the Furies Z 14b	—
5		Dioclesian	Chair Dance Z 17	—
6		Dioclesian	Paspe Z 29	—
7		Dioclesian	Third Act Tune	6
8		Dioclesian	First Act Tune: Hornpipe	7
9		Dioclesian	Dance of Baccanals Z 32d	—
10		Dioclesian	Canaries	9

*Also in suite beginning on page 103.

A similar identification of the music of the less well-known composers has not been possible. (No record has been found, among other things, of Mr. Morgan's first name.) Such identification must await a thematic search of the remaining manuscripts and printed music of these men.

The contents of the four volumes, listed by composers, are as follows:

		Page
Banister, John *(II)*	Suite in 12 movements (Overture in A major)	1
———	Suite in 9 movements (Overture in B-flat major)	88
———	Suite in 12 movements (Overture in C major)	8
Barrett, John	Allemanda	101

INDEX I: COMPOSERS

		MS.	Page
Blow, John	I will hearken what the Lord God will say	Fi 1	138
———	Lord how are they increased	Fi 1	74
———	Movement for strings	Fi 1	6
———	O give thanks unto the Lord	Fi 1	147
———	O God of my salvation	Fi 1	1
———	O Lord I have sinned	Fi 1	8
———	Ponder my words O Lord	Fi 1	210
———	The Kings of Tharsis	Fi 1	131
———	Thy hands have made me (incomplete)	Fi 1	238
———	Thy way O God (chorus only)	Fi 1	230
———	Turn thee unto me O Lord	Fi 1	40
Bond, Capel	Blessed be the Lord	Fi 6	196v
Boyce, William	Get you hence for I must go. Trio in *The Winter's Tale*	Fi 8	26
———	Te Deum in A major	Fi 6	9v
———	The Lord liveth	Fi 6	199v
Broderip, John	Awake up my glory	Fi 6	147v
Brydle, William	Let God arise	Fi 6	119v
———	How long wilt thou forget me	Fi 6	143
Child, William	Praise the Lord O my soul	Fi 1	33
Church, John	I will love thee O Lord	Fi 1	189
———	Praise the Lord O my soul	Fi 1	200
Clarke, Jeremiah	I will love thee O Lord	Fi 4	114
		Fi 6	103v
———	Praise the Lord O Jerusalem	Fi 2	132
———	The Lord is full of compassion	Fi 6	116
———	Suite: Symphony, Gavotte, Air, Hornpipe, Boreè, Prelude, Minuet, Symphony, Air	Fi 9–12	62

		MS.	Page
Clark, N.	O Praise our God	Fi 8	35
Croft, William	Burial Service	Fi 4	86
———	Blessed is the people O Lord	Fi 6	110v
———	Give the King thy judgments	Fi 2	88
———	I will give thanks	Fi 2	61
———	I will sing unto the Lord	Fi 4	48
———	Praise the Lord O my soul	Fi 6	93v
———	Service in B Minor	Fi 3	1
	Te Deum	Fi 3	1
	Jubilate	Fi 3	29
	Sanctus	Fi 3	41
	Gloria	Fi 3	42
———	Service in E-flat	Fi 3	48
	Te Deum	Fi 3	48
	Jubilate	Fi 3	76
———	The earth is the Lords	Fi 4	126
———	We will rejoice in thy salvation	Fi 4	71
Draghi, G. B.	This is the day the Lord hath made	Fi 1	216
Eccles, John	Let us revel and roar	Fi 8	22
Finger, Gottfried	Suite in 9 movements (Overture in A minor)	Fi 9–12	124
———	Suite in 9 movements (Overture in B-flat major)	Fi 9–12	54
———	Suite in 9 movements (Overture in D minor)	Fi 9–12	38
———	Suite in 9 movements (Overture in F major)	Fi 9–12	43
———	Suite in 9 movements (Overture in G major)	Fi 9–12	114
Goldwin, John	O praise God in his holiness	Fi 4	169
Greene, Maurice	Acquaint thyself with God	Fi 5	98
———	Hear O Lord and consider my complaint	Fi 5	130
———	Lord how are they increased	Fi 5	115

		MS.	*Page*
Greene, Maurice	Lord let me know mine end	Fi 5	123
———	My God, my God look upon me	Fi 5	105
———	My soul truly waiteth	Fi 4	190
		Fi 5	55
———	O God of my righteousness	Fi 5	33
———	O God Thou art my God	Fi 5	65
———	O Lord give ear	Fi 5	1
———	O Lord grant the King a long life	Fi 5	74
———	O sing unto God, sing praises	Fi 5	14
———	O sing unto the Lord with thanksgiving	Fi 5	89
———	Sing unto the Lord a new song	Fi 5	41
———	Thou O God art praised in Sion	Fi 5	25
Handel, G. F.	As pants the hart	Fi 6	88v
———[?]	When Phoebus the tops of the hills	Fi 8	30
Hawkins, James	O sing unto the Lord a new song	Fi 4	179
Hine, William	I will magnifie thee	Fi 6	190
Humfrey, Pelham (with Blow and Turner)	I will all way give thanks	Fi 1	160
Humfrey, Pelham	O be joyful in the Lord	Fi 1	90
———	O give thanks unto the Lord	Fi 1	121
———	O praise ye the Lord	Fi 1	104
Isham, John	As Celia was learning	Fi 8	16
Ives, Simon	Thus saith the preacher	Fi 8	4
Jackson, John	The Lord said unto my Lord	Fi 4	148
Keller, Godfrey	Movement in C major	Fi 9–12	70
Kent, James	All thy works praise thee	Fi 6	153v

		MS.	*Page*
Kent, James	Blessed be thou Lord	Fi 6	162v
———	In the beginning was the word	Fi 6	184
———	Lord what love have I	Fi 6	168v
———	Sing O heavens	Fi 6	149v
———	The Lord hath prepared his seat	Fi 6	158
———	When the son of man	Fi 6	180v
———	Who is this that cometh	Fi 6	174
———	Why do the heathen	Fi 6	171
King, Robert	Suite in 10 movements (Overture in E major; Movement 6, Allemanda, by Barrett)	Fi 9–12	98
Knapp, William	Hear ye heavens	Fi 6	135v
———	I said I will take heed	Fi 6	178v
———	I will sing unto the Lord	Fi 6	126v
Morgan, ———	Suite in 9 movements (Overture in B-flat major)	Fi 9–12	24
———	Suite in 9 movements (Overture in F major)	Fi 9–12	12
———	Suite in 12 movements (Overture in G minor)	Fi 9–12	18
Nalson, Valentine	Double Chant	Fi 1	97
Oswald, James	*The Dust Cart Cantata:* As Tinkring Tom	Fi 8	12
Paisible, James	Suite in 10 movements (Overture in G major)	Fi 9–12	30
———	Suite in 10 movements (Overture, 2, 3, Roundo, 5 Mr. Keller, Roundo, 7, 8, 9, Chacone)	Fi 9–12	68
Purcell, Henry (spurious)	I am well pleased	Fi 6	97
Purcell, Henry?	Fie nay prithee John	Fi 8	21
Purcell, Henry	Behold, I bring you glad tidings	Fi 2	30

		MS.	*Page*
Purcell, Henry	Be merciful unto me O God	Fi 2	15
		Fi 4	19
———	*Bess of Bedlam:* From silent shades	Fi 8	5
———	Blessed is he that considereth	Fi 2	50
		Fi 6	114
———	Blessed is the man (chorus only)	Fi 1	230
———	I was glad when they said	Fi 1	178
		Fi 2	41
		Fi 4	137
		Fi 6	128
———	Jack thour't a toper	Fi 8	11
———	Jubilate for Voices and Instruments. (Full score—D major)	Fi 6	78v
———	Julia your unjust disdain	Fi 8	9
———	Man that is born of a woman	Fi 1	26
———	My song shall be alway	Fi 4	102
		Fi 6	124v
———	O give thanks unto the Lord	Fi 2	1
		Fi 6	106
———	Once, twice, thrice	Fi 8	21
———	Sonata No. 1 *a 3* in G minor	Fi 1	251
———	Sonata No. 2 *a 3* in B-flat (fragment)	Fi 1	250
———	Suite in 9 movements (Overture: Bonduca)	Fi 9–12	83
———	Suite in 10 movements from Dioclesian	Fi 9–12	118
———	Suite in 9 movements (Overture: Gordian Knot)	Fi 9–12	74
———	Suite, 12 movements (Overture: Indian Queen)	Fi 9–12	49

		MS.	*Page*
Purcell, Henry	Suite in 10 movements (Overture: Married Beau)	Fi 9–12	79
———	Suite in 9 movements (Overture: The Virtuous Wife)	Fi 9–12	103
———	Te Deum for Voices & Instruments. (Full score—D major)	Fi 6	64
———	The Lord is King and hath put on glorious apparell	Fi 1	84
———	They that go down to the sea	Fi 4	36
———	Thou knowest Lord (The verse included by Croft in his Burial Service)	Fi 4	96
———	When Myra sings	Fi 8	1
Smith, John	Bring unto the Lord	Fi 6	139
———	Lord let me know my end	Fi 6	137v
———	Lord thou art become gracious	Fi 6	141v
———	O how amiable are thy dwelling	Fi 6	130v
Townsend, Roger	I will magnifie thee	Fi 6	143v
———	O praise God in his holiness	Fi 6	100
Travers, John	When Bibo thought fit	Fi 8	33
Turner, William (with Humfrey and Blow)	I will all way give thanks	Fi 1	160
Turner, William	I will magnifie thee O Lord	Fi 1	22
———	See oh see how the flowers adorn the spring	Fi 1	259
Tudway, Thomas	Quare fremerunt gentes	Fi 1	62
———	Sing we merrily unto God	Fi 4	154
———	The Lord hear thee in the day of trouble	Fi 1	50

		MS.	*Page*
Unidentified	Anthem for Christmas day (There were shepherds abiding)	Fi 6	17v
———	Behold I bring you glad tidings (incomplete)	Fi 6	2
———	Favorite Ode, A (From heav'n the land the angelic song)	Fi 6	14
———	God be merciful unto us	Fi 6	145v
———	Instrumental in four parts, ten bars long	Fi 1	259
———	Of battles or sieges	Fi 8	24
———	O praise God in his holiness (fragment)	Fi 1	96
———	Single Chants	Fi 1	95, 96, 97
———	Suite in 10 movements; (Overture in D minor)	Fi 9–12	108
———	Behold God is my salvation	Fi 1	245
———	The watery God (fragment)	Fi 8	36
———	Except the Lord build the house	Fi 6	133v
Wise, Michael	Awake put on thy strength	Fi 1	15
———	Blessed is he that considereth the poor	Fi 1	35
———	How are the mighty fallen	Fi 1	44
———	I will sing a new song	Fi 4	62
Wotton, Nicholas	O sing unto the Lord a new song	Fi 1	174

INDEX II: INITIAL WORDS AND TITLES

		MS.	*Page*
Acquaint thyself with God	Maurice Greene	Fi 5	98
Allemanda	John Barrett	Fi 9–12	101
All thy works praise thee	James Kent	Fi 6	153v
Anthem for Christmas day (There were shepherds abiding)	Unidentified	Fi 6	17v

		MS.	*Page*
As Celia was learning	John Isham	Fi 8	16
As pants the hart	G. F. Handel	Fi 6	88v
As tinkring Tom *(The Dust Cart Cantata)*	James Oswald	Fi 8	12
Awake put on thy strength	Michael Wise	Fi 1	15
Awake up my glory	John Broderip	Fi 6	147v
Behold God is my salvation	Unidentified	Fi 1	245
Behold I bring you glad tidings	Henry Purcell	Fi 2	30
——— (incomplete)	Unidentified	Fi 6	2
Be merciful unto me O God	Henry Purcell	Fi 4	19
Bess of Bedlam (From silent shades)	Henry Purcell	Fi 8	5
Blessed be the Lord	Capel Bond	Fi 6	196v
Blessed be thou Lord	James Kent	Fi 6	162v
Blessed is he that considereth	Henry Purcell	Fi 6	114
———	Michael Wise	Fi 1	35
Blessed is the man (chorus only)	Henry Purcell	Fi 1	230
Blessed is the people O Lord	William Croft	Fi 6	110v
Bring unto the Lord	John Blow	Fi 1	231
———	John Smith	Fi 6	139
Burial Service	William Croft	Fi 4	86
Chant, Double	Valentine Nalson	Fi 1	97
Chants, Single	Unidentified	Fi 1	95, 96, 97
Christ being raised from the dead	John Blow	Fi 1	98
Dust Cart Cantata, The (As tinkring Tom)	James Oswald	Fi 8	12
Except the Lord build the house	Unidentified	Fi 6	133v
Fair Cloe my breast so alarms	Henry Purcell	Fi 8	17
Favorite Ode, A (From heav'n the land the angelic song)	Unidentified	Fi 6	14
Fie nay prithee John	Henry Purcell	Fi 8	21

		MS.	*Page*
From heav'n the land the angelic song (A Favorite Ode)	Unidentified	Fi 6	14
From silent shades *(Bess of Bedlam)*	Henry Purcell	Fi 8	5
Get you hence for I must go (Trio in *The Winter's Tale*)	William Boyce	Fi 8	26
Give ear O Lord unto my prayer	Henry Aldrich	Fi 1	80
Give the King thy judgments	William Croft	Fi 2	88
God be merciful unto us	Unidentified	Fi 6	145v
Hear O Lord and consider my complaint	Maurice Greene	Fi 5	130
Hear ye heavens	William Knapp	Fi 6	135v
How are the mighty fallen	Michael Wise	Fi 1	44
How art thou fall'n from heav'n O Lucifer	John Blow	Fi 1	262
How long wilt thou forget me	William Brydle	Fi 6	143
I am well pleased	Henry Aldrich	Fi 4	1
———	Henry Aldrich (attr. Purcell)	Fi 6	97
Instrumental in four parts, ten bars	Unidentified	Fi 1	259
In the beginning was the word	James Kent	Fi 6	184
I said in the cutting off of my days	John Blow	Fi 1	112
I said I will take heed	William Knapp	Fi 6	178v
I waited patiently	John Blow	Fi 1	184
I was glad when they said	Henry Purcell	Fi 1	178
I will all way give thanks	John Blow, Pelham Humfrey, William Turner	Fi 1	160
I will give thanks	William Croft	Fi 2	61
I will hearken what the Lord God will say	John Blow	Fi 1	138

		MS.	Page
I will love thee O Lord	Jeremiah Clarke	Fi 4	114
		Fi 6	103v
———	John Church	Fi 1	189
I will magnifie thee	William Hine	Fi 6	190
———	Roger Townsend	Fi 6	143v
———	William Turner	Fi 1	22
I will sing a new song	Michael Wise	Fi 4	62
I will sing unto the Lord	William Croft	Fi 4	48
———	William Knapp	Fi 6	126v
Jack thour't a toper	Henry Purcell	Fi 8	11
Jubilate for Voices and Instruments	Henry Purcell	Fi 6	78v
Julia your unjust disdain	Henry Purcell	Fi 8	9
Let God arise	William Brydle	Fi 6	119v
Let us revel and roar	John Eccles	Fi 8	22
Lord how are they increased	John Blow	Fi 1	74
———	Maurice Greene	Fi 5	115
Lord let me know mine end	Maurice Greene	Fi 5	123
———	John Smith	Fi 6	137v
Lord thou art become gracious	John Smith	Fi 6	141v
Lord what love have I	James Kent	Fi 6	168v
Man that is born of a woman	Henry Purcell	Fi 1	26
Movement for strings	John Blow	Fi 1	6
Movement in C major	Godfrey Keller	Fi 9–12	70
My God, my God look upon me	Maurice Greene	Fi 5	105
My song shall be alway	Henry Purcell	Fi 4	102
		Fi 6	124v
My soul truly waiteth	Maurice Greene	Fi 5	55
O be joyful in the Lord	Pelham Humfrey	Fi 1	90
Of battles or sieges	Unidentified	Fi 8	24
O give thanks unto the Lord	Henry Aldrich	Fi 1	170
———	John Blow	Fi 1	147
———	Pelham Humfrey	Fi 1	121
———	Henry Purcell	Fi 2	1
O God of my righteousness	Maurice Greene	Fi 5	33

		MS.	*Page*
O God of my salvation	John Blow	Fi 1	1
O God thou art my God	Maurice Greene	Fi 5	65
O how amiable are thy dwellings	John Smith	Fi 6	130v
O Lord give ear	Maurice Greene	Fi 5	1
O Lord grant the King a long life	Maurice Greene	Fi 5	74
O Lord I have sinned	John Blow	Fi 1	8
Once, twice, thrice	Henry Purcell	Fi 8	21
O praise God in his holiness	John Goldwin	Fi 4	169
O praise God in his holiness	Roger Townsend	Fi 6	100
——— (fragment)	Unidentified	Fi 1	96
O praise our God	N. Clark	Fi 8	35
O praise ye the Lord	Pelham Humfrey	Fi 1	104
O sing unto God, sing praises	Maurice Greene	Fi 5	14
O sing unto the Lord a new song	James Hawkins	Fi 4	179
———	Nicholas Wotton	Fi 1	174
O sing unto the Lord with thanksgiving	Maurice Greene	Fi 5	89
Out of the deep	Henry Aldrich	Fi 1	87
Ponder my words O Lord	John Blow	Fi 1	210
Praise the Lord O Jerusalem	Jeremiah Clarke	Fi 2	132
Praise the Lord O my soul	William Child	Fi 1	33
———	John Church	Fi 1	200
———	William Croft	Fi 6	93v
Quare fremerunt gentes	Thomas Tudway	Fi 1	62
See oh see how the flowers adorn the spring	William Turner	Fi 1	259
Service in B minor	William Croft	Fi 3	1
Te Deum		Fi 3	1
Jubilate		Fi 3	29
Sanctus		Fi 3	41
Gloria		Fi 3	42
Service in E-flat	William Croft	Fi 3	48
Te Deum		Fi 3	48
Jubilate		Fi 3	76
Sing O heavens	James Kent	Fi 6	149v

		MS.	*Page*
Sing unto the Lord a new song	Maurice Greene	Fi 5	41
Sing we merrily unto God	Thomas Tudway	Fi 4	154
Sonata No. 1 *a 3* in G minor	Henry Purcell	Fi 1	251
Sonata No. 2 *a 3* in B-flat (fragment)	Henry Purcell	Fi 1	250
Suite for Strings	John Banister	Fi 9–12	1, 8, 88
———	John Barrett	Fi 9–12	94
———	Jeremiah Clarke	Fi 9–12	62
———	Gottfried Finger	Fi 9–12	38, 43, 54, 114, 124
———	Robert King	Fi 9–12	98
———	——— Morgan	Fi 9–12	12, 18, 24
———	James Paisible	Fi 9–12	30, 68
———	Henry Purcell	Fi 9–12	49, 74, 79, 83, 103, 118
———	Unidentified	Fi 9–12	108
Te Deum in A major	William Boyce	Fi 6	9v
Te Deum for Voices & Instruments	Henry Purcell	Fi 6	64
The earth is the Lords	William Croft	Fi 4	126
The Kings of Tharsis	John Blow	Fi 1	131
The Lord hath prepared his seat	James Kent	Fi 6	158
The Lord hear thee in the day of trouble	Thomas Tudway	Fi 1	50
The Lord is full of compassion	Jeremiah Clarke	Fi 6	116
The Lord is King and hath put on glorious apparell	Henry Purcell	Fi 1	84
The Lord liveth	William Boyce	Fi 6	199v
The Lord said unto my Lord	John Jackson	Fi 4	148
There were shepherds abiding (Anthem for Christmas day)	Unidentified	Fi 6	17v

		MS.	*Page*
They that go down to the sea	Henry Purcell	Fi 4	36
This is the day the Lord hath made	G. B. Draghi	Fi 1	216
Thou knowest Lord (The verse included by Croft in his Burial Service)	Henry Purcell	Fi 4	96
Thou O God art praised in Sion	Maurice Greene	Fi 5	25
Thus saith the preacher	Simon Ives	Fi 8	4
Thy hands have made me (incomplete)	John Blow	Fi 1	238
Thy way O God (chorus only)	John Blow	Fi 1	230
Turn thee unto me O Lord	John Blow	Fi 1	40
Watery God, The (fragment)	Unidentified	Fi 8	36
We will rejoice in thy salvation	William Croft	Fi 4	71
When Bibo thought fit	John Travers	Fi 8	33
When Myra sings	Henry Purcell	Fi 8	1
When Phoebus the tops of the hills	G. F. Handel	Fi 8	30
When the son of man	James Kent	Fi 6	180v
Who is this that cometh	James Kent	Fi 6	174
Why do the heathen	James Kent	Fi 6	171

4 / Repertorium der Quellen tschechischer Mehrstimmigkeit des 14. bis 16. Jahrhunderts

KURT VON FISCHER
Universität Zürich

IM Frühjahr 1965 bin ich auf den Spuren meines verehrten Kollegen Dragan Plamenac in die Tschechoslovakei gefahren, um dort die teilweise noch im altertümlichen Stil gepflegte Mehrstimmigkeit der tschechischen Utraquisten des 15. und 16. Jahrhunderts zu sammeln. Es ist mir eine besondere Ehre und Freude, ein erstes, allerdings in mancher Beziehung nur sehr vorläufiges Resultat dieser, im Hinblick auf die Inventarisierung der Handschriften und Werke in RISM unternommenen Forschungen dem Jubilaren als kleines Zeichen meiner Dankbarkeit überreichen zu dürfen.

Die in der Tschechoslovakei geschriebenen liturgischen, fast ausnahmslos utraquistischen Handschriften des 15. und 16. Jahrhunderts sind unter dem Sammelbegriff Kantional bekannt.[1] Hier ist nun freilich gleich zu bemerken, dass nicht alle unter diesem Begriff zusammengefassten Handschriften auch Kantionalien im engeren Sinne des Wortes, d. h. Handschriften mit Cantionen sind. Vielfach handelt es sich sogar um ausgesprochene Gradualien, oder zumindest um Handschriften, welche in einem ersten Teil Messgesänge, in einem zweiten Teil Cantionen und auch andere Gesänge enthalten. Keineswegs bringen alle tschechischen Gradualien und Kantionalien Mehrstimmiges. Gerade etwa das kunsthistorisch bedeutendste Stück, der Kantional von Litoměřice, enthält ausschliesslich ein-

1. Vgl. u. a. den Artikel "Kantional (tschechisch)" in *Die Musik in Geschichte und Gegenwart,* 7, Sp. 630 ff.

stimmige Gesänge. Ferner ist zu bemerken, dass die älteren Handschriften im allgemeinen vorwiegend lateinische, die jüngeren dagegen fast ausschliesslich tschechische Texte verwenden, wobei zahlreiche tschechisch textierte Stücke als Umtextierungen älterer lateinischer Kompositionen erscheinen.

Ohne hier im einzelnen auf stilistische Fragen eingehen zu wollen, können die verschiedenen Typen tschechischer Mehrstimmigkeit in die folgenden vier Gruppen unterteilt werden:

1. Organale Polyphonie des 14. und 15. Jahrhunderts von der Art wie sie auch im deutschen Raum des Spätmittelalters gepflegt worden ist. Einige stücke zeigen zudem den Einfluss der französischen und italienischen Ars nova.

2. Spezifisch tschechisch-utraquistische Polyphonie in den Gradualien und Kantionalien des 15. und 16. Jahrhunderts. Stilistisch handelt es sich um eine Mehrstimmigkeit, die einerseits noch deutliche Verbindungen mit dem älteren organalen Satz aufweist; dies ist besonders bei den in böhmischer Choralnotation geschriebenen Werken zu beobachten. Andererseits finden sich hier zahlreiche Stücke in schwarzer, im Laufe des 16. Jahrhunderts immer häufiger auch in weisser Mensuralnotation, die satztechnisch den Regeln des späten 15. und 16. Jahrhunderts folgen. Im allgemeinen herrscht aber auch bei diesen Stücken ein Satz Note gegen Note. Ferner ist eine Reihe von Werken in einer choral-mensural gemischten Notation aufgezeichnet. An Texten werden mehrstimmig gesetzt:

a) *Ordinariums-Sätze* (fast ausschliesslich Patrem und Sanctus). Innerhalb dieser Gruppe finden sich die meisten altertümlichen und choral notierten Stücke.
b) *Cantionen,* d. h. Strophenlieder, bei denen die Musik nur zu einer Strophe gesetzt ist.
c) *Cantilenen,* d. h. meist mehrtextige und durchkomponierte Stücke, die man als tschechische Motetten bezeichnen mag.

Die Unterscheidung von Cantionen und Cantilenen ist keine willkürliche. Sie lässt sich expressis verbis in den Handschriften Chrudim, Klatovy und Teplice nachweisen, in welchen in den Überschriften oder im Originalindex (Handschrift Chrudim) deutlich zwischen beiden Formen unterschieden wird. Die Zahl der Stimmen beträgt bei den Ordinariumssätzen zwei oder drei. Die Cantionen sind meist zwei-, oft aber auch dreistimmig, während in den

Cantilenen Drei- und Vierstimmigkeit neben der selteneren Zweistimmigkeit vorherrscht; fünfstimmig mit fünf verschiedenen Texten *(Panis ewus-Pange exul-Panis ecce angelorum-Patribus veteribus-Tantum ergo)* ist die Cantilene in Handschrift Hradec Králové II.A.6, fol. 339v/340 (Franus-Kantional).

3. Niederländische Polyphonie des 15./16. Jahrhunderts, wie sie in einzelnen erhaltenen Stimmbüchern (z. B. in Hradec Králové, Klatovy, Rokycany), vor allem aber in den beiden bekannten Handschriften Prag Strahov, D.G. IV.47 und Hradec Králové II.A.7 (olim Hs. 3955, sog. Cod. Speciálník) überliefert ist. Eine repertoiremässige Verbindung von Stücken des niederländischen Stilkreises mit Werken der Gruppe 2 findet sich im Cod. Speciálník, wo insbesondere ab fol. 428 (neue Hand) zahlreiche Konkordanzen mit den Kantionalien erscheinen.

4. Handschriften des späten 16. und frühen 17. Jahrhunderts, welche einerseits in weisser Mensuralnotation geschriebene Cantionen jüngeren Stils (bis sechsstimmig), andererseits ganze Messezyklen (Proprium und Ordinarium), meist unter Aufgabe der für die Kantionalien normalen Anonymität, mehrstimmig überliefern. Zu diesen gehören etwa die vier Stimmbücher Prag, Staats- und Universitätsbibliothek XI B 1 (dazu als 5. Stimmbuch gehörig: Prag Strahov, Ms. D.A. II.3); zu jenen der Kantional Benešovský (Prag Konservatorium), der Kantional Sedlčanský (jetzt in Prag, Nationalmuseum, ohne Signatur) und die beiden Kantionals, die sich im Bezirksmuseum von Tábor befinden.

Nun folge die Liste der mir bekannten Handschriften der Gruppen 1 und 2, derjenigen Handschriften tschechischer Herkunft also, die entweder ältere organale Mehrstimmigkeit oder anonyme Ordinariums-Sätze, Cantionen und Cantilenen in Kantionalien und Gradualien überliefern.[2]

2. Es sei an dieser Stelle allen Direktoren und Mitarbeitern der von mir besuchten Bibliotheken, Museen und Archiven der ČSSR mein allerbester Dank für ihre überaus grosse Hilfsbereitschaft ausgesprochen. Insbesondere gilt mein Dank Herrn Dr. J. Vanický, Leiter der Musikabteilung des Prager Nationalmuseums, der mir zahlreiche wichtige Informationen zukommen liess und meine Studien in jeder nur möglichen Weise unterstützt hat. Ferner danke ich der Leitung der Handschriftenabteilung der Staats- und Universitätsbibliothek Prag, die mir weit über die vorhandenen Kataloge von J. Truhlář hinausgehende Handschriftenbeschreibungen anfertigen liess.

Auf Literaturangaben wird im folgenden Verzeichnis mit wenigen Ausnahmen verzichtet, da sich die vorhandene Literatur und auch die Handschriftenkataloge nur

Praha, Národní museum, Hs. I.A.17.
Neuutraquistisches Graduale aus Solnice; zweites Viertel 16. Jh. Mehrstimmig sind: tschechisches Sanctus und mehrere tschechische Cantilenen.

Ibid., Hs. I.A.34.
1556 im Auftrage der Literatenbruderschaft von Rychnov nad Kněžnou geschriebenes Kantional mit Advents- und Weihnachtsgesängen. Mehrstimmig ist nur "Radostně Bohu," das u. a. auch in Hs. Hradec Králové II.A.14 steht.

Ibid., Hs. II.C.7.
Sog. Kantional von Jistebnice; um die Mitte des 15. Jh. erfolgte Abschrift eines hussitischen Kantionals von ca. 1420. Mehrstimmig sind: einzelne lateinische Ordinariumssätze (Patrem, Sanctus, Agnus), lateinische und tschechische Cantionen. Es ist dies die bisher wohl älteste bekannte Quelle für mehrstimmige tschechische Lieder.

Ibid., Hs. IV.B.9.
Graduale/Kantional (sog. Kantionale Krolmusův); datiert 1556/57. Mehrstimmig sind: ein tschechisches Sanctus und mehrere tschechische Cantionen.

Ibid., Hs. V.B.5.
Graduale; Mitte 16. Jh. (*terminus ante quem*: 1549). Mehrstimmig sind: tschechische Ordinariumssätze (mehrere Sanctus und Fragment eines Patrem).

Ibid., Hs. XII.A.1.
Graduale aus Plzeň.[3] Datiert 1390 und 1473. Mehrstimmig sind: Versschlüsse eines Liber generationis (14. Jh.) und ein lateinisches Patrem (spätes 15. Jh.).

---

ausnahmsweise mit den mehrstimmigen Stücken der betreffenden Handschriften befassen. Doch sei nachdrücklich auf die wertvolle Beispielsammlung von J. Pohanka, *Dějiny české hudby v příkladech* (Prag, 1958) verwiesen, in der zahlreiche mehrstimmige Stücke veröffentlicht sind. Besonders ist sodann die für die Mehrstimmigkeit der tschechischen Kantionalien des 15. und 16. Jahrhunderts grundlegende Arbeit von D. Orel, *Kancionál Franusův* (Prag, 1922) zu nennen. Ferner vgl. J. Vanický, *Umění vokální polyfonie* (Prag, 1955) und J. Snížková, *Musica polyphonica Bohemiae* (Prag, 1958). Endlich sei auch auf die Neuausgabe von Z. Nejedlý's *Dějiny husitského zpěvu* (6 Bände; Prag, 1954–1956) verwiesen, ein für den hussitischen Gesang grundlegendes Werk, in dem die Mehrstimmigkeit allerdings nur am Rande mitberücksichtigt ist. Zu den Hss. von Hradec Králové vgl. Neuesterns: J. Černý, *Soupis hudebních rukopisů muzea v Hradec Králové,* in Miscellanea musicologica Universitatis Carolinae Pragensis, Tomus XIX, Prag, 1966, 9 ff.

3. Die Mitteilung, dass dieses Graduale, entgegen dem Katalog von Bartoš, nicht aus Prag, sondern aus Plzeň stammt, verdanke ich Herrn F. Fišer aus Litoměřice.

Ibid., Hs. XII.A.23.
Graduale (nicht Antiphonar!) von Pavel Mělnický aus Plzeň. Datiert 1527. Mehrstimmig sind (nur Vorsatzblatt und Nachträge): Fragment eines lateinischen Patrem, ein Sanctus und "Christe iudex."

Ibid., Hs. XII.F.14.
Graduale, möglicherweise aus Jistebnice; geschrieben zwischen 1440 und 1460. Mehrstimmig sind: ein lateinisches Patrem und zwei lateinische Cantionen.

Ibid., Hs. XIII.A.2.
Graduale aus Kolín nad Labem (an der Elbe); geschrieben von Martin Baccalaureus de Wyskytná; datiert 1512. Mehrstimmig sind: lateinische Ordinariumssätze (Patrem, Sanctus), lateinische Cantionen und Cantilenen.

Ibid., Hs. XIII.E.4.
Missale aus Krumlov; geschrieben von Petrus dictus Cleparz de Tym; datiert 1423. Mehrstimmig sind: Versschlüsse der Lektion "In illo tempore intravit Jhesus in quoddam castellum."

Ibid., Hs. XIII.E.8.
Graduale unbekannter Herkunft. 1. Teil (bis fol. 107) 16. Jh.; 2. Teil (ab fol. 108) 15. Jh. Mehrstimmig sind im 2. Teil: lateinisches Sanctus (Fragment) und Agnus; anschliessend zweistimmige Weihnachtslektionen und Benedicamus.

Ibid., Hs. XVI.C.7.
Missale aus dem 14./15. Jh. Im hinteren Deckel eingeklebt: Liber generationis des 14. Jh. mit dreistimmigem Versschluss "Cristus."

Praha, Státní knihovna ČSSR-Universitní knihovna, Hs. IV.H.12.
Teil-Antiphonar des 16. Jh. Provenienz unbekannt (Kloster?). Mehrstimmig sind: zwei lateinische Benedicamus-Tropen.

Ibid., Hs. V.H.11.
Gemischte Hs. wohl noch des 14. Jh. aus der Kollegiumsbibliothek der Karls-Universität. Mehrstimmig sind: Benedicamus-Tropus und Weihnachtslektionen.

Ibid., Hs. V.H.31.
Texths. aus einer Kollegiumsbibliothek (Prag?). Enthält an Musik nur den bekannten Rondellus *Flos florum inter lilia* (vgl. u. a. J. Wolf, *Geschichte der Mensuralnotation* I, 390).

Ibid., Hs. VI.B.24.
Graduale/Kantional aus der Prager Altstadt (Kirche St. Castalin?); 16. Jh. Mehrstimmig sind: mehrere lateinische Sanctus (teils in Choral-

notation, teils in weisser Mensuralnotation); zahlreiche lateinische und tschechische Cantionen und Cantilenen.

Ibid., Hs. VI.C.20a.
Graduale/Kantional aus der Wende des 15./16. Jh.; vermutlich aus dem Besitz des Humanisten Johannes a Choterina. Mehrstimmig sind: lateinische Ordinariumssätze (Patrem, Sanctus, sowie als Nachträge Kyrie und Gloria); lateinische Cantilenen.

Ibid., Hs. VI.G.10a.
Prozessionar des 14. Jh. aus der Georgskirche in Prag (Hradschin). Mehrstimmig ist *Procedentem sponsum.*

Ibid., Hs. VI.G.16.
Wie Hs. VI.G.10a.

Ibid., Hs XI.E.9.
Da elsässisch-süddeutscher Herkunft, nicht zu diesem Repertoire gehörend.

Ibid., Hs. XIII.A.5c.
Graduale des 15./16. Jh. Ist 1605 aus Sedlec nach Prag gekommen. Mehrstimmig ist: ein zweistimmiges lateinisches Patrem.

Ibid., Hs. XIV.G.46.
Antiphonar des 14. Jh. aus der St. Georgskirche Prag (Hrad). Mehrstimmig ist: ein zweistimmiges Amen.

Ibid., Hs. XVII.A.32 (gehört als 2. Band zu Hs. XVII.A.31).
Graduale/Kantional, gestiftet von der Fleischerzunft der Prager Neustadt. Datiert 1567, 1596 und 1611. Mehrstimmig sind: mehrere tschechische Cantionen und Cantilenen.

Ibid., Hs. XVII.A.39.
Graduale/Kantional. Provenienz wie Hs. XVII.A.31./32. Datiert 1574. Mehrstimmig sind: mehrere tschechische Ordinariumssätze und tschechische Cantionen.

Ibid., Hs. XVII.A.41.
Graduale/Kantional; geschrieben auf Kosten der Magdalena vom Goldenen Stern aus der Prager Altstadt. Später im Besitze der Literatenbruderschaft St. Gallus der Prager Altstadt. Datiert 1576. Mehrstimmig sind: einige tschechische Cantionen.

Ibid., Hs. XVII.A.42.
Graduale; geschrieben auf Kosten des Jan Biskup (Bürger von Hradec Králové, geboren in Nové Město); wahrscheinlich bestimmt für die Literatenbruderschaft in Nové Město; datiert 1604. Mehrstimmig sind: mehrere tschechische Sanctus und Patrem.

Ibid., Hs. XVII.B.7, vol. 4.
Kantional (insgesamt 4 Bände) des späten 16. Jh. (Eintragungen datiert 1585 und 1591); aus der Stephanskirche der Prager Neustadt. Mehrstimmig ist nur ein nachgetragenes *Páne Božie.*

Ibid., Hs. XVII.B.8.
Fragmente verschiedener Gradualien und Kantionalien des 16./17. Jh. Mehrstimmig sind: tschechisches Patrem und Sanctus des späten 16. Jh.

Ibid., Hs. XVII.B.19.
Graduale der Literatenbruderschaft St. Gallus (Prager Altstadt) aus der zweiten Hälfte des 16. Jh. Mehrstimmig sind: fünf tschechische Patrem.

Ibid., Hs. XVII.B.20.
Graduale aus Český Brod. Datiert 1559. Mehrstimmig sind: tschechische Sanctus und Patrem, sowie Kyrie und Christe (mit zweistimmigem Versschluss).

Ibid., Hs. XVII.J.17, Fragment XIV.
Blatt des 15. Jh. unbekannter Provenienz. Mehrstimmig ist: zweistimmiges *Biskup zwiediew.* (Vgl. J. Pohanka, Beispielsammlung Nr. 53).

Praha, Archiv pražského hradu, Hs. N. XXIX.
Sammelhs. aus der Wende des 14./15. Jh. aus dem Prager Metropolitanarchiv. Mehrstimmig sind de Versschlüsse eines *Liber generationis.*

Ibid., Hs. E.LXVI.
Herkunft wie Hs. N.XXIX. Hinten und vorn je ein in den Deckel geklebtes Pergamentdoppelblatt des 14. Jh. mit zweistimmigen Lektionen.

Ibid., Hs. K.XXXVII.
Herkunft wie Hs. N.XXIX. Im vorderen Deckel eingeklebtes Vorsatzblatt aus einem Kantional des 15. Jh. mit zweistimmigem Benedicamus-Tropus "et nos dotali letantes."

Ibid., Hs. M.LII.
Herkunft wie Hs. N.XXIX. Pergamentumschlag mit mehrstimmigen Fragmenten (Motetten?) des frühen 15. Jh.

Praha, Museum hlavního města Prahy, Hs. ohne Signatur.
Utraquistisches Graduale aus der Prager Nikolauskirche (Kleinseite), sog. Graduale Malostransky. Mehrstimmig: zahlreiche tschechische Patrem und Sanctus.

Praha, Státní archiv, H. KVš.376 (olim Cod. Vyšehradský V. Cc4).
Graduale/Kantional aus der Mitte des 15. Jh. aus der Vyšehrad-Kirche. Mehrstimmig sind: lateinische Ordinariumssätze, lateinische Cantionen und Cantilenen (ein Stück mit tschechischem Text).

Brno (Brünn), Moravský zemský archiv, Hs. G.12-Sbírka Cerroniho II.265.
Missale romanum des 15. Jh. Vorangestellt ein Faszikel mit einstimmigen Praefationen und "Liber generationis" mit mehrstimmigen Versschlüssen.

Chrudim, Městské museum, Hs. I.2580.
Utraquistisches Graduale/Kantional. Datiert zwischen 1530 und 1549. Fast ausnahmslos lateinische Texte. Mehrstimmig sind: 5 lateinische Sanctus, 4 lateinische Patrem; es folgen 38 mehrstimmige Cantionen (eine davon tschechisch) und 36 lateinische Cantilenen. Diese Hs. ist eine der wichtigsten Quellen für die von den Utraquisten gepflegte Mehrstimmigkeit.

Hradec Králové (Königgrätz), Museum, Hudební oddělení Hs. II.A.6 (olim Hs. 43).
Graduale/Kantional, sog. Franus-Kantional; 1505 von Joannes Franus für die Heiliggeistkirche in Hradec Králové gekauft. Eine Prachths., die zugleich zu den wichtigsten Quellen für die utraquistische Mehrstimmigkeit zählt (vgl. D. Orel, *Kancionál Franusův*). Mehrstimmig sind: zahlreiche lateinische Ordinariumssätze, Cantionen und Cantilenen (zwei davon tschechisch).

Ibid., Hs. II.A.8 (olim Hs. 48).
Graduale. Datiert "Giržik Orfus Malirz z Chotiessyce 1564." Mehrstimmig sind: mehrere tschechische Sanctus und Patrem.

Ibid., Hs. II.A.11 (olim Hs. 47).
Graduale/Kantional (Rorate-Gesänge) aus Hradec Králové; datiert 1585 und 1586 (mit Anhang von 1763). Mehrstimmig sind: ein tschechisches Patrem und ein tschechisches Sanctus.

Ibid., Hs. II.A.13a/b (olim Hs. 44/45).
Zweibändiges Graduale des Matouš Radouš aus Chrudim, geschrieben für die Heiliggeistkirche in Hradec Králové. *Terminus ante quem:* 1584. Mehrstimmig sind: mehrere tschechische Patrem. Auf fol. 256v des zweiten Bandes findet sich eine ganzseitige Abbildung einer Gruppe von singenden Literaten in der Heiliggeistkirche von Hradec Králové; das aufgeschlagene Chorbuch zeigt ein vierstimmiges *Decantabat populus* von J. Rychnovský (publ. von J. Snížková in *Musica polyphonica Bohemiae,* S. 50f.).

Ibid., Hs. II.A.14 (olim Hs. 51).
Kantional, datiert 1599 und 1605 *(termini ante quem),* mit Nachträgen

bis 1652. Mehrstimmig sind: mehrere tschechische Cantionen und Cantilenen.

Ibid., Hs. II.A.15.
Graduale des 16. Jh. Mehrstimmig sind: einige tschechische Patrem und Sanctus.

Ibid., Hs. II.A.44.
Graduale; geschrieben 1586; gestiftet 1597 von Johannes Hradecký (Literatenbruder aus Hradec Králové) für die Marienkirche von Lochenice (bei Hradec Králové). Mehrstimmig sind: zwei tschechische Sanctus und Patrem.

Ibid., Hs. 6351.
Graduale um 1500. Gehörte vermutlich dem Literatenchor von Žiželice (bei Chlumec). Mehrstimmig ist: ein lateinisches Patrem. Den einstimmigen lateinischen Texten sind oft nachträglich tschechische Texte unterlegt.

Ibid., Hs., 8553.
Graduale. Herkunft wie Hs. 6351, jedoch jünger (Einband datiert 1563). Mehrstimmig sind: Mehrere tschechische Patrem und Sanctus.

Jindřichův Hradec, Státní archiv v Trěboni pracovište, Hs. ohne Signatur.
Graduale/Kantional der Literatenbruderschaft von Jindřichův Hradec; datiert 1491. Mehrstimmig sind: lateinisches Sanctus ("Salus honor"), Patrem (lateinisch) und Cantio "Solis praevia" (mit gegenüber anderen Hss. altertümlichem Contratenor).

Klatovy, Okresní Muzeum, Hs. C.3/403.
Graduale/Kantional aus der Werkstatt J. Táborskýs; beendet 1537; vermutlich geschrieben für die Marienkirche Klatovy. Mehrstimmig sind: einige lateinische Patrem und Sanctus, zahlreiche lateinische Cantilenen und zwei lateinische Cantionen.

Křivoklát, Státní Museum (Hradní knihovna), Hs. I.e.10.
Texths. des 14. Jh. Einziges Musikstück: zweistimmiges "Crucifixum in carne."

Litomyšl, Museum, Hs. ohne Signatur.
Zwischen 1561 und 1563 für die Literatenbruderschaft von Litomyšl geschriebenes altutraquistisches Graduale-Kantional. Mehrstimmig sind: tschechische Ordinariumssätze (Sanctus, Patrem, Agnus) und tschechische Cantilenen.

Mladá Boleslav, Museum, Hs. II.A.3.
Utraquistischer Kantional von 1572. Da sich die Hs. gegenwärtig, ihres sehr schlimmen Zustandes wegen, in Prag zur Reparatur befindet,

konnte sie nicht näher untersucht werden. Doch enthält sie bestimmt mehrere mehrstimmige Werke, jedenfalls auch lateinische Cantilenen.

Rakovník, Městské Museum, Hs. II.
Graduale/Kantional aus der Dekanatskirche Rakovnik, enthält vereinzelte Datierungen 1593 und 1594 = *termini ante quem.* Mehrstimmig sind: 6 tschechische Patrem.

Roudnice, Archiv proboštského, Hs. A.
Graduale, vermutlich von Probst Jan Muzofil im Jahre 1591 der Literatenbruderschaft von Roudnice geschenkt. Mehrstimmig sind: einige tschechische Patrem und Sanctus.

Ibid., Hs. B.
Graduale/Kantional für die Weihnachtszeit; um 1600 aus der Dekanatskirche Roudnice. Mehrstimmig sind: mehrere tschechische Cantilenen und Cantionen; ab fol. 158; eine vierstimmige, mensural notierte Marienmesse (Ordinarium und Proprium) im Stil der oben S. 00, unter 4 genannten Messen aus Hs. Praha, Státní knihovna XI B 1.

Rychnov, Okresní Museum, Hs. ohne Signatur.
Utraquistisches Graduale aus der 2. Hälfte des 16. Jh., geschrieben für die Kirche von Kostelec n. Orlicí. Mehrstimmig sind: 8 tschechische Ordinariumssätze (Patrem, Sanctus), sowie mehrere tschechische Cantilenen. Als Nachtrag folgt ein tschechisches Patrem in weisser Mensuralnotation.

Sedlčany, Městské museum na červeném hrádku, Hs. M.3.
Graduale/Kantional aus der Dekanatskirche St. Martin in Sedlčany aus der Mitte des 16. Jh. Mehrstimmig sind: lateinisches Patrem, tschechische Cantionen sowie eine lateinische Cantio.

Ibid., Hs. M.4.
Graduale. Provenienz wie Hs. M.3; *terminus ante quem:* 1593 (vermutlich aber Abschrift eines älteren Graduales). Mehrstimmig sind: ein tschechisches Sanctus und zwei tschechische Patrem, als spätere Eintragung ferner ein vierstimmiges tschechisches Et in terra.

Teplice, Oblastní vlastivědné muzeum, Hs. ohne Signatur.
Neuutraquistisches Graduale von 1560, geschrieben von J. Táborský für die Literatenbruderschaft von Teplice Mehrstimmig sind: mehrere tschechische Patrem, Sanctus und Agnus.

Ibid., Hs. ohne Signatur.
Neuutraquistischer Kantional von 1566. Mehrstimmig sind: zahlreiche tschechische Cantionen (die in älteren Hss. mit lateinischen Texten erscheinen).

Třebechovice, Museum, Hs. 134 (olim 1).
Graduale, datiert 1559. Stammt von der Literatenbruderschaft der Andreas-Kirche in Třebechovice. Mehrstimmig sind: tschechische Ordinariumssätze (Patrem, Sanctus, Agnus) und einige Cantilenen.

Třebenice, Muzeum českého granátu, Hs. ohne Signatur.
Graduale, geschrieben zwischen 1574 und 1583 von Matouš Ornys z Lindperka für die utraquistische Kirche von Třebenice. Prachthandschrift. Mehrstimmig sind: zwei tschechische Sanctus.

Ústí nad Orlicí, Archiv Proboštského, Hs. ohne Signatur.
Utraquistisches Graduale, um 1592 für die Literatenbruderschaft von Ústí geschrieben. Mehrstimmig sind: 5 tschechische Patrem.

Vyšší Brod (Hohenfurt), Klašterní knihovna, Hs. 28[4].
Texths. des 15. Jh.; enthält von fol. 175–183v lateinische Lieder. Mehrstimmig ist: "Huic sit memoria."

Ibid., Hs. 41.
Texths. des 15. Jh.; enthält Musik von fol. 31–34v. Mehrstimmig sind: Tropus "Spiritus et alme," lateinisches "Et in terra" und drei lateinische geistliche Cantionen, alles in weisser Mensural notation.

Ibid., Hs. 42.
Vom Hohenfurter Mönch Przybico im Jahre 1410 geschriebene Hs. Enthält einstimmige Messgesänge und "cantus secundum morem secularem." Mehrstimmig sind: Cantionen und Benedicamus-Tropen (teilweise in roter und schwarzer Notation auf einem System).

Ibid., Hs. LXV.
Zisterzienser Missale des 14. Jh. Auf dem Vorsatzblatt des frühen 15. Jh. steht ein zweistimmiges "Salve Maria regia."

Vodňany, Děkanský úřad, Hs. ohne Signatur.
Kantional aus Vodňany; *terminus ante quem:* 1537; geschrieben von J. Táborský. Der Kantional war noch im späten 19. Jh., vielleicht sogar noch 1930 im Gebrauch. Mehrstimmig sind: tschechische Cantionen und Cantilenen (die in älteren Hss. z. T. mit lateinischen Texten erscheinen), ferner als Nachträge ein tschechisches Patrem und Sanctus.

Wien, Oesterreichische Nationalbibliothek, Hs. 5094.
Sammelhs. mit verschiedenen Blättern verschiedenster Provenienz. Darunter auf fol. 162r–163v drei unvollständige lateinische Patrem vermutlich tschechischer Provenienz.

4. Zu den Handschriften von Vyšší Brod vgl. den Katalog *Xenia Bernardina,* Bd. II (Wien, 1891).

Ibid., Hs. 15501.
Lateinisches Graduale aus Kutná Hora (Kuttenberg), vermutlich aus dem späten 15. Jh. Mehrstimmig ist: ein lateinisches Patrem.

Ibid., Hs. 15503.
Tschechisches Graduale aus Časlav. Datiert 1557, geschrieben von J. Táborský. Mehrstimmig sind: drei Versschlüsse eines tschechischen Kyrie ("Kyrie fons bonitatis").

Ibid., Hs. 15509.
Wie Hs. 15503; datiert 1568. Mehrstimmig sind: zwei Kyrie Versschlüsse (wie Hs. 15503).

5 / Di una lauda nel codice pavese Aldini

FEDERICO GHISI
Università di Firenze e Pisa

NEL vasto repertorio della canzone profana quattrocentesca, soggetta a travestimento spirituale e studiata in precedenti ricerche, mi venne fatto di soffermarmi per il suo particolare interesse storico musicale sull'incipit *Donna sti miei lamenti,* che nei testi di laude edite nel 1489 si canta come *Donna esto mio lamento: Vinitiana* e come *L'amore a me venendo* nella stampa del 1512.

Su questa ultima lauda vorrei richiamare l'attenzione, essendoci pervenuta la melodia nei due codici: 145 Cl. IX della Marciana a Venezia e 361 Aldini della Biblioteca Universitaria di Pavia. Dalla loro stesura musicale è perciò possibile risalire all'intonazione originaria della canzone profana più antica, il cui testo poetico é uno strambotto del Giustiniani per accertata attribuzione.

A documentazione della musica mi valgo della versione esemplata nel XV secolo del codice Aldini, descritto da L. De Marchi e da G. Bertolani nell'inventario dei manoscritti della Biblioteca Universitaria di Pavia. Vi sono raccolti brani vocali sacri e profani, in latino e in volgare, fra i quali a c. 2v–3r la seguente lauda *L'amor ad me venendo* di cui riproduco il testo.[1]

1. Per la difficile lettura del manoscritto sbiadito e consunto, la trascrizione diplomatica è stata redatta dalla Dr. Maria Pia Andreolli dell'Istituto di Paleografia dell'Università di Pavia, e la versione critica curata dalla Dr. Elena Barassi dell'Istituto di Storia della Musica di questa Università, alle quali esprimo i miei più sentiti ringraziamenti per la loro preziosa collaborazione.

L'amor ad me venendo
Sì m'a ferito el core
Sì che en gran fervore
[Io vivo] languendo.

Languesco per dilecto
Che tu mi fay sentire,
Jesu beneditto,
Fame d'amor morire!
Et non possu sufferire,
Amor, cutal ferita,
Jesu, como la vita
Ch'io me vo straziando.

Straziome, e vo pensando
Allo infinito amore:
Chi andandoti scappando,
Tu m'ay ferito el core;
Non possu piuy allore
A ti fare resistencia,
Per che la tua clemencia
Me fae ch'io andar cantando.
[L'amor . . .]

Cantando vao un cantu,
Che li angeli fan festa:
Che tornato m'è in pianto
Ogni mundana festa.
Amor, cum che molestia
Sento le toy sagite!
Sento el cor ferito,
Et vome consumando.
L'amor . . .

Consumato mi è el core;
Non so che m'è venuto,
Che my, gran peccatore,
L'amor m'abia vestito;
Et voy cavar fructu
De la mia feditade,
Giusta al caritati
Che puro me vay chercando.
L'amor . . .

Cha fato m'ay, amore,
Senza el mio volire!
Essendo pien d'orrure,
Ad me volisti venire;
E chi patia tacere
Che non crida amore,
Si che el crepi el core
ad che te va fugendo?
L'amore . . .

Fugito t'o, amore,
Per la mia falsitati,
Et in le cose defora
Possi la mia felicitati;
Et pien di vanitati
Alla morte curriva,
Et non me nascondiva
Come andava saltando.
L'amor . . .

Saltando andava
Alla aeterna morte,
Et may non me pensava
Le mie vie che eran torte.
Che in mare sa gecta
. . . .
Si tucto el mio pecto
Si lavi piangendo!
L'amor . . .

Piangendo per amore
Cussì mi prigare,
Or che sono yo, Signore,
Che tu my voy amare:
Prego, non indusiare,
Fa che en sia suctracto
Dallo aperto costato:
Che dintro sia adormentato!
L'amore . . .

Il contesto poetico mostra passi non sempre di chiaro significato, ma il suo erotico fervore religioso sembra giustificare l'attribuzione al Bianco Ingesuato o a Jacopone da Todi. La forma metrica è quella della ballata con stanze formate da due "mutazioni" di due versi ciascuna e una "volta" di quattro versi, oltre la ripresa iniziale, pure di quattro versi, che ritornella ad ogni stanza l'incipit "L'amore."

Veniamo ora alla musica sopra esemplata, poiché è quanto maggiormente ci interessa. La sua intonazione per lo stesso principio del travestimento spirituale dovrebbe corrispondere alla melodia dello strambotto del Giustiniani *Donna sti miei lamenti,* che per un procedimento meccanico di ripetizione rimane tale e quale alla sua versione profana d'origine, anche se qui risulta riadattata alla veste poetica di una lauda.

A questo proposito troppo numerosi sono gli esempi di strambotti e canti carnascialeschi che di volta in volta hanno rivelato la loro intonazione musicale più antica, anche se esemplata in veste laudistica più recente. Perciò questa stessa versione melodica su testo spirituale, di cui siamo in possesso, dovrebbe pur corrispondere all'altra che si canta invece su "l'aere vinitiano" di *Donna esto mio lamento,* a noi però ancora sconosciuta, ed entrambe le versioni, ammesso siano identiche, rivelarci quel modo di cantare misurato, proprio allo strambotto.

Purtroppo l'esempio musicale qui sopra pubblicato non sembra svelare, malgrado l'aspettativa, il mistero della "vinitiana" e i suoi presupposti e peculiari aspetti stilistici, ritenuti come espressione di un canto estemporaneo, infiorettato da vocalismi alternati ad una intonazione misurata al verso poetico. Infatti, dall'esame della stesura musicale di *Amore ad me venendo* è possibile riconoscere caratteristiche melodiche e armoniche di tarda derivazione arsnovista, senza però riscontrare passi vocalizzati che sembrano decaduti dall'uso, almeno in questo caso, malgrado risultino presenti qua e là in altri esempi di strambotti-laude.

La struttura polifonica a due voci qui appare regolata in modo simmetrico, nota contro nota, persistendo ancora fra le due parti cantate gli intervalli di ottave e quinte consecutive e così pure di quarte e terze; quest'ultime fra la 9–10 battuta si susseguono più volte come le due voci inferiori di un falso bordone.

D'altra parte la stessa espressione melodica del brano rispecchia il gusto musicale dell'epoca che non distingueva il profano dal sacro.

A conclusione di questa breve nota, ogni altra induzione sul famigerato stile musicale della "vinitiana," senza ulteriori documenti di accertamento, non sembra possa convalidare per ora nuove ipotesi, salvo voler avvalorare delle supposizioni avventate.

L'amor ad me venendo.

6 / Historical Awareness in Anton Webern's *Symphony*, Op. 21

SCOTT GOLDTHWAITE
University of Illinois

Much has been written in recent years about Anton Webern's place in contemporary music. The articles in the second volume of *Die Reihe*, for example, deal with various aspects of his style, some in considerable detail. These articles are well known and do not need to be summarized here; suffice it to say that rhythmic, dynamic, intervallic, temporal, phraseological, and other facets of his music have been thoroughly analyzed.

The present study is limited in that it attempts to show Webern's predilection for symmetrical construction in the two movements of the Symphony, Op. 21. The introduction of the second part of Isaak's *Choralis Constantinus*[1], which Webern, as a musicologist, edited, demonstrates that he was captivated not only by the expressive beauty of Isaak's vocal lines but by their contrapuntal erudition as well. He especially points out the ingenious employment of canon and choral color:

> Isaak uses canonic devices very profusely in the second part of the *Choralis Constantinus*—two-part canons at the unison, the fourth above and below, the fifth and octave or the twelfth. It may happen that one part is so derived from another that, entering at the same time as the latter, it imitates it in notes of double the value, or, likewise starting at the same time, transposes the other to the third above. In addition Isaak constructs three-part canons, a four-part one, three double canons and

1. *Denkmäler der Tonkunst in Österreich,* Jahrg. XVI, Vol. 1.

finally two crab canons. Close or more distant imitation, stretti, augmentations, diminutions continually occur. . . .

It is remarkable how Heinrich Isaak achieves widely differing tonal effects with the means at his disposal. . . . Another element is the most delicate observation of tone colour in the various registers of the human voice. This is partly the cause of the frequent radical crossing of parts and of their movement by leap.[2]

There seems to be little doubt that Webern's training in musicology under Guido Adler greatly influenced him in organizing certain compositions written in the serial technique, from the String Trio, Op. 20 (1927) onward. One wonders, for example, whether he would have introduced the subtle symbolism in the String Quartet, Op. 28—in which the first and last movements, respectively, have forty-eight and thirty-two entries of the B-a-c-h tone row—unless he had approached the problem historically. Webern's use of the devices of canon as a technique and as a unifying principle, exemplified in the first movement of the Symphony and the third movement of Cantata No. 1, Op. 29, tempts one to reflect back to the late fifteenth and early sixteenth centuries through the manner in which he employs them. There is a suggestion of the kind of musical concept that produced Ockeghem's *Missa prolationum*—that is, a noticeable preoccupation with intellectual as well as musical principles of construction.

It is true that traditional musical forms in certain of Webern's works function somewhat differently than when used in works based upon tonality and upon thematic repetition and contrast; although the same principles are present they are adapted to serial organization. My examination of two aspects of the Symphony will attempt to show the formal structure and symmetries that are present in the two movements of the work. The first of the two aspects is formal, the second is the instrumentation as related to the form.

The order of the original tone row is well known, and does not require elaborate description here; it is given merely for reference in tabular form. It consists of two hexachords separated by a tritone, the second of which is the retrograde of the first. It has therefore only two forms, O and I.[3]

2. Translation quoted from *Die Reihe,* No. 3, pp. 24–25.

3. O is the original, I the inversion, R the retrograde, RI the retrograde inversion, as in the standard procedure of indicating transpositions.

To determine the symmetries according to Webern's intention, however, it is necessary to view these forms in two ways. O equals an R form and I an RI form, as follows:

O	=	R_6	I	=	RI_6
O_1	=	R_7	I_1	=	RI_7
O_2	=	R_8	I_2	=	RI_8
O_3	=	R_9	I_3	=	RI_9
O_4	=	R_{10}	I_4	=	RI_{10}
O_5	=	R_{11}	I_5	=	RI_{11}
O_6	=	R	I_6	=	RI
O_7	=	R_1	I_7	=	RI_1
O_8	=	R_2	I_8	=	RI_2
O_9	=	R_3	I_9	=	RI_3
O_{10}	=	R_4	I_{10}	=	RI_4
O_{11}	=	R_5	I_{11}	=	RI_5

The O and I forms are:

The first movement begins as a canon using a mirror and retrograde form of the row. The paired entries O–I_8 and I–O_4 (bars 1–2 and 3–4 respectively) bear this out. Not so obvious, however, is the overall form of the movement, which can be determined only by examining the transposition order of the row. In the following schematic plan, column 1 represents the transpositions up to the first double bar and repeat sign, column 2 those from bar 25^b (second ending) to bar 43, and column 3 those from there to the end of the movement.

O			I_7	O	
I_8			I_3	I_8	
I			O_7	I	
O_4			O_{11}	O_4	
I_3	:‖	‖:	O_5	I_3	:‖
O_5			O_1	O_5	
O_9			I_9	O_9	
I_7			I_1	I_7	
I_8				I_8	
O_4				O_4	
O_5				O_5	
I_7				I_7	

Even a casual glance reveals that the third column is a recapitulation of the first and that the second is not, although it employs some of the transpositions of column 1. If one applies the standard custom of giving letters to the sections, including the literal repeats, the formal organization is seen to be that of the earlier sonata form: AA/BABA. One can apply the terms Exposition, Development, and Recapitulation to the sections, but on the basis of serial rather than thematic and tonal principles. Even the "Development" (B) follows the procedure of using some "material" from A. Thus, in a single movement Webern applied two structural principles, the canon and the sonata form, both of which reflect a historical point of view.

If the Janus-like character of the row is shown graphically, it may be seen that the "Development" is further emphasized by the symmetrical organization:

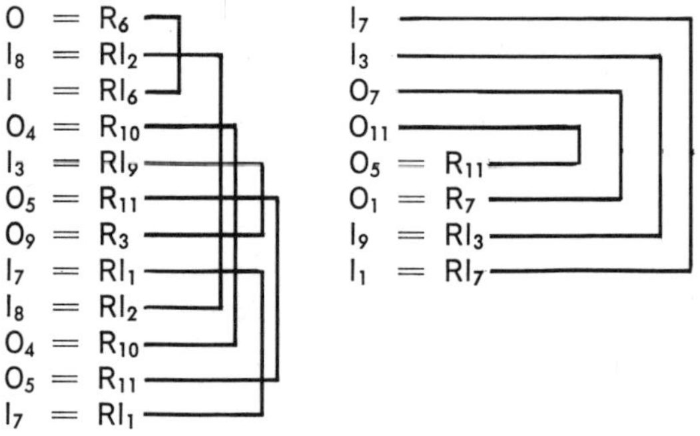

The "Exposition" and "Recapitulation" are not symmetrical in the same way.

Another proof of what seems to have been Webern's intention rests in the scoring[4] of the movement, for he has used the same principles in tone color.[5] (See diagram "Exposition.")

$O(R_6)$ and $I(RI_6)$ use the same number of tones per instrument and the same tone colors. The same is true of I_8 (RI_2) and O_4 (R_{10}), and of O_5 (R_{11}) and I_7 (RI_1); these are in alternating order. O_5 (R_{11}) and I_7 (RI_1) are treated differently, and do not coincide with their previous orderings.

4. So much has been said about Webern's "pointillist" technique in instrumentation that it is not necessary to deal with that subject here. For what it may be worth, one might consider his interest in Isaak's voice crossings.

5. The following symbols are employed: p = pizz., a = arco, m = muted, o = open. Arabic numerals indicate the number of tones per instrument.

EXPOSITION

$O = R_6$	Hn. II 4(O)	Clar. 4	Vla. 4(a)			
$I_8 = RI_2$	Harp 1	Vil. 3(2Pla)	Vln. II 1(a)	Harp 3	Hn. II 2(o)	Harp 2
$I = RI_6$	Hn. I 4(o)	B. Clar. 4	Vla. 4(a)			
$O_4 = R_{10}$	Harp 1	Vla. 3(2Pla)	Vln. I 1(a)	Harp 3	Hn. I 2(o)	Harp 2
$I_3 = RI_9$	Vil. 4(a)	Clar. 4	Hn. 2 4(o)			
$O_5 = R_{11}$	Harp 2	Hn. II 2(1M10)	Vln. I 4(1P3a)	Harp 2	Vla. 2(a)	
$O_9 = R_3$	Vla. 4(a)	B. Clar. 4	Hn. I 4			
$I_7 = RI_1$	Harp 2	Hn. I 2(1M10)	Vcl. 4(1P3a)	Harp 2	Vln. 2(a)	
$I_8 = RI_2$	Vla. 2(a)	Harp 2	Vla. 6(3P3a)	Harp 1	Vla. 1(a)	
$O_4 = R_{10}$	Vln. II 2(a)	Harp 2	Vcl. 6(M3P3a)	Harp 2		
1st ending $O_5 = R_{11}$	Harp 1	Vla. 7(a)	Vcl. 4(M3P1a)			
2nd ending $O_5 = R_{11}$	Harp 1	Vla. 7(a)	Vcl. 3(P)	Harp 1		
1st ending $I_7 = RI_1$	Harp 3	Vcl. 5(M1P4a)	Harp 3	Vla. 1(P)		
2nd ending $I_7 = RI_1$	Harp 1	B. Clar. 3	Vcl. 4(a)	Vla. 3(am)	Harp 1	

The symmetry in the row order of the "Development" is reflected in its instrumentation:

DEVELOPMENT

I_7	Clar. 3	Vln. I 1(a–m)	Harp 2	Vln. I 5(a–m)	B. Clar. 1	
I_3	Vcl. 3(am)	Hn. I 1(m)	Harp 2	Clar. 6		
O_7	Clar. 3	Vln. II 1(a–m)	Harp 2	Vln. II 6(am)		
O_{11}	Vla. 3(a–m)	Hn. II 1	Harp 2	B. Clar. 2	Vcl. 2(am)	Harp 2
R_{11}	Harp 2	Vcl. 2(am)	B. Clar. 2	Harp 2	Hn. II 1	Vla. 3(am)
R_7	Vln. II 6(am)	Harp 2	Vln. II 1(am)	Clar. 3		
RI_3	Clar. 6	Harp 2	Hn. I 1(m)	Vcl. 3(am)		
RI_7	Vln. I 6(am)	Harp 2	Hn. I 1(m)	Vcl. 3(am)		

Here related pairs have related instrumentation: I_7 and RI_7 have almost the same number arrangement but somewhat different scoring. The second member of each of the pairs—I_3 and RI_3, O_7 and R_7, O_{11} and R_{11}—has exact retrograde instrumentation. Again, in the number of notes per instrument I_7, I_3, and O_7 are, with one exception, identical and RI_7, RI_3 and R_7 are quite identical, thus producing a sort of double symmetry.

In view of the foregoing, one might expect the instrumentation of the "Exposition" to be repeated in the "Recapitulation"; that it is not, however, is shown by the following tabulation:

RECAPITULATION

$O = R_6$	Vla. 4(am)	Vcl. 2(a)	Vln. I 6(a)			
$I_8 = RI_2$	Harp 1	Vln. II 2(am)	Hn. II 1(m)	Harp 1	Vln. II 5(am)	Hn. I 2(o)
$I = RI_6$	Vln. I 4(a)	Vla. 2(a)	Clar. 5	Vcl. 1(a)		
$O_4 = R_{10}$	Harp 1	Clar. 3	Harp 1	Vcl. 3	B. Clar. 2	Clar. 2
$I_3 = RI_9$	Vln. I 4(a)	Vla. 2	Vln. I 6			
$O_5 = R_{11}$	Hn. I 2(o)	Vln. II 7(a)	B. Clar. 3			

$O_9 = R_3$	Clar. 1	Vcl. 3(a)	Vla. 2(a)	Clar. 6	
$I_7 = RI_1$	Clar. 2	B. Clar. 2	Vla. 4(a)	Hn. I 1(m)	Vln. II 3
$I_8 = RI_2$	B. Clar. 2	Vln. I 10(am)			
$O_4 = R_{10}$	Vln. II 8(am)	Vla. 4(am)			
$O_5 = R_{11}$	Vla. a(am)	Harp 2	Hn. I 1		
$I_7 = RI_1$	Vla. 9(am)	Harp 2	Vln. II 1(am)	On repetition this tone is two octaves lower in the harp.	

The alternating symmetries of the "Exposition" are not present.

The intended symmetries of the Theme and Variations appear most clearly only when the row orders are shown in their two-faced forms. The orders appear in the O and I forms in the left-hand column of each variation. (See page 72.)

At first glance there would seem to be O and R forms related to Variation I, with its two groups of four entries, within each group. These do not, however, constitute the intended order, which is shown in the lower column of the diagram. Only the scoring, which will be discussed later, reveals the intended symmetry, even though it is obvious that the second group of four repeats the first. In both groups, the entries are also canons, I_3 and O_1, RI_3 and R_1.

Once again, the second variation does not reveal the intended symmetry until one examines the scoring. Rows O_8 and I_7, with which the variation begins, are stated by Horn I with alternating tones as a rhythmic ostinato.

It is clear that Webern intended this ostinato as the passage around whose recognizable tone color the other transpositions were to be symmetrically organized.[6] Its function is somewhat like that of a *cantus firmus*.

6. As will be seen later, this intention is borne out by the scoring of the other rows. A somewhat similar procedure is employed in the second movement of Cantata I, Op. 29, where the vocal entries (except the first), when isolated, form an exactly symmetrical plan.

SYMMETRIES OF THE THEME AND VARIATIONS

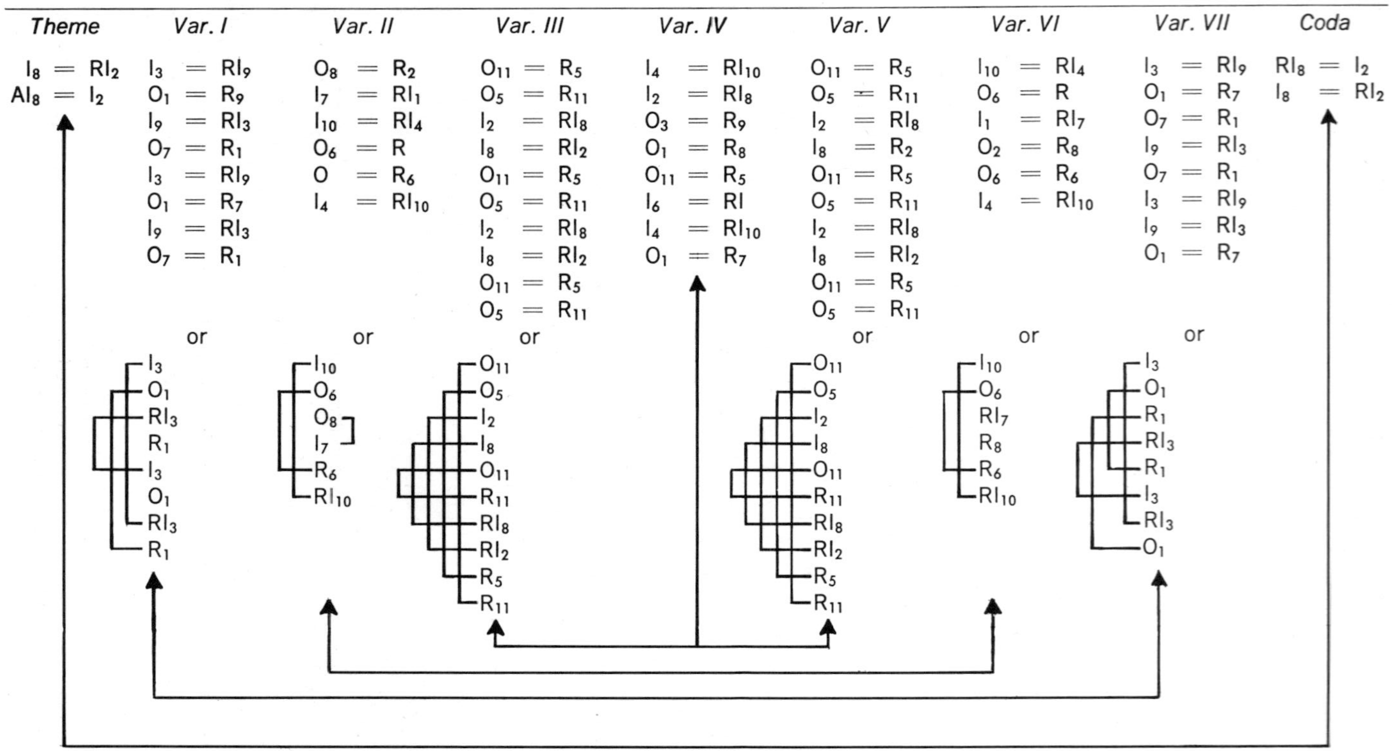

Variation III is again symmetrical, and is arranged in pairs a tritone apart. Moreover, the arrangement is concentric (O_{11} at the beginning, R_{11} at the end, etc.).

The fourth variation is the central one, and its entries are differently ordered. Symmetry is avoided, and the variation is therefore set apart. It may be likened to the hub of a wheel made up of the theme, the other variations, and the coda.

In order of transposition, Variation V recapitulates Variation III. It contains the same repetitions, within itself as well as the same paired entries in the middle. Similarly, Variation VI reflects Variation II with the exception of the two central entries. Here the seventh and eighth transpositions are reversed, with RI_7 in the position of O_8, and with R_8 in the position of I_7. Moreover, the proof of what Webern intended by the position of the first horn in Variation II is shown by a comparison with the above rows (RI_7 and R_8), which are also given to the first horn and in alternation of tones. Here the rows appear in the normal order of entry, as a glance at the preceding diagram will make clear.

The symmetrical plan by now is clear, and one can easily guess that Variation VII will correspond to Variation I, and the Coda to the theme. As in Variations II and VI, there is a slight change in the order of transposition. The Coda is, of course, the mirror of the theme.

Here we have a largely symmetrical plan concentric to the central variation.

It now remains to examine the scoring of each variation, in order to determine Webern's consistency in following row ordering from the point of view of the movement of tone color. Obviously there is no question of scoring by inversion or retrograde inversion; nevertheless, certain correlations are possible. The scoring will be considered by comparing variations that are symmetrically placed in relation to the center—that is, Variation I with Variation VII, Variation II with VI, etc.

In order that the "theme" may be as clear as possible, the same tone color is employed for all twelve tones. The accompaniment is symmetrically distributed between two tone colors.

THEME[7]

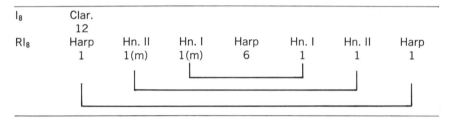

I_8	Clar. 12						
RI_8	Harp 1	Hn. II 1(m)	Hn. I 1(m)	Harp 6	Hn. I 1	Hn. II 1	Harp 1

It might be expected that the Coda, since it is the mirror of the theme, would reflect the scoring of the latter; but it does not. However, since RI_8 is the retrogradation of I_8, a tritone away, Webern has provided an exactly retrograde scoring:

CODA

RI_8	Harp 3	Vln. I 1(a)	Harp 2	Vln. I 3(a)	Vcl. 2(P)	Harp 1
I_8	Harp 1	Vcl. 2(P)	Vln. I 3(a)	Harp 2	Vln. I 1(a)	Harp 3

Variations I and VII, although they are alike in the order of transposition, are not scored alike. Rather, each is considered as a separate problem because of the musical content. Yet in each the same relations between O and R forms and I and RI forms are maintained. In Variation I Webern was very careful to show that repeated row forms do not parallel one another. The eight forms are each divided into two groups of four, so that I_3 of Group One is mirrored by RI_3 of Group Two, O by R_1, R_1 by O_1, etc. Since the entire variation is scored for strings, color is produced by an alternation of arco and pizzicato; and the mirroring of the related rows is emphasized by the repeated use of the same instrument, as well as of the same ordering and number of tones per instrument. Since the row entries are paired in canon, a double symmetry is present. The parallel with Variation VII will be shown in the discussion that follows:

7. The repeated notes in the harp and horns in RI_8 are not counted in the table since they are not new notes of the row.

VARIATION I

I_3	Vln. I 2(a–m) 1(p–m) 2(a–m) 2(p–m) 5(a–m)	
O_1	Vcl. 2(a–m) 1(p–m) 2(a–m) 2(p–m) 2(a–m) 1(p–m) 2(a–m)	canon
RI_3	Vln. II 3(p–m) 2(a–m) 1(p–m) 5(a–m + 1 repeated p) 1(a–m)	
R_1	Vla. 3(p–m) 2(a–m) 1(p–m) 5(a–m + 1 repeated p) 1(a–m)	canon
I_3	Vln. II 1(a–m) 1(p–m + 1 repeated a) 4(a–m) 1(p–m) 2(a–m) 3(p–m)	
O_1	Vla. 1(a–m) 1(p–m + 1 repeated a) 4(a–m) 1(p–m) 2(a–m) 3(p–m)	canon
RI_3	Vln. I 5(a–m) 2(p–m) 2(a–m) 1(p–m) 2(a–m)	
R_1	Vcl. 2(a–m) 1(p–m) 2(a–m) 2(p–m) 2(a–m) 1(p–m) 2(a–m)	canon

But another relation must also be taken into account. Each pair of row entries, as has been mentioned, is in canon. This arrangement accounts for the note distributions of I_3 O_1 in the first group, which are very similar, whereas RI_3 and R_1 are identical. The second group follows a reverse order: I_3 O_1 are identical, RI_3 R_1 are similar.

Although the order of entry for the rows in Variation VII is slightly different from that in Variation I, the basic relation of the rows is the same. This again is borne out by the instrumentation, which though entirely different from Variation I in tone color, employs the same parallel principle.

VARIATION VII

I_3	Clar. 2	Harp 2	Vla. 2(p)	Hn. I 2(o)	Clar. 2	Harp 2
O_1	B. Clar. 2	Harp 2	Vln. II 2(p)	Hn. II 2(o)	B. Clar. 2	Harp 2
R_1	Vcl. 2(a)	Clar. 3	Hn. I 1(o)	Vcl. 3(p)	Clar. 1	Vla. 2(a)
RI_3	Vln. I 2(a)	B. Clar. 3	Hn. II 1(o)	Vln. I 3(p)	Clar. 1	Vln. II 2(a)
R_1	Harp 2	B. Clar. 2	Hn. I 2(o)	Vln. II 2(p)	Harp 2	B. Clar. 2
I_3	Vln. II 2(a)	B. Clar. 1	Vln. I 3(p)	Hn. II 1(m)	B. Clar. 3	Vln. I 2(a)

RI_3	Harp 2	Clar. 2	Hn. I 2(o)	Vla. 2(p)	Harp 2	Clar. 2
O_1	Vla. 2(a)	Clar. 1	Vcl. 3(p)	Hn. I 1(o)	Clar. 3	Vcl. 2(a)

However, there are again, as in Variation I, pairs in canon, though slightly different as to order. As a result there is another relationship of scoring due to the canons; that is, numbers of notes per instrument as well as similar tone color.

VARIATION I

canon	I_3	
	O_1	(similar to I_3 in number
canon	RI_3	(identical
	R_1	in number)
canon	I_3	(identical
	O_1	in number)
canon	RI_3	
	R_1	(similar to RI_3 in number)

VARIATION VII

canon	I_3	(identical
	O_1	in number)
canon	R_1	(identical
	RI_3	in number)
canon	R_1	(identical
	I_3	in number)
canon	RI_3	(identical
	O_1	in number)

A comparison of the scoring of Variations II and VI shows an interesting parallel. In the latter, where the scoring is restricted to wind instruments, Horn I nevertheless serves much the same function as in Variation II. It announces two rows in alternating notes, and becomes a center around which the other rows are organized. (See page 71.)

The symmetry of the instrumentation in both variations is so exact as not to need discussion in detail. The only deviation in the retrograde rows is the substitution in RI_{10} of Variation II, of three notes by the bass clarinet for the two cello notes and one bass clarinet note in I_{10}.

Variations III and V are, again, very different in instrumentation even though, as has been shown, they are exactly alike in row structure. Variation III is canonic and follows the same principles of scoring that have been observed in Variations I and VII; the retrograde rows mirror the originals and inversions as far as possible, and in the canons the allocation of notes is comparable. Variation V, however, is unique. Since the variation is entirely chordal, instrumental symmetry is observable only by careful study. The unique

VARIATION II

I_{10}	Vcl. 2(a)	B. Clar. 1	Harp 1	Clar. 1	Vla. 1(p)	B. Clar. 1	Vln. II 1(p)	B. Clar. 1	Harp 1	B. Clar. 1	Harp 1
O_6	Clar. 2	Harp 1	B. Clar. 2	Vla. 1(p)	B. Clar. 1	Vla. 1(p)	Harp 1	Clar. 1	Harp 1	Clar. 1	
O_8	Hn. I 12(o)										
O_7	Hn. I 12(o)										
R_6	Clar. 1	Harp 1	Clar. 1	Harp 1	Vla. 1(p)	B. Clar. 1	Vla. 1(p)	B. Clar. 2	Harp 1	Clar. 2	
RI_{10}	Harp 1	B. Clar. 1	Harp 1	B. Clar. 1	Vln. II 1(p)	Clar. 1	Vla. 1(p)	Clar. 1	Harp 1	B. Clar. 3	

VARIATION VI

I_{10}	B. Clar. 12	Canon
O_6	Clar. 12	
RI_7	Hn. I 12(4–o, 1–m, 7–o)	
R_8	Hn. I 12(o)	
R_6	Clar. 12	
R_{10}	B. Clar. 12	Canon

VARIATION III

O_{11}	Vln. I 1(p)	Vla. 2(a)	Clar. 3	Vln. II 3(a)	Hn. I 2(o)	Harp 1			canon
O_5	Vcl. 1(p)	Vln. II 2(a)	Vla. 3(a)	Clar. 3	Hn. II 2(m)	Harp 1			
I_2	Hn. I 1(o)	Harp 1	Vln. I 1(p)	Clar. 3	Vla. 3(a)	Hn. II 2(m)	Harp 1		canon
I_8	Hn. II 1(m)	Harp 1	Vcl. 1(p)	Vln. II 3(a)	Clar. 3	Hn. I 2(o)	Harp 1		
O_{11}	Hn. II 1(m)	Harp 1	Vln. I 2(a)	Hn. I 1(m)	Harp 3	Vcl. 2(a)	Harp 1	Hn. I 1(o)	Retrograde Instr.
R_{11}	Hn. I 1(o)	Harp 1	Vcl. 2(a)	Harp 3	Hn. I 1(m)	Vln. I 2(a)	Harp 1	Hn. II 1(m)	
RI_8	Harp 1	Hn. I 2(o)	Clar. 3	Vln. II 3(a)	Vcl. 1(p)	Harp 1	Hn. II 1(m)		canon
RI_2	Harp 1	Hn. II 2(m)	Vla. 3	Clar. 3	Vln. I 1(p)	Harp 1	Hn. I 1(o)		
R_5	Harp 1	Hn. II 2(m)	Clar. 3	Vla. 3(a)	Vln. I 2(a)	Harp 1			canon
R_{11}	Harp 1	Hn. I 2(o)	Vln. II 3(a)	Clar. 3	Vcl. 2(a)	Harp 1			

features are the allotting of exactly the same number of tones per instrument in each row and the use of the harp for notes 4, 5, and 6 in each row; these notes are thus central, and are preceded and followed by 2 + 2 in different tone colors used in chord successions. These tone color changes in rows are not to any great extent aurally perceptible. (See page 78.)

VARIATION V

O_{11}	Vla.	Vcl.	Harp	Vln. II	Vln. I	
	2(a)	2(a)	4	2(a)	2(a)	
O_5	Vln. I	Vln. II	Harp	Vcl.	Vla.	Retrograde Instr.
	2(a)	2(a)	4	2(a)	1(a)	
I_2	Vln. II	Vln. I	Harp	Vla.	Vcl.	
	2(a)	2(a)	4	2(a)	2(a)	
I_8	Vcl.	Vla.	Harp	Vln. I	Vln. II	Retrograde Instr.
	2(a)	2(a)	4	2(a)	2(a)	
O_{11}	Vla.	Vcl.	Harp	Vln. II	Vln. I	
	2(a)	2(a)	4	2(a)	2(a)	
R_{11}	Vln. I	Vln. II	Harp	Vcl.	Vla.	Retrograde Instr.
	2(a)	2(a)	4	2(a)	2(a)	
RI_8	Vln. II	Vln. I	Harp	Vla.	Vcl.	
	2(a)	2(a)	4	2(a)	2(a)	
RI_2	Vcl.	Vla.	Harp	Vln. I	Vln. II	Retrograde Instr.
	2(a)	2(a)	4	2(a)	2(a)	
R_5	Vla.	Vcl.	Harp	Vln. II	Vln. I	
	2(a)	2(a)	4	2(a)	2(a)	
R_{11}	Vln. I	Vln. II	Harp	Vcl.	Vla.	Retrograde Instr.
	2(a)	2(a)	4	2(a)	2(a)	

Within limitations, the principle of paired scoring (O_{11}—O_5, etc.) of Variation V is similar to that of Variation III. The difference is that in Variation III the pairs, except for the central one, have nearly parallel scoring (O_{11} O_5, etc.), whereas in Variation V the second row of each pair is a kind of retrograde despite its chordal structure.

Since Variation IV is the central one, around which the other variations are symmetrically placed, it is treated somewhat differently: that is, there are no mirrored entries between the first and second groups of four rows. In scoring, some correspondences occur in the numbers of notes per instrument. In distribution I_4, I_2, O_1, and the final O_{11} are alike, the last two reversing the first two; O_8 and I_4 are similarly related. The first entry of O_1 (Group One) and I_6 are somewhat different from one another.

VARIATION IV

I_4	Clar. 2	Vcl. 2(a)	Vla. 2(a)	Hn. I 2(m)	Vln. II 2(a)	Clar. 1	Hn. I 1(m)	
I_2	Hn. II 2(m)	Vln. II 2(a)	Vln. I 2(a)	Vcl. 2(a)	Hn. I 2(m)	Harp 1	B. Clar. 1	
O_3	Hn. I 2(m)	Hn. II 2(m)	Vln. II 2(a)	Vla. 2(a)	B. Clar. 1	Hn. II 2(m)	Hn. I 1(m)	
O_1	B. Clar. 2	Clar. 4	Vln. I 2(a)	Hn. II 1(m)	Harp 2	Hn. II 1(m)		
O_1	Clar. 1	Hn. I 1(m)	Vcl. 2(a)	Clar. 2	Vln. I 2(a)	Vcl. 2(a)	Clar. 2	
I_6	Hn. II 1(m)	Hn. I 1(m)	B. Clar. 1	Hn. II 1(m)	Vln. I 2(a)	Vla. 2(a)	Hn. II 2(m)	Hn. I 2(m)
I_4	Harp 1	Hn. II 2(m)	Harp 1	Vla. 2(a)	Hn. I 2(m)	Clar. 2	B. Clar. 2	
O_{11}	Harp 1	B. Clar. 1	Hn. I 2(m)	Vln. II 2(a)	Vcl. 2(a)	Vln. II 2(a)	Hn. II 2(m)	

The object of this essay has been to examine only two facets of the Symphony, Op. 21—its formal organization and its scoring. The latter reinforces the former, and at the same time emphasizes small segments by instrumental color, especially where canons are employed. Even where the use of precisely the same tone color in retrograde is impossible, a similar one is substituted (string pizzicato for harp, for example).

Webern reflects his abundant knowledge of older forms and techniques in the construction of this Symphony, and he adapts them to serial composition. The historical implications can hardly be ignored.

7 / Another Barbingant Mass

CHARLES HAMM
University of Illinois

Among the handful of works attributed to Barbingant—all of which, curiously enough, are printed in the *Opera Omnia* of Jacob Barbireau[1]—is a single Mass, the *Missa Terribilment*, two voices of which parody an anonymous bergerette. We know nothing of Barbingant's life except that he must have been active as a composer around and shortly after the middle of the fifteenth century. Though his preserved output is slight, he is assured a small niche in the history of the cyclic Mass because this work appears to be one of the very earliest parody Masses.

There is, however, another Mass, which is anonymous in the two manuscripts which preserve it, but which is surely by Barbingant. It is found in S.P. B.80 (Rome, San Pietro, MS. B.80), on folios 39r–48v, and in Tr.89 (Trent, Castello del Buon Consiglio, 89), on 306v–315. The Credo is incomplete in S.P. B.80; the scribe apparently turned one page too many of his model, missing an entire opening and leaving out the "Et incarnatus" and "Et in spiritum" sections.

My initial identification of this as a Barbingant Mass was based on a passage in the third book (Capitulum II) of Tinctoris'

1. Jacobus Barbireau, *Opera Omnia*, ed. Bernhard Meier, 2 vols., Corpus mensurabilis musicae 7 (Rome: American Institute of Musicology, 1954–1957). For an excellent discussion of this matter see C. W. Fox, "Barbireau and Barbingant: a Review." *Journal, American Musicological Society*, XII (1960), 79–101.

Proportionale musices.[2] Here, in a discussion of various "errors" made by certain of his contemporaries in the notation of proportions, he observes: "Multi vero per praedictum temporis imperfecti majorisque prolationis signum taliter reversum Ͽ sesquialteram quod etiam deterius est per impletionem notarum denotabilem, ut Barbingant in suo 'Et in terra' autenti prothi mixti. . . ."

In the "Domini fili unigenite" duo in the Gloria of the Mass in question, the superius has a signature of Ͽ, against ¢ in the other voice; the entire brief passage is in coloration in the top voice, and the effect is the replacement of two semibreves by three (colored) semi-

EX. 1. Gloria, *Domini fili unigenite.*

breves (see Example 1). The Mass has a finalis of D, with a range from A to f′. I have been unable to find this unusual mensural usage in the Gloria of any other Mass from the same period. The signature seems unnecessary, incidentally, since coloration alone would have brought about the same effect, and the scribe of Tr.89 has not bothered to record the mensural sign. It should be pointed out that this is by no means an isolated example of a simplification by this particular scribe of a passage he considered difficult or obscure.

It is apparent immediately that this Mass has many general similarities to the *Missa Terribilment,* which is also found in S.P. B.80. All five sections of both are organized in a O–¢–O pattern, with the change to *tempus imperfectum diminutum* and the change

2. Coussemaker, *Scriptorum,* IV, 171–72. My first, tentative identification of the composer of this Mass on the basis of Tinctoris' remarks was made in "The Manuscript San Pietro B.80," *Revue belge de Musicologie,* XIV (1960), 43.

back to *tempus perfectum* taking place at the same point in the text of the two. In both works *tempus perfectum* moves in semibreves and minims, with many semiminims and a scattering of fusae, and with suspended dissonance allowed on the minim; in both, there are two varieties of *tempus imperfectum*, clearly differentiated from one another: in one, movement is in breves and semibreves, with dissonance on the semibreve, whereas in the other the movement is in semibreves and minims, with dissonance occurring on the minim.

Similarities of general structure are found within individual sections. The contrasting *tempus imperfectum* section of the Kyrie is of the semibreve–minim type in each, and in the Gloria it is of the breve–semibreve variety. And such exact correspondence as that between the Sanctus of the two Masses reaffirms that they must indeed be by the same composer:

Missa Terribilment		*Missa sine nomine*
○ (semibreve–minim), a 3	Sanctus	○ (semibreve–minim), a 3
○ (semibreve–minim), a 2	Pleni sunt	○ (semibreve–minim), a 2
₵ (breve–semibreve), a 3	Osanna	₵ (breve–semibreve), a 3
₵ (semibreve–minim), a 2	Benedictus	₵ (semibreve–minim), a 2
"ut supra"	Osanna	○ (semibreve–minim), a 3

At first glance the *Missa sine nomine* appears to be a tenor Mass. The Kyrie and Agnus break down into the expected three sections, the middle movements into five; the five sections match in finalis and show melodic similarity in the tenor:

	Section				
	1	2	3	4	5
Kyrie	D	D			D
Gloria	D	D	D	A	D
Credo	D	D	D	A	D
Sanctus	D	D	D	A	D
Agnus Dei	D	D			D

Apparently a *cantus firmus* has been split into five fragments, with the first, second, and fifth used for the tripartite movements and all five for the others. The belief that we are dealing with a tenor Mass is strengthened when it is observed that the parallel sections are themselves broken into smaller fragments with identically patterned cadences. For instance, in the large Section 1 outlined in the diagram above, important structural cadences in the tenor have the following pattern:

Section 1

Kyrie	D			F		D
Gloria	D	A		F	F	D
Credo	(D)	A	A	F		D
Sanctus	D	A		F		D
Agnus Dei	D	A		F		D

We should expect either to find the *ur*-tenor in the Kyrie, with additions in succeeding sections to accommodate longer texts, or to be able to piece together the *ur*-tenor from the Gloria and Credo, with subtractions for shorter sections. Section 5 of the tenor looks very much the same:

Section 5

Kyrie	G	D	A		D
Gloria	G	D		F	D
Credo	G	D	A	F	D
Sanctus	G	D	A		D
Agnus Dei	G	D	A	F	D

From this we should anticipate no difficulty in reconstructing the original of the tenor from the Credo and Agnus, although we should note that phrases have been omitted from the other sections.

But when we turn to the music itself, the idea that this is a tenor Mass does not hold up. The first five or six notes of the tenor of each movement agree, but the melodic correspondence goes no further. Not even the most liberal attitude toward melodic coloration, not even the assumption that we are dealing with a decidedly irrational treatment of a *cantus firmus*, will permit the identification of a tenor common to all five movements of the Mass. Here, for example, is the tenor of each movement for the first part of Section 1, through the cadence on A (Example 2).

No analysis of the tenor will reveal similarity except in the beginning phrases. The line may move to cadences on the same scale degrees in the successive movements, but it cannot be analyzed as variation of a common melodic source. Indeed, if the first note of the tenor of Sections 2, 3, and 4 is dropped an octave, the melodic shape of the beginning of each of these becomes almost identical with that of the first section. The tenor at each of these sectional beginnings is simply a "melodic" line resulting from the pitch movement of a part that temporarily takes over the function of a bass line, with a con-

EX. 2. Section I, tenor.

tour determined by movement to those notes required by conventional phrase-beginning harmonic patterns. In other words, the tenor is clearly a bass part here—a further indication that the work is not a tenor Mass, since such Masses usually draw on a liturgical melody, a secular tune, or sometimes a melodic voice from another polyphonic composition. Also, tenor Masses are commonly identified in manuscripts by a title standing at the head of the entire Mass, or by some few words of text written under the borrowed melody. There is no such information about this Mass in either of the manuscripts in which it is found, nor does Tinctoris refer to it by such a title.

Since the *Missa Terribilment* is a parody Mass, it is quite possible that our Mass is of the same type. In the former, each of the movements and many of the internal sections begin with both the superius and the tenor parodying the model chanson for a number of measures, whereas the contratenor is mostly free, drawing on the chanson only rarely in the middle or at the ends of phrases. As in many parody Masses, the borrowed material is treated much more freely and in more irregular fashion than was customary in a tenor Mass.

But in the *Missa sine nomine*, even though both the superius and the tenor voices show some melodic similarity at sectional beginnings, closer analysis reveals that it is not a parody Mass. The superius and the tenor both often follow their model in the *Missa Terribilment* at important structural points—beginnings of movements, beginnings of internal sections, changes of mensuration, ends of sections—for stretches so long that it would be possible with little difficulty to reconstruct these two voices of the chanson, if that had not been preserved. But in the present Mass the superius behaves just as we have seen the tenor behave: a common motif of a few notes can be traced at corresponding points in the various movements, but even though this voice, like the tenor, may move to cadences on the same note in the same order, it is impossible to trace recurring melodic material after the initial few notes. Here, as an example, are the beginnings of the superius in Section 5 in each movement. The initial note is D, and a triad is quickly outlined. Four of the five continue to a first cadence on the A above the first note; but no matter how determined an effort one makes to analyze these and succeeding phrases as variations on a common melodic source, the results are negative (Example 3).

EX. 3. Section V, superius.

During the first three decades of the fifteenth century, composers became interested in establishing musical relationships between the paired Mass items or among the movements of a partial or complete Mass Ordinary cycle. These relationships were at first quite general: common clefs; common mensural patterns; common finalis; the same number of voices, with the same disposition of text; often a common head motif, at first of only a few notes in the superius, later of a longer sequence in two or even three voices. Soon, more thorough and complex methods of organization were developed, in tenor, paraphrase, and parody cycles. These latter techniques have occupied scholars of later fifteenth-century music, so much so as to obscure a recognition that Masses based on other principles of organization continued to be written.

The Barbingant *Missa sine nomine* is such a Mass. It is organized, first of all, tonally. Each movement has a finalis of D; all larger internal sections also have a D finalis, with the exception of the penultimate of the three middle sections, which for contrast ends on A, the dominant in a later harmonic-tonal sense. Again for contrast, cadences within the five larger sections are often on F, A, or (rarely) G, though D cadences predominate at this level also. Since the Mass is not based on a *cantus firmus*, this unification around a dominating tone, with excursions to related tones, was a conscious device, not something already present in a borrowed melody.

The Mass is further unified by its general structure. Each of the five movements has a basic O–¢–O design, with contrast of three and two-part writing:

Kyrie	O (a3)		¢ (a3)		O (a3)
Gloria	O (a3)	O (a2)	¢ (a3)	C 2(a2)	O (a3)
Credo	O (a3)	O (a2)	¢ (a3)	C 2(a2)	O (a3)
Sanctus	O (a3)	O (a2)	¢ (a3)	¢ (a2)	O (a3)
Agnus Dei	O (a3)			¢ (a2)	O (a3)

It is also unified by melodic motto. Corresponding sections of the five movements begin with common melodic material in both superius and tenor—only a few notes in the top voice, but sometimes more in the tenor.

The Mass, dating probably from after the mid-century, is an example of the survival of an earlier sort of Mass in a time when newer techniques were becoming popular. Incidentally, the compositional devices used here can also be observed in certain sections of the *Missa Terribilment*. The duo sections of the Sanctus and Agnus Dei are free, in that they do not draw on the chanson which is parodied elsewhere. Both are in ¢ and occur at corresponding places in the structure of their respective movements. Both come to a first cadence on D, then move to A, to F, and finally back to D. There is melodic similarity in both voices at the beginnings of these two duo sections and at the beginnings of internal sections. In these free sections of what is otherwise a parody Mass, Barbingant uses precisely those methods of organization found throughout the "free" *Missa sine nomine;* the similarities are so marked that even had Tinctoris not told us the Mass was by Barbingant, we should have guessed it was on the basis of style.

8 / *Fors seulement* and the Cantus Firmus Technique of the Fifteenth Century

HELEN HEWITT
North Texas State University

IT WAS August Wilhelm Ambros who first called attention to *Fors seulement*, a French "rondeau cinquain" of the fifteenth century, and more specifically to the unusually large number of musical settings bearing the incipit of this rondeau. In the third volume of his *Geschichte der Musik* Ambros expressed the opinion that *Fors seulement* seemed to have served as a touchstone for the setting of a secular chanson as did *L'Homme armé* for the composition of a Mass.[1] He listed the various arrangements known to him: Ockeghem's original setting in the Dijon Codex,[2] the eight

This essay is a slightly expanded version of a paper read at the annual meeting of the American Musicological Society held at Berkeley, in December 1960.

While writing his doctoral dissertation on "The Albums of Marguerite of Austria," Dr. Martin Picker also became involved with the *Fors seulement* problem, and he thought of writing an article on some of the pieces. As it happened, I had submitted the title of my paper before becoming aware of Dr. Picker's special interest in *Fors seulement*. He was most helpful to me in many ways during the preparation of my paper. I am pleased to have this opportunity of expressing my appreciation. Through correspondence we discovered that we were in substantial agreement at every turn in regard to decisions that had to be made. This statement is borne out by his article in *Annales musicologiques*, as well as by his published dissertation: Picker, "Albums," and Picker, *Albums*. (See the List of Sources following this essay, in which *sigla* have been prepared for the citation of manuscripts and early printed works; modern articles and books will be cited by the surname of the author only, if no confusion will arise; otherwise, by the surname followed by a short title.)

1. Ambros, *Geschichte*, III, 57.

2. *Ibid.*; also *n.* 2, apparently Kade's addition. See List of Sources, Dijon 517, and the Annotated Concordance, No. 1.

works in the Basevi MS. in Florence,[3] and the six compositions published by Petrucci in *Canti B* and *Canti C*.[4] Since four of these works occur in both the Basevi MS. and either *Canti B* or *Canti C*, the actual total is eleven, not fifteen, as Ambros thought.

Some years later, Otto Kade published Obrecht's arrangement (from Ambros' score) among the musical examples constituting Volume V of the *Geschichte*. In his introduction he itemized eighteen arrangements[5] (not including Obrecht's setting), but if duplicates are disregarded, the true total is fourteen. Brumel's setting, for example, is listed as three different compositions: the first, by "Al. Agricola" (after Petrucci 1504[3] *Canti C*); the second, by Brumel (after Florence 2439); and the last, by an anonymous composer (after Munich 1516, although Kade cites the older call number "Codex 204"). Other errors make this list as unreliable as that in Volume III. Kade's comment is interesting, however: "With this list of song material, surely not yet complete, I have wished merely to give an impetus to more rigorous researches which are so lacking in this field. For I am firmly convinced that comparative studies, which in other fields enjoy such splendid success, would work only to the greatest advantage in the study of our own art, not merely in the individual case of the piece or song, but for the art in general, for the cultivation of the art of an entire period."[6]

In 1925, the late Otto Gombosi encountered the *Fors seulement* problem while making his study of the style of Obrecht.[7] He mentioned in his book that he knew of thirty-two works called *Fors seulement*, but had been unable to obtain them all. He then stated the basic problem more clearly by pointing out that there exist certain compositions "whose connection with the *Fors seulement* song has hitherto not been clarified."[8] He felt that "in spite of the

3. See List of Sources, Florence 2439.

4. See List of Sources, Petrucci 1502[2] *Canti B* and Petrucci 1504[3] *Canti C*.

5. Ambros, *Geschichte*, V, xix. Kade added Nos. 25, 31, 32, and 35 (see Annotated Concordance at end of article).

6. *Ibid.*

7. See List of Sources, Gombosi, *Obrecht*. As early as 1910, Eduard Bernoulli extracted Ockeghem's superius from seven of the compositions in St. Gall 461 for comparison of notation, but, although valuable in its way, this study has no direct bearing on the present narrow one. See Bernoulli's *Studie*, pp. 81–83. Gustave Reese, in *Music in the Renaissance* (New York, W. W. Norton, 1954), *passim*, discusses seven of the *Fors seulement* chanson settings in some detail: Nos. 1, 4, 5, 6, 20, 26, and 30.

8. Gombosi, *Obrecht*, p. 16.

wealth of source material, important compositions that could provide connecting links between quite different pieces with different *cantus firmi* seem . . . to be lost."[9]

Since Gombosi wrote these prophetic words, the development and use of microfilm have made the sources more readily accessible. More manuscripts have also become known, so that today there exists sufficient material for presenting a somewhat more complete account of the career of the rondeau *Fors seulement.* But no claim is made that this study will contain the final word on this subject, for one cannot predict what the future may disclose in the way of additional settings of *Fors seulement.*[10] This short essay can only sketch the barest outline of a family tree—the genealogy of *Fors seulement.*

Thirty secular works called *Fors seulement* have survived, and two motets employing sacred words, although based on a secular *(Fors seulement)* cantus firmus. Three other secular pieces remain incomplete because one or more part-books of the original sets are missing today.[11] A List of Sources, placed at the end of this discussion, names the manuscripts and early printed volumes which transmit these thirty-five settings. An Annotated Concordance then shows the location of the compositions in manuscript or print.

The composers of twenty-one of the thirty-five compositions are known; the composer of one work is *incertus,* since it is attributed to Josquin in one source and Ghiselin in another; thus, thirteen settings are anonymous. Ambros stated that "the Roman Costanzo Festa made an arrangement of the song,"[12] and Kade identified the source of Ambros' knowledge in a footnote: "Costanzo Festa's song is

9. *Ibid.*

10. Even since these words were written in the fall of 1960, the "second Copenhagen chansonnier" (Copenhagen 1848) and a manuscript at Cividale, Italy, have become known to me. I am greatly indebted to Dr. Plamenac for permitting me to have a copy of his film of Copenhagen 1848; it contains our settings Nos. 14 and 31. I am also indebted to Dr. Lewis Lockwood of Princeton University for a copy of the *Fors seulement* from Cividale (Museo Archeologico, MS. 59), a manuscript otherwise containing only sacred music. (A Table of Contents was distributed in connection with Dr. Lockwood's paper read in Washington, D. C., at the annual meeting of the American Musicological Society, December 1964.) I have not included this late setting of *Fors seulement* found in Cividale, since I can find in it no musical connection with the material discussed here. Its text is the original rondeau *Fors seulement l'attente,* except that the words "la mort" occur directly after "Fors seulement." The piece is attributed—inscrutably—to "Andreas pleni."

11. Nos. 11, 12, and 21.

12. Ambros, *Geschichte,* III, 57.

mentioned by Aron in the *Aggiunta des Toscanello.*"[13] This composition has not yet come to light, however, so that it has been assigned no number in this study. An alphabetical List of Composers follows the Annotated Concordance.

Six sources reflect a local interest in the gathering of settings of *Fors seulement.* Twelve settings, for example, are grouped together at the beginning of St. Gall 461; seven arrangements are found at the very end of Vienna 18746. A full report on these grouped compositions follows the List of Composers.

Fors seulement—either poetry or music—appears nearly one hundred times in the old manuscripts and prints. The poetry alone is found in five purely literary sources: four manuscripts and one print, *Le Jardin de plaisance,* published in Paris, *c.* 1501. The thirty-five musical settings appear in thirty manuscripts, from the Dijon Codex of *c.* 1475 to the Cambrai MS., dated 1542. They are also found in eleven early prints from Petrucci's *Canti B* of 1502 to Le Roy and Ballard's *Premier livre de chansons a trois parties* of 1578.

We do not know the precise date of composition of any of these works, yet a rather satisfactory chronology can be established based on the dates of sources in which they appear. The rondeau itself must have been written before 1470, the date assigned the Berlin MS. that once belonged to Cardinal de Rohan[14] and in which the poem appears. This is the earliest appearance of the rondeau. Some five years later the original three-part setting of the words by Johannes Ockeghem was inscribed in the Dijon Codex. This work is the fountainhead of the stream of compositions that borrowed from it in the ensuing decades.[15] It is preserved in six different manuscripts. In three of them, the two upper parts appear on the folios in the positions appointed by tradition for superius and tenor; in the other three, their positions are reversed. Some decision on terminology was necessary for use in the Table below in which analyses are made of the treatment of Ockeghem's materials in later arrangements of *Fors seulement.*[16]

13. *Ibid., n.* 2.

14. List of Sources, Berlin 78.B.17.

15. Its opening and closing measures appear on p. 122 below. The voices are given as found in Paris 1597, St. Gall 461, and Rome C. G. XIII, 27.

16. See pp. 120–21.

As may be observed, the two upper parts are identical for the first four measures, after which one part takes an upward, the other a downward turn. The range of the voice leading upward is somewhat higher than that of the other, although the parts cross during measures 49–53. Partly because of its range, but mainly because of its cadence (leading-tone, tonic), it was decided to call this voice the superius, regardless of its entering last—as the tenor usually does. The voice that tends downward, although it is the upper voice at the start, closes with the traditional tenor ending: supertonic, tonic; this voice will be called the tenor. Ockeghem has, in fact, constructed a cadence for three voices in a manner considered ideal during this period.[17]

With a terminology thus established, we may say that the "superius" was the part more frequently borrowed for use as a cantus firmus. If the tenor were borrowed, it could be placed (ideally) only in the tenor of the new work; if it were placed elsewhere, the "displaced" tenor ending would make difficulties for the arranger and preclude the formation of the favored structure. The superius, on the other hand, could function only uneasily as a "tenor," so that again ingenuity would be required of the arranger. A cadence was not impossible, of course; it merely could not have the ideal structure. It may have been these very difficulties, in part, that stimulated these composers and persuaded them to place the borrowed part in a different voice. Ockeghem's original setting is written in the Aeolian mode, each of its voices closing on the final, A. In Ghiselin's arrangement, No. 20, Ockeghem's superius serves as alto. Ghiselin does not change its pitch-level, but adds one flat to its signature, thus changing its mode to transposed Phrygian. The other parts are also given a signature of one flat, and the composition closes in transposed Aeolian. Since the cantus firmus closes G-natural, A, the formation of a V-I cadence is impossible. Thus Ghiselin has the A sustain for four measures, in order to give himself time to construct a proper cadence. Since this note is the fifth of the mode of the work as a

17. On p. 123 I have given three sample cadences, all of which may be considered "ideal." The tenor is found in the middle voice of a three-part work; in the voice next above the bass in a four-part work; and in the middle voice of a five-part work. In No. 19, Ockeghem's soprano (in the second tenor of this arrangement) had been completed in m. 94; this polyphonic cadence has taken shape by mm. 97–99.

whole, the problem is a comparatively simple one. Tenor, soprano, and bass can fall into the ideal cadential pattern quite easily within four measures.

It is frequently because of the composer's inability to have the other parts cadence when the cantus firmus does, that the number of measures of the arrangement is greater than Ockeghem's original seventy. On the other hand, non-observance of the nine measures of rest that open Ockeghem's superius has shortened arrangements of this voice.

In the Analyses below the signs for *plus* and *minus* are used to indicate the transposition of the cantus firmus up or down for use in the "arrangement." When it is transposed down a fifth or a twelfth, it is given a signature of one flat and its mode is therefore transposed Aeolian. In De Silva's arrangement (No. 3) the mode of the work as a whole is the same, transposed Aeolian. In this work Ockeghem's superius is kept as superius, and there is no conflict between the individual voice and the work as a whole. A more interesting situation exists in Nos. 14–18. In each of these arrangements Ockeghem's superius has been transposed down a twelfth to become the lowest voice of the composition. One flat is added to the signature and the voice is now in transposed Aeolian. The other voices show a signature of one flat, as well, but these compositions are all written in transposed Dorian. Since, in this transposed position, the cantus firmus now closes on D, it cannot support the tonic triad in transposed Dorian. The same solution is found by all the composers of Nos. 14–18: a G, the final of transposed Dorian, is added to the end of the cantus firmus. In Paris 2245 only, the cantus firmus is notated at its original treble pitch, but given a canon directing that it be performed a twelfth lower. No note is added at the end of the cantus firmus, nor is any rest given. Perhaps the performer would instinctively have added the necessary tonic in performance.

No. 3, by De Silva, is also notable for its very low pitch. It is a four-part work, and Ockeghem's superius, transposed down a twelfth, is still the "superius." The three highest voices all cover the same compass, F to b-flat, but the lowest voice ranges from d down to B_1-flat of the contra octave. A companion piece is the five-part work by Willaert, No. 35, which, however, employs a more "normal" range, the two octaves from F up to f′. It, also, is written *ad aequales voces*.

No. 24, the motet *Maria mater gratiae*, is interesting, for the cantus firmus is transposed down an octave, yet is given a signature of one flat. The borrowed voice was Ockeghem's tenor, so that the supertonic-tonic ending of this voice has now become a half-step progression, and its mode the transposed Phrygian. In measures 66 and 73, the anonymous composer has the bass rise above the cantus firmus in the second tenor (or second bass, as it is called in Brussels 228) to take advantage of the progression B-flat, A in a Phrygian cadence. In several other passages he lets the bass drop out, and the cadence is constructed with the cantus firmus as the lowest-sounding voice. This half-step progression, so characteristic of the Phrygian mode, is also found a number of times in the bass—usually at the end of a motive of varying lengths and differing beginnings. This motive recurs, though irregularly, somewhat in the manner of an ostinato, and this treatment is suggestive of the service for which the motet was intended, the Litanies of Loreto.

Nos. 2–27 all borrow from Ockeghem's original setting (No. 1), though they vary in their effect and in their quality. No. 20, by Jean Ghiselin, may be considered representative of the group. It contains some rather modern-sounding sequential modulations, measures 22–25, and a touch of stretto in the three highest parts, measures 63–69.

And now come two compositions that were unknown to Otto Gombosi: Nos. 28 and 29. They provide connecting links between Ockeghem's work and the group of pieces showing what may be called the "new" cantus firmus—a melody not deriving from Ockeghem's original setting.[18] This melody seems to have been originally a tenor, for it closes supertonic, tonic. It is found in the superius of No. 28, an anonymous work of which four voices occur in Bologna Q.19,[19] and a fifth voice (labeled *Quinta vox*) in St. Gall 463. While the superius rests, the first eight measures of Ockeghem's tenor are heard prominently in the alto. Meanwhile the three lowest voices treat in imitation and sequence a motive perhaps inspired by the ascending triad found at the start of Ockeghem's contra.[20] No. 28 seems to be an arrangement of the "new" cantus firmus, not its ultimate source.

18. The melody in its entirety is given on p. 123.

19. See Edward Lowinsky, "The Medici Codex," *Annales musicologiques*, V (1957), 61–178; pp. 98–106 deal with Bologna Q.19. Dr. Lowinsky states that this manuscript was written for Diane de Poitiers.

20. See p. 124 for the first four measures of No. 28; see also pp. 122–23 for several related motives drawn from various pieces among the thirty-five being studied here.

No. 29, an anonymous three-part work, found in London Add. 35087, Antico 1520[6] *Chansons a troys,* and Formschneider 1538[9] *Trium vocum carmina,* provides a second connecting link between Ockeghem's original setting and those compositions based on the "new" cantus firmus. It refers to Ockeghem's work by quoting six measures of his contra, contracted to five, at the beginning of its superius; it then paraphrases measures 7–10 in its measures 6–9. No. 29, like No. 1, also opens with a duet. The tenor rests for eight measures and then sounds its first note as the duet forms a cadence in measure 9. From measure 10 on, the outer parts treat in imitation an ascending scale line that may have been derived from Ockeghem's contra by filling in the thirds and omitting the repetitions. In the soprano, the scale rises from a′ to e″ before turning; in the contra the interval is enlarged to nearly an octave ranging from d to c′. (A similar situation exists at the beginning of the work where a motive covering a fifth in the soprano is imitated in the contra by the same motive extended to a sixth.) The tenor of No. 29 contains the melody termed here the "new" cantus firmus.

The composition of this piece shows an interesting design. In the setting of the first line of text, the tenor phrase is split into two parts at the caesura (the rests fall in measures 14–15), but the outer parts bridge over this break in the continuity. All three voices unite in a strong cadence at the close of the second half of the tenor phrase, measure 19. A similar pattern may be observed in the setting of the second line of text: note the imitation in all three voices, measures 20–24, the rest in measure 27 of the tenor, and the cadence for all voices in measure 30. For the remaining lines of the refrain the tenor shows no break at the caesura; but imitation at the start of the phrase links soprano and tenor, and a cadence marks the close of each voice. With such an abundance of imitation, the work is well balanced and integrated. The effect of the writing is a smooth and natural sound, and the whole seems so homogeneous that one is inclined to believe that this work may be the source of the "new" cantus firmus—an original work prefaced by a duet that acknowledges Ockeghem's work as the original setting of *Fors seulement.*

No. 30, probably by Matthaeus Pipelare,[21] was published by

21. Although both editions of *Canti B* attribute the piece to "Pe. de la Rue," five manuscripts ascribe it to Pipelare. The sheer weight of evidence seems to declare *Canti B* in error.

Petrucci in *Canti B* in 1502. It lies at the very heart of the *Fors seulement* problem. A desire to understand this particular setting furnished the stimulus for the present study.

Pipelare's work seems to have been modeled on No. 29.[22] It, too, opens with a duet, and, in general, produces much the same serene atmosphere. The "new" cantus firmus appears in its tenor part. The texture, however, is now enriched by the addition of an alto; the duet is made much more elaborate and is lengthened by four measures. Pipelare has also invented a rhythmically more interesting head-motive for the duet. It seems to refer to Ockeghem's contra, but by way of the contra of No. 29, which, in its imitation of Ockeghem's motive sounds A, C, and F, whereas, Ockeghem's motive sounds A, C, and E. (These may all be seen on pages 122–23.) Pipelare also marks the end of the duet by the entrance of the other voices. He cadences at the first caesura, however, as well as at the close of the first phrase of the cantus firmus in the tenor. He writes a homophonic passage to introduce phrase two, which enters in the tenor in measure 26. No discernible system of imitation has been discovered.

22. Picker, *Albums*, pp. 74–75, comments on the relationship between Nos. 29 and 30 as follows: "The most probable source of Pipelare's *cantus firmus* is the three-part composition herein transcribed (Appendix A, no. 2). [No. 29] These two works have much in common beside their tenors. Both have a long opening duo preceding the entrance of the tenor—the clearest points of imitation in either work. The anonymous setting quotes the opening of Ockeghem's contra, and is thus a link between Ockeghem's rondeau and other compositions based on its tenor. Pipelare introduces many cadences at the same points in relation to the tenor as does the anonymous setting. The similarity is closest in measures 22–23, where the three lower voices of Pipelare's chanson are identical with the three voices of the anonymous work. The unusually close texture of Pipelare's composition (SSST) may be explained by its dependence on the similar texture of the three-part work (TrST)."

Hellmuth Christian Wolff, *Die Musik der alten Niederländer (15. und 16. Jahrhundert)* (Leipzig: Breitkopf & Härtel, 1956), p. 201, feels that "die klar gezeichnete Polyphonie Ockeghems ist von Brumel durch einen dickeren klangvollen Satz harmonischer Art [No. 6] verdrängt worden. Die Stimmführung ist freier und bewegter. Ähnliches zeigt die Komposition von *Pipelare* [No. 30], der den Bass der Ockeghemschen Fassung aufgriff und ihn verziert von Durchgangsnoten, Wiederholungen u. ä. umspielen liess:" (He quotes 19 measures of No. 30.)

Ronald Cross, however (in "Matthaeus Pipelare: A Historical and Stylistic Study of His Works," diss., New York University, 1961, pp. 95–102 dealing with the settings containing the "new" cantus firmus), believes that Pipelare, departing from tradition, wrote a completely independent setting of *Fors seulement* (p. 99): "The melody itself [tenor] . . . is related to Ockeghem's chanson only in the first few notes. . . ." He feels that the other works showing this melody as a cantus firmus (including No. 29) derive it from Pipelare. The reader will want to consult these pages for himself and make his own decision. Cross's dissertation appeared on microfilm after my original paper was read in California; the latter contains, therefore, none of Cross's ideas.

This work seems to have one earmark of the "arrangement" for many "arrangements," although borrowing a voice from some other work, allow the remaining voices to ignore it, sometimes even using motives completely unrelated to the cantus firmus.

No. 31 provides an interesting deviation from the cantus firmus technique, for this work by Antoine de Févin must be considered a parody of No. 30.[23] It uses in its superius and tenor all of the phrases of the "new" cantus firmus except the first two. The first line of the poem *Fors seulement* is sung in Nos. 29 and 30 to measures 9–19 of the "new" cantus firmus. These two short phrases are not used by Févin. Instead, one finds the motive of Pipelare's opening duet and the superius he wrote as an accompaniment to measures 15–18 of the "new" cantus firmus. (See page 125 for the motives of Pipelare's composition [No. 30] and Févin's parody of it [No. 31].) The lineage seems clear. Pipelare modeled his work on No. 29; then Févin produced a parody of Pipelare's work. In the course of the transformation of the opening theme, all traces of Ockeghem's contra seem to have been lost.

It is also important to mention that there occurs in connection with Févin's parody a second text beginning *Fors seulement*, a text perhaps intended as a poetic parody. Much has been written about there being two texts beginning *Fors seulement—Fors seulement l'attente* and *Fors seulement la mort*—but less has been said of a third set of words which are found in No. 14 in certain manuscripts, *Fors seulement contre ce que ay promis*, or the text *Du tout plongiet*, which Brussels 228 gives for three of the four voices of Brumel's *Fors seulement*, No. 6, or of various substitute Latin texts that might be used, if desired. (*Exortum est in tenebris*, for example, is found with No. 30, Pipelare's setting, in the Segovia MS.) Perhaps all these divergences were merely local manifestations and should therefore not receive undue attention. One notices, for example, that the Pepys MS. 1760 in Cambridge—which carries considerable weight as the only manuscript source to give the name of the composer of No. 31, Févin—shows the original text, *Fors seulement l'attente*, under each of the three parts. (The only exception to this statement is in line

23. This work is discussed by Joseph Schmidt-Görg in his book *N. Gombert, Kapellmeister Karls V., Leben und Werk* (Bonn, 1938), p. 189, and by Edward Clinkscale in his doctoral dissertation, "The Complete Works of Antoine de Févin" (New York University, 1965), I, 181 f.

one, where "la mort" is inserted between "seulement" and "l'attente," although in the superius only.)[24]

Nos. 32, 33, and 34 need be discussed only briefly. Although the setting by Blanckenmüller is called *Fors seulement*, it uses no cantus firmus; it does find a place in this group of works, however, for its second half leans heavily on measures 50–55 of No. 31.[25] The exact repetition of ten measures at the end is an effective touch—the only actual repetition of all voices noticed during the study of this material.

No. 33, an anonymous work from the Cambrai MS., borrows the "new" cantus firmus and places it in the tenor. So much liberty is taken with the number of rests separating the phrases, however, that the arrangement is some thirteen measures longer than Pipelare's arrangement (No. 30), and seventeen measures longer than No. 29. Anticipatory imitations of the cantus firmus by the soprano are introduced fairly regularly, although usually during rests in the cantus firmus, so that a kind of dialogue results. At measure 45, however, it is the alto that anticipates the entrance of the cantus firmus in the tenor, measure 50. During this alto statement the tenor is given an accompanimental phrase (as the bass rests) that is not a part of the borrowed cantus firmus.

No. 34 is a motet by Verdelot, which borrows the "new" cantus firmus, transposes it down a fifth, and places it in the alto.

The last setting to be considered in this study is the five-part work by Willaert, No. 35, which may be found in the Kriesstein publication of 1540. Ambros characterized it as "an almost magnificent show-piece, compared with the many older, smoothly capable settings of this same song."[26] It is of extraordinary interest to find here in the superius the tenor of Févin's parody. To establish even more firmly the connection between the two pieces, Willaert quotes the four opening measures of Févin's contra in his second tenor; later in the piece he introduces a brief treatment of the dotted motive first heard in the "new" cantus firmus (see page 123, No. 29, tenor, measures 50–51), but later developed in all voices by both Févin

24. See the Annotated Concordance, No. 31, for modern books which give the complete text of *Fors seulement la mort.*

25. See p. 125, last staff, for the motive that is developed in sequence and imitation by Févin and then by Blanckenmüller.

26. Ambros, *Geschichte,* III, 523.

and Blanckenmüller. The text is the second text beginning "*Fors seulement la mort.*"

Thus, in this chain of compositions, which is shown graphically on page 126, five different cantus firmi have emerged: Ockeghem's superius, his tenor, his contra, the "new" cantus firmus, and, finally, Févin's tenor.

In conclusion, attention is directed once again to No. 28, a one-time "missing link," whose existence Gombosi suspected. It may be regarded as a symbol of the virtual compulsion that prompted these composers to weld together the links in this chain and of the interest in *Fors seulement* that continued through several generations of composers, "Van Ockeghem tot Willaert."

LIST OF SOURCES WITH *SIGLA*

In this List of Sources with *Sigla* are reported "Manuscripts" (A), "Early Printed Books" (B), and "Modern Editions and Studies" (C) that contain one or more of the thirty-five settings of *Fors seulement.*

The manuscripts are listed alphabetically according to the city in which they are found; the contemporary publications are listed by publisher; and the modern sources are listed alphabetically by author of article or book, or editor of complete works.

Bibliographical details of modern editions of a few manuscripts and early printed books will be found in section C. The number following the publisher's name in section B is taken from *Recueils imprimés: XVIe-XVIIe siècles (Répertoire International des Sources Musicales)*, edited by François Lesure (Munich, 1960).

A. Manuscripts

Augsburg 142^{a}

Augsburg, Staats- Kreis- und Stadtbibliothek, MS. 142^{a} (*olim* 18)

No. 25

Basel F.X. 1–4

Basel, Universitäts-Bibliothek, MSS. F.X. 1–4

No. 30

Berlin 78. B.17 (poetry only)
Berlin, Kupferstichkabinett, MS. 78. B.17 (Hamilton 674)
Nos. 1–30

Bologna Q.19
Bologna, Civico Museo Bibliografico Musicale, MS. Q.19
(Diane de Poitiers Codex)
Nos. 3, 7, 28, 30

Bologna R.142
Bologna, Civico Museo Bibliografico Musicale, MS. R.142
No. 11

Brussels 228
Brussels, Bibliothèque Royale de Belgique, MS. 228
(Album de Marguerite d'Autriche)
Nos. 6, 24, 30

Brussels IV.90, Tournai 94
Brussels, Bibliothèque Royale de Belgique, MS. IV.90
Tournai, Bibliothèque de la Ville, MS. 94
No. 30

Cambrai 124
Cambrai, Bibliothèque de la Ville, MS. 124 (125–28)
No. 33

Cambridge 1760
Cambridge, Magdalen College, MS. Pepys 1760
No. 31

Copenhagen 1848
Copenhagen, Kongelige Bibliotek, Ny Kgl. Samling, MS. 1848–2°
Nos. 14, 31

Cortona 95–96, Paris 1817
Cortona, Biblioteca Comunale, MSS. 95, 96 (Altus and Superius part-books only)
Paris, Bibliothèque Nationale, Nouv. acq. fr. 1817 (Tenor part-book only; Bassus part-book wanting)
No. 12

Dijon 517
Dijon, Bibliothèque Publique, MS. 517
No. 1

Florence 164–67
Florence, Biblioteca Nazionale Centrale, MS. Magl. XIX, 164–67
Nos. 25, 30

Florence 2439
Florence, Biblioteca del Conservatorio di Musica "L. Cherubini," MS. 2439 *(Fondo Basevi)*
Nos. 4, 5, 6, 8, 14, 16, 20, 26

London Add. 35087
London, British Museum, MS. Additional 35087
No. 29
London Add. 31922
London, British Museum, MS. Additional 31922
No. 31
London Lansdowne 380 (poetry only)
London, British Museum, MS. Lansdowne 380
Nos. 1–30
Munich 1516
Munich, Bayerische Staatsbibliothek, Mus. MS. 1516
Nos. 6, 31, 32
Paris 1596
Paris, Bibliothèque Nationale, Fonds fr. 1596
No. 14
Paris 1597
Paris, Bibliothèque Nationale, Fonds fr. 1597
Nos. 1, 30
Paris 1719 (poetry only)
Paris, Bibliothèque Nationale, Fonds fr. 1719
Nos. 1–30
Paris 1722 (poetry only)
Paris, Bibliothèque Nationale, Fonds fr. 1722
Nos. 1–30
Paris 2245
Paris, Bibliothèque Nationale, Fonds fr. 2245
No. 14
Regensburg C.120
Regensburg, Proske-Bibliothek, MS. C.120 *(Codex Pernner)*
Nos. 4, 5, 6, 20, 22, 30
Rome C. G. XIII, 27
Città del Vaticano, Biblioteca Ap. Vaticana, Cappella Giulia, MS. XIII, 27
No. 1
Rome Vat. 11953
Città del Vaticano, Biblioteca Ap. Vaticana, Codicetto Vat. lat. 11953 (Bassus part-book only)
No. 20
St. Gall 461
St. Gall, Stiftsbibliothek, MS. 461 (*Fridolin Sichers Liederbuch,* 1545)
Nos. 1, 4, 5, 6, 14, 15, 17, 20, 22, 23, 26, 30
St. Gall 463
St. Gall, Stiftsbibliothek, MS. 463 *(Aegidius Tschudis Liederbuch)*

(Superius and Altus part-books only)
Nos. 10, 28, 31

St. Gall 464
St. Gall, Stiftsbibliothek, MS. 464 *(Aegidius Tschudis Liederbuch)* (A duplicate of the Superius of St. Gall 463 and Bassi of five- and six-part works only)
Nos. 10, 28

Segovia
Segovia, Catedral, MS. (without number)
No. 30

Vienna 18746
Vienna, Oesterreichische Nationalbibliothek, MS. 18746 (five part-books)
Nos. 2, 9, 10, 18, 19, 24, 27

Vienna 18832
Vienna, Oesterreichische Nationalbibliothek, MS. 18832 (Tenor and Bassus part-books only; other books missing)
No. 21

Washington Laborde
Washington, D. C., Library of Congress, MS. Laborde, M 2. 1L25 Case
No. 1

Wolfenbüttel 287
Wolfenbüttel, Herzog August–Bibliothek, MS. 287 Extravag.
No. 1

B. Early Printed Books

Aich [1519]^{5} *Lieder*
In dissem Buechlyn fynt man LXXV. hubscher Lieder myt Discant. Alt. Bas. und Tenor. lustick zu syngen. Auch etlich zu fleiten, schwegelen und anderen musicalisch Instrumenten artlichen zu gebrauchen. Cologne, Arnt von Aich, n.d.
No. 30

Antico 1520^{6} *Chansons a troys*
Chansons a troys. A. Antico, L. A. Giunta, 1520.
Nos. 29, 31

Attaingnant 1534^{6} *Liber quartus*
Liber quartus XXIX. musicales quatuor vel quinque parium vocum modulos habet. . . . Paris, P. Attaingnant, 1534.
No. 34

[Egenolff] [c. 1535]^{14} *Lieder*
[Lieder zu 3 & 4 Stimmen]—[Frankfurt a. M., C. Egenolff, n.d.].
Nos. 30, 31

Formschneider 1538^{9} *Trium vocum carmina*
Trium vocum carmina a diversis musicis composita. Nuremberg,

H. Formschneider, 1538.
Nos. 14, 29, 31
Kriesstein 1540[7] *Cantiones*
Selectissimae necnon familiarissimae cantiones.... Augsburg, M. Kriesstein, 1540.
No. 35
Le Roy et Ballard 1578[14] *Premier livre*
Premier livre de chansons a trois parties composé par plusieurs autheurs. Paris, A. le Roy et R. Ballard, 1578.
No. 31
Petreius 1541[2] *Trium vocum cantiones*
Trium vocum cantiones centum, à praestantissimis diversarum nationum ac linguarum musicis compositae. Tomus primus. Nuremberg, J. Petreius, 1541.
No. 31
Petrucci 1502[2] *Canti B*
Canti B. numero cinquanta. Venice, O. Petrucci, 1502.
No. 30
Petrucci 1504[3] *Canti C*
Canti C. N° cento cinquanta. Venice, O. Petrucci, 1504.
Nos. 4, 6, 13, 20, 26.
Vérard, *Le Jardin de plaisance* (poetry only)
Le Jardin de plaisance et fleur de rethoricque. Paris, Antoine Vérard, n.d. Facsimile edition: I. *Reproduction en fac-similé de l'édition publiée par Antoine Vérard vers 1501* (Paris, 1910); II. *Introduction et Notes,* by Eugénie Droz and Arthur Piaget (Paris, 1925).
Nos. 1–30

C. Modern Editions and Studies

Ambros, August Wilhelm, *Geschichte der Musik.* 3d ed. Leipzig, Leuckert, 1887–1911. Vol. III, ed. Otto Kade (1891); Vol. V, ed. Otto Kade (1911).

Bernoulli, Eduard, *Aus Liederbüchern der Humanistenzeit: Eine bibliographische und notentypographische Studie.* Leipzig, 1910.

Bernoulli, Eduard, and Hans Joachim Moser (eds.), *Das Liederbuch des Arnt von Aich (Köln um 1510). Erste Partitur-Ausgabe der 75 vierstimmigen Tonsätze.* Kassel, 1930.

Burbure, Léon de (ed.), *Étude sur un manuscrit du XVIe siècle.* Brussels, 1882. (Study of Florence 2439)

Cross, Ronald, "Matthaeus Pipelare: A Historical and Stylistic Study of His Works." Part I, 307 pp., text; Part II, 160 pp., music. (Unpublished Ph.D. dissertation, New York University, 1961.)

Droz, Eugénie, Geneviève Thibault, and Yvonne Rokseth (eds.), *Trois chansonniers français du XVe siècle* (*Documents artistiques du XVe*

siècle, IV). Paris, 1927. Fasc. I, *Bibliothèque de Dijon, MS. 517 (ancien 295), folios 1–56.*

Eitner, Robert, "Eine Handschrift von Egidius Tschudi," *Monatshefte für Musikgeschichte,* VI (1874), 131–34.

Eitner, Robert, "Mitteilung," *Monatshefte für Musikgeschichte,* XIX (1887), 59.

Françon, Marcel (ed.), *Albums poétiques de Marguerite d'Autriche.* Cambridge, Mass., and Paris, 1934. (In part after Brussels 228; poetry only.)

Gachet, Émile (ed.), *Albums et oeuvres poétiques de Marguerite d'Autriche, Gouvernante des Pays-Bas. Publications de la Société des Bibliophiles Belges, séant à Mons,* XVII. Brussels, 1849. (In part after Brussels 228; poetry only.)

Giesbert, Franz Julius (ed.), *Ein altes Spielbuch. Liber Fridolini Sichery (um 1500) mit drei, vier und fünf Stimmen für Blockflöten oder beliebige andere Instrumente übertragen.* Édition Schott No. 2439. Mainz, 1936. (After St. Gall 461.)

Gombosi, Otto, *Jacob Obrecht: Eine stilkritische Studie. Mit einem Notenanhang.* Leipzig, 1925.

Gröber, Gustav (ed.), "Zu den Liederbüchern von Cortina" *Żeitscchrift für romanische Philologie,* XI (1887), 371–404. (After Paris 1817; poetry only.)

Hewitt, Helen (ed.), *Canti B. Numero Cinquanta.* Chicago: University of Chicago Press, 1967. *Monuments of Renaissance Music,* Edward E. Lowinsky, General Editor, Vol. II.

Lesure, F., and G. Thibault, *Bibliographie des éditions d'Adrian Le Roy et Robert Ballard (1551–1598).* Paris, 1955. *Publications de la Société française de Musicologie, IIme Série, Tome 9.*

Löpelmann, Martin (ed.), *Die Liederhandschrift des Cardinals de Rohan (XV. Jhrt.), nach der Berliner Hs. Hamilton 674. Publikationen der Gesellschaft für romanische Literatur,* XLIV. Göttingen, 1923. (After Berlin 78. B.17; poetry only.)

Maldeghem, R.-J. van (ed.), *Trésor musical: Collection authentique de musique sacrée et profane des anciens maîtres belges.* 29 vols. Brussels, 1865–1893. (*"Sacrée"* or *"profane"* following a short title will distinguish between the two volumes published each year by Van Maldeghem.)

McMurtry, William Murl, "The British Museum Manuscript *Additional 35087:* A Transcription of the French, Italian, and Latin Compositions with Concordance and Commentary." 229 pp., text; pp. 230–414, music. (Unpublished Ph.D. dissertation, North Texas State University, 1967.)

Picker, Martin (ed.), *The Chanson Albums of Marguerite of Austria. A Critical Edition and Commentary.* Berkeley: University of California Press, 1965. (In part after Brussels 228.)

Picker, Martin, "The Chansons Albums of Marguerite of Austria: MSS. 228 and 11239 of the Bibliothèque Royale de Belgique, Brussels." *Annales musicologiques,* VI (1958–1963), 145–285.

Reese, Gustave, "Maldeghem and His Buried Treasure: A Bibliographical Study." *Music Library Association Notes,* VI (1948), 75–117.

Renier, Rodolfo, "Un mazzetto di poesie musicali francesi," *Miscellanea di filologia e linguistica: In memoria di Napoleone Caix e Ugo Angelo Canello* (Florence, 1886), pp. 271–88. (After Cortona 95–96; poetry only.)

Seay, Albert (ed.), *Pierre Attaingnant, Transcriptions of Chansons for Keyboard (1531). Corpus mensurabilis musicae,* 20. Rome: American Institute of Musicology, 1961.

Shipp, Clifford Marion (ed.), "A Chansonnier of the Dukes of Lorraine: The Paris Manuscript *Fonds français 1597.*" 580 pp. (Unpublished Ph.D. dissertation, North Texas State University, 1960.)

Smijers, Albert (ed.), *Treize livres de motets parus chez Pierre Attaingnant en 1534 et 1535. Quatrième Livre.* Paris, Éditions de l'Oiseau-Lyre, 1960.

Wolf, Johannes (ed.), *Jacob Obrecht, Werken: Wereldlijke Werken.* Amsterdam and Leipzig, n.d.

ANNOTATED CONCORDANCE OF THIRTY-FIVE SETTINGS OF *FORS SEULEMENT*

1. Dijon 517, f. 25′–26 Okeghem. Three stanzas; refrain in highest of three voices.

   Paris 1597, f. 36′–37, Anon. Complete text; refrain in superius, tenor.

   Rome C. G. XIII, 27, f. 104′–105 (97′–98), Anon. The incipit "Frayres y dexedes me" appears in the superius.

   St. Gall 461, pp. 2–3, Ockenhem. Incipit in the superius only.

   Washington Laborde, f. 99′–100, Anon. Complete text in superius.

   Wolfenbüttel 287, f. 43′–45, Anon. Complete text in superius.

This setting is published after Dijon 517 in Droz, pp. 48–49; after Paris 1597 in Shipp, pp. 388–92; after St. Gall 461 in Giesbert, pp. 2–3, and Gombosi, *Obrecht, Anhang,* No. 9. The superius of St. Gall 461 occurs in Bernoulli, *Studie,* pp. 81–83.

This work was an original setting of the "rondeau cinquain" "Fors seulement" by Johannes Ockeghem. The poem (without music) is found in Berlin 78. B.17 (f. 69), London Lansdowne (f. 251), Paris 1719 (f. 34), Paris 1722 (f. 72′), and Vérard, *Le Jardin de plaisance* (f. 115); the complete text also appears with Ockeghem's music as described above.

The refrain (first stanza) is found in several settings and publishing details are part of the concordances of these pieces given below. Löpelmann, *Liederhandschrift,* No. 77, is an edition of the poem in Berlin 78. B.17; Françon, *Albums,* Appendix XII, gives the text as in Paris 1719 and Appendix XI as in Vérard, *Le Jardin de plaisance.* Eitner, "Mitteilung," p. 59, No. 4, gives the text after Dijon 517. Cross, Vol. II, p. 14, gives the text after Paris 1597.

Of the thirty-five works studied here, Nos. 2–27 use one or another of the voices of Ockeghem's original setting as a cantus firmus. Nos. 28 and 29 borrow a few measures only.

2. Vienna 18746, No. 56 (f. 57–57′; f. 62–63; f. 52′–53; f. 56′–57; f. 55′–56), Rue. Incipit in each of the five voices.
   Vienna 18746, No. 56a, Anon. Superius, contra, and bass only; duplicates of the corresponding voices of No. 56.

   This work is published in Gombosi, *Obrecht, Anhang,* No. 13. The bass and second tenor are in canon at the fifth above, the bass showing a signature of one flat. There is a brief five-part stretto near the end.

3. Bologna Q.19, f. 2′–3, Andreas de Sylua. Incipit in each of four voices.

   All voices are written on the bass staff. This is written "ad aequales voces," yet at one point the lowest voice descends to the B-flat below the bass staff.

4. Florence 2439, f. 23′–24, Hobrecht. Incipits in all four voices.
   Regensburg C.120, pp. 320–23, Hobrecht. Incipits in superius and alto only.
   St. Gall 461, pp. 12–13, Obrecht. "F" only, in alto.
   Petrucci 1504[3] *Canti C*, f. 4′–5, Ja. Obreht. "Forseulement" in each of four voices.

   This work is published after St. Gall 461 in Giesbert, pp. 12–13; after Petrucci 1504[3] *Canti C* in Wolf, *Obrecht,* pp. 14–16, No. 6, and in Ambros, *Geschichte,* Vol. 5, pp. 29–33. The alto of St. Gall 461 appears in Bernoulli's *Studie,* pp. 81–83.

   The last note of the cantus firmus in the alto functions as the fifth of the tonic chord in the final chord.

5. Florence 2439, f. 19′–20, Rue. "Fors seullement" in each of four voices.
   Regensburg C.120, pp. 326–27, P. de la Rue. Incipits in soprano and tenor.
   St. Gall 461, pp. 14–15, Pirson. "F" only, in the alto.

   Published after St. Gall 461 in Giesbert, pp. 14–15; alto of St. Gall 461 given in Bernoulli's *Studie,* pp. 81–83.

   At the start La Rue introduces a motive unrelated to the cantus firmus; this motive is brought back from time to time during the course of the work.

6. Brussels 228, f. 18′–19, Anon. Superius, "contra" and "baricanor" give the refrain of the rondeau "Du tout plongiet," the remaining stanzas appearing below the music. The tenor gives the first line only of "Fors seulement."

Florence 2439, f. 20′–21, Brumel. The incipit "Fors seullement" appears in each voice.

Munich 1516, No. 2, Anon. Incipit "Fors seulement" in each voice. The work is transposed up a fifth.

Regensburg C.120, pp. 324–25, An. Brumel. Incipits in superius and alto only.

St. Gall 461, pp. 16–17, Brumel. "F" only, in soprano and alto.

Petrucci 1504[3] *Canti C,* f. 5′–6, Alexander. "Forseulement" (only) in all four voices. The work is transposed up a fifth.

Published after St. Gall 461 in Giesbert, pp. 16–17; after Brussels 228 in Picker, *Albums,* pp. 237–41; and presumably after Brussels 228 in Maldeghem, *Trésor musical (profane),* Vol. XXI (1885), No. 13, attributed to Pierre de la Rue (=Reese, "Maldeghem," No. 334); after Regensburg C.120 in Wolf, *Obrecht, Beilage* 2, pp. 85–87; alto of St. Gall 461 appears in Bernoulli's *Studie,* pp. 81–83.

In this work all voices start out together. Only Brussels 228 gives the text beginning "Du tout plongiet." The other sources give either the incipit "Fors seulement" or no words at all. The attribution in Petrucci 1504[3] *Canti C* to "Alexander" is undoubtedly erroneous. Petrucci *Canti C* and Munich 1516 notate the work a fifth higher with a signature of only one flat; the other sources show two flats.

7. Bologna Q.19, f. 9′–11, Antonius Diuitis. Three lines of "Fours seullement" appear in the alto; four other voices show only the incipit.

The cantus firmus (in the alto) is used here in augmentation, making this the longest of the thirty-five settings.

8. Florence 2439, f. 21′–22, Pipelare. Incipit in each of four voices.

Published in Cross, Vol. II, pp. 11–13.

The first eighteen measures of Pipelare's setting are in two-part writing, a duet for tenor and bass being answered by one for soprano and alto.

9. Vienna 18746, No. 55 (f. 56′–57; f. 61′–62; f. 51′–52; f. 56; f. 55), Anon. Incipit in each of five voices.

A motive unrelated to the cantus firmus in the alto opens all of the other voices except the bass. Curiously, the cantus firmus begins the work in measure one.

10. Vienna 18746, No. 51 (f. 53′–54; f. 58′–59; f. 48′–49; f. 53′; f. 52′–53), Anon. Incipit in each of five voices.

St. Gall 463–64, No. 194. St. Gall 463 has the superius and altus; St. Gall 464, a duplicate alto and a "quinta vox" (bass) not in St. Gall 463. The two tenors of Vienna 18746 are lacking. All voices have only textual incipits.

After the alto sounds the last note of the cantus firmus, it sustains for ten measures while the remaining voices complete their parts. A "puzzle canon" in French calls for a transposition of the part as notated.

11. Bologna R.142, f. 57′, Josquin a sei. Incipit in tenor. (The remaining part-books are missing today.)

Ockeghem's superius appears here with the inscription "Josquin a sei." Unfortunately none of the parts written by Josquin appears to have survived.

12. Cortona 95–96, Paris 1817, No. 22, Anon. The refrain appears in the three part-books.

This work is also incomplete; soprano and alto appear in Cortona 95–96, the tenor in Paris 1817, but the bass part-book is missing.

13. Petrucci 1504[3] *Canti C,* f. 23′–25, G. Reingot. Incipits in four voices.

Reingot uses so many notes of short duration that the cantus firmus seems to be in augmentation. Ockeghem's superius occurs in the tenor, but ten measures of his tenor are quoted by Reingot's soprano before the cantus firmus starts.

14. Copenhagen 1848, p. 427, Anon. Incipit in highest of three voices.

Florence 2439, f. 52′–53, J. Ockeghem. Refrain text in the superius; incipits in two lower voices.

Paris 1596, f. 7′–8, Anon. All three voices have the refrain of "Fors seulement contre ce que ay promys" and the two other stanzas are below the music to complete the rondeau.

Paris 2245, f. 16′–17, Okeghem. The text of "Fors seulement contre ce quay promys" is complete in this MS. The contra shows the refrain of "Fors seulement lactente."

St. Gall 461, pp. 4–5, Ockengem. Incipit "Fors solament" in the contra. The initial note of each part is longer by the value of a breve than it is in the other sources.

Formschneider 1538[9] *Trium vocum carmina,* No. 47, Anon. The words "Fors seulement" are written by hand in both the tenor and "Bassus" part-books of the print.

Published after St. Gall 461 in Giesbert, pp. 4–5; after Florence 2439 in Gombosi, *Obrecht, Anhang,* No. 10; the contra of St. Gall 461 appears in Bernoulli's *Studie,* pp. 81–83.

There seems to be no reason why Ockeghem could not have arranged one of the voices of his original setting. Gombosi, however, cast a doubt on his authorship of No. 14 (*Obrecht, Anhang,* No. 10). In Paris 2245 the cantus firmus is notated at its original pitch, with the words "Canon Royal" indicating a transposition down a twelfth. This MS. belonged to the Duke of Orleans, who became King of France in 1499. The MS. is dated 1496, and Louis of Orleans had already been notified that he would be the next king of France as Louis XII. It is quite possible that the word "royal" in this canon was hinting that the transposition should be that of the "twelfth."

15. St. Gall 461, pp. 18–19, Jo. Agricola. Incipit in the lowest of four voices.

Published in Giesbert, pp. 18–19; the bass, only, is found in Bernoulli's *Studie,* pp. 81–83.

The only manuscript containing this work seems to be attributing it to "Jo." Agricola rather than "Alexander." One may at least question whether "Jo. and Agricola" was meant, "Jo." referring to Ockeghem who contributed the *cantus firmus.*

16. Florence 2439, f. 22′–23, De Orto. Incipits in four voices.

Nos. 14, 15, 16, and 17 have Ockeghem's superius in the lowest voice; the final of the mode of this borrowed voice is the dominant of the mode of the work as a whole. In the last three works mentioned, the composer merely adds a downward leap of a fifth at the end of the cantus firmus. In No. 14, a three-part work, however, Ockeghem has the contra drop out, so that the two upper parts conclude the work alone.

17. St. Gall 461, pp. 20–21, Anon. "F" in alto and bass, only, of four voices.

Published in Giesbert, pp. 20–21; only the bass appears in Bernoulli's *Studie,* pp. 81–83.

18. Vienna 18746, No. 52 (f. 54–54′; f. 59–60; f. 49′–50; f. 54; f. 53–53′), Anon. Incipits in all five voices.

19. Vienna 18746, No. 54 (f. 55′–56; f. 60′–61′; f. 50′–51′; f. 55′; f. 54′–55), Anon. Incipits in all five voices.

The transposition of the cantus firmus down a thirteenth places it in the Ionian mode. After a cadence on C, the last note of the cantus firmus, that voice rests for three measures and then sounds an E, the dominant of the Aeolian mode, in which the work closes. The final chord has three roots and two fifths, but no third, even though all five parts are represented.

20. Florence 2439, f. 17′–18, Ghisling. Incipits in four voices.

Regensburg C.120, pp. 332–335, Verbonet. Incipits in soprano and alto.

Rome Vat. 11953, f. 13–14, Anon. "Forsoloment" only. Bass part-book only; others missing. Notated a fifth lower than in other sources.

St. Gall 461, pp. 10–11, Verbonet. "F" in soprano and alto.

Petrucci 1504[3] *Canti C,* f. 37′–39, Ghiselin. Incipits in all voices.

Published after St. Gall 461 in Giesbert, pp. 10–11; after Petrucci *Canti C* in Gombosi, *Obrecht, Anhang,* No. 11.

This work is unusual in its selection of a cantus firmus. The first part of the work draws on Ockeghem's tenor; the second part uses the second half of Ockeghem's superius. The sequential modulations, mm. 25–30, and the three-part stretto, mm. 66–73, are effective.

21. Vienna 18832, No. 38, Anon. Incipits in tenor and bass. This work is incomplete, since other part-books are missing.

22. Regensburg C.120, pp. 328–31, De La Val et Jo. Incipits in superius and alto only, of four voices.

St. Gall 461, pp. 22–23, Anon. "F" in tenor only.

Published after St. Gall 461 in Giesbert, pp. 22 23.

The second part of the composer attribution in Regensburg C.120 may have reference to "Jo" Ockeghem, composer of the cantus firmus in the tenor.

23. St. Gall 461, pp. 24–25, Jacobus Romanus. "F" in superius and alto only, of four voices.

Published in Giesbert, pp. 24–25.

Owing to certain paleographical peculiarities in St. Gall 461, this composer's name remains in doubt. Giesbert agrees with the reading "Romanus"; Gombosi and others, however, have read it differently: "Thoman," for example.

24. Brussels 228, f. 23′–24, Anon. The full text of "Maria mater gratie" appears in all five voices. The voice containing the cantus firmus is labeled "Fors seulement" as well, and the canon "In dyapason" is added. When the canon is realized, this voice becomes the second lowest.

Vienna 18746, No. 50 (f. 52′–53; f. 57′–58; f. 47′–48; f. 52′–53; f. 51′–52), Anon. Incipits in all voices. The cantus firmus is marked "Fors seullement" and "In subdyapason."

Published after Brussels 228 in Picker, *Albums,* pp. 257–64, and presumably after Brussels 228 in Maldeghem, *Trésor musical* (*sacrée*), Vol. XIX (1883), No. 3, pp. 7–9, attributed to La Rue (=Reese, "Maldeghem," No. 315).

This Latin hymn forms a part of the "Litanies of Loreto" (see *Liber usualis* [Paris, Tournai, Rome: Desclée & Socii, 1953], p. 1863), but in a few lines differs slightly from the present-day reading. The hymn consists of two stanzas and an "Amen." The melody of the *Liber usualis* is not related to the music of the polyphonic setting.

25. Augsburg 142[a], f. 40′–42, Anon. Incipit in the highest of four voices.
Florence 164–67, No. 60, Anon. The refrain of the rondeau is given in all four voices.

The single word "Canon" appears with the alto in Florence 164–67, but is lacking in Augsburg 142[a]; a *custos* placed on the line a fifth above the first note indicates the exact pitch at which the cantus firmus should start. The mode of the cantus firmus is thus changed from Aeolian to Phrygian. The final alto E sustains for eight measures while the lower parts perform a sequential passage. The work as a whole is in the Aeolian mode.

26. Florence 2439, f. 18′–19, Ghisling. "Fors seullement," only, in each of four voices.
St. Gall 461, pp. 6–7, Josqin Deprecz. "F" in alto only.
Petrucci 1504[3] *Canti C,* f. 51′–52, Anon. Incipits in all voices.

Published after St. Gall 461 in Giesbert, pp. 6–7; after Petrucci *Canti C* in Gombosi, *Obrecht, Anhang,* No. 12 ("Josquin des Près oder Ghiselin[?]").

It is interesting that all three works using Ockeghem's contra place it in the alto; two of the three use a canon to indicate the transposition, only the present work writing it out as it is to be performed, at the octave above.

27. Vienna 18746, No. 53 (f. 54′–55′; f. 60–60′; f. 50–50′; f. 54′–55; f. 53′–54), Anon. Incipits in all five voices.

The cantus firmus (Ockeghem's contra) is written at its original pitch. An accompanying canon reads "In dyapason ascendende," which brings it into the position of alto in the new work.

Three of the lower parts start together on D or A, the superius following after eight measures. All make one or more repetitions and eventually leap a third in imitation of the cantus firmus. Mensuration canon comes to mind.

28. Bologna Q.19, f. 3′–4, Anon. Incipits in all four voices.
St. Gall 463–64, No. 193, Anon. Textual incipits only. St. Gall 463 shows one voice in the Discantus part-book, and one voice labeled both "Vagans" and "Quinta vox" in the Altus part-book. St. Gall 464 (f. 9–10) gives a duplicate superius and a bassus. When the "Vagans" of St. Gall 463 is placed beneath the four voices of Bologna Q.19, a five-part work results. Each part-book of the St. Gall manuscripts gives the word "Quinque," meaning that the composition is for five voices.

This setting is one of the connecting links between Ockeghem's original setting and the works exhibiting the "new" cantus firmus. The latter occurs here in the soprano, the alto showing measures 2–9 of Ockeghem's tenor. The three lowest voices treat in imitation and sequence a motive perhaps inspired by Ockeghem's contra.

29. London Add. 35087, f. 80′–81, Anon. Incipits in each of three voices, the soprano having more than one line of text.

Antico 1520^{6} *Chansons a troys,* No. 19, Anon. "Supranus" (f. 10′–11) and "Bassus" (f. 60–60′) only, with refrain of "Fors seullement latente." (Tenor part-book is missing.)

Formschneider 1538^{9} *Trium vocum carmina,* No. 46, Anon. Three voices. Notated a fifth lower than in the other sources. "Fors seulement" has been written by hand in the tenor part-book of the Jena copy. The work has a signature of one flat.

Published after London Add. 35087 in Picker, *Albums,* pp. 477–78, and McMurtry, "Manuscript *Additional 35087,*" pp. 337–40.

This work is the second connecting link, for the "new" cantus firmus occurs in the tenor, while the soprano shows seven measures of Ockeghem's contra, followed by three measures that elaborate the corresponding measures of Ockeghem's original work. The opening duet features Ockeghem's contra and thus gives recognition of Ockeghem's work as the original setting of "Fors seulement." This composition may be the one from which later composers borrowed the "new" cantus firmus.

30. Basel F. X. 1–4, No. 118. "Mathias Pipilari" in the tenor part-book; "M. P." in other books; incipits in all four books.

Bologna Q.19, f. 1′–2, Piplare. Incipits in all four books.

Brussels 228, f. 17′–18, Anon. Refrain in all four voices.

Brussels IV.90, f. 22′–23′, Anon. Refrain (superius); Tournai 94, f. 22–22′, Anon. Refrain (tenor). Other books missing.

Florence 164–67, No. 61, Anon. Refrain in all voices.

Paris 1597, f. 60′–61, Anon. Refrain in superius; other voices, incipits only.

Regensburg, C.120, pp. 336–37, Pipelare. Incipit "Forseulement" in soprano and alto.

St. Gall 461, pp. 8–9, M. Pipelare. "F" in alto.

Segovia, f. 92, Matheus Pipelare. A Latin text (Psalm 112:4), "Exortum est in tenebris" appears complete in all voices.

Aich $[1519]^{5}$ *Lieder,* 19, 12, 74, 35, Anon. Incipits in all voices.

[Egenolff] $[c. 1535]^{14}$ *Lieder,* Vol. I, No. 31, Anon. Superius only, with textual incipit.

Petrucci 1502^{2} *Canti B,* f. 31′–32, Pe. de la Rue. Incipits in superius and alto.

This work has been published after Brussels 228 in Picker, *Albums,* pp. 233–36; after Florence 164–67 in Seay, No. 10, and in Wolf, *Obrecht, Beilage* No. 3, pp. 88–90; after Paris 1597 in Shipp, pp. 485–89; after St. Gall 461 in Bernoulli's *Studie, Beilage* XII, pp. 98–99, and Giesbert, pp. 8–9; after Aich, *Lieder,* in Bernoulli-Moser, No. 72, pp. 126–27; after Petrucci 1502^{2} *Canti B* in Hewitt, *Canti B,* pp. 168–71; after "a private library of Rome" in Maldeghem, *Trésor musical (profane),* Vol. I (1865),

No. 6, attributed to Pipelare, but with a substitute text "Quand vers le soir" (=Reese, "Maldeghem," No. 555) and in Vol. XXI (1885), No. 12, attributed to Pipelare, but transposed up a third (=Reese, "Maldeghem," No. 557).

The attribution to La Rue in Petrucci *Canti B* is undoubtedly erroneous. This piece seems to have been modeled on No. 29 although it thickens the texture to four parts and presents a more elaborate opening duet.

31. Cambridge, Pepys 1760, f. 58′–60, Anth. de Fevin. Refrain, only, of "Fors seulement l'attente" in each of three voices.

Copenhagen 1848, pp. 102–03, Anon. Refrain in superius.

London Add. 31922, f. 104′–105, Anon. "Fors solemaut" only, in the contra.

Munich 1516, No. 129, Anon. Incipit in each voice. The work is transposed down a fifth, and has one flat in the signature.

St. Gall 463, No. 46, Anon. Superius only, with refrain of another rondeau, "For seulement la mort."

Antico 1520[6] *Chansons a troys,* No. 6, Anon. "Supranus" (f. 4–4′) and "Bassus" (f. 52′–53) only, with refrain of "Fors seullement la mort" in both voices. Tenor part-book is missing.

[Egenolff] [c. 1535][14] *Lieder,* Vol. III, No. 51, Anon. Superius only, with incipit "Fors seulement."

Formschneider 1538[9] *Trium vocum carmina,* No. 31. "Jöskin" is written by hand in the tenor of the Jena copy. The work is here written a fifth lower than in other sources.

Le Roy and Ballard 1578[14] *Premier livre,* f. 14′–15, Févin, "Fors seullement la mort" in each part-book.

Petreius 1541[2] *Trium vocum cantiones,* No. 73, Anon. Incipits in all three voices.

Published after Petreius, *Trium vocum cantiones,* in Wolf, *Obrecht, Beilage* No. 4, pp. 90–92, attributed to "Josquin(?)."

The text beginning "For seulement" but continuing "la mort" is published after St. Gall 463, No. 46, in Ambros, *Geschichte,* Vol. V, p. xix; in Eitner, "Handschrift," pp. 132–33; and in Wolf, *Obrecht,* p. xviii. See also Lesure-Thibault, *Bibliographie,* p. 192, No. 218.

This work is a parody of No. 30; the motives found in it are also those of No. 29, with the exception of the opening motive which relates to No. 30 but has no connection with No. 29. In St. Gall 463 text beginning "Fors seulement la mort" appears; in Cambridge Pepys 1760 there appears to be a confusion between "Fors seulement la mort" and "Forseulement l'attente" in the first line of the superius; elsewhere this manuscript shows the text of Ockeghem's original setting.

32. Munich 1516, No. 131, Jörg Blanckenmüller. "Forseulement," only, in each of three voices.

This is a curious piece, having no cantus firmus and seeming to consist, in its first half, of nothing more than an exercise in writing approaches to cadences. The final measures (mm. 40–60) are based on mm. 50–55 of No. 31. The exact repetition of mm. 40–50 in mm. 50–60 is a rarity in this period.

33. f. 144′ (in each part-book), Anon. "Forseullement," only, in each of four voices.

Published in Maldeghem, *Trésor musical (profane),* Vol. XVIII (1882), pp. 8–9, with a substitute text ("O qu'à bon droit") presumably selected by Van Maldeghem himself (=Reese, "Maldeghem," No. 72).

The "new" cantus firmus appears here in the tenor. Several of its phrases are anticipated in one or another of the upper parts. A reference to the opening motive of No. 31 is noticed in measure 25 of the alto.

34. Attaingnant 1534[6] *Liber Quartus,* f. 9′–10, Verdelot. A Latin text beginning "Infirmitatem nostram" in the four highest of five voices. The lowest voice has two incipits "Quaesumus domine" and "Forseulement."

For several other early prints that contain this work, see Edward E. Lowinsky, "A Newly Discovered Sixteenth-Century Motet Manuscript at the Biblioteca Vallicelliana in Rome," *Journal of the American Musicological Society,* III (1950), 173–232 (see 206, 223).

Published after Attaingnant, *Liber Quartus,* in Smijers, *Treize livres,* IV (1960), No. 17, pp. 99–102.

Verdelot has written a five-part motet, using the "new" cantus firmus in the alto. The text is very similar to a Post Communion prayer to be used "In any Tribulation."

35. Kriesstein 1540[7] *Cantiones,* No. 43, Adrianus Willart. "Fors seulement la mort" appears complete in each of five voices written "ad aequales voces."

This text was first found in Févin's parody; his tenor is also found as the soprano of Willaert's work, thus establishing another cantus firmus in this chain of compositions. The source of the borrowing is further confirmed by the quotation of four measures of Févin's contra in the second tenor of Willaert's composition.

LIST OF COMPOSERS OF THE SETTINGS OF *FORS SEULEMENT*

Name of Composer	*No.*
Agricola, Jo.	15
Blanckenmüller, Georg	32
Brumel, Antoine	6
Divitis, Antonius	7
Festa, Costanzo	—
Févin, Antoine de	31
Ghiselin, Jean	20
La Rue, Pierre de	2, 5, (30)
La Val, de	22
Obrecht, Jacob	4
Ockeghem, Johannes	1, 14
Orto, Mabriano de	16
Pipelare, Matthaeus	8, 30
Prez, Josquin des	11
Reingot, Georg	13
Romanus, Jacobus	23
Silva, Andreas de	3
Verdelot, Philippe	34
Willaert, Adrian	35
Incertus (Josquin *or* Ghiselin)	26

The numbers in this table are those given the settings in the Annotated Concordance. Parentheses designate a false attribution.

SETTINGS OF *FORS SEULEMENT* FOUND IN GROUPS IN CERTAIN SOURCES

No.	*St. Gall* Stifts-bibliothek MS. 461 *Sichers Liederbuch*	*Florence* Conserva-torio L. Cherubini MS. 2439 *Basevi MS.*	*Venice* Petrucci: *Canti B* and *Canti C*	*Regensburg* Proske-Bibliothek MS. C.120 *Codex Pernner*	*Bologna* Civico Museo Bibliografico Musicale MS. Q.19 *D. de Poitiers Codex*	*Vienna* Oester-reichische National-bibliothek MS. 18746
4.	Obrecht	Obrecht	Obrecht	Obrecht		
6.	Brumel	Brumel	*Alexander*	Brumel		
20.	Ghiselin	Ghiselin	Ghiselin	Ghiselin		
26.	*Josquin*	*Ghiselin*	Anon.			
30.	Pipelare		*La Rue*	Pipelare	Pipelare	
22.	Anon.			De La Val		
5.	La Rue	La Rue		La Rue		
14.	Ockeghem	Ockeghem				
16.		De Orto				
8.		Pipelare				
13.			Reingot			
15.	Agricola					
1.	Ockeghem					
23.	Romanus					
17.	Anon.					
7.					Divitis	
3.					De Silva	
28.					Anon.	
2.						La Rue
9.						Anon.
10.						Anon.
18.						Anon.
19.						Anon.
24.						Anon.
27.						Anon.

The conflicting attributions for No. 26 and those thought to be incorrect in *Canti B* and *Canti C* are set in italics.

ANALYSES: TREATMENT OF OCKEGHEM'S MATERIALS IN LATER ARRANGEMENTS OF *FORS SEULEMENT*

No.	Composer	No. of Parts	C.f. was Ock.'s	C.f. now in:	Transposition	Other borrowing from Ock.	Imitation of c.f.	Imitation of ind. mot.	Mode of c.f.	Mode of Arr.	No. of mm.
1	Ockeghem	3									70
2	La Rue	5	S in S		0	H in T1 & A T_7 in T2 & B	–	–	Ae	Ae	76
3	De Silva	4	S in S		-12^b	H in AB	–	–	TrAe	TrAe	65
4	Obrecht	4	S in A		–4	T_{10} in S	TB	–	Ph	Ae	72
5	La Rue	4	S in A		-5^b	—	–	STB	TrAe	TrD	67
6	Brumel	4	S in A		-5^b	—	–	–	TrAe	TrD	62
7	Divitis	5	S in A		-5^b	—	–	STB	TrAe	TrD	111
8	Pipelare	4	S in A		–8	T_{10} in T	SB	–	Ae	D	73
9	Anon.	5	S in A		–8	—	–	STT2	Ae	D	57
10	Anon.	5	S in A		–8	T_{10} in S	–	–	Ae	Ae	82
11	Josquin	6	S in T		0	?	?	?	?	?	70?
12	Anon.	4	S in T		–8	T_{10} in A	–	–	Ae	D	74
13	Reingot	4	S in T		–8	T_{10} in S	–	AB	Ae	Ae	73
14	Ockeghem	3	S in C		-12^b	T_3 in T	–	–	TrAe	TrD	63
15	Agricola	4	S in B		-12^b	H in S T_3 in T	–	–	TrAe	TrD	63
16	De Orto	4	S in B		-12^b	H in A & T T_9 in S	–	–	TrAe	TrD	71
17	Anon.	4	S in B		-12^b	H in A	–	ST	TrAe	TrD	64
18	Anon.	5	S in T2		-12^b	H in T2B H_2 in S	–	–	TrAe	TrD	61
19	Anon.	5	S in T2		–13	T_7 in S C_5 in A	–	–	I	Ae	99
20	Ghiselin	4	1/2T + 1/2S in A		0^b	T_{10} in B S_6 in S	T	–	TrPh	TrAe	75
21	Anon.	4	T in T		0	?	?	?	?	?	70?
22	De La Val	4	T in T		0	—	–	SAB	Ae	D	72

No.	Composer	No. of Parts	C.f. was Ock.'s	C.f. now in:	Trans-position	Other borrowing from Ock.	Imitation of c.f.	Imitation of ind. mot.	Mode of c.f.	Mode of Arr.	No. of mm.
23	Romanus	4	T	in S	0	H in B T_{14} in A	–	–	Ae	Ae	70
24	Anon.	5	T	in T2	-8^{b}	—	–	SAT	TrPh	TrPh	76
25	Anon.	4	C	in A	+5	H in S	TB	–	Ph	Ae	77
26	Incertus	4	C	in A	+8	T_3 in T & B T_{10} in S	–	–	Ae	Ae	72
27	Anon.	5	C	in A	+8	—	ST T2B	–	Ae	Ae	76
28	Anon.	5	"new" c.f.	in S	0	Ockeghem's T_8 in A	–	TT2B	D	D	54
29	Anon.	3	"new" c.f.	in T	0	O's C_9 in S O's C_3 in C	–	–	D	D	54
30	Pipelare	4	"new" c.f.	in T	0	—	–	SB	D	D	58
31	Févin	3	—		(-5^{b}) *	—	–	ST	–	TrD	59
32	Blanckenmüller	3	—		(-5^{b})	—	–	–	–	TrD	60
33	Anon.	4	"new" c.f.	in T	–8	"new" $c.f._6$ in S	S	AB	D	D	71
34	Verdelot	5	"new" c.f.	in A	-5^{b}	—	–	STT2B	TrD	TrD	60
35	Willaert	5	T of No. 31	in S	-5^{b}	C_4 of No. 31 in T2	A	–	TrD	TrD	59

Key to symbols: S(uperius), A(ltus), T(enor), B(assus), C(ontra); "+4" means "up a fourth"; "—5*b*" means "down a fifth, with a signature of one flat." A numeral used as a subscript indicates the number of measures borrowed; e.g., "T_{10} in S" means that 10 mm. of Ockeghem's Tenor appear in the Superius of the new work. "H" denotes the "head-theme" used by Ockeghem in both his upper voices. "Ind. mot." stands for "independent motive," i.e., one having no connection with Ockeghem's original setting. Ae(olian), D(orian), Tr(ansposed), etc.

*Parentheses indicate a work using one flat in all voices although no continuous c.f. is present. Nos. 34 and 35 also use this lower pitch level; c.f. of No. 34 was originally a fifth higher; that of No. 35 is found at both levels.

No. 1. Ockeghem, beginning and ending.

Motives based on Ockeghem's contratenor.
No. 19. Anon., mm. 1–3.

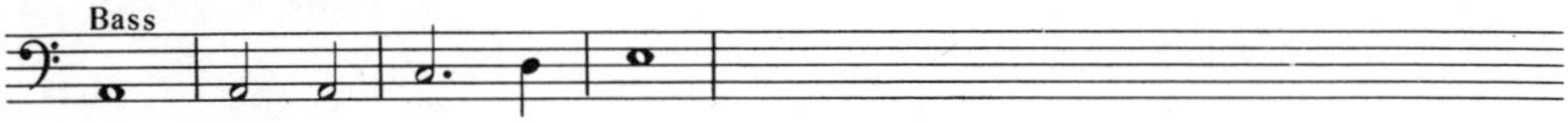

No. 25. Anon., mm. 10–13.

No. 28. Anon., mm. 1–2.

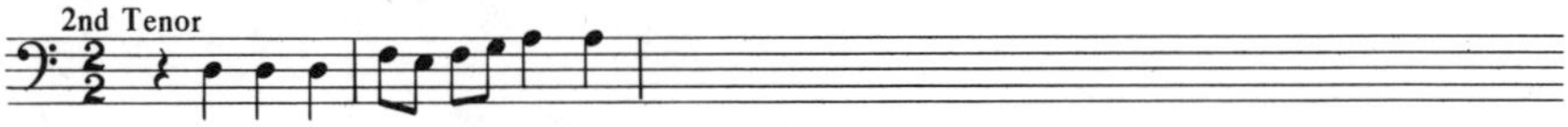

No. 29. Anon., mm. 1–5, mm. 45–47.

No. 30. Pipelare, mm. 1–6.

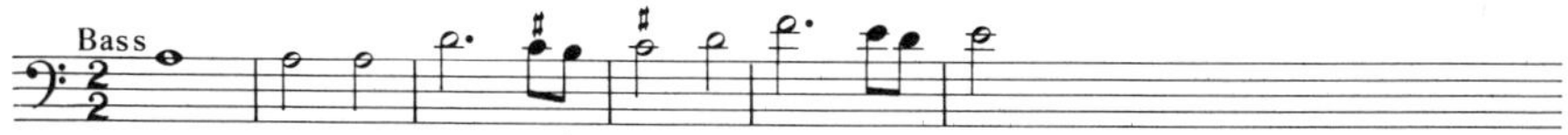

No. 31. Févin, mm. 1–4.

Typical final cadences in 3, 4, and 5 parts.

No. 29. Anon., mm. 52–54.

No. 30. Pipelare, mm. 56–58.

No. 19. Anon., mm. 97–99.

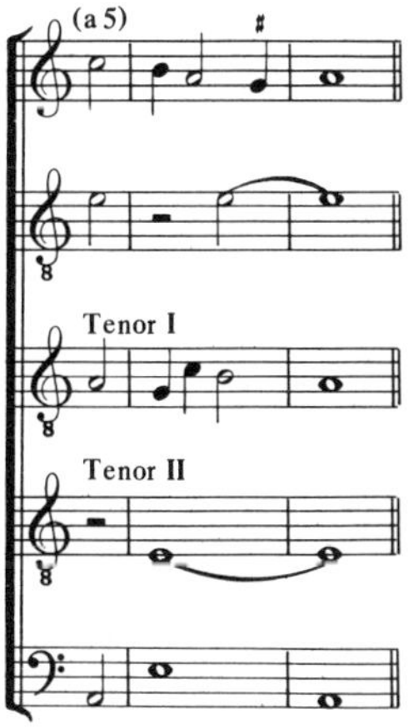

The "new" cantus firmus.
No. 29. Anon.

Beginnings of principal works discussed in text.

No. 29. Anon.

No. 28. Anon.

No. 31. Févin.

No. 35. Willaert.

Comparison of themes from Pipelare's *Fors seulement l'attente* and Févin's parody *Fors seulement la mort.*

FORS SEULEMENT "VAN OCKEGHEM TOT WILLAERT"

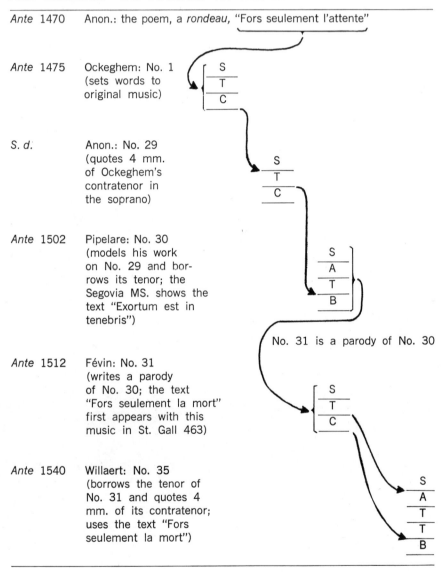

Ante 1470	Anon.: the poem, a *rondeau,* "Fors seulement l'attente"
Ante 1475	Ockeghem: No. 1 (sets words to original music)
S. d.	Anon.: No. 29 (quotes 4 mm. of Ockeghem's contratenor in the soprano)
Ante 1502	Pipelare: No. 30 (models his work on No. 29 and borrows its tenor; the Segovia MS. shows the text "Exortum est in tenebris")
Ante 1512	Févin: No. 31 (writes a parody of No. 30; the text "Fors seulement la mort" first appears with this music in St. Gall 463)
Ante 1540	Willaert: No. 35 (borrows the tenor of No. 31 and quotes 4 mm. of its contratenor; uses the text "Fors seulement la mort")

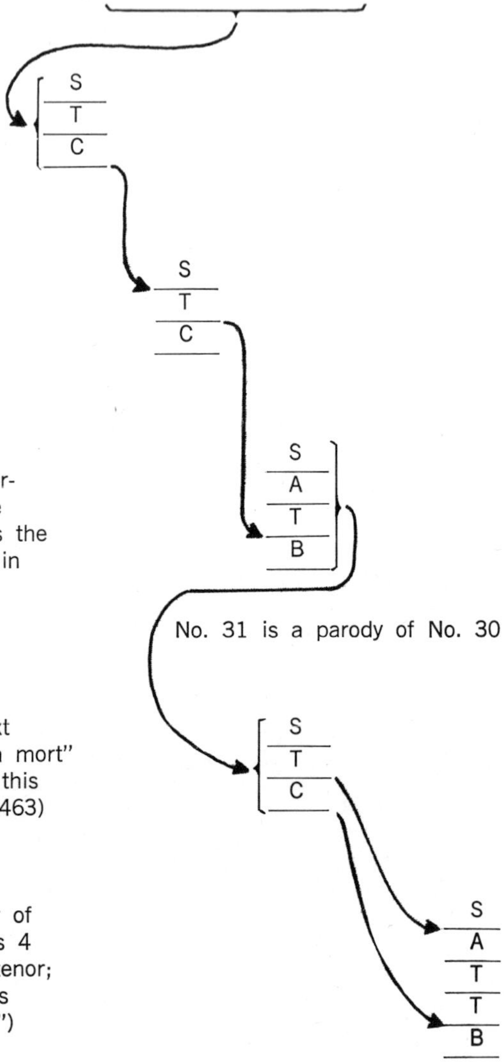

9 / The Choir in Fifteenth-Century English Music: Non-mensural Polyphony

ANDREW HUGHES
University of North Carolina

IN the informative fifth chapter of *Studies in Medieval and Renaissance Music*, Manfred Bukofzer discusses the beginnings of choral polyphony and finds the earliest evidence in the large Italian sources of the 1430's and 1440's.[1] His conclusion that Italy was the homeland of the style, despite an early English contribution in the carol manuscripts,[2] must now be modified in the light of further evidence.

The medieval choir as a body was used only for plainsong, and was thus unaccustomed to mensural singing even in monophony. Certain individual singers were no doubt familiar with mensuration; but even supposing that all of them were, since before the late fifteenth century there were no books large enough for many persons to read simultaneously, the problem remains of how polyphonic and rhythmic music can have been learned and performed. Certainly singers of that time must have had exceptional memories, and it is perhaps possible that the parts were learned individually and sung together from memory. But, to take an example, single parts in a

The main part of this article was read as a paper to the fall meeting of the Mid-West Chapter of the American Musicological Society, in Chicago, 1964.

1. For instance, Bologna, Conservatorio, MS. Q.15 and Modena, Estense MS. α.X.1.11. M. F. Bukofzer, *Studies in Medieval and Renaissance Music* (London, 1951), Chap. 5.

2. London. British Museum MS. Egerton 3307 and Oxford, Bodleian Library MS. Arch. Selden B.26.

polyphonic piece may rest for lengthy passages, and such rests would have to be counted correctly: thus, the choir as a body would have to learn the new art of "counting the bars" while silent. Quite aside from the inaccuracy with which such long rests are often written, there are also the difficulties of rhythmic complexity, of the constant contraction and expansion of the "bar"-length, and the complete absence of actual barlines in the music used for the memorizing. Polyphonic chaos would have resulted if memory had been the sole guide. A highly developed art of choral conducting is another possibility; but of this there is no evidence. That there may have been copies of the music for each person, a still further possibility, must surely be discounted for several reasons: manuscript material was expensive and copyists' time valuable; moreover, not a single example of multiple copies or of small part-books has come down to us. Perhaps a temporary method of writing, for instance on a blackboard or slate, was used.

The likelihood, then, must be that the first attempts at choral singing of polyphony would have been with non-mensural music that was simple to the extreme in other respects also. There would thus have been a stylistic distinction between solo and choral polyphony. The lack of any such distinction bothered Bukofzer,[3] who proposed that only one voice-part of a section marked "chorus" was intended for choir, the other parts being for instruments (or, as I would suggest, solo voices). This argument still throws little light on the transition to choral participation in all voices; nevertheless, I believe Bukofzer's contention to have been correct as far as it went.

The evidence put forward here, although circumstantial, inconclusive, and perhaps open to various interpretations, concerns a number of seemingly unrelated features, all of which, however, in my opinion, do fit together to make a sensible pattern. This evidence suggests that choral polyphony was developed along two different but largely contemporaneous lines: beginning with non-rhythmic monophony or chant, one line progressed through non-rhythmic polyphony, the other through rhythmic monophony; these two eventually coalesced into full choral polyphony as we know it.

The first of these approaches, which I believe to be English in the earliest instances, can be clearly seen in a fragmentary manuscript

3. Bukofzer, *Studies,* p. 179.

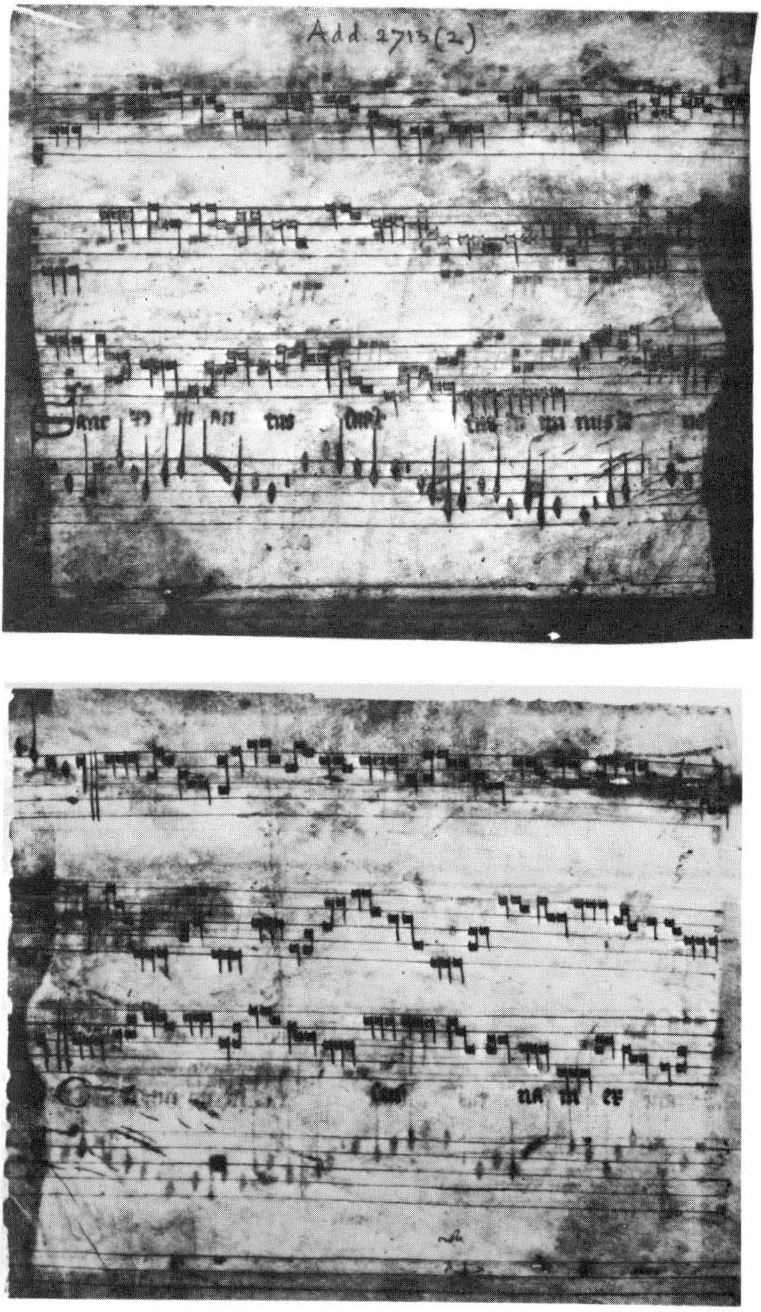

PLATE I. Cambridge University Library MS. Add. 2713
Top: folio 2r *Bottom:* folio 2v

from Cambridge,[4] ironically enough noted but not described by Bukofzer.[5] There are two small leaves, each originally part of a larger leaf, with music on both sides: the verso of each may be a continuation of the recto (the designations verso and recto are my own; since the leaves are mutilated it is now impossible to state which was the binding margin). A facsimile of one leaf is shown in Plate I, and the music of both leaves is transcribed in its entirety in Example 1.

EX. 1a. Credo (Cambridge, MS. Add. 2713, fols. 1r, 1v).

4. University Library MS. Add. 2713.
5. *Musical Quarterly*, XLIV (1958), 6.

* Clefs conjectural

EX. 1b. Sanctus (Cambridge, MS. Add. 2713, fols. 2r, 2v).

*Clefs conjectural

It is clear that the two-part sections are fairly florid, whereas the three-part sections are extremely simple. The latter are in fact written in symbols with no mensural significance, here transcribed conventionally as crotchets; only two places, both perhaps through an error, call for the use of any difference in rhythmic values in the transcription. On the other hand, it may be worth noting that there is frequent vocalization on repeated notes, and that unless sung with glottal stops, such passages would introduce new rhythmic values, the length of which would be determined by the number of times the note symbol was written. Example 2 shows an alternative transcription of part of the facsimile, in which repeated notes of the same pitch have been replaced by a single note of the relevant value. The result is a good deal more sophisticated than the original, and, excepting a few crudities, quite closely resembles mensural music with its hemiolas and occasional lengthened or shortened bars. It is not possible to put the conventional ligature brackets into such a transcription; accordingly, later examples of this kind retain their original form so that ligatures can be shown.

EX. 2. Sanctus (Cambridge, MS. Add. 2713, fol. 2r), alternative transcription.

The stylistic differentiation in these pieces surely implies a distinction between solo and chorus. Plainsong, which might have established an English origin for the music, is unfortunately not used. Unfortunate, too, is the lack of any indication of date, although the alternation of two and three parts, together with the style of the duets and their tentative use of imitation, would suggest a date about 1450.

Let us now work with the hypothesis that music written in the three-part style of this fragment indicates choral participation. Pieces in the same style can be traced in English sources through the late fifteenth century and into the sixteenth. Taverner's *Playn Song Mass,*[6] composed throughout in a slightly more elaborate four-part version of the technique, is the origin of the term "playnsong style," now applied to pieces written in this way, mainly using one note-value.

From the years between 1450 and 1500, there are several other pieces entirely in "playnsong style" in English manuscripts. Two more occur in the Bodleian MS. Lat. lit. b 5, a mid-fifteenth-century York Gradual (for use by the choir, of course) containing a "Deo gratias" written in non-mensural symbols with no plainsong, and a similar setting of the hymn *Veni creator spiritus* with the chant in the middle voice (Example 3).

EX. 3a. "Deo gratias" (Oxford, Bodleian, MS. Lat. lit. b 5, fol. 22v).

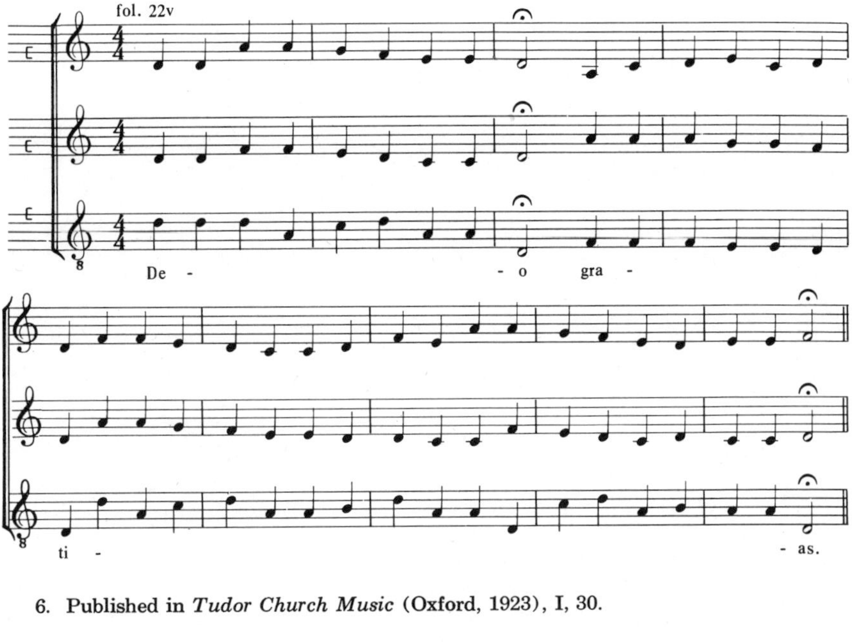

6. Published in *Tudor Church Music* (Oxford, 1923), I, 30.

EX. 3b. *Veni creator Spiritus* (Oxford, Bodleian, MS. Lat. lit. b 5, fol. 86v).

Incidental matters of interest are the cadences of both pieces and the lack of any significant parallel movement. Both compositions are noted in separate parts. These features suggest a date well into the fifteenth century.

From the second half of the century the Pepys MS. 1236, datable c. 1460–1465,[7] gives one "playnsong piece." Once again the symbols have no mensural significance. Example 4 shows the setting of *Salve*

EX. 4. *Salve festa dies* (Cambridge, Magdalene College, Pepys MS. 1236, fol. 81v).

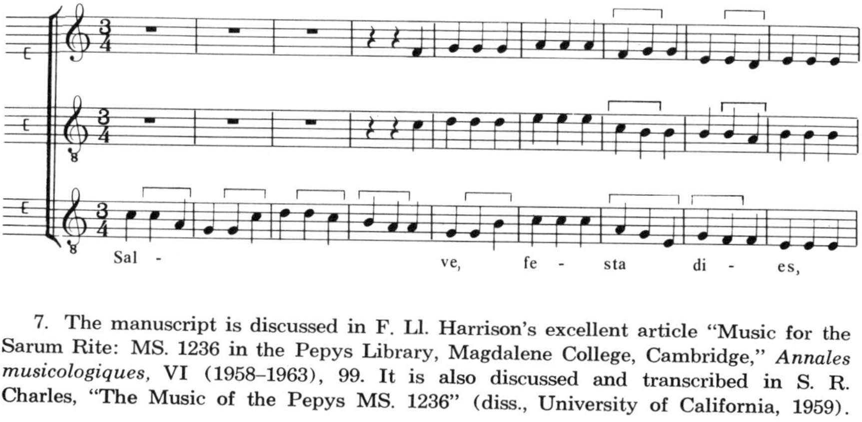

7. The manuscript is discussed in F. Ll. Harrison's excellent article "Music for the Sarum Rite: MS. 1236 in the Pepys Library, Magdalene College, Cambridge," *Annales musicologiques*, VI (1958–1963), 99. It is also discussed and transcribed in S. R. Charles, "The Music of the Pepys MS. 1236" (diss., University of California, 1959).

festa dies, folio 81v, with the plainsong perhaps ornamented in passages of the top voice. The piece is followed by a more florid two-part setting of a subsequent stanza of the same hymn. Whether this is intended as a solo continuation is not clear, even though that would seem most likely. Certain dissimilarities in the notation may perhaps indicate that the two-part section is a later addition. That the clefs are not alike may be accounted for by the use of a different pen. But the "playnsong" music is noted in separate parts, and the florid duet appears in score on the facing page, not using the space left below the "playnsong" section. The notation of the "playnsong" passages from the Cambridge fragments mentioned first is very similar in appearance to the notation of this "playnsong" passage, but no definite connection between the two can be established from the slim evidence available. The symbols, although distinctive, have few of the individual characteristics from which scribal relationship can be deduced.

"Playnsong" pieces also occur in the late fifteenth-century Ritson manuscript.[8] One work in particular, a Mass (lacking the Kyrie) by Petyr,[9] is entirely in this form of notation. So too are the *Salve festa dies*, *[Sancta] Maria virgo intercede*, *Salve regina misericordie* (with the trope *Virgo, mater ecclesie*), *Anima mea liquefacta*, and *Nunc Jesu te petimus*.[10] All these works, and Petyr's Mass, are written in separate parts, and before the beginning of the voices in many of these is a symbol of uncertain meaning which could be a *c* joined to the abbreviation for the *-us* ending: i.e., *c[hor]us*. The symbol appears with numerous other pieces in the manuscript, as does the term "chorus" in full. Interestingly enough, in the *Salve regina* the trope text is set for only two voices, as is usual in the settings of this piece,[11] and here the symbol is sometimes replaced by ∝. Liturgically the trope was always sung by soloists, and a distinction between solo and chorus is certainly intended. In the polyphony this is shown by the use of florid music for the duets.

These are all the "playnsong-style" pieces known to me from English sources. I would suggest, however, that a few isolated items written more conventionally but still based on simple monorhythmic chords may represent the same type in a more refined style. One such piece, in a sixteenth-century hand, is from the Bodleian MS. Lat. lit. e 14, a fifteenth-century Franciscan Ritual (Example 5). The ultimate development of the style must surely be in the simple settings of such works as the Taverner Mass mentioned earlier and the Preces and Responses of William Byrd.[12]

We can be fairly sure, then, that a choral style using simple polyphonic music flourished in England, at least from the 1450's. To

8. British Museum MS. Add. 5665. The manuscript is discussed and transcribed in Catherine K. Miller, "A Fifteenth-Century Record of English Choir Repertory: British Museum Add. MS. 5665; A Transcription and Commentary" (diss., Yale University, 1948).

9. Fol. 111v et seq., described by F. Ll. Harrison in *Die Musik in Geschichte und Gegenwart* under "Petyr" as "in einer choralartigen Notierung aufgezeichnet."

10. Fols. 119, 119v, 121v, 126v, 128v respectively.

11. F. Ll. Harrison, "An English 'Caput'," *Music and Letters*, XXXIII (1952), 204–06.

12. P. C. Buck, ed., *Tudor Church Music*, octavo ed. 1st ser., No. 32.

EX. 5. *Adoramus te* (Oxford, Bodleian, MS. Lat. lit. e 14, fol. 56v).

introduce a further complexity, however, it would seem probable that "playnsong" settings were not intended for what I shall term the "professional" choirs of long standing. More probably, they were intended for the newly established colleges and choir schools that were founded in large numbers in fifteenth-century England.[13] Here a beginners' style of polyphony would have been much in demand. Several features lead me to make this assertion. First, the settings was well known at the time. Second, three of the manuscripts are of do not often include a plainsong; when they do, the chant is one that provincial origin. The Pepys book probably came from somewhere in Kent, and was used at a singing school in which boys figured prominently.[14] There are numerous references to boys in the manuscript, and it includes the chant *Crucis signo* for the Feast of the Boy Bishop, an important occasion in the medieval school.[15] The Ritson manuscript almost certainly came from the West Country, and was probably used at Exeter.[16] Similarly, the manuscript Lat. lit. b 5 was, according to W. H. Frere, clearly designed for a village

13. See F. Ll. Harrison, *Music in Medieval Britain* (London, 1958), Chap. 4.

14. S. R. Charles, "Music of Pepys MS.," pp. 36–37, and R. L. Greene, "Two Medieval Musical Manuscripts: Egerton 3307 and some University of Chicago Fragments," *Journal, American Musicological Society*, VII (1954), 12–13.

15. Kathleen Edwards, *The English Secular Cathedrals in the Middle Ages* (Manchester, 1949), pp. 323–34.

16. J. Stevens, *Music and Poetry in the Early Tudor Court* (Lincoln, Nebraska. 1961), p. 5.

church in the diocese of York.[17] Third, the composition and (in some pieces) the notation of the music itself give evidence of unprofessional, even unskilled, musicians and scribes.[18]

The appearance of choral polyphony in the newest establishments, however, would surely imply a longer tradition in professional choirs such as those of the Chapel of the Royal Household and St. George's Chapel, Windsor. The extant records for these two choirs indicate that an increasing number of clerks were employed in the early fifteenth century. Even in 1413, the household accounts appertaining to the Chapel Royal show the names of twenty-seven clerks; for 1421, they show the names of forty-one clerks and sixteen "pueri."[19] Large choirs are, of course, known earlier than the fifteenth century, and there is some evidence that not all the members participated at all times. For instance, John Wyclif, who died in 1384, writes in "Of feigned contemplative life": "for whanne ther ben fourty or fyfty in a queer thre or foure proude & lecherous lorellis* schullen knacke† the most devout seruyce [so] that noman schal here the sentence, & alle othere schullen be doumbe & loken on hem as foolis."[20]

In other passages from the same work, Wyclif seems to have had polyphony in mind in such contexts. Nevertheless, surely significant in the records of the 1410's and 1420's is the frequent and largely unprecedented mention of "pueri." Although it may have been possible to find one or even two or three countertenors or male altos for the performance of the high voices in solo polyphony, the number required for choral polyphony might well have been excessive. Boys' voices were the obvious answer to the increasing demand for numbers of singers with a high vocal range.

But what polyphony exists for the professional choirs? Although there is little definite indication that the numerous fourteenth-century descant settings were performed chorally, they are really

17. W. H. Frere, "The Newly-found York Gradual," *Journal of Theological Studies,* II (1901), 587.

18. J. Stevens, *Music and Poetry,* p. 6.

19. For 1413: London, Public Records Office MSS. E101 404/21 & 406/21, etc. For 1421: MS. E101 407/4.

20. F. D. Matthew, ed., *Early English Text Society,* LXXIV (1880). The Old English letter *thorn* in this quotation has been modernized to *th.*

**Lorel:* a worthless person, a rogue (*OED*).

†*Knacke:* probably, from other references in Wyclif's writings, to sing in a florid manner and with many short notes.

remarkably similar in style to "playnsong," apart from their evident technical superiority (see Example 6).

EX. 6. *Mater ora Filium* (Oxford, Bodleian, MS. Barlow 55, fol. 4r).

In such settings there is little or no rhythmic difficulty; the chant, in the middle voice, if present at all, is sung in one note-value throughout, as are the other voices for the most part. In addition, melodic parallels make for more simplicity. The advance from this almost entirely chordal and often parallel descant to the slightly more florid descant pieces of the Fountains manuscript[21] and the Old Hall manuscript[22] is easy to follow. Unfortunately, although there is evidence suggesting choral performance of other items in Old Hall,[23] for descant there is nothing conclusive. Nevertheless, in one or two pieces a single voice is occasionally split into two notes for one beat—an obvious impossibility for a soloist. The only voice to split is the middle voice, which bears the plainsong and might any-

21. British Museum MS. Add 40011B. My complete edition of this manuscript is to appear in the *Early English Church Music* series. Examples are printed in Bukofzer, *Studies*, pp. 88–90.

22. A. Ramsbotham, H. B. Collins & Dom Anselm Hughes, eds. (3 vols., 1933–1938). A new edition is in preparation by Margaret Bent and the author for The American Institute of Musicology.

23. See my article, "Mensural Polyphony for Choir in 15th Century England," *Journal, American Musicological Society*, XIX (1966), 352–69.

way have had more than one singer to emphasize it. There is, too, a possibility (though only a slight one, since plainsong is involved) that the division, in which one note is often written in red, may indicate alternative or successive rather than simultaneous notes. Despite the lack of evidence for choral participation, descant does seem the likely origin of and example for the non-professional "playnsong" pieces. Moreover, the consistent use of three individual voice ranges, as is typical of the style, makes a homogeneous texture sound well; in styles where the pieces constantly cross one another, contrasting timbres are necessary.

The origins of descant style itself are impossible to describe here, but the simplicity of a note-against-note setting is as old as polyphony itself. The stage at which the choir took over, if fourteenth- and fifteenth-century descant is indeed choral, can only be hinted at in this study. Did it begin with the first polyphonic settings of portions of the liturgy in which the choir or congregation took part? Primarily, of course, medieval polyphony uses only the solo sections of chant; choral sections, or settings of choral texts, performed by soloists would violate correct liturgical observance—always an important consideration, especially in England. An examination of the problem would certainly involve liturgical inquiries, and the sole comment possible at present is that the earliest known English settings of, for instance, items of the Ordinary of the Mass are a good deal earlier than the earliest known Continental settings. Compare some items of the Worcester Fragments with the Machaut Mass. That the English may well have begun the adoption of the choir for polyphony seems a possibility. Nevertheless the Continent cannot have been far behind, for numerous pieces of polyphony written in a style similar to that of "playnsong" also occur in European manuscripts. That this sort of notation, with all its possible implications, was very widespread may also be deduced from a wide range of manuscripts now in Prague (National and University Library MS. VI.C.20a) Engelberg (MS. 314) and Verona (Bibl. Capit. Codex DCXC), as well as elsewhere.[24]

In a discussion of solo as opposed to choral participation in ritual music, the question of liturgical propriety must always be considered.

24. I am indebted to Charles Hamm of the University of Illinois for this information.

Of the items in "playnsong" notation extant in England, all are suitable for choral singing. The Sanctus and Credo of the Cambridge fragments and the whole of Petyr's Mass are settings of the Ordinary; and apart from the intonations of the Gloria and Credo not set to polyphony, in the liturgy these are entirely choral. So is the "Deo gratias," the choral response to the priest's "Ite missa est."[25]

Veni creator spiritus is a hymn. The rubrics for the piece vary, but all agree that it is begun by one or more soloists, seven being the usual number, and that subsequent verses are sung *alternatim* by the choir.[26] The intonation of the first line is preserved in the setting (see Example 2). We should not, however, assume that since this intonation was normally sung by seven soloists, all the parts were sung by a similar number. It is known that three was the usual number to sing from one book of plainsong;[27] and if each part of a polyphonic piece were to have been written out separately, three would have been the most likely number. The choir was probably no larger than nine or twelve for a three-part piece.

The two versions of *Salve festa dies* are settings of the choral refrain of the processional hymn, sung first and then after every solo verse.[28]

Sancta Maria virgo (in which the first word, a solo intonation, is not set polyphonically), *Anima mea* and *Adoramus te, Christe* are votive or processional antiphons in which choral participation would have been normal. *Nunc Jesu* (usually *Christe*) *te petimus* is the

25. Although one of the manuscripts of Machaut's Mass has the words "Ite missa est" as well as "Deo gratias" written under the polyphony, the polyphonic performance of the priest's words would be liturgically quite incorrect.

26. *Breviarium ad Usum Sarum,* ed. F. Proctor and C. Wordsworth (3 vols.; Cambridge, 1882–1886, I, mviii ("deinde procedant praedicti septem seniores ad gradum altaris. . . . omnes simul incipiant hunc Hymnum *Veni Creator.* . . . Chorus vero . . . prosequatur"). *The Use of Sarum,* ed. W. H. Frere (2 vols.; Cambridge, 1898–1901): I. 204 ("Deinde . . . episcopus . . . incipiens alta voce [ymnum] *Veni creator* . . . et ita totus ymnus cantetur [et] ut primus versus a clericis secus altare assistentibus cantetur, secundus [versus] a toto choro, et ita alternatim [omnes versus tocius] ymni cantentur"). See also the *Hereford Breviary* (London, 1904), I, 390-91, and the *Customary of St. Augustine's, Canterbury and St. Peter's, Westminster* (London, 1902), I, 3, 14, 385.

27. Harrison, *Music in Medieval Britain,* p. 103, *n.* 1.

28. *Graduale Sarisburiense,* ed. W. H. Frere (London, 1894), Plates 116, 134 ("In die [Paschae, Ascensionis, Pentecostes] ad processionem prosa *Salve festa* etc. Chorus idem repetat post unumquemque versum").

third verse of the ninth respond at Matins of the Dead, and would liturgically have been sung by a soloist. However, this text may also be an antiphon, "part of *Sancte Deus, sancte fortis* which was commonly sung as a Jesus-antiphon."[29]

The votive antiphon *Salve regina* also follows liturgical practice. The antiphon itself, and the exclamations *O clemens, O pia, O dulcis Maria,* set in three parts, would be sung chorally; the intervening trope text, set in two parts, would be sung by soloists.[30] The stylistic distinction has been mentioned.

The ritual use of solo or choir is thus retained in all the "playnsong-style" compositions. The same is true of the more refined pieces in descant style: these are settings of the Ordinary of the Mass or of devotional antiphons. To my knowledge, there is only one that does not fall into either of these groups: this is the *Nunc dimittis* from the Magdalene College MS. 267. Although the accompanying antiphon is not included, the piece is clearly a setting of the canticle for Compline, using the fifth psalm-tone untransposed. The absence of transposition is a characteristic of migrating chants; the first one or two notes of the tone occur in the lowest voice, the rest in the middle part. The liturgical performance of the canticle requires the alternation of two halves of the choir, a division emphasized in the music.[31] The liturgical designation of the music thus dictates the specific method of performance.

EX. 7. *Nunc dimittis* (Oxford, Magdalen College, MS. 267, fol. 89v).

o - cu - li me - i sa - lu - ta - re tu - um:

* The first few lines are missing.

29. Harrison, *Music in Medieval Britain,* p. 174.
30. *Ibid.,* p. 82.
31. *Ibid.,* p. 58.

Quod pa - ra - sti an-te fa-ci-em o-mni-um po-pu-lo - rum:

Although a detailed discussion of the second approach to choral polyphony—the approach through mensural monophony—cannot be presented here, an undocumented and very generous synopsis of the main features will serve to place the non-mensural "playnsong" and partly mensural descant styles in their proper context.[32] Concurrently with the fifteenth-century use of these two styles, composers seem to have been experimenting with choral participation in one voice of certain florid polyphonic pieces. In some of these the experiment takes the form of a rhythmicizing and melodic ornamentation of plainchants which liturgically were to be sung by choir; its complexity is greatest when the chant appears in the highest voice. Although there are very early fourteenth-century examples of this technique, its most consistent application is to be found only after about 1400, in the later layers of the Old Hall manuscript and in some other English sources between 1400 and 1470. It is worth noting that in a few of the Old Hall pieces the highest voice divides into two parts in the final section, thus expanding the choral participation into two upper voices. Choral singing in some such pieces seems, especially in the Old Hall manuscript, to be quite specifically implied by the use of texts written in black ink, contrasting with red ink for solo two-part sections. This use of black and red ink in place of the Continental terms "chorus" and "duo" or "unus" is also to be found in other English sources such as the Eton Choir Book, from the decades around 1500.

32. Complete details and documentation are in my article, "Mensural Polyphony for Choir in 15th Century England," *Journal, American Musicological Society,* XIX (1966), 352–69.

Performance by choir of only the lowest part of a piece may be implied by the use of a more or less unrhythmicized voice (i.e., a part using only one note-value) accompanied by florid upper parts. Disregarding isorhythmic works, in which this contrasting of upper and lower voices is normal, such pieces are infrequent in English sources. The Pepys manuscript contains a hymn and a Communion, and the Ritson book an Alleluia, written in this way. Plainsong and liturgical observance again confirm the possibility of choral singing. Non-rhythmic inner parts are very scarce: the only examples known to me are three antiphons from the Ritson manuscript.

If the choir was added to florid polyphony in this way, a single upper or lower—or occasionally an inner—part at a time, the influence of the apparently thriving non-mensural styles, in which each part was already choral, would soon have brought about full choral participation on each part of mensural pieces. We may surely agree that such a situation had been reached by the beginning of the sixteenth century. It is noteworthy that the appearance of choral performance for each voice coincides with the virtual disappearance of stylistic distinctions between individual voices.

Several other features, notably the significance of unison passages, faburdens, sections marked "chorus" in certain carols, and liturgical clues[33] are of help in amplifying and substantiating the conclusions reached in this study. Much work remains to be done, especially with Continental sources, but it is clear that the English were prominent in the early development of this important innovation. Their love of blending voices, of sonority and sweetness, was probably decisive in the emergence of choral polyphony.

33. See, for instance, Harrison's discovery regarding an Alleluia in the Pepys MS.: *Annales musicologiques,* VI (1958–1963), 109.

10 / Ockeghem à Notre-Dame de Paris (1463–1470)

FRANÇOIS LESURE
Bibliothèque Nationale, Paris

Les archives de Notre-Dame de Paris, conservées en gros depuis le XIVe siècle, continuent d'attendre l'historien qui les mettra en oeuvre. Elles sont, n'en doutons pas, une mine extrêmement riche pour l'histoire musicale, les travaux publiés jusqu'à ce jour n'en donnant qu'une idée très insuffisante.[1] André Pirro semble avoir dépouillé pour lui-même minutieusement ce fonds, conservé aujourd'hui aux Archives nationales. Au lieu d'en faire l'objet d'une étude particulière, il en dissémina les résultats, comme il le fit pour beaucoup d'autres de ses dépouillements, dans le cours de son *Histoire de la musique de la fin du XIVe à la fin du XVIe siècle* publié en 1940. C'est ainsi qu'il révéla incidemment au sujet de J. Ockeghem que "le 8 août 1463, il n'était encore que sous-diacre, quand les chanoines de Notre-Dame l'admirent parmi eux, quelques semaines après avoir conféré la même dignité à Nicaise Dupuis, premier chapelain de Philippe le Bon (LL.120, p. 502 et 518)." Voici quelques renseignements supplémentaires sur les rapports entre cette illustre maîtrise et le trésorier de Saint-Martin de Tours.

Ce n'est pas le musicien en personne qui se présenta le 8 août 1463 devant le chapitre de Notre-Dame, mais un certain Pierre Moceti, "procurator . . . venerabilis et circumspecti viri magistri

1. Le principal est celui de F. L. Chartier, *L'ancien chapitre de Notre-Dame de Paris et sa maîtrise* (Paris, 1897), qui, plus que sur les archives originales, s'est fondé sur les résumés faits au XVIIIe s. par le chanoine Sarasin.

Johannis Okeghem, subdiaconi, nostri Regis prothocapellani." Il s'agissait de prendre possession d'une chanoinie rendue vacante par la mort de Nicolas Merchant. Moceti prêta serment, fut installé dans le choeur et au chapitre, enfin paya les droits usuels de 22 livres, 10 sols pour Ockeghem.[2] A son tour, ce dernier se présenta le 26 août suivant: "Receptus fuit in persona et juravit in forma ac fuit installatus in choro et capitulo."[3]

Dans les mois suivants il n'est pas question à nouveau du musicien, retourné remplir ses devoirs auprès du roi. Mais la vie du chapitre est surtout marquée par des visites illustres: en octobre, avec le même faste que s'il s'agissait du roi, celle de Radegonde de Piémont, soeur du roi, femme du fils aîné du duc de Savoie, au son des orgues et de "Marie" et "Jacqueline," les grosses cloches de l'église; le 7 novembre celle du duc de Savoie; le 6 mars 1464 celle du duc de Berry.[4]

Une délibération du 15 mars 1464 revient sur le cas d'Ockeghem: "Maistre Henry Lefevre, commissaire en Chastelet, par vertu de certaines lettres royaulx et commission du prévost de Paris, a fait commandement que on face joyr Me Jeh. de Okeghem des fruitz, distribucions et revenues de la prébende de Paris, a laquelle il a esté receu par vertu de certaines lettres apostoliques . . . " Ockeghem n'avait-il pas pu jouir des bénéfices afférant à sa prébende ? Le problème juridique parait avoir été délicat—soit pour un motif de non-résidence, soit pour celui de cumul—si bien que la réponse du chapitre fut différée . . . "attentis statutis ecclesie." Finalement, après deux jours de réflexion, le 17 mars, une réponse clairement positive fut donnée: "Aux commandemens faiz a nous, doien et chapitre de l'église de Paris par honorable homme maistre Henry Lefevre, commissaire de par le roy nostre sire en son Chastelet de Paris, nous, doien et chapitre, respondons que, en obéissant au mandement de nostre Saint Pere le pape et expectative par luy concédée a la requeste du roy . . . a vénérable et discrete personne maistre Jehan de Okeghem, nous avons receu led. Okeghem en possession des chanoinie et prébende de céans et n'empeschons point que led. Okeghem ne soit maintenu par led. comissaire en sa possession

2. Archives nationales, LL.120, p. 518 (Pl. I).
3. *Ibid.*, p. 525 (Pl. II).
4. *Ibid.*, pp. 541, 547, 581.

dessusdicte et qu'il ne joysse selon les status et communes observances de lad. église."[5]

En 1466 Ockeghem est noté comme absent dans les listes canoniales,[6] mais l'année suivante, le 11 septembre, le chapitre délibère sur une nouvelle affaire de prébende le concernant: "Guillaume Barbeau, huissier des requestes, a segnefié la mainlevée faite es requestes du Palays au prouffit de Me Jehan de Okeghem de la prébende de Paris litigieuse entre led. Okeghem et feu Me Henry Megret par le trespas dud. Megret . . . "[7] Malgré l'issue heureuse de ce litige, le premier chapelain du roi ne parait pas avoir conservé longtemps son canonicat à Notre-Dame.

La dernière apparition d'Ockeghem dans les archives de la cathédrale de Paris a lieu le 22 août 1470.[8] Elle nous permet d'assister à une sorte d'échange triangulaire de prébendes, entre Amisius Gombert, prêtre licencié en droit et conseiller du roi, Louis Collebart,[9] et Ockeghem, l'enjeu étant constitué par des chanoinies à St-Martin de Tours, St-Benoît-le-Bientourné et Notre-Dame. Ainsi apprend-on qu'Ockeghem fut un certain temps titulaire de la chapelle St-Louis à l'église St-Benoît de Paris. Là encore il procéda par procuration, sa résignation ayant été faite en son nom par un certain Jean Barbier.

5. *Ibid.*, pp. 584–85 (Pl. III et IV).
6. *Ibid.*, LL.121, p. 63.
7. *Ibid.*, p. 193.
8. *Ibid.*, p. 457 (Pl. V).
9. M. Brenet (*Musique et musiciens de la vieille France* [Paris, 1911], pp. 39–40) note entre 1472 et 1474 un chapelain ordinaire de la chapelle du roi avec la graphie L. Colebert ou Collebert.

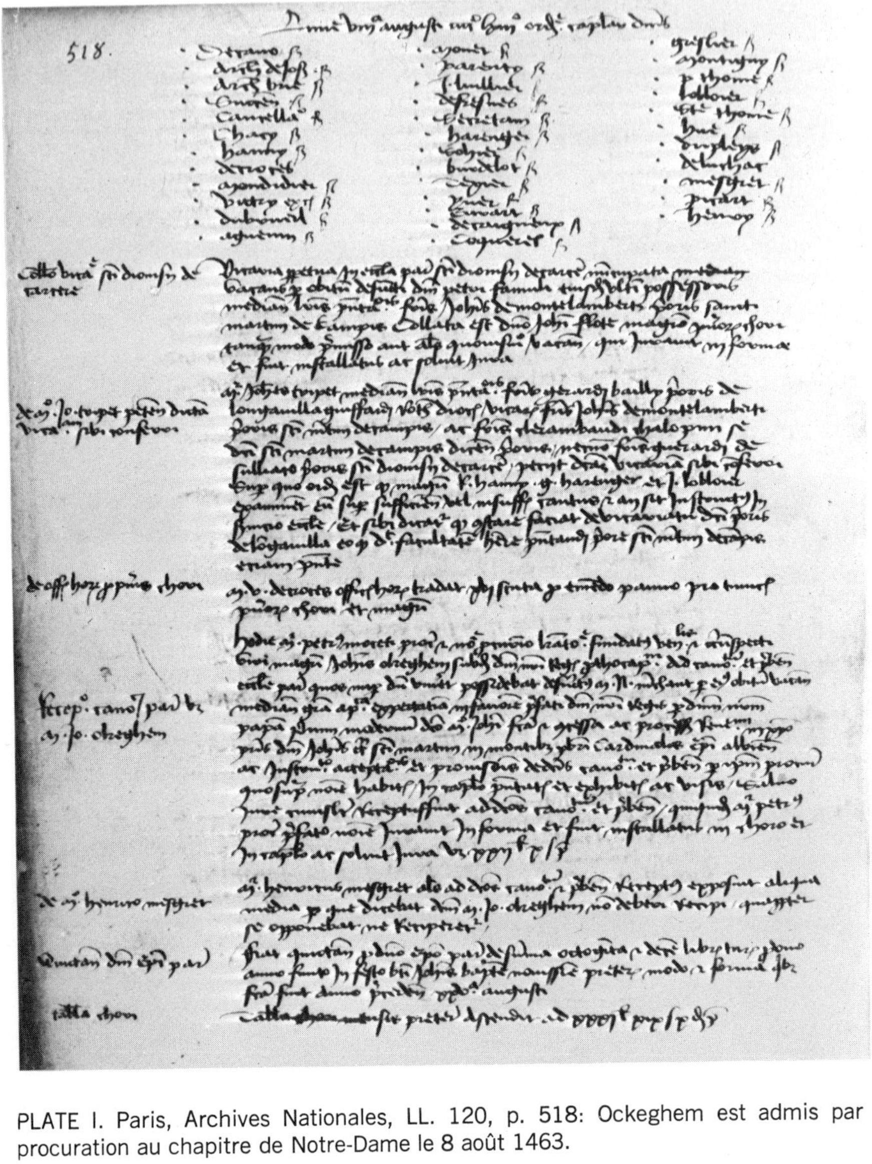

PLATE I. Paris, Archives Nationales, LL. 120, p. 518: Ockeghem est admis par procuration au chapitre de Notre-Dame le 8 août 1463.

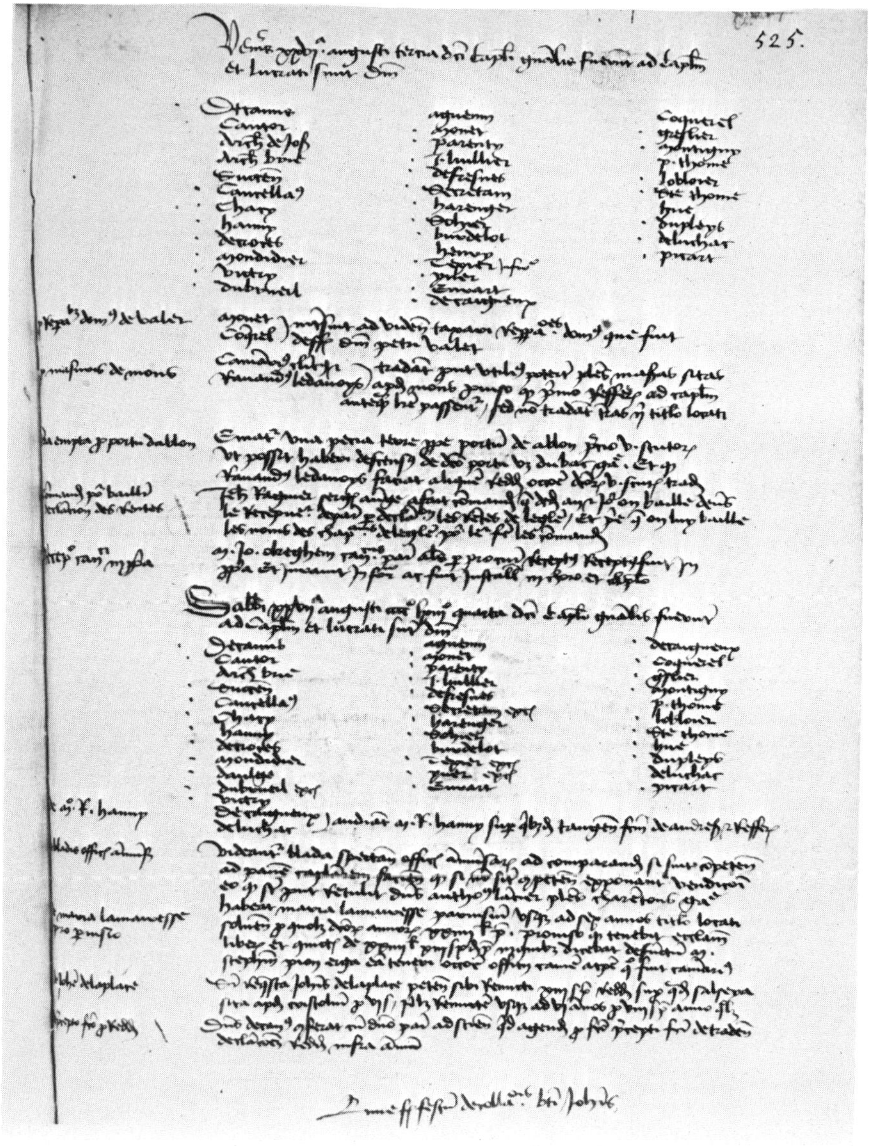

PLATE II. Paris, Archives Nationales, LL. 120, p. 525: Ockeghem est reçu en personne et installé au chapitre de Notre-Dame le 26 août 1463.

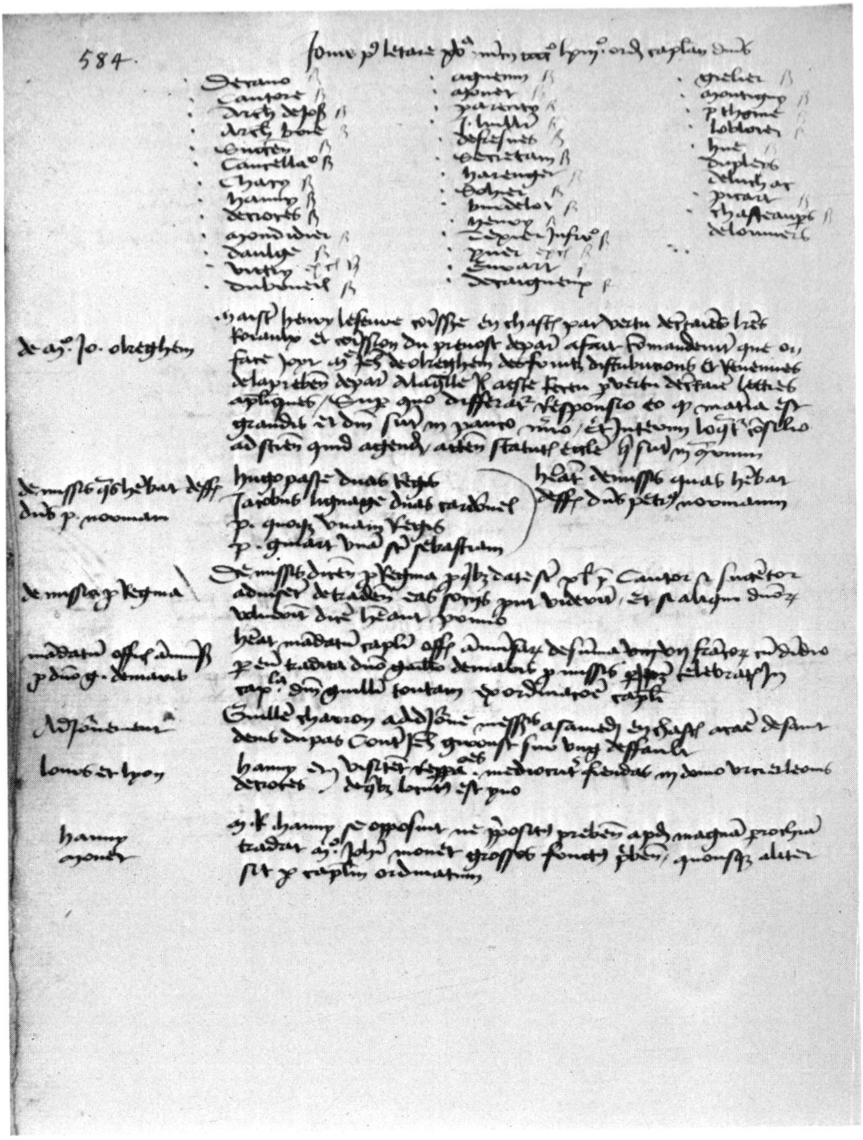

PLATE III. Paris, Archives Nationales, LL. 120, p. 584: Le 15 mars 1464, le chapitre de Notre-Dame est sommé de "faire jouir" Ockeghem des revenus de sa prébende.

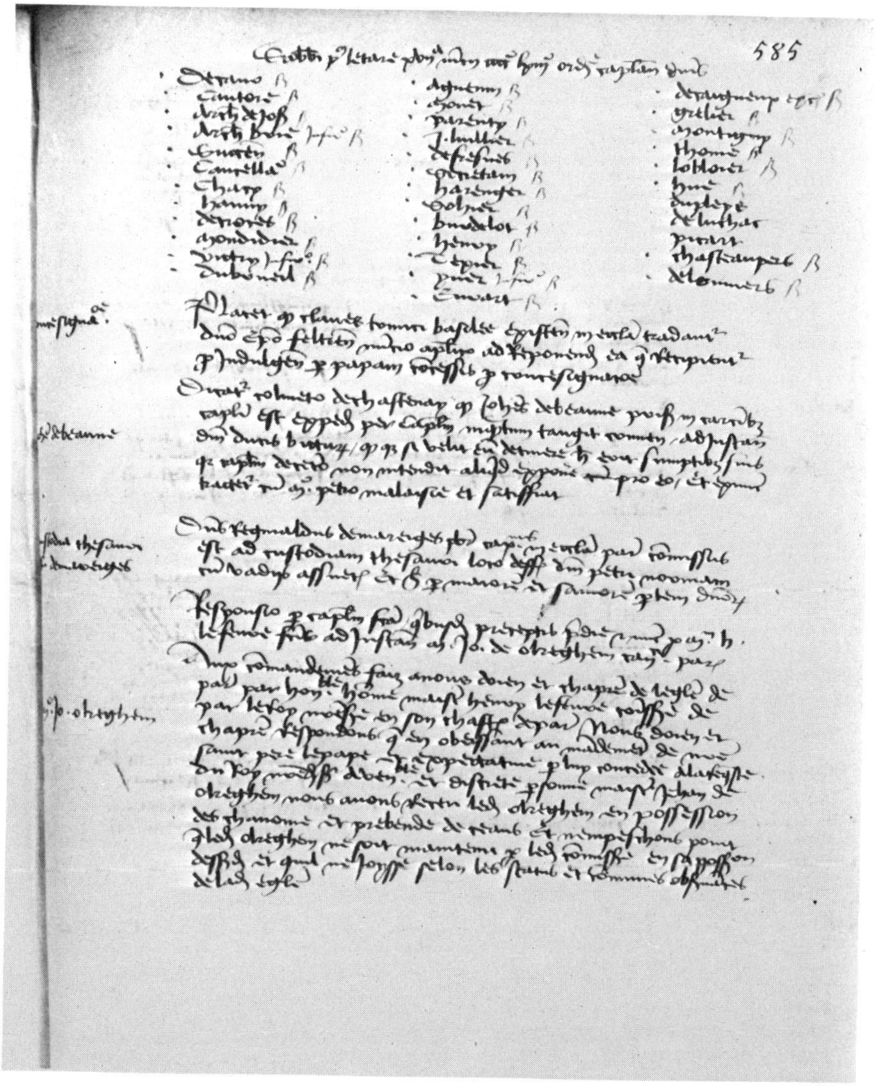

PLATE IV. Paris, Archives Nationales, LL. 120, p. 585: Le 17 mars 1464 le chapitre de Notre-Dame répond favorablement au "mandement" concernant la prébende d'Ockeghem.

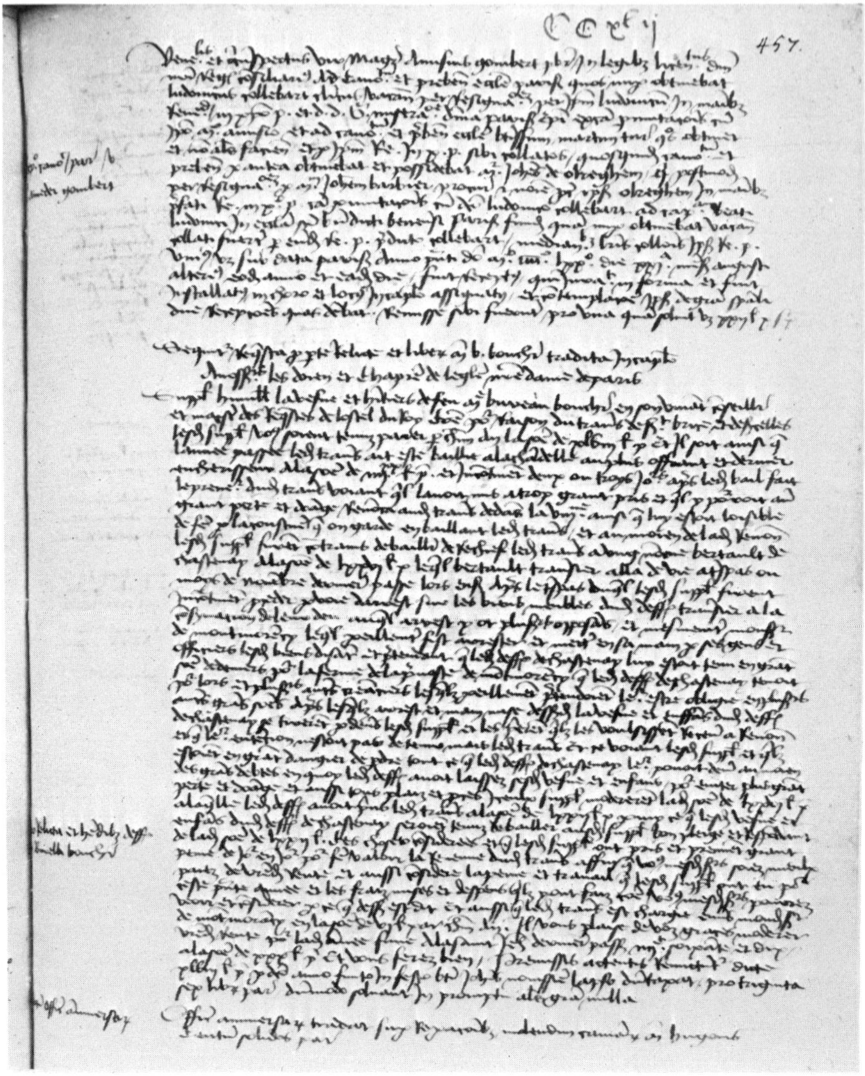

PLATE V. Paris, Archives Nationales, LL. 120, p. 457: Ockeghem apparaît pour la dernière fois dans les archives de Notre-Dame le 22 août 1470.

11 / Ockeghem's Canon for Thirty-six Voices: An Essay in Musical Iconography

EDWARD E. LOWINSKY
University of Chicago

No Netherlandish composer has suffered more from misinterpretation in the histories of music than Johannes Ockeghem. It cannot be denied that the composition of a canon for thirty-six voices played a considerable part in blackening his name. Fétis[1] resolutely refused to believe that Ockeghem ever composed such a canon, notwithstanding his familiarity with Guillaume Crétin's[2] testimony and Glareanus' reference.[3] He was convinced that the work was mythical.

Ambros,[4] who did not know the canon either, found it impossible to disbelieve the literary evidence, particularly since he discovered new testimony in Ornitoparchus' treatise of 1517.[5] He surmised that

1. F. J. Fétis, *Biographie universelle des musiciens* (8 vols.; 2d ed., Paris, 1860–1865), VI, 365: "Je le répète, une telle composition était absolument impossible au temps d'Okeghem."

2. Er. Thoinan, *Déploration de Guillaume Cretin sur le trépas de Jean Okeghem* . . . (Paris, 1864), p. 29:

> C'est luy qui bien sceut choisir et attaindre
> Tous les secretz de la subtilité
> Du nouveau chant par sa subtilité,
> Sans ung seul poinct de ses reigles enfraindre
> Trente-six voix noter, escripre, et paindre
> En ung motet . . . .

3. Henricus Glareanus, *Dodekachordon* (Basel, 1547), p. 454: "Quippe quem constat triginta sex vocibus garritum quendam instituisse." But Glareanus adds that he never saw the work—"Eum nos non vidimus".

4. August Wilhelm Ambros, *Geschichte der Musik* (Breslau, 1868), III, 174.

5. Andreas Ornitoparchus, *Musice active micrologus* (Leipzig, 1517), fol. k3v: "Nam Joannem Okeken mutetum 36. vocum composuisse constat."

no more than six or nine voices were notated with a six- or fourfold canon emerging from each part; he referred to Josquin's Psalm *Qui habitat in adjutorio*, written in the form of a canon for twenty-four voices developed from four notated parts, as an analogous example. However, he found the loss of "Ockeghem's monster motet" hardly regrettable, since "under the mountainous burden of such an obbligo the hand of the master must have been paralyzed."

Ambros' designation of the canon, which he admittedly did not know, as a "monster motet" has colored the appreciation of Ockeghem's canon to this day.

Since Riemann's transcription[6] (based on Eitner's[7] identification of the canon of literary fame with the anonymous "Deo gratia[s]" in Petrejus' third volume of psalms dated 1542), it has been known that at no time are more than eighteen voices singing in the thirty-six-part motet. This moved Alfred Orel[8] to say that the "apparent monster," under closer examination, takes on a simpler shape.

But the technical aspect has continued to dominate the evaluation of the work. Johannes Wolf,[9] probably skeptical of Eitner's identification, wrote: "A marvel of technique must have been his 36-part motet. . . ." Charles van den Borren,[10] one of the few authors who subjected the work to a painstaking analysis, found it a "purely scholastic exercise." Otto Ursprung[11] spoke of Ockeghem's motet and similar works as "monstrous canons," and he added that such com-

6. Hugo Riemann, *Handbuch der Musikgeschichte* (3 vols.; 2d. ed., Leipzig, 1919–1922), II[1], 239–49.

7. Robert Eitner, *Bibliographie der Musik-Sammelwerke* (Berlin, 1877), p. 311. It might be added that Petrejus' publication of 1542 begins with the twenty-four-part canon of Josquin, referred to above, and concludes with the anonymous thirty-six-part canon "Deo gratia[s]." For the rest, the edition contains mostly compositions for four and five voices. Riemann contended that the placement of the two canons, Josquin's at the beginning and the anonymous (= Ockeghem's) canon at the end, implied a value judgment and an adverse criticism of Ockeghem's work. Laurence K. J. Feininger, *Die Frühgeschichte des Kanons* (Emsdetten, 1937), p. 46, points out that the position of the "Deo gratia[s]," which concludes the three-volume series of psalms, is to be interpreted simply as an analogy to the conclusion of the Divine Service. For reasons to be developed later, we believe that Eitner's identification is correct. It should be added that the canon was printed a second time, without indication of the author, again in Nuremberg, in the *Cantiones triginta selectissimae,* edited by Clemens Stephani of Buchau, published by Ulricus Neuber in 1568.

8. In Guido Adler, ed., *Handbuch der Musikgeschichte* (2 vols.; Berlin, 1930), I, 304.

9. *Geschichte der Musik* (3 vols.; Leipzig, 1925–29), I, 79.

10. *Études sur le quinzième siècle musical* (Antwerp, 1941), p. 222.

11. *Die katholische Kirchenmusik* (Potsdam, 1931), p. 169.

positions were destined not for the church but for "chamber music of a general spiritual nature." Joseph Schmidt-Görg[12] relegated the composition to the realm of "kanonische Spitzfindigkeiten."

Why Ockeghem, who ordinarily limited himself to compositions for three, four, and five voices, should have aspired to write a canon for thirty-six voices is a question. If he was, as is generally assumed, motivated by technical considerations, why should he not have tried his hand at other canons for eight, twelve, or sixteen parts? Why do we have only this one multivoice canon, and what is the reason for the unprecedented number of parts in a musical tradition that cultivates three- to five-part writing?

It is the burden of the present argument that technique was the least of Ockeghem's concerns in composing this canon—that the canon was merely the instrument needed to carry out an idea. The idea that prompted Ockeghem to such an extraordinary enterprise had been for many centuries an integral part of the Christian mystical vision; it went back in part to the Neoplatonic, in part to the Jewish prophetic tradition, notably to Isaiah and Ezekiel, and was nourished by various ancient mythologies as well. It was the concept of the heavenly music of the angels sung in praise of God.

Ockeghem's motet, the number of its parts, the canonic construction, and its whole technique can be explained in terms of the angelic music[13] it was designed to echo.

The central work on the celestial hierarchy is the treatise of that name[14] written by the mysterious Dionysius Areopagita[15] about A.D. 500. It was destined to become the most influential and popular book on angels during the Middle Ages. According to Dionysius

12. "Niederländische Musik des Mittelalters und der Renaissance," *Kriegsvorträge der Rheinischen Friedrich-Wilhelms-Universität Bonn a. R.*, LXVI (Bonn, 1942), 16.

13. The most recent and most thorough treatment of the subject is in Reinhold Hammerstein's *Die Musik der Engel* (Bern and Munich, 1962). I should also like to refer to the article by Charles de Tolnay, "The Music of the Universe: Notes on a Painting by Bicci di Lorenzo," *Journal, Walters Art Gallery*, VI (1943), 83–104. This excellent study was unknown to Hammerstein.

14. *De Caelesti Hierarchia;* see the edition entitled *Dionysiaca* (2 vols.; published by the Société de St. Augustin, Desclée de Brouwer & Cie., Bruges, no authors, 1937), which assembles two Greek texts and nine Latin translations, together with a French version.

15. For a recent critical summary of the various attempts at identification of Dionysius, also called by some writers Pseudo-Dionysius, see the edition by René Roques, Günter Heil, and Maurice de Gandillac of *Denys l'Aréopagite, La Hiérarchie Céleste* (Paris, 1958), pp. v–xix.

Areopagita, whose ideas were taken up by St. Gregory and the later scholastics, there were three hierarchies of angels, each ordered in three choirs: Seraphim, Cherubim, Thrones; Dominations, Virtues, Powers; Principalities, Archangels, Angels.

The mystical writers of the Middle Ages developed certain ideas on the angelic chant in praise of God. Contrary to Hammerstein's belief,[16] their ideas of angelic hymns, and of liturgical music as an echo of the heavenly music, go back to Dionysius Areopagita, who in his description of the highest hierarchy of angels says: "Therefore the Sacred Scriptures offer to the earthborn hymns that reveal the eminence of these sublime lights to us in sacred form. Indeed, some of these spirits, to use human metaphors, cry out with a voice like roaring waters: 'Blessed be the glory of the Lord in this place'; others call to each other that famous and venerable chant: 'Holy, Holy, Holy, Lord of hosts, the earth is full of thy glory.' These magnificent hymns of the angelic spirits we have already explained to the best of our ability in the treatise on divine chants."[17]

To the characteristics of angelic chant as developed throughout the Middle Ages belong the following: The angels sing

1) as with one voice ("una voce"),
2) unceasingly ("sine fine"),
3) in alternating choirs ("alter ad alterum"),
4) beating their wings with a tone as of roaring waters,
5) always in praise of God, on texts of psalms, Alleluia, Sanctus, Gloria, or Benedictus.[18]

At least the third, fourth, and fifth characteristics of angelic chant are rooted in Dionysius' description. The stipulation "una voce" by no means excludes harmonic or polyphonic song.[19] Hildegard of Bingen (c. 1150) describes angelic music in terms suggesting

16. R. Hammerstein, *Die Musik,* gives an excellent account of angelic singing and the evolution of this concept in the Middle Ages. However, it is not correct that "Bei Pseudodionysius ist allerdings nicht ausdrücklich vom Gesang der Engel die Rede. Immerhin weist das Wort *Χορός,* bzw. *chorus* auf diesen Zusammenhang" (p. 26).

17. See *Dionysiaca,* II, 863–65. See also Roques et al., *La Hiérarchie Céleste,* p. 118, where the treatise on divine chants is referred to as "fictitious or lost" (*n.* 5). A reason why this work should be presumed fictitious is not given.

18. Hammerstein, *Die Musik,* p. 70 (also pp. 25, 45, 58–59).

19. Eric Peterson, *The Angels and the Liturgy,* trans. R. Walls (New York, 1964; 1st ed., *Das Buch von den Engeln,* 1935), p. 28, takes the "una voce" literally. Basing his opinion on theological authority alone, the author also argues that "the worship which is offered to God in heaven makes use of no mechanical instrument but only the voice of angels" *(ibid.)*. Accounts of mystical visions, literary testimony, and the

unity in harmony. She likens it to "the voice of a great multitude" which "unites harmonically in praise of the celestial inhabitants. For such harmony celebrates the glory and honor of the heavenly citizens in unity of mind and heart" ("ut vox multitudinis in laudibus de supernis gradibus in harmonia symphonizat, quia symphonia in unanimitate et in concordia gloriam et honorem coelestium civium ruminat").[20]

To the same period belongs the famous vision of Tundalus. He reports that the music of the nine angelic choirs consists of "voces diverse consonantes."[21] Somewhat later, Caesarius of Heisterbach (1177–1240) describes the heavenly music as sung by "voces multae et diversae," and its harmony as "concors illa diversitas."[22]

If Ockeghem wished to create a sounding likeness of the unity of angelic harmony he could not have chosen a better means than canon, which mirrors unity and produces harmony. If he desired to imitate the chain of acclamations from one to the other ("alter ad alterum"), he could hardly have selected a more appropriate technique than the nine-part canon in which the voices enter one after another a bar apart, in ever swelling chorus. If he intended to emulate the alternating choirs, he could not have done better than to let each new nine-part canon come in at the end of a preceding nine-part canon. If he hoped to echo the tremendous sound of roaring waters, he had to go completely beyond the three- or four- or five-part harmony of his time. Thus he used eighteen real voices in the fifteenth century, an utterly unprecedented event in the history of concerted music. If Ockeghem meant to depict the nine angelic choirs, the number of thirty-six participating voices suggested itself quite logically; if he aspired to reproduce the aspect of never-ending praise, what better way than to compose a canon that could be easily and endlessly repeated? Since the ternary meter of each bar was divided into two units of tonic and one of dominant, the music could go on and on. If the lilting meter and the graceful rhythm suggested dance, this

---

innumerable paintings of angelic concerts showing the whole instrumentarium of the Middle Ages—some of which contain identifiable references to polyphonic music—roundly contradict this view.

20. Hammerstein, p. 56. The accumulation of terms such as "harmonia," "symphonia," "concordia," and "symphonizare," makes it extremely unlikely that Hildegard thought of song in unison.

21. *Ibid.*, p. 66.

22. *Ibid.*, pp. 85–86.

too fitted the medieval vision, according to which dance and procession accompanied the chanting of the angels.[23] Finally, the chief characteristic of angelic chant is its purpose of praising God. The "Deo gratia[s]" of the Petrejus text fulfills this condition.

If every single aspect of Ockeghem's motet can be shown to flow forth from its iconographic intent, the traditional interpretation of the canon as a mammoth exercise in counterpoint must be abandoned. Even as the painters of the age never ceased to be fascinated by the topic of angelic music—a topic endlessly discussed by theologians, treated by mystics, and embellished by poets—so the greatest musician of his time, Johannes Ockeghem, rose to the challenge of depicting the nine angelic choirs in audible tones.

But if this new interpretation is accepted, the question arises whether Ockeghem's contemporaries could have remained unaware of his intention. Since the theory of the time deals exclusively with the practical aspects of composition, not with questions of meaning, we must rely on implicit rather than explicit testimony.

Dragan Plamenac, in a justly famous essay,[24] has assembled contemporary literary evidence on Ockeghem's canon. In particular he published a French poem written by Nicolle Le Vestu for a poetic contest at Rouen in 1523 in celebration of the Immaculate Conception. For such contests the competitors were given an "argument" in verse, on which they were to elaborate in a "chant royal." Le Vestu's poem, preceded by the "argument" of an unknown author, whom Plamenac hypothetically (and very persuasively) identifies with Guillaume Crétin, deals with the "motet exquis, chef d'oeuvre de nature," as the steadily recurring refrain line calls it—that is, with the thirty-six-voice canon by "Okghem."[25] Although the poem had been published before, Plamenac is the first historian of music to discover this highly interesting document.

23. *Ibid.*, pp. 47–49.

24. "Autour d'Ockeghem," *Revue musicale*, IX (1928), 26–47.

25. The first lines of the "chant royal" present the composer as "Okhem, tres-docte en art mathematique,/Aritmeticque, aussy geometrie,/Astrologie, et mesmement musique." It does not seem necessary to identify Le Vestu's Okhem with the scholastic philosopher William of Occam, as was done in the first publication of the poem in Abbé A. Tougard's work, *Les trois siècles palinodiques* (Rouen–Paris, 1898), II, 285. The branches of knowledge attributed to the composer are after all none other than the traditional subdivisions of the quadrivium of which music was a part—arithmetic, geometry, astronomy, and music—and which are correctly summarized as

From the vantage point of our interpretation it is easy to find elements in the "chant royal" that may lead us to believe that its author was indeed well acquainted with the intended meaning of the musical work. In the second verse, Le Vestu writes as follows:

> Cestuy Okghem, usant moult de praticque
> Et theorique en toute symphonie,
> Si bien garny a cest oeuvre autenticque
> De chant mistique et parfaicte armonie.[26]

The angels are believed to have "knowledge of supernatural mysteries";[27] their song, imbued with the fervor of the divine arcana, is the "chant mistique."[28]

This meaning comes out more clearly in the last verse:

> Se ung tel motet je attribue et applicque
> A ton pudicque et sainct Concept, Marie,
> Ne soys marrye en tant que chant celicque
> Ny angelicque au tien ne s'apparie.

> (If such a motet I attribute and apply to thy holy
> immaculate conception, Mary, do not be sorrowful, for
> no heavenly or angelic chant matches thine.)

What Le Vestu is saying here implies his clear knowledge that the "motet exquis" was originally intended to present the heavenly concert of the angels. However, following the time-honored tradition of parody and contrafactum, he "applies and attributes" it to the Immaculate Conception of the Virgin. Such a reinterpretation was the more natural because Mary's Assumption and Coronation, in the

---

"art mathematique." It is much easier to explain why Ockeghem—who, incidentally, could very well have been a good mathematician—should be credited with knowledge of the quadrivium than it is to explain why Occam, who lived more than a century earlier, should be praised, in verse two, as "... usant moult de praticque/Et theorique en toute symphonie."

26. Plamenac, "Autour d'Ockeghem," p. 38.

27. "[T]he angels' knowledge of God's revelation in creation and Redemption ... is what gives their *Sanctus* cry its Eucharistic significance" (see Peterson, *Angels and Liturgy*, p. 5; also p. 54, *n.* 12).

28. Speaking of the angels' ceaseless praise of God, Peterson (p. 20) says: "The song of praise." And again later (p. 41): "[T]he *Sanctus* cry of the angels is represented in the liturgies as mystical praise—*theologia*. During their singing it is as 'crying and saying' is not supposed to be a natural 'crying and saying,' but a *mystical* though the angels are beside themselves." This is why St. Gregory the Great, in describing the "mystical" life of the angels, speaks of their "being drunk with the sacred wine of wisdom" (*ibid.*, p. 69, *n.* 1).

traditional iconography, are represented as occurring in the presence of singing and playing angels.[29]

Among the various sources containing Le Vestu's poem is the manuscript franç. 1537 of the Bibliothèque Nationale, written in 1523, which accompanies the poem with a miniature showing Ockeghem and his chapel singers. Published for the first time in Plamenac's article (and since then republished in innumerable histories of music), it shows Ockeghem's musicians singing a "Gloria in excelsis" from a choirbook mounted on a large lectern.[30]

The lectern is surmounted by two figures of the angel announcing the blessed tidings to Mary. Even though this would suggest the feast of the Annunciation, the "Gloria" may still refer to the angelic concert, the original theme of Ockeghem's canon. The singing angels' praise of God is considered part of a heavenly liturgy, of which the earthly liturgy is but an echo.[31] There is community between angelic and human worship. The biblical testimony to, and origin of, the angelic chant is the "Gloria in excelsis" of the angels on Christmas night (St. Luke 2:14), whose hymns of praise are heard by the shepherds.[32] Is it mere coincidence that Ockeghem and his singers are presented as intoning the "Gloria in excelsis" in the miniature accompanying the poem in celebration of the master's "motet exquis"? Is it likewise coincidence that the number of singers, including Ockeghem himself—who was famous for his beautiful voice, and who is presented in the miniature as singing with his musicians—comes to nine? Or might the illuminator, working in close collaboration with the poet, have wished to emphasize with the number nine both

29. Hammerstein, *Die Musik,* pp. 232–36, and the accompanying illustration; see further Emanuel Winternitz, "On Angel Concerts in the 15th Century: A Critical Approach to Realism and Symbolism in Sacred Painting," *Musical Quarterly,* XLIX (1963), 450–63, with illustrations.

30. For a beautiful reproduction in color see Plamenac's recent article on Ockeghem in *Die Musik in Geschichte und Gegenwart,* IX (1961), Plate 117. Curiously enough, no one, in discussing this group portrait, has ever clearly identified the composer. I confess that only the clarity of the colored reproduction in *MGG* and, in particular, the stunning red of his choirgown, contrasting vividly with the dark hues of the other singers' gowns, made it clear to me that the man standing to the right of the lectern was Ockeghem. It is also clear that the right hand of the composer resting on the lectern is used to tap the beat. Standing taller than his singers, Ockeghem offers a striking picture of handsome strength, bearing out contemporaneous descriptions (see Edward E. Lowinsky, *The Medici Codex of 1518,* Monuments of Renaissance Music, III–V [Chicago, 1968], III, 67).

31. See Peterson, *Angels and Liturgy,* pp. 11–13, 30.

32. Hammerstein, *Die Musik,* p. 30.

the intimate relation between the chanting of the nine angelic choirs and the chanting of nine human singers and the enormous distance between them?[33]

There is a possible hint at angelic music even in the reference by Glareanus, who was not acquainted with the work but obviously did know of its fame. The word he uses in describing it is "garritus," which denotes not only the chatter of human beings but also the warbling of birds.[34] Now it is important to remember that Glareanus considered music his avocation, that his chief profession was that of a humanist, and that he prided himself on his mastery of Greek. In the Greek tradition the ecstatic language of the seer is at times compared with the twittering of the swallow.[35] It is possible, therefore, that Glareanus thought of the ecstatic praise of the angels in the sight of the Ineffable when he referred to Ockeghem's canon as "garritus."

The concept of angelic music was familiar to the musicians of the Middle Ages, not only from the Scriptures, the liturgy, the Church Fathers, the mystics, and the poets and painters, but also from the theorists of music. Aurelianus Reomensis, in his *Musica disciplina* of the ninth century, refers to the Apocalypse and its description of heavenly music ("habentes citharas Dei"); he regards the liturgical office as an imitation of the angels' singing ("quando in hoc angelorum choros imitamur"[36]) and he believes that the antiphonal character of liturgical singing is an attempt to imitate the singing of the Seraphim in alternating choirs.[37]

The thirteenth-century theorist Elias Salomon, in his *Proemium*

33. On the distance between earthly and heavenly orders, liturgies, and singing, see Hammerstein, pp. 32 ff.

34. And this is the way in which Peter Bohn in his German translation (*Publikationen älterer praktischer und theoretischer Musikwerke,* XVI [Leipzig, 1888], 409) put it: "Es steht nämlich fest, dass er ein gewisses Gezwitscher von 36 Stimmen eingerichtet hat."

35. Lycrophon, in his *Alexandra* (v. 1460), calls the prophetess Cassandra a swallow; Aeschylus, in his *Agamemnon* (v. 1050), has Clytemnestra speak of the "incomprehensible twittering of swallows" in reference to Cassandra (see E. Mosiman, *Das Zungenreden* [Tübingen, 1911], p. 42; for other quotations, from Aristophanes and Virgil, see Hermann Güntert, *Von der Sprache der Götter und Geister* [Halle, 1921], pp. 57–58).

36. See Gerbert, *Scriptores ecclesiastici de musica sacra potissimum,* I, 30a.

37. "Antiphona dicitur vox reciproca, eo quod a choris alternatim cantetur: quia scilicet chorus, qui eam cepit, ab altero choro iterum eam cantandam suscipiat, imitans in hoc Seraphim, de quibus scriptum est: *Et clamabant alter ad alterum: Sanctus, sanctus, sanctus Dominus Deus Sabaoth*" (*ibid.*, p. 60a).

scientiae artis musicae, held that "music was created together with the angels. For it is proper to them to praise God; and this was, before the advent of our Lord, sung by prophets and other saints: *Praise Him all His angels. Praise Him with the sound of the tuba,* etc. And all song and the fine art of singing was hallowed at the Nativity of our Saviour as is written: Today Christ was born; today our Saviour appeared; today angels sing on earth, and archangels jubilate; today all exult singing: Glory to God on high, alleluya."[38] Salomon also pointed to the role of the angels at the Assumption of Mary. He believed that the plainchant was regulated by the angels, the holy prophets, and St. Gregory.[39]

The fourteenth-century theorist Marchetto da Padova, in the peroration of his *Pomerium,* addressed the singers as follows: "I beseech all singers: sing to our Lord, sing, for He is the King of all the earth, sing wisely! The celebrated herald of Christ, David, prophet excelling among prophets, commanded conformity between the Church Triumphant, which sings praises and hymns to our Lord assiduously through the triple hierarchy of the angels, and of the Church Militant, which sings this praise seven times daily. . . ."[40]

The same author, in his *Lucidarium* (Tract I, Ch. 2), said: "[T]he greatness of music captures all that lives, and all that does not live: it[s praise] is sung without end in the harmonious chant of angels, archangels, and all saints singing before God, Holy, holy, holy."[40a]

Machaut (c. 1300–1377), a poet as well as a composer, in a poem dedicated to Music, wrote in this same tradition:

38. "[C]um ipsa creatione angelorum eamdem [ars musicae] creatam fuisse; nam proprium est eis laudare Deum: et quod ante adventum Domini per prophetas et alios sanctos fuerat vaticinatum: *Laudate eum omnes angeli eius. Laudate eum in sono tubae.* . . . [E]t in eius nativitate Salvatoris nostri totus cantus et bona ars cantandi fuit canonizata per hoc, quod sequitur: *Hodie Christus natus est, hodie Salvator noster apparuit, hodie in terra canunt angeli, laetantur archangeli: hodie exultant cuncti dicentes: Gloria in excelsis Deo alleluia*" (Gerbert, *Scriptores,* III, 17a).

39. "[C]antum planum, et bene ordinatum per angelos, et per sanctos prophetas, et per beatum Gregorium" (*ibid.,* p. 17b).

40. Marcheti de Padua, *Pomerium,* ed. Giuseppe Vecchi, Corpus scriptorum de musica, VI (Rome, 1961), p. 209.

40a. [M]agnitudo musices capit omne quod vivit, et quod non vivit: hanc concentus Angelorum, Archangelorum, Sanctorumque omnium ante conspectum Dei Sanctus sanctus sanctus dicentes, sine fine decantant" (Gerbert, *Scriptores,* III, 66a).

J'ai oy dire que li angles
Li saint, les saintes, les archangles
De vois delié, saine et clere
Loent en chantant Dieu le Père
Pour ce qu'en gloire les a mis
Com justes et perfais amis:
Et pour ce aussi que de sa grace
Le voient adès face à face;
Or ne peulent li saint chanter
Qu'il n'ait musique en leur chanter:
Donc est musique en Paradies. . . .[41]

Georgius Anselmus of Parma, in his treatise *De musica* dated as of 1434, wrote of the "nine orders of celestial spirits."[42] His account is distinguished from others by his comparison of the angelic choirs with the Sirens' song in the mystical account of the heavens given by Plato in the Republic, X, 617b. Anselmus' reference is to this passage: "And the spindle turned on the knees of Necessity, and up above on each of the rims of the circles a Siren stood, borne around in its revolution and uttering one sound, one note, and from all the eight there was the concord of a single harmony."[43] "Our theologians, however," continued Anselmus, "more appropriately call these spirits angels, and divide them into nine orders, giving each order its own name." Anselmus then proceeded to a precise description of the nine orders (attaching each order to one of the nine spheres of medieval astronomy[44]) and of the celestial harmony they produce. Anselmus' ideas were given wider circulation by Franchino Gaffurio in his *Theorica musicae* of 1480, in which Anselmus is quoted almost literally.[45]

41. After a quotation by Marius Schneider, *Die Ars nova des XIV. Jahrhunderts in Frankreich und Italien* (Wolfenbüttel–Berlin, n.d.), pp. 75–76, from Chichmaref, *Guillaume de Machaut, Oeuvres,* I, 10.

42. Georgius Anselmus Parmensis, *De musica,* ed. Giuseppe Massera, Historiae musicae cultores biblioteca, XIV (Florence, 1961), pp. 103–06.

43. See *The Collected Dialogues of Plato,* ed. Edith Hamilton and Huntington Cairns, Bollingen Series, LXXI (New York, 1961), p. 841.

44. For a typical description of the nine spheres, consisting of the seven planets, the eighth sphere of the fixed stars, and the ninth sphere of the *primum mobile* on which the twelve signs of the zodiac are fixed, see Lynn Thorndike's account of the universe as seen by the fourteenth-century Geoffrey of Meaux (*A History of Magic and Experimental Science* [New York, 1934], III, 292).

45. See Gaetano Cesari's facsimile edition of the Milanese reprint of 1492 (Rome, 1934), fol. a4 recto and verso, and the quotation in the footnote to p. 105 of Massera's edition of Anselmus' treatise.

The fifteenth-century composer-theorist Adam von Fulda invoked, in his treatise of 1490, the vision of "Cherubim and Seraphim proclaiming with untiring voice Holy, Holy, Holy" (from the Te Deum).[46]

This tradition continues in the sixteenth century, when Zarlino wrote, also in a chapter on the praise of music: "Our theology, placing the angelic spirits in Heaven, divides them into nine choirs and three hierarchies, as Dionysius Areopagita says. They are constantly in the presence of the Divine Majesty, and they never cease singing Holy, Holy, Holy, Lord God of hosts, as is written in Isaiah."[47]

To prove the thesis that Ockeghem intended to create a musical likeness of the angelic concert in praise of God, we have presented evidence of various kinds: inner evidence resting on the nature of the composition, on its unprecedented character (which demands explanation), and on a structure explicable in its every facet as a precise analogy to the traditional ideas of angelic music; literary evidence produced one generation later, in which the canon is referred to as a "chant mystique," that is by a term that could have been used only in reference to the "musica coelestis"; and the circumstantial evidence (which could easily be doubled and tripled) that the musical literature of the Middle Ages abounds in references to the music of the angels.

All of this evidence seems seriously compromised by the evidence in the first print of the canon in Petrejus' psalm collection of 1542. Here the composition carries the heading "Novem sunt musae." The print of 1568 by Ulricus Neuber varies this inscription slightly to "Musis ter trinis. . . ." The two sources transmitting the canon seem to attribute it to the nine Muses instead of to the nine angelic choirs.

How serious a challenge is this evidence to the interpretation developed thus far? We can in fact dispose of the argument by means of the following observations:

46. "Cherubim et Seraphim incessabili voce proclamant Sanctus, Sanctus, Sanctus" (*Adami de Fulda Musica,* Gerbert, *Scriptores,* III, 339b). See, for the three last named theorists, Hermann Abert, *Die Musikanschauung des Mittelalters und ihre Grundlagen* (Halle, 1905), p. 144.

47. "[L]a Theologia nostra ponendo nel cielo gli spiriti angelici, diuide quelli in nuove Chori & tre Hierarchie, come scrive Dionisio Areopagita. Queste sono di continuo presenti al conspetto della Divina maestà, & non cessano di cantare Santo, Santo, Santo, Signore Iddio de gli esserciti, come è scritto in Esaia" (*Le Istitutioni harmoniche* [Venice, 1558], pp. 5–6).

1) The Muses are Greek deities. Traditionally, they are known as individual goddesses protecting the various arts and branches of scholarship. If Ockeghem had had the nine Muses in mind, nine voices would have sufficed, there being no choirs of Muses.

2) In that event, the use of canon would also have been inappropriate, inasmuch as each Muse standing for her own individual art should have been represented by her own melodic line.

3) A composition by Ockeghem in honor of the Muses would constitute a unique phenomenon in the composer's oeuvre. There are no manifestations in his work of any interest in humanism or of sympathy with the humanistic movement. Ockeghem, among the outstanding composers of the fifteenth century, was perhaps the most uncompromising representative of the belief that music's dignity lay in its service to divine worship.

How then is the inscription of the two Nuremberg prints to be explained? For one thing, it is not necessarily to be read as a title to the composition; it may be regarded as a humanistically inspired direction for the solution of the canon. In the time-honored manner of canon writing, the inscription "Nine are the Muses" would then simply indicate a nine-part canon. Ockeghem would not himself have used such a motto. If anything, he would have said "Nine are the angelic choirs."

Why did the Nuremberg editors choose the humanistic motto? One reason, I believe, lies in the Protestant faith of Nuremberg, to which this imperial town was officially converted in the year 1525.[48] Although Luther believed firmly in the existence of angels, he rejected as sacrilegious the claims of Dionysius Areopagita to an intimate knowledge of the heavenly hierarchies: "In the *Cherubim* and *Seraphim* he [Luther] does not recognize angels at all."[49] Georg Forster, the editor of Petrejus' collection of psalm settings, was a Lutheran. A physician by profession, a musician by avocation, he was also a solid humanist who knew Latin and who had studied Greek with Melanchthon and Garbicius in Wittenberg. There, in 1540, he met Luther, who accepted him into his famous table sodality.[50]

48. Friedrich Roth, *Die Einführung der Reformation in Nürnberg, 1517–1528* (Würzburg, 1885), pp. 194 ff.

49. Julius Köstlin, *The Theology of Luther* (2 vols.; Philadelphia, 1897), II, 326.

50. See *MGG,* IV (1955), cols. 568–74.

Georg Forster had been a choirboy in the court chapel of Heidelberg; he belonged to the circle of gifted young composers who had gathered around Lorenz Lemlin, the director of the court chapel: Caspar Othmayr, Jobst vom Brandt, and Stephan Zirler.[51] Long after their years of common study, these men remained attached to each other. Clemens Stephani of Buchau, in the preface to his posthumous edition of Brandt's *Geistliche Psalmen* of 1573, speaks of common plans made by Forster, Othmayr, and Brandt.[52] Clemens Stephani was the editor of the 1568 print which, as mentioned above, contains the second publication of Ockeghem's canon. There can be little doubt that in his canon inscription on the nine Muses, he followed the example of Georg Forster.

Among the Protestant editors of Catholic church music, no activity was more common than the adapting of old texts and ideas to the new faith. Thus it is understandable that all allusions to the "chant mystique" of the angels should disappear, that the nine angelic choirs should be replaced, inadequately to be sure, by the nine Muses—Nuremberg was a center of humanism—and perhaps even that the composer should not be mentioned, since Ockeghem's name stood squarely and unambiguously for France and Catholicism, the former being highly unpopular in contemporaneous Germany, the latter being bitterly combated by the adherents of the new faith.

However, at least two fifteenth-century theorists wrote of the nine Muses in connection with the nine angelic orders. It is observed by Georgius Anselmus Parmensis (and by Franchino Gaffurio, quoting him in his *Theorica musicae*), after having described the angelic order residing in the ninth sphere: "Therefore some poets posited the Muse Urania there, she who, of the nine Muses, whom they imagined to be the daughters of Jupiter and Memory, embraces and exceeds every sweetness of expression."[53] To be sure, this is only a juxtaposition, but it is not impossible that, in the form of the well-known treatise of Gaffurio, it could account for the replacement of the nine angelic orders by the nine Muses in the Nuremberg prints.

While painters and poets competed with each other in representing angelic concerts, Ockeghem's attempt to do the same in sound

51. See Hans Albrecht, *Caspar Othmayr* (Kassel and Basel, 1950), p. 9.
52. *Ibid.*, p. 31.
53. *Op. cit.*, p. 104. For Gaffurio, see note 45.

remained rather isolated.[54] Only when we come to the seventeenth century do we find, in a fresh resurgence of musical mysticism, another instance of a thirty-six-voice canon written in imitation of the angelic choirs. Preceding the title page of Athanasius Kircher's *Musurgia universalis*, published in Rome in 1650, we see a full-page woodcut that combines pagan and Christian symbols in praise of music (Plate I). Below, on the left side, Pythagoras points with a

54. Dr. Kathi Meyer-Baer has kindly drawn my attention to Robert Wylkynson's nine-part *Salve Regina* in the Eton Choirbook (see Frank Ll. Harrison's edition, *Musica Britannica*, X, 90–100). In the note pertaining to it (p. 147) Professor Harrison writes as follows: "In each of the initial letters in the first opening, which were pasted in place, is written the name of one of the nine choirs of angels, thus: Quatruplex, Seraphyn; Triplex, Cherubyn; Primus Contratenor, Dominaciones; Tenor, Potestates; Primus Bassus, Angeli; Medius, Troni; Secundus Contratenor, Principatus; Inferior Contratenor, Virtutes; Secundus Bassus, Archangeli. At bottom of right-hand page: 'Antiphona hec Cristi laudem sonat atque Marie/Et decus angelicis concinit ordinibus. . . .'" Wylkynson's *Salve Regina*, and in particular its initials and the accompanying poem, demonstrate the vigor of the ancient tradition of the nine angelic choirs, a tradition which is unquestionably responsible for the choice of the unusual number of nine voices.

The same composer wrote a thirteen-part round (Eton Choirbook, *Musica Britannica*, XII, 135) on the text of the Apostles' Creed. Each of the articles of the Creed is assigned to one of the Apostles in accordance with a pseudo-Augustinian tradition (see Harrison's note on p. 171 of the volume cited). The work begins with the words "Jesus autem transiens" from the Antiphon to the Magnificat on the Third Sunday in Lent. Certainly, the thirteen voices are meant to represent Jesus and the twelve Apostles. The two works, probably written in the first decade of the 16th century, corroborate our interpretation of Ockeghem's thirty-six-voice canon directly as well as indirectly—indirectly because of the possible connection between theological numbers and the number of voices in a composition.

Attention should likewise be drawn to a painting by Marten de Vos that reached a wide public in the form of an engraving by Johann Sadeler, dated 1587 (the best reproduction is Illus. 3 in the catalogue *Die Singenden in der graphischen Kunst: Ausstellung anlässlich des XV. Deutschen Sängerbundfestes in Essen*, 1962). The engraving carries the following caption at the top: TRIUMPHUS CHORI ANGELICI DE PACE HOMINIBUS PER INCARNATIONEM VERBI DIVINI FACTA.

In this representation two spheres are contrasted: the lower sphere shows the shepherds astonished, indeed terrified, as the heavens open and the angel announces Christ's birth; the higher sphere shows a choir of nine angels surrounded by crowds of little putti. Each of the nine angels holds a sheet of music in legible notation with the text "Gloria in excelsis Deo." Max Seiffert, in his article "Bildzeugnisse des 16. Jahrhunderts für die instrumentale Begleitung des Gesanges und den Ursprung des Musikkupferstiches," *Archiv für Musikwissenschaft*, I (1918), 49–67; 56, identified the composition on the engraving as Andreas Pevernage's nine-part "Gloria in excelsis." A third reproduction and additional information are found in J. A. Stellfeld, *Andries Pevernage* (Louvain, 1943), opp. p. 91 (description on p. 92).

Finally, it should be mentioned that the Vienna choirbook MS. 11.778 and MS. Cappella Sistina 41 transmit the canon of the middle voices in the four-part Sanctus of Josquin's Mass *L'homme armé sexti toni* with the motto "Duo Seraphim clamabant alter ad alterum," after Isaiah 6:2–3 (see Helmuth Osthoff, *Josquin Desprez* [2 vols.; Tutzing, 1962–1965], I, 166).

PLATE I. Athanasius Kircher, *Musurgia universalis,* Rome, 1650, frontispiece.

wand to the cave where the mythical blacksmiths are at work, producing diverse intervals with their hammers of differing sizes and weights. His right arm rests on a rectangular block on which we see the harmony-producing numbers one to six—Zarlino's famous *senario* containing the proportions of the consonances from the octave (1:2) to the minor third (5:6)—and three squares of differing dimensions, combined into an appealing geometric pattern.[55] Proportion governs the world of sound as well as that of shape. At Pythagoras' feet lie primitive ancient instruments. On the right, Music appears as a beautiful, richly adorned young woman—the Muses were invariably represented as women—holding a cornett in her hand, surrounded by the rich instrumentarium of the Baroque. Perched on her head is a nightingale, symbol of music in nature. The earthly group is designed to illustrate sketchily, in a bird's-eye view, the progress of music from its mythical origins in the time of Pythagoras to what in 1650 was its present state, this being illustrated in the complexity and variety of the contemporary instruments.

Behind the figures of Pythagoras and Music there opens a view of a beach with the ocean framed by hills and distant mountains. Dancing on the beach are the diminutive figures of nine satyrs, and in the water are eight dancing sea-gods. Presumably, they all sing while they dance. From the most ancient times, in both Eastern and Western traditions, dancing and music have belonged together. Toward the right, a man leaning on a cane calls up to the mountain, "Pascite ut ante Boves." A dotted line shows the angle of refraction at which the word "Boves" echoes back as "Oves" and comes down upon a shepherd walking with his sheep. This is evidently a little illustration of the working of acoustics, a subject in which Kircher was much interested.[55a] On the right, the winged horse rearing from

55. The same figure of three squares appears in John Harington's correspondence with Isaac Newton printed in Book X of John Hawkins' *A General History of the Science and Practice of Music* of 1776 ([New York: Dover Publications, 1963], I, 410–11). Harington demonstrates the presence of all musical intervals from the minor second to the major seventh in this figure. Since the correspondence between Harington and Newton took place in the year 1693, whereas the same figure with the numbers 1, 2, 3, 4, 5, 6 appeared on the frontispiece of Kircher's work of 1650, it is unlikely that Harington is indeed, as Hawkins believed, "the author of this discovery."

55a. Aside from parts of the *Musurgia* dealing with acoustics, Kircher devoted a whole book to the subject—the *Phonurgia nova,* published in the year 1673.

the highest step of the staircase, as though ready to soar to the high cliff above, represents Pegasus, a companion of the Muses and a symbol of immortality.

The lower sphere denotes the "musica instrumentalis." The globe floating in the center with the symbols of the zodiac, and the inscription from Job 38:37, "Quis concentum coeli dormire faciet? (Who shall still the harmony of the spheres?)," symbolizes "musica mundana," the music of the spheres. On the globe, Apollo, his streaming curls held together by a laurel wreath, is seated holding a kithara in his right hand and Panpipes in his left, representing string and wind instruments respectively.

Finally, crowning the music of the heavens and the mortals is the "musica coelestis" of the angels symbolized in the *Canon Angelicus 36 Vocum in 9 Choros Distributus.* The banderole with the canon and the inscription is held by two six-winged cherubim; a corona of angels surrounds the circle of the sun, with an inscribed triangle and three ears denoting the Trinity, and an eye symbolizing God.

Added to the inscription is the remark, "cuius resolut*ionem* vide fol. 584" (Plate II). Here we find the name of the composer, the Roman master of canonic writing, Romano Micheli, and the resolution of the canon. Although nearly two hundred years had passed since the earlier thirty-six-voice canon was composed, that of Micheli is inferior in every respect to Ockeghem's. Since it is built on a triadic motif, contrapuntal problems are eliminated. It is easy to use the motif both *recte* and *inverse,* and to set nine choirs for four parts rather than four parts in nine-part canons. Nevertheless, Kircher invites the reader's admiration for the ingenuity with which the canon is set so as to avoid all obvious unisons—a result that Micheli achieves by clever use of pauses and of numerous octaves and double octaves. Unisons nevertheless occur throughout, although they are not allowed to begin at the same time.

Compared with the heavenly monotony of Romano Micheli's canon based on one single harmony, Ockeghem's canon seems rich indeed.[56] It is hardly possible to exaggerate the immense difficulties

56. To do justice to the latter work we must take into account Laurence Feininger's critique of Riemann's transcription in *Die Frühgeschichte des Kanons,* pp. 45–48. Feininger has pointed out a series of errors in the original edition and in Riemann's transcription. Having studied the whole evolution of canonic writing, he has become convinced that Ockeghem is the author of the thirty-six-voice canon.

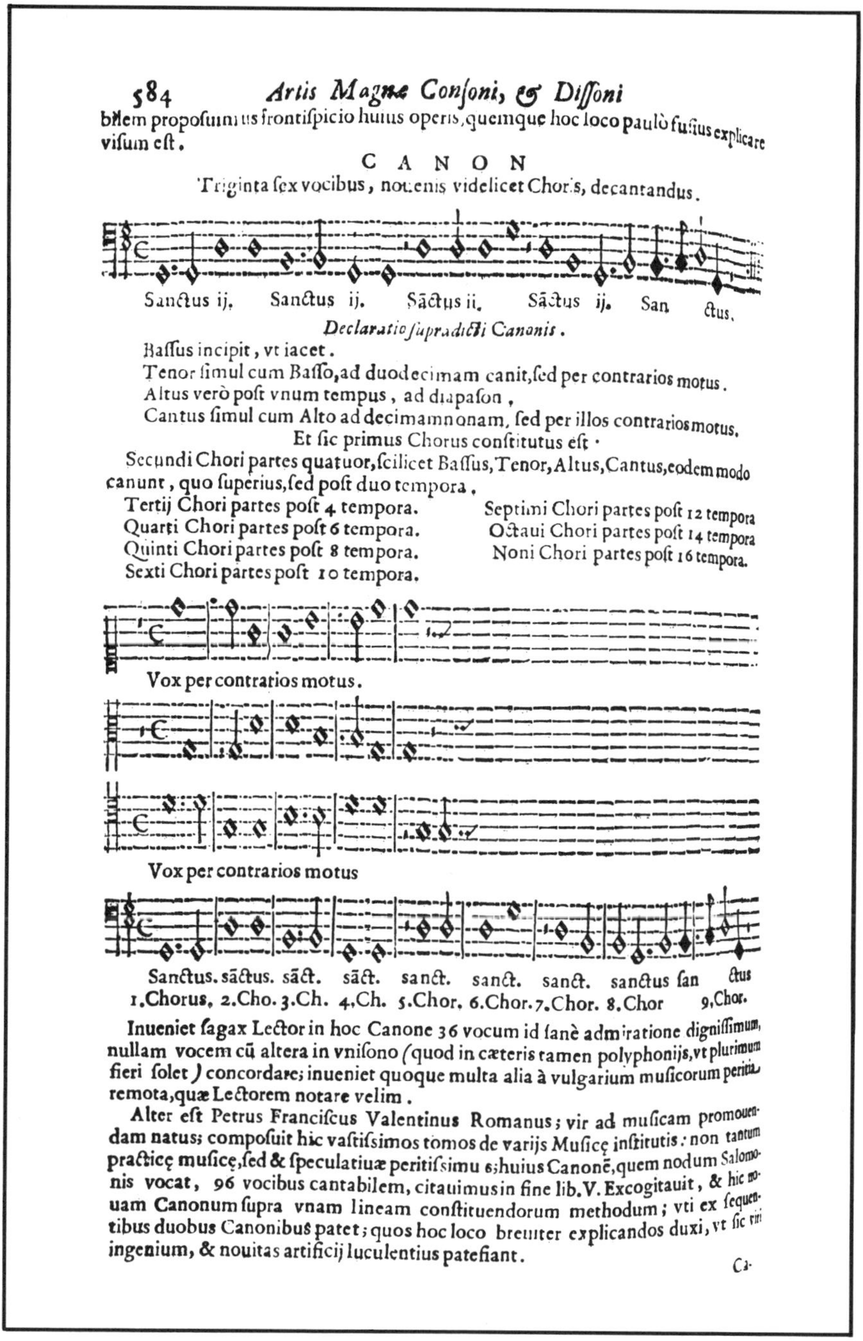

584 *Artis Magnæ Consoni, & Dissoni*

bilem proposuimus frontispicio huius operis, quemque hoc loco paulò fusius explicare visum est.

CANON

Triginta sex vocibus, nouenis videlicet Choris, decantandus.

Sanctus ij, Sanctus ij. Sãctus ii. Sãctus ij. San ctus.

Declaratio supradicti Canonis.

Bassus incipit, vt iacet.
Tenor simul cum Basso, ad duodecimam canit, sed per contrarios motus.
Altus verò post vnum tempus, ad diapason,
Cantus simul cum Alto ad decimamnonam, sed per illos contrarios motus.
Et sic primus Chorus constitutus est.

Secundi Chori partes quatuor, scilicet Bassus, Tenor, Altus, Cantus, eodem modo canunt, quo superius, sed post duo tempora.

Tertij Chori partes post 4 tempora.
Quarti Chori partes post 6 tempora.
Quinti Chori partes post 8 tempora.
Sexti Chori partes post 10 tempora.
Septimi Chori partes post 12 tempora
Octaui Chori partes post 14 tempora
Noni Chori partes post 16 tempora.

Vox per contrarios motus.

Vox per contrarios motus

Sanctus. sãctus. sãct. sãct. sanct. sanct. sanct. sanctus san ctus
1.Chorus, 2.Cho. 3.Ch. 4.Ch. 5.Chor. 6.Chor. 7.Chor. 8.Chor 9.Chor.

Inueniet sagax Lector in hoc Canone 36 vocum id sanè admiratione dignissimum, nullam vocem cũ altera in vnisono (quod in cæteris tamen polyphonijs, vt plurimum fieri solet) concordare; inueniet quoque multa alia à vulgarium musicorum peritia remota, quæ Lectorem notare velim.

Alter est Petrus Franciscus Valentinus Romanus; vir ad musicam promouendam natus; composuit hic vastissimos tomos de varijs Musicę institutis: non tantum practicę musicę, sed & speculatiuæ peritissimu s; huius Canonẽ, quem nodum Salomonis vocat, 96 vocibus cantabilem, citauimus in fine lib. V. Excogitauit, & hic nouam Canonum supra vnam lineam constituendorum methodum; vti ex sequentibus duobus Canonibus patet; quos hoc loco breuiter explicandos duxi, vt sic viri ingenium, & nouitas artificij luculentius patefiant.

Ca-

PLATE II. Athanasius Kircher, *Musurgia universalis*, Rome, 1650, p. 584.

involved in setting a four-fold canon for nine parts each; and this is the problem that Ockeghem set for himself. The four canon melodies are so conceived that each bar contains an alternation between tonic and dominant, the former having two beats, the latter one; accordingly, they must be so written that the tones on beats one and two are F, A, or C, and so that the tones on beat three are C, E, or G. Variation is achieved by passing notes, by syncopated dissonance, by the use of rests, and by rhythmic diversity. At the same time, the four melodies must be so planned as to produce a sound harmonic combination. If anything speaks for Ockeghem's authorship, it is the indisputable rhythmic genius with which the canon is executed (see Plates III and IV). The result of the metric and rhythmic diversity achieved by the subtle use of rests, of triplets, of syncopations, and of carefully gradated movements of differing speeds is a total rhythmic flow of infinite suppleness, of constant motion and unending variety.

We have anticipated the problem of authenticity. Bertha Wallner, in her study on Virdung,[57] was the first scholar to question Eitner's identification of the "Deo gratia[s]" in Petrejus' psalm collection with the famous thirty-six-voice canon by Ockeghem. She had discovered a letter by Sebastian Virdung in which the composition was described as consisting of six six-part canons. Since the letter was dated 1504, not even a decade after Ockeghem's death, Wallner took Virdung's testimony seriously, as is even more understandable if we consider that Virdung was a versatile and competent musician, theorist, composer, and singer at the court chapel of Heidelberg. Bertha Wallner's doubts were shared by Dragan Plamenac[58] (and others) for the same reason.

But Virdung's letter allows a different interpretation. It is true that he wrote: "[A] master of all composers, whose name was Johannes Ockeghem, and, as I believe, he was a provost at Thueren [Tours] where St. Martin is [located], or a bishop. He made a motet for six voices. Each voice is a canon for six parts, and together thirty-

57. Bertha Wallner, "Sebastian Virdung von Amberg," *Kirchenmusikalisches Jahrbuch* (1911), 85–106, esp. 97–98, 103–04.

58. See his aforementioned essay and his recent article in *MGG*, IX (1961), cols. 1825–38; 1834.

six voices."[59] Virdung added a brief description of the *Missa prolationum* and mentioned the *Missa cuiusvis toni*—all works that were available at the Heidelberg court chapel. But now comes the crux of the matter: referring to the canon and the *Missa prolationum*, he said: "[T]hese two things we have here with us and also a Mass *c[uius]vis toni*, but [they are] altogether incorrectly written"[60]—a remark that explains the purpose of the letter, in which Virdung asked Count Palatine Ludwig of Bavaria to furnish the court chapel of Heidelberg with correct copies of the three works. If Virdung succeeded in acquiring a correct copy of the canon, then it is very likely that Georg Forster, first publisher of the canon, obtained his copy of it at the Heidelberg court chapel, where he had been a choirboy.

Virdung's description of Ockeghem's canon as consisting of six times six voices, then, was based on nothing more than imagination or possibly hearsay—not, at any rate, on his knowledge of the work from a correct copy. Virdung may not have had more than two or three parts of the canon. Or he may even have had all four of them; but he had never worked them out, since a canon for four times nine voices was so unprecedented an enterprise that he persuaded himself that two parts must be missing. Indeed, nothing in the letter refers to an actual performance of the canon. This eliminates the only objection so far raised to the identification of the "Deo gratia[s]" with Ockeghem's thirty-six-voice canon.

But there is more to be said for Ockeghem's authorship; if Virdung's description of the canon may be dismissed on his own testimony that he did not possess a correct copy, his ascription of the canon to Ockeghem constitutes the earliest contemporary testimony for that composer's authorship of a work that amazed contemporaries and later generations alike. All these pieces of evidence speak of one canon for thirty-six voices, not of two canons; all of them ascribe that one canon to Ockeghem. Taking into account

59. "[E]in meister aller c(om)ponisten, Hatt geheissen Johannes/ockeghem, vnd als ich wen, der ist ein probst Zu thüren, da sant martin ligt / oder bischoff gewest ist, Der hatt ein mütett mit sex stymmen gemacht. Der stymmen / itlich ist ein füg mit sex stymmen, vnd alzüsamen XXXVI stymm" (Bertha Wallner, *loc. cit.*, p. 97).

60. "[D]ye zwey Ding haben wir / hye aussen bey vns vnd ein mess c(uius)vis toni, aber aller Ding vngerecht geschrieben . . ." (*ibid.*, p. 98).

PLATE III. *Top* J. Petreius, *Tomus tertius psalmorum selectorum,* Nuremberg, 1542, Discant, no. 40.
Bottom J. Petreius, *Tomus tertius psalmorum selectorum,* Nuremberg, 1542, Tenor, no. 40.

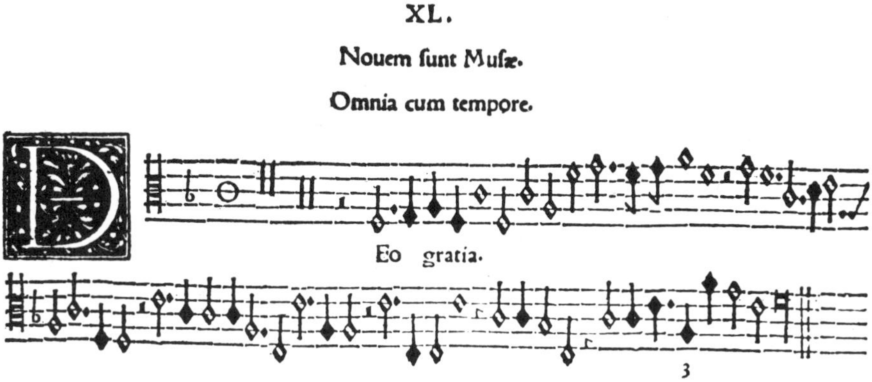

PLATE IV. *Top* J. Petreius, *Tomus tertius psalmorum selectorum,* Nuremberg, 1542, Alto, no. 40.
Bottom J. Petreius, *Tomus tertius psalmorum selectorum,* Nuremberg, 1542, Bass, no. 40.

the extraordinary character of the undertaking as well as the unanimity of literary and theoretical evidence, the assumption that two such works existed may safely be ruled out. It is intrinsically unlikely; it is also completely unsupported by any evidence whatever.

Finally, the musical character of the work in no way goes counter to Ockeghem's style or technique. He was interested in canonic writing; he never shied away from technical difficulties. The melodic and, in particular, the rhythmic ingenuity of the composition, always considering the unheard-of difficulty of constructing a fourfold canon having nine parts in each canon, makes for its easy acceptance into the body of Ockeghem's authentic works.

Ockeghem has often been characterized as a mystic among composers, but on no evidence other than a subjective interpretation of certain stylistic features of his music.[61] In understanding the celebrated canon as Ockeghem's answer to the age-old challenge of visionaries, poets, and painters to the musicians, as his conception of the ecstatic song of the angelic choirs surrounding the Divine Majesty of God, we have tangible testimony of his mystical outlook. Far from being moved by the ambition to do the technically well-nigh impossible, he is motivated by the *visio Dei.*[62] Such an understanding calls for a transformation of the traditional image of the composer (and the traditional evaluation of the canon) from one representing a proud exhibitionism of technique to one expressing the heroic humility of an artist willing to undergo the most extreme difficulties in the service of an idea, in an attempt to create in sound the effect of a mystical vision.

If Ockeghem's canon for thirty-six voices was an answer to the challenge of painters, poets, and visionaries, Josquin's canon for twenty-four parts may well have been an answer to Ockeghem's unprecedented enterprise. It has been observed by Riemann and others following him that Josquin's canon exceeds Ockeghem's in technical difficulty, since even though he reduces the number of written parts, he does engage all twenty-four voices simultaneously in the unfolding of the canon.

Josquin constructs his work in four canons of six parts each. Did

61. See notably Manfred F. Bukofzer, *Studies in Medieval and Renaissance Music* (New York, 1950), pp. 291–92.

62. Ockeghem's great contemporary, Nicholas of Cusa, philosopher and mystic, wrote a treatise *De visione Dei.*

he, too, have a symbolic idea in mind? We cannot write another essay here. Suffice it to formulate the following suggestion:

Josquin may have chosen the number twenty-four to represent the twenty-four elders of the Book of Revelation.[63] Adam of Fulda mentions, next to the angels, the twenty-four elders singing God's praise as they fall on their faces before His throne.[64] Zarlino follows in this tradition when, in Chapter Two of the first book of his *Istitutioni harmoniche*, on the praise of music, he testifies that not only the angels, but also "the twenty-four elders stand before the immaculate Lamb, and with the sound of citharas and with high voices sing a new song to God on high."[65] The early Christian philosopher and theologian Origen made a significant distinction

63. The twenty-four elders come from the apocalyptic vision of St. John. In Revelation 4:4 they are described as follows: "And round about the throne were four and twenty seats: and upon the seats I saw four and twenty elders sitting, clothed in white raiment; and they had on their heads crowns of gold. . . ." Revelation 5:8 adds to this description: ". . . and four and twenty elders fell down before the Lamb, having every one of them harps, and golden vials full of odors, which are the prayers of saints."

"These elders constitute a puzzle, since their exact counterparts are not to be found in Jewish sources. It is possible that John obtained the suggestion for these elders, who sing God's praises, from a verse in the little apocalypse in Isaiah, 'For the Lord shall reign in Zion and in Jerusalem and shall be glorified before the elders' (Isa. 24:23 LXX). It has also been proposed that they represent the twelve tribes (or patriarchs) combined with the twelve apostles, as in 21:12–14, where the names of the twelve tribes are inscribed on the twelve gates of the New Jerusalem with those of the twelve apostles on the twelve foundations."—*The Interpreter's Bible*, ed. George Arthur Buttrick et al. (12 vols.; New York, 1952–1957), XII, 402. Many other suggestions follow in that work. But the decisive aspect of the twenty-four elders as rendered in medieval church sculpture is that they are human figures wearing crowns, holding musical instruments and chalices in their hands (see, e.g., the representation of the twenty-four elders at the abbey church of Moissac; cf. Meyer Schapiro, "The Romanesque Sculpture of Moissac," *Art Bulletin*, XIII [1931], 249–350, 464–531, esp. 464 ff.).

That the iconographic tradition of the twenty-four elders had a long life can be seen from the *Adoration of the Lamb* by Jodocus a Winge, likewise engraved by Johann Sadeler and dated as of 1588 (see Seiffert, p. 57 of article cited in note 54). In the lower part of the picture, crowds of people worship the Lamb; in the higher part, God is seated in the center surrounded by clouds of angels. But in a semicircle grouped around Him sit the twenty-four elders with crowns on their heads, each one playing a harp. The picture, on the open pages of four tall part-books, carries the four-part motet *Dignus es*, by Andreas Pevernage.

It might be added that Aurelianus Reomensis, in the description of heavenly music referred to above, probably had the twenty-four elders in mind when he characterized the "heavenly citizens" as holding harps in their hands.

64. "[E]t viginti quatuor seniores ceciderunt in facies suas in conspectu throni, et cecinerunt canticum" (Gerbert, *Scriptores*, III, 339b).

65. "Stanno poi li ventiquattro vecchi inanzi all'Agnello immaculato, & con suono di Cetere & altissime voci cantano all'altissimo Iddio vn nuovo canto" (p. 6).

between the singing of angels and that of men when he wrote: "To man, the singing of psalms is appropriate: but the singing of hymns is for angels and those who lead a life like that of the angels."[66] According to the Alexandrian theologians, "the psalm corresponds to the *active* life and the hymn by contrast to the contemplative life."[67] Josquin chooses a Psalm—No. 90 in the Catholic Bible, No. 91 in Protestant versions—for his canon: "Qui habitat in adiutorio Altissimi, in protectione Dei caeli commorabitur." The psalmist sings of God and of the angels (verses 11–12), but, throughout, he deals with the relation between God and man, and with the angels as God-appointed guardians of man. Whereas the text can hardly be made to fit Ockeghem's canon, which, in consequence, sounds more like a twittering ("garritus") of birds, Josquin so sets the text that it can be comprehended; it is human speech.

It is thus that Josquin's canon for twenty-four parts may perhaps be understood as an answer to Ockeghem's canon for thirty-six voices. Ockeghem sings of the angelic praise of God, Josquin of the human soul in search of God and in need of the angels. Josquin's canon is a symbol of Christian humanism; Ockeghem's, of Christian mysticism.[68]

66. Quoted in Peterson, *Angels and Liturgy,* p. 27.

67. *Ibid.*

68. After completing this study I found the article by Walther Krüger, "Ein neunchöriger Sanctus-Kanon," *Musik und Kirche,* XXV (1955), 180–83, which deals with Romano Micheli's canon on the illustrated title page of Athanasius Kircher's *Musurgia universalis.* Although I fully agree with Krüger's interpretation of the canon—an interpretation that is of course suggested by Kircher himself—I believe that he is mistaken in identifying the figure seated on the globe with St. Cecilia, and consequently the middle area with church music. Kithara, Panpipes, and laurel wreath are fitting attributes for Apollo (who, with his long hair, indeed resembles a woman), but they are quite unsuitable for St. Cecilia, who converted from paganism to Christianity and who cannot therefore be represented through Greek instruments. Krüger's interpretation of the three sides of music on Kircher's title page as secular, ecclesiastic, and heavenly should be replaced by instrumental (and therefore human), cosmic, and celestial music. Strangely enough, Krüger mentions Ockeghem's canon without the slightest hint at the possibility of a symbolic interpretation. He writes (p. 182): "Im übrigen ist daran zu erinnern, dass ja auch schon die Niederländer derartige vielstimmige Kanons geschrieben haben, man denke etwa an Ockeghems 36stimmige Motette mit sechs notierten Stimmen für je sechsfachen Kanon oder an das anonyme 36stimmige Deo gratias mit Kanonvorschrift 'Novem sunt musae'!" Obviously, the author still believes in the existence of two different canons for thirty-six voices.

12 / Musical Areas Reconsidered: A Critique of North American Indian Research

BRUNO NETTL
University of Illinois

MUSICALLY, the North American Indians are a rather compact group, and we probably know more about them than about culturally, racially, and numerically analogous areas. This rather thorough knowledge of a group of musical styles in a large number of tribal units, and with relatively few musical components, is probably responsible for the several attempts to provide statements of geographic distribution. It has been possible to learn enough about a fairly large number of these tribal units to make such statements, and the kind of information available for the various tribes about which we know something has been sufficiently similar, and has been stated with enough similarity, to enable us to make the comparisons necessary for indicating these distributions.

Statements of geographic distributions are at the heart of ethnomusicological tradition. For decades, scholars have said that culture X sings thus and so, and that island Y has this or that instrument. From such statements followed others, indicating that culture A and culture B had similar music, whereas cultures C and D differed. This manner of thought, for better or worse, gave ethnomusicology part of its character, as symbolized by its earlier name, comparative musicology. From general comparisons and impressionistic statements of similarity it was only a step to the attempt at a precise delineation of areas; and the interest in distribution studies of the Kulturkreis type, as well as in the less ambitious culture areas which Americans were establishing, provided models for the discussion of music areas. Music areas, more or less coinciding, were outlined by George Herzog, by Helen Roberts, and most recently by myself for North America; by Waterman and Merriam for Africa; and in a less formal sense by many scholars for Europe, Asia, and Oceania. The musical area was regarded somewhat as a microcosm of the culture area; the latter was determined by separate but interdependent elements of culture involving all aspects of living, whereas the musical area consisted of presumably separable but interdependent traits in music. Whether musical traits are as separable as culture traits may, of course, be argued.

The purpose of establishing musical areas has been two-fold: primarily, an area is a convenient way of organizing knowledge in a field which depends on comparison for its everyday thinking; secondarily, it may provide clues both to the nature of change in music and to the nature of history—an area which some colleagues consider outside our purview, but which I regard as necessary for the understanding of the present musical culture of even a non-literate society. In the past, some of us who worked with the musical-area concept took much for granted, and may have tended to be unmindful of many implications in attempting to establish such units, on the assumption that musical areas, and culture areas, were alike a concrete phenomenon that simply waited to be discovered and identified.

My task here is to try to show what modifications are now indicated in the scheme of musical areas in North America with which I began work over ten years ago. At the same time, I should like to make some remarks about the concept of musical areas. It now seems clear that those areas are not necessarily there, simply awaiting discovery; but I still think the concept is useful, if approached with suitable caution.

The basis of the present critique is the division of the continent north of Mexico into six music areas, some of them with subdivisions: (1) the East, including the woodlands, with the exception of the "wild rice" area of the upper Great Lakes; (2) the Plains-Pueblo area, subdivided into Pueblo, typical Plains and certain Plateau tribes, Prairie, and Upper Lakes sub-areas; (3) the Athabascan, consisting of Apache and Navajo; (4) part of the Great Basin, including the Paiute, the Northern Ute to an extent, and Northern California (i.e., Modoc, Klamath, Yahi, Yokuts); (5) the California-Yuman area, comprising the Yuman and Central California tribes; and (6) the Eskimo–Northwest Coast areas, including the classical coast cultures, the Coast Salish, and the Eskimo, and subdivided along these lines. The divisions are based on material generally available about twelve years ago, and on the notion that *a* music, i.e., a tribal repertory, is homogeneous, or at least that whatever portion of it can be regarded as reflecting conditions previous to contact with outside influences is homogeneous. This notion sometimes made it possible to decide upon the placement of a culture in an area on the basis of an extremely small sample. Whether the assumption of homogeneity was justified is open to question; but thus far it has not been proved wrong in many of the cases explored here. On the other hand, the assumption that a so-called primitive tribal repertory is *ipso facto* homogeneous is obviously no longer acceptable.

On the whole, the areas were arrived at in a manner similar to that evidently used for culture areas by Wissler and Kroeber: a single, outstanding, striking trait which correlates roughly with a group of less concrete and perhaps more questionable isoglosses has been the determining factor. The striking main traits may, in the culture areas, be associated with contrasting aspects of life; along the Northwest Coast, it is the Potlatch ceremony and a distinctive style in art; in the Plains, it is dependence on the buffalo. Similarly, the music areas are sometimes distinguished primarily by non-coordinate traits of music. Thus, a music area may be based mainly on traits present in it and not found elsewhere, although their distribution within it may be uneven. This is true of the moderate complexity of drum rhythms for the Eskimo and Northwest Coast cultures, and of antiphonal and responsorial singing in the East. An area may, on the other hand, be based on the considerable prevalence of a trait which is also found elsewhere, but with a much lower degree of frequency. This is true of the California–Yuman area, which is characterized mainly by the prevalence of the so-called rise form and contour, a technique which is present in a very large proportion of its songs, but which also is found occasionally in the songs of certain Northwest Coast, Southeastern, Basin, and Northeastern cultures. Again, an area may be determined by its style of voice production, a trait generally more characteristic of a whole repertory than are other traits in the stylistic superstructure of a music. This is true of the Plains–Pueblo area, which is held together only loosely in other respects. But elsewhere, singing style and vocal technique have not been used as a main differentiating trait; thus, the Athabascan area includes several different kinds of vocal production, and there is evidently considerable difference between the Navajo and the Apache in this respect.

In spite of the criticisms that may be directed at the way in which the various areas have satisfied diverse criteria for their establishment, we cannot retreat altogether from the idea of musical areas. North American Indian music does not emerge in a picture of confused diversity; neither is there complete homogeneity, or even a uniform diversity correlating with geographical distance. That there is certainly some correlation of musical homogeneity with cultural homogeneity has been indicated by the old musical-area scheme, which was arrived at independently of culture-area considerations.

What are we to do with the large amount of information available? Can we organize it into significant units of any kind? Should we return to the position that North American Indian music is essentially a single style unit? Could we, on the other hand, take the view that each tribe has a style which can be understood only in its own terms, and whose similarity to or difference from that of its neighbors is essentially irrelevant to ethnomusicological considerations? Let me suggest that for now we retain the idea of supratribal areas, but that we examine the concept, give it added sophistication, and make it capable of expressing more precisely the cultural and musical facts that it serves to organize for us. No such elevation of the musical-area concept to a more sophisticated level will be accomplished in one short article. But I should like to make a few suggestions, which I hope may help us to move in that direction.

I should like, for one thing, to suggest altering the picture of six more or less coeval musical areas into one which distinguishes between what we may perhaps call "good" and "bad" areas. In other words, there are, according to this way of thinking, certain areas which have the traditionally required degree of homogeneity and of trait clustering; and there are others in which this concept doesn't work so well. A "good" area, it seems to me, should have some traits that are present there and not elsewhere; it should have one or two predominant types of structural song or composition; and a reasonably homogeneous singing style should be evident in a majority of its tribal repertories.

With this outline as a criterion, we could select the typical Plains tribes, along with certain neighboring Prairie and Plateau groups, as constituting a "good" musical area. We find here a fairly distinctive singing style, difficult to describe but easy to identify, with high tessitura (except for song endings), vocal tension or lack of "width," and pulsations. There is also the characteristic terrace-shaped contour and the binary form with incomplete repetition; both contour and form are found elsewhere, but they are more prevalent as well as somewhat specialized in the Plains repertories. The relation of the Plains to the Pueblos, however, is not as strong, and if we insist on adding the Pueblo styles to those of the Plains, we do so at the expense of having a weaker or less "good" area. Yet because Plains influence has been strong for a long time in the Eastern Pueblos, and many of their songs are in the classical Plains style, it is necessary for us to take cognizance of the relationship.

Another "good" area is the Yuman-Californian, which is characterized by a trait not found elsewhere with anything like the same degree of prevalence. Possibly another may be the Great Basin, where paired-phrase patterns (though they do not appear in every song) and the large proportion of simple forms and small ambits seem to me to outweigh the presence of certain forms typical of the Plains. Some other areas, however, must be regarded as unsatisfactory according to the new criteria. One such area is the East, which does not exhibit the required internal homogeneity. The similarity of style in some parts of the East to the Plains style is as great as that within certain portions of the Eastern area. The Athabascan area is "poor," since it contains too small a group of cultures to satisfy all of the above criteria; and its internal homogeneity, in view of the small size of the area and the few cultures represented, is also insufficient. Some of the Apache styles seem more closely related to those found in the Plains than had been thought earlier. But the difference between Navajo and Plains or Pueblo music seems sufficiently great to preclude incorporating the Navajos into the old Plains-Pueblo area. Furthermore, the Eskimo and Coast-Salish groups seem tied together by too thin a thread to constitute an area analogous to one so close-knit as the California-Yuman.

Before making concrete suggestions for revision, I must point out that a good deal of new raw material has become available, and that some of this material changes the stylistic picture of certain areas. Without going into the details of bibliography, let me say that the major contributions since the early 1950's have been those on Iroquois, Apache, and Northern California music. The availability of old recordings in Library of Congress pressings, and the recent attention given to singing styles, must also have their effect. Generally speaking, the new material has not affected the orientation as much as might have been expected. The revisions indicated below are based mainly on criticisms of method and of concept, rather than on the availability of new raw material. It should be pointed out, however, that recent publications show the characteristics once claimed for the Eastern area to be less prevalent in Iroquois music than had been thought; rather, the East shares Plains characteristics to a greater degree than was indicated earlier. Rhythmic simplicity, a trait once regarded as Athabascan, is not as strongly represented in Apache or even in Navajo music as was thought in the past. Furthermore, a large area of simple styles in Northern California and Southern Oregon is now indicated by Modoc, Klamath, Chukchansi Yokuts and Yahi music, whose character was formerly regarded simply as an isolated remnant of an archaic layer, or as a subtype of the paired-phrase pattern of the Great Basin. Even these simple styles, however, do not exhibit the formerly expected homogeneity. For example, the songs sung by Ishi, the only Yahi Indian informant and probably the only informant ever found who can be said with some certainty to have grown up without any influence from Western civilization, knew songs which had come, or whose style evidently had been borrowed, from tribes and areas outside his own. Thus, although the songs he knew were primarily of simple structure, with two similar phrases, he sang one song that clearly had the "rise" pattern of the Yuman style, and a few others reminiscent of the terrace contours of the Plains.

Presumably these songs that did not fit into Ishi's repertory were imported to the Yahi from the outside. We may presume that the intrusion was of fairly recent date. If the Yahi repertory had been sampled one hundred years earlier, would the same non-Basin songs have been included? All of this brings us to the problem of time perspective in the study of Indian musical areas. We have samplings of music from many tribes representing possibly (1) the repertory immediately before white contact and (2) the influences, more often indirect than direct, of European civilization. The time of first contact, however, differs greatly from area to area, as does the magnitude of white influence. Thus it is probable that the proportion of Plains-style songs in some of the Great Basin and Eastern Pueblo repertories has increased within the last hundred years. It is obvious that in dealing with geographic distribution we cannot ignore the time factor, even though we may have difficulty in assessing its importance, and even though it may sometimes appear a hindrance.

Having given some attention to the concept of musical areas, let us consider briefly some suggestions for a revised scheme. As a working hypothesis it seems possible to divide the repertories into five areas (some new, others corresponding to older ones), as follows: (1) a large and not very homogeneous area consisting of the East, the Plains, part of the Plateau, and the Eastern Great Basin, together with the Pueblo and Eastern Apache tribes; (2) the Eskimo which has certain similarities to (3) the Northwest Coast and Coast Salish; (4) the Western Basin and Northern California; and (5) the California-Yuman area, plus the Navajo. Joining the East with the Plains region seems advisable in view of similar vocal techniques, and of certain similar forms. Breaking up the old Athabascan area seems logical in view of its lack of cohesion. The non-strophic nature of many Navajo songs, along with the relatively smooth and relaxed-sounding manner of singing, makes the joining of Navajo and Yuman styles a possibility. The presence of a large proportion of Plains-style songs in the music of the Ute, and perhaps in that of some of the Shoshone, makes their inclusion with the Plains advisable. In a primitive form, the paired-phrase pattern—i.e., one phrase repeated with modifications—is found in a number of Northern and even of Central California tribes; here it is probably related to the slightly more sophisticated paired-phrase patterns of the Great Basin, which appear to predominate among Western Basin tribes such as the Paiute. Similarities between Eskimo and Northwest Coast tribes seem too slight to allow us to continue viewing them as one area, though perhaps our old Eskimo-Northwest Coast area is no more heterogeneous than our new one consisting of the Eastern, Plains, Pueblo, and surrounding tribes. Thus possibly we could assume two large, heterogeneous areas—the Eskimo-Northwest and the Eastern-Plains-Pueblo-etc.—and two smaller, more homogeneous ones, i.e., the Western Basin and the Yuma-California-Navajo. Perhaps this division may indicate something about the history of singing styles. Could it be that the areas with more mobile cultures developed more heterogeneous but more widely distributed styles? Many interpretations are possible, but they must all be tested against the relatively small amount of concrete data. In any event, the areas suggested here follow more closely than the old ones the pattern of A. L. Kroeber's culture areas.

Definitive conclusions are not attempted and would not be appropriate here. It is clear that the problem of the geographical distribution of musical traits, and of their use for historical study, becomes more complicated as more data are provided. If the concept of "musical areas" is valid at all, it must be regarded as a concept with much flexibility. It is evident that different areas developed not only with distinctive stylistic features but with varying amounts of tolerance for extraneous segments of repertory, with varying degrees of stability or rates of change, and with different kinds of interaction among the components of style. And finally, in spite of these problems, the work of classifying tribal repertories, of attempting to measure the degrees of difference and similarity among them, and of studying the relation between musical and other cultural findings, is bound to provide us with more insight into the nature of the musical behavior of groups of people—even though, like the anthropologists with their culture areas, we may never find complete satisfaction or agreement on the distribution of musical styles.

WORKS CITED

Herzog, George, "Musical styles in North America," *Proceedings*, 23d International Congress of Americanists, 1928, pp. 455–58.

Kroeber, Alfred Louis, *Cultural and Natural Areas in Native North America* (Berkeley, 1947).

Merriam, Alan P., "African Music," in William R. Bascom and Melville J. Herskovits, eds., *Continuity and Change in African Cultures* (Chicago, 1959), pp. 49–86.

Nettl, Bruno, *North American Indian Musical Styles* (Philadelphia, 1954).

Roberts, Helen H. *Musical Areas in Aboriginal North America* (New Haven, 1936).

Wissler, Clark, *The American Indian* (New York, 1922).

13 / The Duo Texture of Mozart's K. 526: An Essay in Classic Instrumental Style

WILLIAM S. NEWMAN
University of North Carolina

I HAVE always been grateful for that familiar story about the six blind men who came to report on the elephant, and who each got a decidedly different "view." It serves me here by way of recalling the diversity of views held toward Mozart in this remarkable heyday of Mozart worship and scholarship. One scholar, seeking to account for Mozart's universal genius, views him especially as an unparalleled melodist; a second as the master architect of musical form; a third as a superb organizer of harmony and tonality; a fourth as one of the most subtle and fluent manipulators of phrase syntax; a fifth as the most flawless of craftsmen; a sixth as an expert weaver of musical textures.[1]

In my own experience the last of these views, that pertaining to texture, provides one of the prime clues to the Mozart style, and to the Classic style in general.[2] However, the term "texture" itself introduces a broad, many-faceted concept, and one, this time, that is capable of several distinctly different subviews (recalling another highly useful analogy in the arts, that of wheels within wheels). In

1. This study follows up my contribution, on classic instrumental texture, to the Stanford University conference on Mozart and the Classic Style. July 6–8, 1965. In part, the six views just listed (among various others that have been and might well be argued) relate to the six refreshingly different views presented at this conference, in which the other participants were Eva Badura-Skoda, Daniel Heartz, Anna Amalie Abert, Jan LaRue (by proxy), and Leonard Ratner.

2. W. S. Newman, *The Sonata in the Classic Era* (Chapel Hill: The U. of North Carolina Press, 1963), pp. 119–31, *et passim*.

the first place, the word "texture" is relatively new to the language of musicology, new enough that up to now it has scarcely found a place in the standard music dictionaries.[3] Borrowed, like various other musical terms, from the visual arts, texture in its broadest sense simply means the way the notes are put together.[4] But, to labor our analogy a bit more, one blind man "sees" it as a matter mainly of the total sonority and the varied euphony that result; another as the skill in voice-leading in each of the melodic and harmonic strands; a third as the independence or subordination of the separate parts in predominantly polyphonic or homophonic styles; a fourth as the rhythmic activity and interplay of the several parts; a fifth as the style of accompaniment, especially in homophony; a sixth, among others, as a matter of give and take as well as balance between instruments and/or voices. Furthermore, the consideration of each of these subviews might well be influenced in turn by the medium, whether solo keyboard, chamber group, orchestra, chorus, or opera.

The emphasis in the present discussion will be on the last of these subviews of texture, that of give and take and of balance in scoring; and the medium selected here is the instrumental chamber music of Mozart, more particularly the Sonata for Piano and Violin in A major, K. 526, which would be my own nomination for the freshest and most skillful of Mozart's works in this duo category. The emphasis on scoring, especially the scoring of the instrumental duo, permits us to concentrate on a significant point of arrival in Classic musical texture. That is, in Mozart's chamber music we can find the completion of a cycle of development in duo treatment that began with what I have called the "melo/bass" disposition in early-, high-, and late-Baroque chamber music,[5] that passed through a kind of missing link in what I have called the "accompanied clavier" setting in pre-Classic and even high and late Classic chamber music,[6] and

3. An exception is the full-page entry in the first edition of Willi Apel's *Harvard Dictionary of Music* (1944).

4. W. S. Newman, *Understanding Music* (2d ed.; New York: Harper & Row, 1961), pp. 105–29.

5. W. S. Newman, *The Sonata in the Baroque Era* (Chapel Hill: U. of North Carolina Press, 1959), pp. 50–53, 63–65, *et passim;* with further references.

6. See Newman, *Classic Era,* pp. 98–105, *et passim,* and "The Accompanied Clavier Sonata," in *Musical Quarterly,* XXXIII (1947), 327–49; both with further references.

that ended or culminated in the full partnership of the true duo during the high-Classic Era. Although it is impractical here to attempt even a summary of that cycle of development, with its variety of origins, performance practices, and chief manifestations, we might at least recall the first two phases through one illustration of each, so as to put our third and final phase into better perspective.

The "melo/bass" disposition, or what Bukofzer aptly discussed as a "polarity" of thorough-bass and melody instrument(s),[7] might well be recalled with a quotation from one of Handel's best known "solo" sonatas for violin and thorough-bass, that in D major (Example 1, after the new *Hallische Händel-Ausgabe*, Vol. IV/4,

EX. 1. *Sonata for violin and thorough bass* in D major—Handel.

p. 28). This example is sufficient to remind us of the predominance of the "solo" part, and of the subordination and complementary or supporting function of the bass, including the rapid harmonic rhythm it engenders. The "accompanied-clavier" setting might well be recalled, from among the countless examples in later eighteenth-century catalogues and collections, with a quotation from the opening movement of a delightfully transparent yet pointed "Sonata per cembalo o piano-forte con accompagnamento d'un violino" in A major, Op. 6, No. 2, by Franz Anton Rössler or Rosetti (Example 2, after the Antonio Zatta edition in Venice of about 1781). This example illustrates the reversal of relations during this critical period

7. Manfred Bukofzer, *Music in the Baroque Era* (New York, W. W. Norton, 1947), p. 11.

EX. 2. Beginning of movt. I of the *Sonata per cembalo o piano-forte con accompagnamento d'un violin* in A major—Rössler (Rossetti).

of transition from harpsichord to piano, in which the keyboard now predominates, and the violin serves merely to fill out the texture. The violin's new subordination is confirmed here not only by its much less active part but by the relatively lower level of volume prescribed in its dynamic indications.

The accompanied-clavier setting expired only after having reached such extreme disproportions of scoring as are still to be found in the earlier nineteenth century, for example in Chopin's Piano Trio in G Minor, Op. 8 (1828–1829). But at least a half century before its expiration, examples of the true duo began to appear. Those of Mozart were not the first. Before him, in Paris in 1768, Boccherini had published a pioneer example of real distinction in his Sonata III in B-flat major, Op. 5. But Mozart was the first important composer to write true duos consistently—that is, in the later years of his short life. Actually, the presumed total of forty-four sonatas that he left for keyboard and violin (characteristically, in that period, more than twice the number of his solo keyboard sonatas) progresses from four sets totaling sixteen sonatas, still typical of the accompanied clavier setting (1762–1766), to the set of six possibly spurious "Romantic sonatas" (originally K. 55–60, c. 1775?), in which tentative approaches to the duo idea occur, and thence (from 1768) to the true duos that are his only sonatas for keyboard and violin to be found in popular editions. Related to this arrival at the true duo style was Mozart's growing preference for the piano over the harpsichord. To the Sonata in A under consideration here, K. 526, Mozart gave the title "Sonata per Piano-forte e Violino . . . ," no longer with even the alternative of the harpsichord, but with the listed order of instruments still deriving from the practice and titles of works for the accompanied clavier. The date of the composition of this work is 1787, which is also the year of the first edition.[8] The work adheres to Mozart's almost invariable sonata cycle of three movements in the order of fast—slow—fast, in this instance a *Molto Allegro* in sonata form, an *Andante* in binary design, and a *Presto* in sonata-rondo form.

With texture as our special view of Mozart and the Classic instrumental style, in this little study, and with the duo scoring as our special subview, we may now pay final homage to our overworked elephant story by examining K. 526 according to six successive sub-subviews: the balance between the two instruments; the fullness of the part-writing; the euphony of the scoring; the contrapuntal activity and other busy-ness within the texture; the technique of the voice-leading; and the idiomatic treatment of the individual instruments. In each of these aspects Mozart's heritage from the accompanied-clavier setting must be borne in mind. (In the references to K. 526 that follow, Roman and Arabic numerals, respectively, designate the movement and measure number, so that I/14 would mean the first movement, measure 14. The text used here is Serie 18, No. 42 of Mozart's *Werke;* the autograph has been lost since World War II, and the volume of the Mozart *Neue Ausgabe* that will contain this work—Serie VIII, Werkgruppe 23, Band 2—had not yet appeared as of this writing [summer 1965].)

Perhaps still reflecting the predominance of the keyboard in the accompanied setting, the balance in the division of main melodic ideas between the two instruments is not exact. A simple statistical tabulation reveals, for example, that in the first movement the piano takes the lead more than half of the time and the violin less than a

8. Hoffmeister in Vienna, Plate 128; see also 6th ed. (1964) of Köchel *Mozart Verzeichnis,* p. 590; and O. E. Deutsch, *Musik-Verlags-Nummern* (Berlin: Merseburger, 1961), p. 14.

fourth of the time, the remainder being shared by the two instruments equally. Of course, in any true duo, then or since, the piano is the instrument more likely to be given solo passages. In any event, the total effect is of partners of equal or nearly equal importance. In

EX. 3. Beginning of movt. I of the *Sonata per piano-forte e violino* in A major (K. 526)—Mozart.

fact, except for the opening theme in the finale, every main theme in the sonata is stated first by one of the instruments and then restated antiphonally by the other through an interchange of melodic and other textural responsibilities. So it is with the very opening of the sonata (Example 3, I/1–20), in which the piano takes the lead and is literally on top for the first eight measures, the violin for the next nine measures; the piano then returns to dominate the cadence of the double period in the remaining three measures. Although the violin is subordinate in that opening passage, it continues to employ one of the main means of accompaniment in the traditional accompanied setting: that is, it moves in parallel thirds and sixths below the top line of the keyboard part. Two other clear vestiges of—or, at least, resemblances to—those accompaniment techniques may be seen in this sonata; for example, the violin supplies a slower, filler part for the main theme of the finale (Example 4, III/1–8), and it accompanies the second theme of the *Andante*, slow movement with a simple broken-chord figure (Example 5, II/29–33). To be sure, the piano now departs from the tradition of the accompanied setting by employing the same subordinate styles when *it* is doing the

EX. 4. (K. 526) Beginning of movt. III.

EX. 5. (K. 526) Extract from movt. II.

accompanying. Perhaps, in this consideration of balance between instruments within the texture, it is more important to note how little of the accompanied setting still remains in K. 526, and how often, without a prevalence of actual polyphonic writing, each part has something significant to offer to the mainstream of musical ideas. There are further vestiges of the accompanied setting in other late duos by Mozart (and in the earlier, similar duos by Beethoven, too)—for example, the violin's doubling at the unison, its long sustained notes during rapid keyboard figures, and its outlining of the faster keyboard part, all in the first movement of Mozart's Sonata in E-flat for piano and violin, K. 481, at measures 17–18, 126–128, and 28, respectively.

In part-writing, the high-Classic norm for solo keyboard music was three parts as against the typical two parts in the early Classic era. But even including the violin, the writing is most often only in three parts in K. 526, as can be seen from Examples 3 to 5 above. Today, with our purist attitude toward Classic music, we tend to remark on the economy and efficiency of its texture. In fact, until fairly recently I had always heard that familiar interchange between

Mozart and the Emperor as a complaint by the Emperor that there were "so few notes" in *Die Entführung*, with Mozart replying, "Just so many as are needed, Your Majesty." But Niemetschek, the source of the story, puts it the opposite way, with the Emperor complaining of the "extraordinary number of notes, dear Mozart."[9] Perhaps the Emperor's reaction was not only to the increasing fullness of texture in high Classic music but to the illusion of still greater fullness that a skillful composer can achieve through the rapid shift of registers within or between the individual parts. The works of J. S. Bach often shift registers rapidly within a single line, so that one part gives the illusion of two (or so that, for example, the two parts of the *Allemande* from his Partita II in C minor have the fullness of four). Mozart is more likely to shift registers between the parts, as in Example 6 (III/56–59). Of course, there are also numerous passages

EX. 6. (K. 526) Extract from movt. III.

that literally make use of more parts, and other passages that make use of fewer parts. Mozart was much less inclined than Bach to stick to a set number of parts throughout a piece. At the start of the *Andante* middle movement there is, in effect, only one part in measures 1 and 3, since the piano is playing alone in octaves. Similarly, there are two parts when the violin joins in measures 2 and 4, three when the piano plays alone in measure 5, four when the violin rejoins in measure 6, and a peak of five different "parts" in measure 7, after which the texture rapidly thins until there is again the effect of one part only in measures 8 and 9 (Example 7, II/1–9). Here, then, is an exceptionally clear example of a familiar means of enhancing the effect of tension and relaxation while leading to and away from a melodic and harmonic peak. Only for fleeting moments

9. Newman, *Classic Era*, p. 500.

EX. 7. (K. 526) Beginning of movt. II.

is there literally but a single part, and then almost exclusively in the piano, as in the rising, nearly chromatic scale of I/192–94.

Euphony, our third sub-subview of Mozart's texture as revealed in his duo scoring, means here the blending of sounds, by whatever means, that produces his extraordinarily sweet and precise sonorities. It is no problem to cite some of the special means of blending in K. 526. But any team of experienced performing musicians will agree that not just this or that isolated passage but the whole sonata "sounds," tells acoustically, and makes its point transparently, satisfyingly, and completely. One might start with Example 7, just quoted, in which a sharp contrast is achieved by the relatively wide spacing that separates the serious piano octaves below, in steady eighth-notes, from the more plaintively decorative utterances played in broken phrases by the violin above. In the coda of this movement, the same effects are heightened by the still wider spacing, as well as by the octaves now broken by the piano and the still shorter utterances of the violin (Example 8, II/84–87). The harmonically opulent

EX. 8. (K. 526) Extract from movt. II.

EX. 9. (K. 526) Extract from movt. III.

sound of chromatic double-thirds is exploited deliciously over repeated bass notes in the piano, and is doubled still more opulently at the octave when the violin enters, in the closing theme of the finale (Example 9, III/133–42). The sheer variety and imagination of the euphony in Mozart's mature chamber music never fails to surprise. Thus, for twelve measures at the close of the first movement of K. 526 there is a change of style in the scoring of every other measure (Example 10, I/231–42). After a rare measure of violin

EX. 10. (K. 526) Extract from movt. I.

unaccompanied, and an answer to its run in the pianist's left hand while the violin tops the pianist's right-hand chords, come a sequence of chromatic dominant chords with the violin doubling the descending chromatic line at the octave above, then a bit of eighteenth-century hocket between the two instruments, then two measures of piano alone, while the right hand makes a melodic elaboration of bare left-hand chords, then a single bass line doubled at both the octave and the sixteenth above in the piano while the violin plays another descending run, and finally two full cadential chords, with a total of nine notes each between the two instruments.

In spite of such variety, with the violin joining or opposing both or either of the hands in the piano part in almost every conceivable way, it is interesting to note the infrequency, now, of what had been a favorite Baroque setting—that is, the "trio" setting, in which two high parts (for example, two violins, or two manuals of the organ, or the violin and keyboardist's right hand as in J. S. Bach's sonatas for violin and realized keyboard) intertwine in more rapid or florid notes over a slower-moving bass or, often, a steady "running" bass. Example 3, above, from the start of K. 526, bears some resemblance to the old practice, although the frequent intertwining of the upper parts on an equal basis is absent. The few closer resemblances that do occur take us to our fourth sub-subview, that of the contrapuntal or related activity within the texture. Thus, the development of that opening theme brings a few measures of actual intertwining and close imitation between the upper parts (Example 11, I/120–25). Such

EX. 11. (K. 526) Extract from movt. I.

passages provide the chief contrapuntal activity in this sonata, in the total absence of fugues or even fughettas. A bit of close imitation in a different disposition, and of a freer sort, involving all three parts, was seen in Example 6 above. In Example 12 (III/220–35) we see an interchange of melodic and accompanimental blocks that might

EX. 12. (K. 526) Extract from movt. III.

qualify for the eighteenth-century term "ars combinatoria,"[10] which refer to what was sometimes a calculated permutation of melodic or other units within or between the individual parts. In addition to these sorts of melodic counterpoint, one must not overlook the fresh counterpoint of rhythmic interests that goes on constantly, either as part of the melodic counterpoint (Example 13, III/275–78) or in

10. As developed and discussed in an illuminating paper read by Professor Leonard Ratner of Stanford University at the Mozart conference cited earlier, and also at the national meeting of the American Musicological Society in Washington, D. C., December 27–29, 1964.

EX. 13. (K. 526) Extract from movt. III.

conjunction with figures that are less significant thematically (as at the close of II/87–89).

The voice-leading in K. 526 leaves little to be said beyond exclaiming over Mozart's impeccable craftsmanship, his precision in the conduct of each line or strand in the piano and violin parts, and the expressive purposefulness that is the result. Example 7, above, in which new separate strands are added and subtracted, makes as convincing an example as any. The prevailing three-part texture, of course, requires more skill and precision to sound complete in all its directions than four-part writing. Even in the relaxation of part-writing principles that characterized *galant* and high-Classic scoring for piano, Mozart is not to be caught napping over details that determine high standards of voice-leading.[11] For example, between the separate strands of the Alberti bass, or of other broken-chord figures of the period, it is common to find parallel fifths and octaves that would not have been permitted had the same notes been written as simultaneous chords. But Mozart usually eschews even these parallelisms, and when he does permit them it is clearly with his own musical justifications. We have already had an example of this in Example 5 above—namely the violin's broken-chord figure across the barline from measures 29 to 30. The parallel root-position triads defined by the two broken chords do not offend the ear, both because they occur in five-part writing (including each strand of the broken chords as one part), with the bass moving in contrary motion, and

11. How fully conscious Mozart was of such details is vividly illustrated by the sort of corrections he made in the composition notebook of his pupil Thomas Attwood (as ably discussed in the paper read by Dr. Heartz at the Stanford Mozart conference).

because the barline in this instance separates the thesis of one short melodic segment from the arsis of the next.

Finally, the idiomatic treatment of the individual instruments in Mozart's duo scoring is to be examined. Virtuosity is not exploited for its own sake in K. 526, as it is in the freer displays of others among the instrumental and vocal pieces of Mozart. But the outer movements are inherently virtuosic, especially the spirited finale of this sonata, which is a near "perpetuum mobile." In that movement such passages as were quoted in Example 12 make far greater demands of the violinist, by way of finger and bow dexterity, than would ever have been tolerated in an accompanied-clavier setting. And such rapid passages as those given to the pianist's left hand at measures 91 to 101 in this movement, or Example 13 (recalling the contemporary praise for Mozart's left-hand prowess[12]), suggest that only pianists of considerable technical accomplishment are likely to get by unscathed in a performance up to tempo. In any event, the left hand of the piano part is unusual in this work for its variety, interest, and thematic participation. Remarkable is the total absence of Alberti bass, a device that had been so much a mainstay of the accompanied sonata and that still served abundantly in other mature works by Mozart (as well as throughout much of Beethoven's keyboard writing). However, other traces of those simple, unobtrusive styles of accompaniment that contributed so much to the slower harmonic rhythm and to the fluency of the Classic style do still appear, in moderation, in K. 526. In the absence of the Alberti bass one finds other broken-chord accompaniments (such as the triplet figure in I/20–28). There are also repeated notes and "murky" or "pom-pom" basses (both, for example, in III/47–55). There are block chords (I/130–135) and even an anticipation of the "um-pah-pah-pah" style (III/109–115) that was to pervade Romantic writing for the keyboard. Mozart is able to give these figures some musical significance of their own, as with the broken-chord figure in our Example 5 above and its continuation in augmentation in the succeeding measures (33–34), although he never quite elevates them to the independent esthetic facts that Beethoven makes of the murky bass in the first movement of Op. 13, or of the Alberti bass in the finale of Op. 27, No. 2.

12. A. Hyatt King, *Mozart in Retrospect* (London: Oxford U. Press, 1955), p. 257.

14 / Vincenzo Galilei's Arrangements for Voice and Lute

CLAUDE V. PALISCA
Yale University

VINCENZO Galilei is remembered chiefly as a theorist and polemicist. But in his daily professional activity these roles were subordinated to his work as a lutanist and composer. Indeed, his writings were most often stimulated by problems he met in musical practice. The dialogue called *Fronimo*[1] (1568; 2nd edition 1584) undertakes to explain through a large number of examples the rules for intabulating music for the lute. His *Dialogo della musica antica et della moderna* (1581) began as a disquisition on instrumental tuning, particularly on the differences between lute and keyboard tuning. His subsequent pamphlet, the *Discorso* (1589), grew out of his controversy with Gioseffo Zarlino on questions of tuning. The manuscript treatise on counterpoint drafted during Galilei's last years (1589–1591) reflects his recognition of the cleavage between the academic rules of composition as they were taught and as they were practiced by leading composers, particularly in the instrumental field.

Documents are not lacking for Galilei's notable achievements as an arranger for the lute and as a composer. A book of intabulations of madrigals and *ricercari* (1563), two books of madrigals (1574 and 1587), a set of two-part counterpoints (1584), and many intabulations and original compositions in the two editions of *Fronimo*, 1568

1. For information concerning the works cited in this and the next paragraph, see my article, "Galilei," in *Die Musik in Geschichte und Gegenwart*, IV, cols. 1265–70.

and 1584, make up the music printed in his lifetime. The largest collection of his compositions remains in manuscript, and is still not available in transcription aside from seventeen compositions edited by Fabio Fano.[2] This is the 280-page book of lute intabulations, mainly of independent instrumental dances, preserved among the Galileo manuscripts in the Biblioteca Nazionale Centrale in Florence.

Perhaps the uniquely characteristic legacy of Galilei's vocation as a lutanist is in the two small collections of arrangements for lute and voice, airs, dances, and *romanesche* found at the back of two copies of the rare edition of *Fronimo* printed at Venice in 1568. The two copies, which must have belonged to Galilei, both contain manuscript appendices, mostly in his hand. One copy is in the Landau-Finaly collection at the Biblioteca Nazionale Centrale of Florence under the call number Landau-Finaly MS. Mus. 2, and is notable for its so-called "pseudo-monodies." It was first discovered by Alfred Einstein while it was still in the private library of Baron Horace de Landau. The other copy of *Fronimo* with a manuscript appendix is in the Biblioteca Riccardiana of Florence and bears the signature F.III.10431. The existence of this manuscript appendix, which contains only three pages of music, all of them instrumental, has not been previously reported in print.

My main purpose here is to draw attention to the arrangements for voice and lute in the Landau-Finaly copy of the *Fronimo* of 1568. The twelve songs with lute accompaniment thus preserved are precious remnants of a popular art of singing to the lute that has left only scant traces in Italy. A secondary purpose is to provide a description and inventory of the two little known sources that are the subject of this article.

The Landau volume has only lately been accessible to the public. Until about 1948 it belonged to the library of Baron Horace de Landau. Its presence there is already recorded in the printed catalogue of 1885,[3] but no mention is made of the manuscript appendix, which was first reported by Alfred Einstein in 1937. At that time, because of limitations imposed by the owner upon his use

2. "La Camerata Fiorentina" in *Istituzioni e monumenti dell' arte musicale italiana* (Milan, 1934).

3. *Catalogue des livres manuscrits et imprimés composant la bibliothèque de M. Horace De Landau-Finaly*, I (Florence, 1885), 522–23.

of it, Einstein did not feel free to describe it in any detail.[4] The library then belonged to Madame Hugo Finaly, who in 1903 had inherited it from her uncle Horace de Landau (d. 1902). She continued to add to the collection, and her will expressed the wish that her son, Horace Finaly, should retain it for life, after which it was to be sold. Through the bequest of Horace Finaly—he died in New York on May 19, 1945—the *Fronimo* volume went, along with other precious items, to the City of Florence. These items now form the Horace Landau Memorial Collection in the keeping of the Biblioteca Nazionale Centrale.[5]

The first edition of *Fronimo* of 1568 is less well known than the much expanded and revised edition of 1584. Although there are seventeen copies of the later edition, according to the latest inventory in *RISM*, *Recueils imprimés*, only eight complete copies of the 1568 edition, and one that is incomplete, are known.[6]

The manuscript supplement to the Landau-Finaly copy consists of twenty folios, on each page of which ten sets of six lines for tablature have been ruled by hand. With the exception of folios 14r and 20, all pages contain music, either in tablature or in mensural notation. Although the binding that combines into a single volume the printed book and its manuscript supplement is of comparatively recent date—probably from the nineteenth century—there is reason to believe that the two were united by Galilei himself. Even before the leaves of the appendix were trimmed and gilt-edged along with those of the *Fronimo*, they must have been cut to fit this volume (dimensions: 21.5 x 32 cm.), since the manuscript pages have normal

4. "Galilei and the Instructive Duo," *Music and Letters,* XVIII (1937), 360–68.

5. See Anita Mondolfo, "La biblioteca Landau-Finaly," in *Studi di bibliografia in memoria di L. de Gregori* (Rome, 1949), pp. 265–85. I first studied the manuscript in 1951, before it was catalogued, through the courtesy of Miss Mondolfo, who kindly permitted a film to be made of it at that time. The contents of the manuscript pages have since been described by Bianca Becherini in *Catalogo dei manoscritti musicali della Biblioteca Nazionale di Firenze* (Kassel, 1959), p. 132, No. 110. The inventory of the music there is not entirely accurate.

6. The 1568 edition is not listed in *Répertoire international des sources musicales* (hereafter abbreviated to RISM), *Recueils imprimés.* However, Claudio Sartori has included an inventory of five libraries that possess copies of it in his *Bibliografia della musica strumentale italiana stampata in Italia fino al 1700* (Florence, 1952), pp. 28–29.. To those listed there should be added the Landau and Riccardiana copies under discussion, and those of the civic libraries of Bergamo and Rimini. The copy that Sartori notes as once in the Wolffheim collection is now in the Library of Congress.

margins all around. The Landau copy of *Fronimo*, moreover, has further traces of the author's handiwork: corrections in a faded red ink to two of the printed tablatures, those on pages 12 and 29. The hand cannot be identified, because the scribe aimed to imitate so far as possible the style of printed numbers; but the nature of the corrections suggests that the composer was responsible.

These circumstances might not be sufficient to persuade one that the book and manuscript belonged together, but for the existence of the parallel coupling in the copy of the same edition now at the Biblioteca Riccardiana. The 1568 *Fronimo* in the Riccardiana has hand-written corrections identical with those of the Landau copy, and, like it, contains appended twenty folios of paper ruled for tablature. They are uniform in size with the book and are bound with it, untrimmed, in a loose parchment folder. Only three pages of the Riccardiana copy contain tablatures, all but part of the third page in Galilei's hand. The other pages are ruled but contain no music. This copy too was probably Galilei's. He must have been in the habit of supplementing his personal copies of this book with additional arrangements and compositions. The purpose of including the additional pieces may have been to provide material either for performance or for use as illustrative pieces in teaching.

Another circumstance that suggests a link between the printed book and the Landau MS. is the chronological proximity, as will be seen, of the material of the MS. and of the publication. Five of the items in the MS. (counting "seconde parti" as separate items) occur in the printed book in slightly more literal transcriptions, suggesting that the MS. grew out of the printed book.

Folios 1r–6v and 13r–19r follow a uniform scheme: the voice part is on the left-hand page and the intabulated lute accompaniment on the one opposite, except for the page opposite 13v, which is blank. Evidently this format was not contemplated when the extra sheets were first added to the book, for all twenty folios were originally ruled with six-line systems. When Galilei decided to use some of the left-hand pages for the vocal lines, he had to scratch out the lowest line of each six. The superfluous line still shows clearly in photographs.[7] The eleven pages in the middle (folios 7r to 12r) are filled

7. Cf. facs. in *MGG,* IV, Plate 54.

with independent lute tablatures. All are *passamezzi* and *romanesche* but two, which are arrangements of popular songs. Folio 19v was used to notate another arrangement of a part-song, and folio 20 was left blank. Only one composer is identified in the manuscript: Giacomino, probably Bernardino Giacomini, for *Caro dolce ben mio.*

Close study of this layout of material reveals that the manuscript was incorrectly bound into the book. Folios 12v and 1r, containing respectively the voice and the lute parts of Palestrina's *Vestiva i colli,* should be facing one another. The series of folios 1 to 6 and 13 to 19 belong after folio 12, and folios 7 to 12 constitute the first six folios of the manuscript in its original state. My table shows what the original sequence of numbers must have been. Galilei evidently put the first eleven pages (now folios 7r to 12r) to the use they were intended for—lute tablatures. Then he decided to alternate voice parts and intabulated accompaniments (folios 12v, 1r–6v, 13r–19r) and was forced to adapt the six-line tablature for five-line staves on the left-hand pages. He used up the verso of folio 19 for an intabulation of a madrigal. Folio 20 remained blank.

Except for two pages, the Landau MS. is entirely autograph. This can be ascertained by comparing the notational mannerisms with those of the MS. lute-book of 1584, and with a stray tablature in the volume containing a translation of the *Harmonics* of Aristoxenus.[8] The handwriting in the texts and titles also matches the hand in the manuscript treatises.[9] The tablatures on folios 1r and 2r, however, are in a different hand, although the titles of the madrigals intabulated on those pages, *Vestiva i colli* and *Cosi le chiome mie,* are in Galilei's hand. That none of the other lute accompaniments are thus labeled suggests that Galilei may have marked the pages that were to receive the tablatures with the intention of filling them in later. Someone else did so, but less faithfully and skillfully than was Galilei's custom.

The Landau appendix appears to be approximately contemporary with the printed book. Every one of the vocal models that can be identified first appeared in print in some form earlier than 1569. For the eight items so identified, the first known publication dates, as

8. Florence, Biblioteca Nazionale Centrale, MS. Gal. 6. Facs. page in Fano, ed., *La Camerata Fiorentina,* p. 96; MS. Gal. 8, fol. 38v.
9. MSS. Gal. 1 to 4.

may be seen from the table, are: two in 1555, one in 1560, one in 1561, two in 1566, one in 1568, and one in 1569. The single watermark that is visible throughout the manuscript pages belongs to papers represented by Zonghi's tables of Fabriano papers under numbers 897–906.[10] They are found in archive documents dated between 1527 and 1572. The closest in dimensions to that of our MS. is No. 904, dated 1566.

The lute pieces are of little assistance in dating. Two of them, the *romanesca* on folio 7r and that on folio 8v, became respectively *Romanesca sesta* and *Romanesca quarta* in the MS lute-book of 1584, where they were used as subjects for variation. One such variation, of the *Romanesca sesta,* already appears on folios 11v–12r of our MS. In each of the *romanesche,* the 1584 version has regular 2/2 barring, whereas the MS. version is without measure bars. The printed versions also introduce some rhythmic or harmonic elaborations or simplifications. The lute pieces thus tell us only that our MS. is earlier than 1584. All the circumstances considered, the most likely date seems to be circa 1570.

The compilation falls into the period of Galilei's career when he was engaged principally in teaching, playing, and composing for the lute. This was before he became engrossed in the study of ancient music. We know that his wife and family lived at Pisa in the 1570's, but he must have spent a great deal of time in Florence. He surely lived there from 1572 onward, although his family did not join him until 1574. During these years he was undoubtedly employed to entertain at the home of Giovanni de' Bardi, who was a lavish host, and at homes of other patrons. The 1584 edition of the *Fronimo,* for example, is dedicated by Galilei to "my most honored patron, Signore Jacopo Corsi." It is known that Galilei sang as well as played, from a letter of Pietro Bardi, written many years later, relating that Galilei had sung his own monodic compositions at Bardi's house around 1582. It may be assumed, then, that he customarily sang to the lute popular songs, madrigals, and other vocal compositions, as well as poetry set to standard airs. All that remains of this part of his repertory are the arrangements in the Landau copy and the airs in the Riccardiana copy of the *Fronimo* of 1568.

10. Aurelio Zonghi, "Le marche principali delle carte fabrianesi dal 1293 al 1599," in *Zonghi's Watermarks* (Hilversum, 1953).

Although it is generally assumed that the singing of polyphonic compositions by a single voice to lute or other accompaniment was a widespread practice in sixteenth-century Italy, little evidence survives in the form of written arrangements. The printed arrangements of Bossinensis,[11] Willaert,[12] and Verovio,[13] and the manuscript book of Cosimo Bottegari,[14] are among the few collections extant. To these, which give the voice part, should be added lute-books that include with the intabulations the texts to be sung.[15]

The Galilei arrangements differ in some important respects from other known collections of this kind. The arrangements of Bossinensis, Willaert, and Bottegari consist of single voice parts for soprano, or occasionally tenor, with intabulated reductions of the remaining parts provided below the voice part. Galilei's are bass parts accompanied by lute-reductions of all the parts. Pietro Bardi, in his letter of 1634, referred to Galilei as a tenor,[16] but at such a distance of years he could well have been mistaken, and these arrangements, clearly for a bass voice, were probably intended for Galilei himself. Their range is from F to d′, though they are notated variously in tenor, baritone, and bass clefs.[17]

11. Franciscus Bossinensis, *Tenori e contrabassi intabulati col sopran in canto figurato per cantar e sonar col lauto. Libro primo* (Venice, 1509); *Libro secondo* (1511). A similar collection is *Frottole de Misser Bartolomio Tromboncino et Misser Marcheto Carra con Tenori et Bassi tabulati et con soprano in canto figurato* (1520). An example from the second book of Bossinensis is transcribed along with the vocal model in Benvenuto Disertori, "Contradiction tonale dans la transcription d'un 'Strambotto' célèbre" in Jean Jacquot, ed., *Le luth et sa musique* (Paris, 1958), pp. 39–40. Others may be seen in Oswald Körte, *Laute und Lautenmusik* (Leipzig, 1901), pp. 158–61. The manuscript studied by Geneviève Thibault in "Un manuscrit italien pour luth des premières années du XVIe siècle," *ibid.*, pp. 43–76, includes similar arrangements but omits the voice part. Cf. the reconstructions, *ibid.*, pp. 67–76.

12. *Intavolatura de li madrigali di Verdelotto da cantare et sonare nel lauto, intavolati per Messer Adriano* (Venice, 1536; 1540).

13. Simone Verovio, *Ghirlanda di fioretti musicali* (Rome, 1589); *Diletto spirituale* (Rome, 1585).

14. Modena, Bibl. Estense, MS. Mus. C.311. Cf. Carol MacClintock, "A Court Musician's Songbook: Modena MS. C.311," *Journal, American Musicological Society,* IX (1956), 177–92. This manuscript is edited by Dr. MacClintock in *The Bottegari Lutebook* (Wellesley, Mass., 1965).

15. E.g., Florence, Bibl. Naz. Cent., MS. Magl. XIX, 168, dated 10 maggio 1582; Magl. XIX, 109, late sixteenth century.

16. Angelo Solerti, *Le origini del melodramma* (Turin, 1903), p. 145.

17. The arrangements of Verovio, from which the singer chooses his voice part out of the three parts on the left-hand page and a keyboard or lute reduction of the composition from the right-hand page, would produce for a bass about the same result as the arrangements of the Galilei MS.

Galilei's choice of the bass part, since evidently this fit his range, was probably mainly a matter of convenience. But a deeper reason for preferring this part for at least some of the songs is suggested by a statement in his *Dialogo della musica antica et della moderna.* There he demonstrated that the bass voice was the one that gave a contrapuntal composition its "air": "[C]he la parte graue sia veramente quella che dà l'aria (nel cantare in consonanza) alla Cantilena. . . ."[18] In the word "aria," Galilei vaguely comprehended melodic and harmonic movement. By "cantare in consonanza" Galilei meant polyphonic singing in general, but he intended by this qualification to exclude any kind of melody-dominated music, such as popular songs, which would not normally be sung polyphonically. In the imitative compositions of the manuscript—for example, *Vestiva i colli,* or *Ancor ch'io possa dire*—where the parts are of equal importance, the bass deserved precedence in Galilei's opinion, because it was the harmonic foundation. Galilei firmly opposed Zarlino's contention that the tenor was the part that governed a composition: "It is to be understood that the lowest part, and not the tenor, as it pleases Zarlino, is that which reigns and governs and gives the air to the composition; and wherever the bass part does not vary its notes, the composition is not varied, or only little varied."[19] The arrangement of the anonymous ottava rima, *Se ben di sette stelle* (transcribed in the musical appendix to this article), demonstrates how effective the bass part in a polyphonic texture is when it is set in relief by soloistic performance, because it is the part which moves, as Galilei implies, with greatest harmonic compulsion.

The singing by a solo voice to the accompaniment of instruments enjoyed a vogue at about this time, according to Vincenzo Giustiniani. He wrote of the practice in his *Discorso sopra la musica de' suoi tempi,* dated around 1628:

In the holy year of 1575 or slightly later there began a new manner of singing very different from the previous one, and this was continued for a number of years afterwards. This was the manner of singing with a solo voice over an instrument, as for example, that of a certain Neapolitan,

18. (Florence, 1581), p. 76.

19. *Il primo libro della prattica del contrapunto* (1589–1591), Florence, Bibl. Naz. Cent., MS. Gal. 1, fol. 76v. On this question see my article, "Vincenzo Galilei and Some Links between 'Pseudo-Monody' and Monody," *Musical Quarterly,* XLVI (1960), 348.

Gio. Andrea and Sig. Giulio Cesare Brancacci and the Roman, Alessandro Merlo, who sang bass voices of twenty-two notes with a variety of *passaggi* new and grateful to the ears of all. These singers stimulated composers to write works to be sung by several voices as well as by a single one to the accompaniment of an instrument in imitation of these singers and also of a certain woman called Femia, but achieving greater invention and artfulness. There resulted various villanelle in a style intermediate between madrigals in contrapuntal style and villanelle.[20]

Giustiniani found two novel features in the new manner: the cult of the solo singer and the improvised passage work. Solo singing itself was not novel, but its increasing use to render composed music, as opposed to that improvised over standard airs, constituted a new trend. Galilei's collection must be regarded as a product of the vogue observed by Giustiniani, although its music belongs to an intermediate category. It is neither composed for nor improvised by a solo voice, but is adapted for solo performance from composed polyphonic music. Giustiniani's characterization of the favored style as falling between the madrigal and villanelle fits all but a few of Galilei's arrangements.

Years later, even after espousing the monodic principle proclaimed by Girolamo Mei,[21] Galilei continued to defend the performance of part-music by one voice with instrumental accompaniment, particularly when the music had a tuneful top voice. He wrote around 1591:

. . . per essempio nel cantare questa tale aria come t'haggio lasciato vita mia. dico che cantando il soprano di cotale aria sopre ad uno stromento che suoni tutte le sue parti, si domanda cantare proschorda; et il cantarne piu si domanda cantare sinfone et in consonanza. et quante piu parti canteranno nell'istesso tempo tostomeno sara compresa tale aria dal senso, et operera con meno efficacia negl'animi di quelli che l'ascoltano la sua natura: il qual soprano si puo ancora cantare nella uoce d'un tenore che torni bene.[22]

20. Italian text printed in Solerti, *Le origini,* pp. 106–07.

21. See my *Girolamo Mei; Letters on Ancient and Modern Music* (Rome: American Institute of Musicology, 1960).

22. This statement was inserted in Galilei's essay, *Dubbi intorno a quanto io ho detto dell'uso dell'enharmonio con la solutione di essi,* Florence, Bibl. Naz. Cent., MS. Gal. 3, fol. 70r–70v, but subsequently it was crossed out and not used. The essay is from about 1591. The use of the words "proschorda" and "sinfone" points to an earlier discussion of Plato's criticism of certain accompaniments used by his contemporaries. See my article in *Musical Quarterly,* XLVI, 355. The song mentioned is printed there on p. 348.

(For example in singing an air such as *Come t'haggio lasciato vita mia,* I say that when the soprano is sung to an instrument that plays all the parts, this is called singing *proschorda;* and to sing more parts is called *synphonon* or "in harmony." The greater the number of parts that sing at one time, the less will the air be grasped by the sense and the less efficaciously will its character work upon the souls of those who listen to it. It will also turn out well if such a soprano is sung by a tenor.)

The compositions Galilei selected for transcription are about equally divided between those in imitative style (Nos. 10–11, 12–13, 14, and 18) and those homophonically set (Nos. 21, 22, 19, and 16). Two, Nos. 20 and 15, are in a mixed style. The imitative compositions are favorite works of such well-known composers as: Palestrina, Lassus, and Striggio. Among the homophonic songs, several are anonymous, and are unknown outside this manuscript: *Vattene o sonn'e maj, Pur viv'il bel costume,*[23] and *Si gioioso mi fann'i dolor miej.*[24] One other song, *Se ben di sette stelle,*[25] has also not been identified. It is probable that one of the criteria for selection was the melodiousness of the bass part. Other criteria may be inferred from Galilei's description of three compositions of the MS., in a short essay drafted in 1591, as possessing "great beauty of air." The three pieces are *Pur viv'il bel costume, Si gioioso mi fann' i dolor miei,* and *Vivo sol di speranza* (seconda parte of *Aspro core*).[26] By "beauty of air" Galilei seems to have meant simplicity of texture, clarity of harmonic movement, and rhythmic vitality, as well as melodic distinctiveness in the leading voice.

The treatment of the original in Galilei's accompaniments ranges from almost absolute fidelity to the part-writing to a free chordal sketch. The key of the original is preserved in every one of the identifiable compositions. The importance of keeping the part-movement intact in a transcription for lute is repeatedly emphasized in the *Fronimo.* But this requirement was a stricture imposed upon instrumental transcriptions; it is not surprising that Galilei often departed from it in the accompaniments. At one extreme is the lute

23. No other compositions on these two texts have been found.

24. Not based either on Vincenzo Ruffo's madrigal on this text in his *Primo libro di madrigali cromatici a 4 v.,* 1556, or on Bernardo Lupacchino's setting in his *Il primo libro di madrigali a 5 v.,* 1547.

25. Not based on Bartolomeo Spontoni's madrigal on this text in his *Il primo libro di madrigali a 4 v.,* 1558.

26. In the essay named above, note 22; see *Musical Quarterly,* XLVI, 358.

accompaniment for Striggio's *Ancor ch'io possa dire.* Except for the final measures, where Galilei has varied the harmony and bass, and for a few ornamental runs, this intabulation is a faithful transcription of the six-part madrigal. More typical is the free lute accompaniment for Lasso's sonnet *Fiera stella.* It is instructive to compare the opening measures of this with the original five-voice setting and with Galilei's faithful intabulation in the *Fronimo.*

The transcription printed in *Fronimo* is fussy in its preservation of the details of the original composition, extending even to attempts to reproduce the five-part texture. The manuscript accompaniment adheres less slavishly to the original. The harmony is almost always maintained, but it is no longer possible to trace Lassus' individual

EX. 1. Lassus, *Fiera stella.*

1a. Original five-voice setting.

1b. *Fronimo,* 1568.

1c. Landau MS.

* Tablature erroneously repeats these two beats, shifting the barline a half value until corrected at measure 9.

voice parts. From the third measure on, Galilei even abandons the thread of the top part. In one place (measure 5) he chooses the C major chord over Lassus' C minor.

The loss of the top part of a composition in imitative texture as *Fiera stella* may not seem serious; but the absence of the original top line in a homophonic song such as Giovanni Ferretti's *Dolce mi saria uscir d'affanno* does appear to violate a statement once made by Galilei, that in such songs the soprano has the "air."[27] In this song Galilei's accompaniment departs from the soprano melody as often as it preserves it—perhaps so as to detract less attention from the part that is sung. The one part in which Galilei respects the original in every detail, however, is the bass. This is true of all the arrangements, except at times when the bass has lengthy pauses, and Galilei has borrowed a fragment of an interior part to fill the gaps. No ornamentation appears in the solo voice parts, therefore, but one

27. *Ibid.*, p. 348.

cannot exclude the possibility that the singer would have embellished them in the manner of the time, particularly where there are large skips.

The appendix to the Riccardiana *Fronimo* is of a much different character from the one just described. The collection of music is what dance-band musicians today would call "fake-books"—musical notebooks in which they jot down standard tunes and their chords as guides to improvisation. Each piece in this MS. consists of a single musical period. Today's tune collectors would call such a unit a "chorus"; in the sixteenth century it would have been referred to as an "aria" or air. The short span of the pieces here is in contrast to the instrumental compositions in the Landau MS., which are several periods long—for example, the *Romanesca con quattro parti* on folio 7r, which utilizes the *romanesca* pattern of ten measures four times over. In the first three pages of the Riccardiana fascicle—the only pages utilized—Galilei notated nine pieces in tablature; a tenth incomplete piece is in a different hand, which resembles the second hand of the Landau MS. Each of the nine items by Galilei provides raw material for improvisation or variation. The tenth item is itself a variation on the passamezzo of No. 9. Another notable feature of the series of airs is that they are all in the tonality of C, most of them minor, but Nos. 1, 4, 5, and 8 are in major. This uniformity may have served to provide a standard point of reference for transposition, which is easily effected on the lute by a change in the tuning. In a number of the pieces the notation is more explicit than what Galilei was accustomed to use. In all but Nos. 4 and 5, dots under the figures indicate the use of the index finger. In Nos. 1, 2, and 8, dots are placed also after the figures in certain chords, evidently, to indicate immediate dampening. (In the transcription of No. 1 these latter dots are placed above or below the note.)

The numbers belong to several categories: standard tunes, dances, single variations of the standard patterns of the *romanesca* and *passamezzo antico*, and airs for the singing of poetry. The stock airs or tunes are No. 1, *Germini*, and No. 6, *Era di maggio*.[28] The

28. A variant of this melody, in mixed triple and common time, and repeating each phrase, is in Florence, Bibl. Naz. Cent., Magliabecchi, Classe XIX, No. 108. It is printed in Federico Ghisi, "Alcune canzoni a ballo del primo cinquecento" in *Festschrift Hans Engel,* ed. Horst Heussner (Kassel: Bärenreiter, 1964), p. 132. The text given there—"Era di Maggio, era la Primavera,/ Ch'ogn'albero produce il suo bel fiore"—fits the tune in the Galilei MS.

variations on standard patterns are: No. 2, on the *romanesca,* and No. 9, on the *passamezzo antico.* No. 10 is a variation, unlabeled, of the *passamezzo* of No. 9. Dance airs are No. 3, a *gagliarda;* No. 7, another *gagliarda;* and No. 8, a *contrapasso.* The *passamezzo* is, of course, likewise a dance.

Perhaps the most valuable items in the group are the two airs for the singing of poetry. Such airs are not abundant in manuscripts and even less so in printed sources. No. 4 is an air for the singing of sonnets, and No. 5 an air for singing capitoli. The air for capitoli is identical to that for sonnets except for the omission of the third measure.

The collection is thus a small compendium of the diverse kinds of music a lute-player was expected to supply for social functions. To play for dancing and for theatrical performances, to improvise instrumental interludes, and to provide the accompaniment for poetic recitation: such were the lutanist's typical obligations in the service of his patrons.

CONTENTS: LANDAU-FINALY MS. MUS. 2, BIBLIOTECA NAZIONALE CENTRALE, FLORENCE

No.	*Folio Voice*	*Folio Intab.*	*Tuning*	*Text Incipit or Title*	*Composer & No. of Parts*	*Concordance and Remarks*
1		7r		Romanesca con 4 parti	[Galilei]	MS. Gal. 6, 20r–20v: "Romanesca sesta"
2		7v		Pass'e mezzo	[Galilei]	
3		8r		Pass'e mezzo	[Galilei]	
4		8v		Romanesca con 4 parti	[Galilei]	MS. Gal. 6, 77r–77v: "Romanesca 4ª"
5		9r		Acas'un giono [sic] con la seconda parte	[pop. song prob. **arr.** by Galilei]	
6		9v–10r		Romanesca con 4 parti	[Galilei]	
7		10v–11r		Romanesca con 4 part	[Galilei]	
8		11v–12r		Romanesca con 4 part	[Galilei]	MS. Gal. 6, 81v–82r: "sopra la medesima [Romanesca 6ª]"
9		12r		Bella man di valore		
10	12v	1r	A	Vestiva i colli	[Palestrina] a 5	RISM 1566[3]: *Desiderio*
11	1v	2r	A	[2da parte:] Cosi le chiome mie		**Fronimo* 1568, p. 15 **Fronimo* 1584, p. 47 Casimiri *Opere* IX, 117 Lute part not autog.
12	2v	3r	G	Fiera stella sel cielo ha forza in noi	[Lassus] a 5	Boetticher 1555 α: *Il 1º lib. mad. a 5,* Venice, A. Gardano.
13	3v	4r	G	(2da parte:) Ma tu prend'à diletto		**Fronimo* 1568, p. 129 *Sämt. Werke* II, 50

No.	Folio Voice	Folio Intab.	Tuning	Text Incipit or Title	Composer & No. of Parts	Concordance and Remarks
14	4v	5r	D	Io son ferito ahi lasso	[Palestrina] a 5	RISM 1561^{10}: *3º lib. delle Muse a 5* **Fronimo* 1568, p. 146
15	5v	6r	A	Vivo sol di speranza rimembrando [2da parte of *Aspro core*]	[Lassus]	Boetticher 1560 β: *1º lib. di Mad. a 4*, Venice, A. Gardano. *Bottegari MS., fol. 36r, attr. to G. D. da Nola
16	6v	13r	A	Vattene o sonn'e maj		
17	13v	missing		Madonna O felice quel giorno		Cf. Galanti, *Le Villanelle* under "O felice quel giorno"
18	14v	15r	A	Ancor chio possa dire	[A. Striggio] a 6	RISM 1591^{10}: *Melodia Olympica*, 1594^{7}, 1611^{11} **Fronimo* 1568, p. 153
19	15v	16r	G	Si gioioso mi fann'i dolor miej		
20	16v	17r	A	Se ben di sette stelle		
21	17v	18r	G	Dolce mi saria uscir d'affann'e pen e da martire	[G. Ferretti] a 5	*Il 2do Lib. delle canzoni alla Napolit. a 5*, Venice, G. Scotto, 1569, 2/1574, 3/1578, 4/1581
22	18v	19r	G	Pur viv'il bel costume		Partially printed *Mus. Quart.*, XLVI, 359
23		19v		Caro dolce ben mio à 4 del Giacomino	[Bernardino Giacomini?]	

*Intabulation varies.

THEMATIC INDEX OF ANONYMOUS AND UNIDENTIFIED COMPOSITIONS IN THE LANDAU-FINALY MS. MUS. 2

(Except where indicated, note values have been halved. Bar lines through the staff are those of the manuscript.)

No. 5. *A cas un giorno con la seconda parte,* fol. 9r.

No. 9. *Bella man di valore,* fol. 12r.

No. 16. *Vattene o sonn'e maj,* fols. 6v, 13r (see full transcription on page 224).

No. 17. *Madonna O Felice quel giorno,* bass part only, fol. 13v (original note values).

Madonna O fe - li - ce O fe - li - ce quel gior- no O fe - li - ce‿ho - ra

No. 19. *Si gioioso mi fann'i dolor miej,* fols. 15v, 16r (see full transcription on pages 226–28).

No. 20. *Se ben di sette stelle,* fols. 16v–17r (see full transcription on page 228).

No. 22. *Pur viv'il bel costume,* fols. 18v–19r.

Pur viv'-il bel cos - tu - me Pur viv' - il bel cos - tu - me

No. 23. *Caro dolce ben mio a 4 del Giacomino,* fol. 19v.

CONTENTS: F. III.10431, BIBLIOTECA RICCARDIANA

1. Folio Ir. Germini.
2. Folio Ir. Romanesca.
3. Folio Ir. Gagliarda.
4. Folio Iv. Aria de sonetti.
5. Folio Iv. Aria de capitoli.
6. Folio Iv. Era di maggio
7. Folio Iv. Gagliarda.
8. Folio Iv. Contrapasso.
9. Folio 2r. Pass'emezzo.
10. Folio 2r. [Passamezzo].

TRANSCRIPTIONS

(All note-values have been halved. Bars through the staff are in the manuscript tablature; added barlines do not penetrate the staff. Added mensuration signs are in brackets. Where there is a conflict between the original sign and the modern time signature, the original is above the staff.)

LANDAU-FINALY MS.

No. 16. *Vattene o sonn'e maj* (Landau-Finaly, MS. Mus. 2, fols. 6v, 13r).

que - ste mem - bra le - gar le - gar quan - to
n'hai tol - to o meste lu - cj pian- ge - te Si ch'el
uostro pian - to ma - don - n'er - ror co - no- sch'e non in - gan -
no o meste lu - cj pian - ge - te si che'l uostro pian - to ma -

don - n'error co - no - sch'e non in - gan - no

No. 19. *Si gioioso mi fann'i dolor miej* (Landau-Finaly, MS. Mus. 2, fols. 15v, 16r).

Si gio-io-so mi fann'i do-lor mie-j don - na don-
na per a-mar uo - i che sempr'a-mand'ogn'hor morir uorre-j
che sempr'a-mand' ogn' hor mo - rir uor-re - j mo-rir uor-re-

j et fra me di-co po - i se tal gio - ia m'ar-
re - ca il mio mar - ti - re hor che fa - rà'l mo - ri - re hor
che fa - rà'l mo - ri - re hor che fa - rà'l mo - ri - re hor che
fa - rà'l mo - ri - re se tal gio - ia m'ar - re- ca il mio

No. 20. *Se ben di sette stelle* (Landau-Finaly, MS. Mus. 2, fols. 16v–17r).

stel - le ar - dent'e bel- le Ti cing' il
bion - do crin lie - ta co - ro - na.
Mentr'a di - por - to in questa part'en quel - le Vaj con la ua - ga
fi - glia di la - to - na Pur t'ac - ce - ser'il cor l'em -

- pie fa - cel - le. Del fie - ro-ar-
cier di - gni - do on- de ne suo - na Il li-do an- co- ra
il li - do an -co - ra e'l a - ve - no - sa spon - da.
Chel mar di Cre - ta

RICCARDIANA *FRONIMO*

No. 1. *Germini* (Riccardiana F. III. 10431, fol. 1r).

No. 4. *Aria de sonetti* (Riccardiana F. III. 10431, fol. 1v).

No. 6. *Era di maggio* (Riccardiana F. III. 10431, fol. 1v).

15 / Early Venetian Libretti at Los Angeles

NINO PIRROTTA
Harvard University

CURIOSITY, the seed of science, needs time and favorable conditions to develop into full knowledge. But when, during a recent visit to Los Angeles, my curiosity was aroused by a collection of Venetian libretti preserved there in the Music Library of the University of California, time was inexorably short. Similar collections exist in some other libraries; but nobody, to my knowledge, has ever undertaken to describe any of them, still less to inquire how much they resemble one another, and whether or not they may have had a common origin. To answer such plain questions would require no little time and labor, and all that I can do is to scatter the seed of my curiosity, hoping, as the farmer does, that it will bear good fruit.

The set at Los Angeles consists of more than one hundred volumes, in all-parchment bindings possibly of the late eighteenth century. On the spine of each volume the title *Raccolta de' Drammi*, lettered in gold on a leather tag, is supplemented by the year, or years, of the libretti included. Slight variations in the external measurements correspond to variations in the size of the small 12° format typical of such libretti (roughly 6 x 3 inches). I had the opportunity to examine only the first four volumes of the collection, which cover the first seven years of operatic activity in Venice. Even this was made possible only by the courtesy and liberality of the U.C.L.A. library system and of its music librarian, Mr. Frederick Freedman.

The spine of the first volume is stamped with the years 1637–38–39. It came as a surprise, therefore, on opening the volume, to find myself confronted with "LA DEIANIRA DEL SIG. MALATESTA LEONETTI. Opera recitatiua in Musica. . . . IN VENETIA Per ANGELO SALVADORI Libraro a San Moisè MDCXXXV." The excitement of a possible discovery quietly subsided, however, when I learned from the editor's dedication that the work had come from Rome, and from the author's original dedication to Cardinal Antonio Barberini, dated Fossombrone, September 8, 1631, that the "opera" had been planned for staging "con suoni, canti, & balli," on the occasion of the Cardinal's visit to that town. Lack of time and ill health had prevented Leonetti from perfecting his text in time, and from having it set to music.

Even as an unborn opera, *La Deianira* is remarkable for its use of the term "opera" at least four years (eight, if we consider Leonetti's dedication) before its earliest known occurrence.[1] Also interesting is the ending of the work, which presents six strophes to be sung by a female chorus and danced by youths and damsels, followed by six additional strophes of a "corrente del balletto," and by two final lines for "tutti i chori." For the rest, the opera has some rather archaic features: it is divided into five acts; Hercules' battles backstage are only verbally reported to the audience; and finally, the acts are divided by a moralizing, unidentified "choro," quite distinct from the specific choruses of youths, damsels, priests of Juno, etc., all of which take an active part in the dialogue and the action.

Following *La Deianira,* the four volumes I examined include all the expected titles for the years 1637 to 1643, each represented by at least one libretto (see the Appendix). G. Badoaro's texts for *Il Ritorno d'Ulisse in patria* and *Le Nozze d'Enea con Lavinia* (Nos. 17 and 18) are both in manuscript; comparison with other existing copies might establish whether or not they belong to small manuscript editions (so to speak) that were circulated instead of printed libretti at the time of the original performance.[2] G. F. Busenello, like

1. The term is found in both libretto and scenario of *Le Nozze di Teti, e di Peleo* (1639); see Donald J. Grout, *A Short History of Opera* (New York, 1947), p. 3.

2. Wolfgang Osthoff, "Zu den Quellen von Monteverdis 'Il Ritorno di Ulisse in Patria,'" *Studien zur Musikwissenschaft,* XXIII (1956) 69, lists seven manuscript libretti of *Il Ritorno* in various Venetian libraries, of which list he assigns only one,

Badoaro, also seems to have been unwilling to have his texts printed when they were set to music; however, he had them published later in a single volume (*Hore ociose*, Venice, 1656), each with an individual frontispiece and pagination. Abstracts from this print are included in Vol. 2 (Nos. 10, 11, and 14) and Vol. 3 (No. 30) of the Los Angeles collection. B. Ferrari's *La Ninfa avara*, published in 1642 as an individual libretto (although with the date misprinted as 1662), also appears in Vol. 2 in an abstract from the author's *Poesie drammatiche* of 1644 (No. 16); it is preceded and followed, however, by manuscript pages reproducing title page, dedication, etc., and an appended *intermedio*, just as they appear in the 1642 libretto. G. Strozzi's highly successful *La Finta pazza* is present with no less than three different editions (Nos. 15, 19, and 20); *L'Arianna* (Nos. 9 and 13), *La Venere gelosa* (Nos. 32 and 33), and *L'Egisto* (Nos. 34 and 35) are each represented by two different editions.

In sharp contrast with such evident striving for completeness, the collection includes very few examples of scenari: only one in Vol. 1 (No. 6)[3] and two in Vol. 3 (Nos. 24 and 26).[4] For the rest, a scenario—i.e., the description, scene by scene, of what happens on stage—is sometimes incorporated into a libretto, as, for instance, in the first edition of *La Finta pazza* (No. 15, pp. 7–21) and in *Amore innamorato* (No. 21, pp. 11–17). Strozzi's *La Finta savia* has a general "Argomento Historico" supplemented by extensive individual

---

No. 5, to the 17th century. Los Angeles No. 17, "1641 Il Ritorno d'Ulisse in Patria di C.B.C.V.," reproduces the title of Osthoff's No. 5 almost literally, and seems also to belong to the 17th century. The other copies in Venice have longer title pages, giving composer and theater, and qualifying Badoaro as "Nobile Veneto," whereas No. 5 and the Los Angeles copy have "G.V." (= Giureconsulto Veneto?). Manuscripts of *Le Nozze d'Enea* also exist in Venice, but they have not been thoroughly investigated. An unpaged copy in the Library of Congress is given by the printed catalogue as "probably 17th century." Los Angeles No. 18, written in a minute 17th-century handwriting (22 lines of text per page), has both pagination and 8° signatures.

3. "BREVE ESPOSITIONE Della festa Teatrale Del Signor ORATIO PERSIANI, Posta in Musica dal Sig. FRANCESCO CAVALLI Da recitarsi nel TEATRO DI S. CASCIANO. L'Opera è intitolata LE NOZZE DI TETI, e di Peleo" (no imprint, no date). The list of characters on p. 3 reappears with the same typographical setting in the libretto; the latter, however, omits the information that the performers "parte sono stati conceduti all'Auttore da diuersi Potentati. E parte sono stipendiati nella Cappella della Serenissima Republica Veneta."

4. "ARGOMENTO. Et SCENARIO DEL BELLEROFONTE . . . Da rappresentarsi nel Teatro Nouissimo" (Venice, Surian, 1642), and "ARGOMENTO Et SCENARIO DI NARCISO, ET ECCO IMMORTALATI . . . Da rappresentarsi in Musica nel Teatro di San Gio. e Paolo" (no imprint, no date).

"argomenti" for the prologue, the "intermezzi," and every single scene.

We are so used to seeing libretti sold at the doors of our opera houses as to take it for granted that libretti were always printed for, or before, the first performance of an opera. The evidence we can gather from the libretti now under examination tends to negate such an assumption, at least for the earliest phase. It is well known, for instance, that Ferrari's *Andromeda* and *Maga fulminata* (Nos. 2 and 3) contain detailed narratives of the way in which the two operas *had been* staged.[5] A note appended to Strozzi's *Delia* (No. 4) warns the reader that more than three hundred lines of the printed text "*have been* omitted in the performance," these being "the poet's trills," which had to give way to the passages of the singers. Again Ferrari, commending his *Armida* (No. 7) to the doge Francesco Erizzo, expresses hope that the latter's name shall protect her not against adverse reactions of opera-goers, but against "the horrors of oblivion." The libretto of Ferrari's *Ninfa avara* (No. 16), performed in 1641, was printed in 1642. Finally, we have seen that both Badoaro and Busenello seem to have prevented the printing of libretti at the time in which their texts were represented with the music of Monteverdi or Cavalli.[6]

Most usual at the time of the performance—or even earlier, judging from the strong advertising flavor of some title pages[7]—was the printing of a scenario, seldom exceeding twenty-four pages, i.e., one single 12° fascicle. Very few of these small pamphlets have been preserved; but in fact we cannot be sure that none existed, even for operas for which none has survived. Although libretti were evidently conceived as library items, the occasional and utilitarian character of the scenari, added to their extreme frailty, exposed them all too

5. The dedication of *L'Andromeda,* dated May 6, 1637, states that the opera had been represented two months earlier—probably an understatement, since Carnival ended that year on February 24. The description of the performance is reproduced by Simon T. Worsthorne, *Venetian Opera in the Seventeenth Century* (Oxford, 1954) pp. 168–69.

6. This is in part a continuation of the courtly habit of publication after the event, for the sake of prestige. It may also be that the printing of a libretto had to wait for at least the first reactions of the audience, lest the dedicatee resent the homage of an unsuccessful opera. Anyway, it was the librettist's business; and the poets, not yet a professional lot, were most concerned with their own literary glory and with the benefits to be secured through a well-placed dedication. Thus, they always got the lion's share, while the rest received only passing mention, if any at all.

7. See note 3.

easily to the danger of obliteration. To be sure there was some tendency to replace the function of a scenario with the printing of a libretto;[8] even so, the majority of libretti were so much more concerned with the glorification of the poets that even composers' names were usually omitted, not to speak of the names of singers, dancers, or stage designers.

From the latter category a third sort of print originated, which did not appear very frequently, and which is best characterized in connection with the short-lived activities of the Teatro Novissimo (1641–1647). The emphasis placed by these activities on stage design and machinery was responsible for such publications—in addition to those of the usual sort—as *Il Cannocchiale per la Finta pazza,* a scenario of fifty-five pages focusing, as the title points out, on the visual aspect of the opera; a folio edition of *Il Bellerofonte,* including ten plates of stage designs; and M. Bisaccioni's *Apparati Scenici Per lo Teatro Novissimo di Venetia Nell'anno 1644,* a narrative of *La Venere gelosa* illustrated by twelve plates (some of them belonging to other productions).[9]

In spite of the diversity of such publications, or perhaps because their publishers' interests and aims were so varied, we can seldom be sure of the precise date of the original performance, or of a repetition, of any given opera. We rely with great confidence on a tradition based on Bonlini's and Groppo's catalogues, without realizing that these authors did not have any better sources of information than do we about operas that had been performed one century before their own time. They, too, when faced with the same difficulties as we encounter today, may have been misled by the unconscious projection into the past of customs that prevailed at their own time.[10]

To such misleading projections belongs the view that every

8. See *Amore innamorato* (No. 21), "da rappresentarsi in Musica nel Teatro di S. Moisè l'Anno 1642," as well as *Il Bellerofonte* and *La Venere gelosa* (Nos. 23 and 32), whose title pages contain similar expressions announcing the performance. The theater in San Moisè seems never to have had scenari printed for its productions; in the other theaters the habit was discontinued after 1655.

9. None of these items, all reflecting the aggressive personality of Giacomo Torelli, are included in the Los Angeles collection. The last two among them were dedicated respectively to Ferdinand I of Tuscany and Cardinal Antonio Barberini; plates from both are reproduced in Worsthorne, *Venetian Opera.*

10. Consultation of a microfilm of MS. Cl.VII, 3226 of the Biblioteca San Marco in Venice, containing the expanded version (unpublished) of Groppo's catalogue, made me only more aware of such shortcomings. I want to express here my thanks to Mr. Charles Troy for letting me consult his microfilm.

printing of a libretto was determined by a new series of performances in a different year or season. Thus, the existence of two Venetian libretti of *L'Arianna* has led to the notion, unsupported by any other piece of evidence, that Monteverdi's thirty-year-old opera was first given to inaugurate operatic activity at the theater in San Moisè in the autumn of 1639, and later repeated during the regular season of 1640.

I strongly doubt that the custom of an autumn season was already established in 1639. In fact, a quick glance at the 1639 libretto of *L'Arianna* may suffice to bring about the realization that its printing was not related to any performance. It was a purely literary publication, reproducing the 1608 text without any mention of theater or composer; nor did it contain any of the marks which in the 1640 libretto were used to indicate numerous lines, mainly in the choruses, that were then omitted in the performance.[11] Quite a different situation is evident just in the title page of the 1640 libretto, "L'Arianna del Sig. Ottavio Rinuccini Posta in Musica dal Sig. Claudio Monteverdi. Rappresentata in Venetia l'Anno 1640 . . ." Venice was too proud of its most famous musician to let his name pass unnoticed; in addition to the title page, the printer's dedication also mentions the performance and praises Monteverdi, and a sonnet by Ferrari extols him as the "Oracolo della Musica." What is most relevant to our present purpose, however, is that, although the 1639 libretto merely reproduces the original prologue,[12] this appears in the 1640 print in a version addressed to the Venetian doge.

More complex is the case of *L'Adone*, which is likewise associated with Monteverdi's last years even though the traditional attribution to him of the music has recently been rejected.[13] That the composer was Manelli is made clear by the latter's dedication of the libretto to Antonio Grimani (one of the owners of the theater in San Giovanni e Paolo), and particularly by the following passage: "So had I the

11. See Library of Congress, *Catalogue of Opera Librettos Printed before 1800*, prepared by O. G. T. Sonneck (Washington, D.C., 1914) I, 141.

12. This is the prologue addressed to Carlo Emanuele of Savoy, printed in the 1608 editions of Florence, Mantua, and Venice, but already modified on the occasion of the Mantuan performance of May 28, 1608, because the Duke did not attend his daughter's wedding.

13. See Anna Amalie Abert, *Claudio Monteverdi und das musikalische Drama* (Lippstadt, 1954), p. 128.

good fortune, in representing it [*L'Adone*] in music, not to be one of the humblest professors of this art, while the theater of Your most Illustrious Lordship, in which it was performed, is the noblest of all that exist today in Italy."[14] To be sure, the passage also implies that *L'Adone* had already been performed before the date of the dedication, December 21, 1639; but the time during which the performance must have taken place is narrowed down to a few days by a letter from Bologna, also printed in the libretto, in which the poet Paolo Vendramino deplores Manelli's decision to present *L'Adone* in his absence—that is "without those lights that are most needed for its staging." "It *shall be* your task," he then warns, "to give it that diligence and study that I am not able to give, and which, nevertheless, are deserved by any performance of an opera in Venice."[15] Up to December 16, 1639, the day on which this letter was written, no news of the performance had reached Bologna; it is clear, then, that the presentation on stage of *L'Adone* must have preceded Manelli's dedication by no more than one week. I am inclined to think that the presumed date of the dedication is that of the day following the first performance.[16]

Whatever scant evidence we have seems to indicate that autumn was, at this time, the season in which operatic companies traveled to perform in places other than Venice. As the poet of *L'Adone* had recently moved from Venice to Bologna, so I would suggest that the opposite journey had been made only a few weeks earlier by the

14. P. 4: "Così io nel rappresentarla musicalmente hauessi hauuto ventura di non essere uno de gl'ultimi professori dell'arte, come il Teatro di V.S. Illustrissima, nel quale si è rappresentata è il più nobile di quanti hoggidì n'habbia l'Italia."

15. P. 6: ". . . toccherà à lei di darli quello studio, e quella diligenza, che io non hò potuto, e che merita il far recitare un'Opera à Venezia."

16. We can gather, then, from *L'Adone* that fierce competition led to pushing forward as much as possible the opening of the winter season. Placed in the regular 1640 season, *L'Adone* fills the gap that would otherwise exist in the record of the theater in San Giovanni e Paolo. Similarly, if we postpone the date of *L'Incoronatione di Poppea,* and anticipate the date of *L'Egisto* (placing both of them in the regular season of 1643, rather than in improbable autumn seasons), the rate of two operas per year, adopted for some time by that theater, is re-established. (The date 1642 in the 1656 libretto of *L'Incoronatione* may indicate an early opening of the winter season.) Puzzling are the opening lines in the preface of *L'Egisto:* "Per non lasciare perire la Doriclea ho formato con frettolosa penna l'Egisto . . . scusa la qualità del suo essere, perchè nato in pochi giorni si può chiamare più tosto sconciatura, che parto dell'intelletto." They do not seem to add any credence to the date 1642 appearing on the Viennese score; furthermore, there is no record of a *Doriclea* before 1645.

Manelli troupe. My reason for believing this is the evidence, recently uncovered by Wolfgang Osthoff, that the troupe had performed Manelli's own *Delia* and Monteverdi's *Ritorno d'Ulisse* in Bologna.[17] Osthoff places the Bolognese performances in 1640, after the first Venetian performance of *Il Ritorno*, which he convincingly dates in 1640, instead of the traditional 1641.[18] It seems more likely to me that Monteverdi's new opera had an "out-of-town" trial before its 1640 appearance in Venice—namely, at Bologna in the late autumn of 1639.

This is no academic shuffling of dates. In both the 1639 Venetian reprint of *L'Arianna* and the Bolognese performance of *Il Ritorno* (in which he had no direct participation) I see Monteverdi's shrewd yet cautious moves toward a full re-entry on the operatic scene. It was not proper for the head of the ducal chapel of San Marco, now a priest, to show any eagerness to become involved in the most thoroughly secular form of musical activity and in the never very reputable milieu of the public stage. Yet Monteverdi, old in years but still young in spirit, must have been thrilled at first by the activity of the "foreign" troupe of Ferrari and Manelli (whom he may have encouraged to settle in the theater in San Casciano),[19] and even more tantalized in 1639, when his own pupil, Cavalli, and many of his singers in San Marco began their own operatic activity.[20] The latter obviously established a favorable precedent for the master's still unavowed goal; yet it is remarkable that Monteverdi's operas were all performed in the theaters in which Ferrari and Manelli acted as producers.[21] He probably believed that collaboration

17. Wolfgang Osthoff, "Zur Bologneser Aufführung von Monteverdis 'Ritorno d'Ulisse' im Jahre 1640," *Anzeiger der phil.-hist. Klasse der Oesterreichischen Akademie der Wissenschaften* (1958), 155–60.

18. According to Osthoff ("Bologneser Aufführung," p. 155), the title of the pamphlet celebrating the Bolognese performance is the following: "Le Glorie della Musica Celebrate dalla Sorella Poesia, Rappresentandosi in Bologna la Delia, e l'Ulisse Nel Teatro de gl'Illustriss. Guastavillani. In Bologna MDCXXXX. Presso Gio. Battista Ferroni." It seems to me that the date may refer to the printing, not necessarily to the performance.

19. Monteverdi's son Francesco had already collaborated with them in a 1636 Paduan performance of *L'Ermiona,* music by F. Sances. See Bruno Brunelli, *I teatri di Padova* (Padova, 1921), p. 74.

20. See note 3, above.

21. Ferrari and Manelli seem to have assumed control of the theaters in San Moisè and San Giovanni e Paolo in 1639, when Cavalli took over as a kind of artistic director in the theater in San Casciano.

with his own dependents would have harmed his lofty position of authority in San Marco.

Badoaro's letter to Monteverdi, missing in the Los Angeles libretto of *Il Ritorno,* but prefacing the corresponding seventeenth-century manuscript in Venice, stresses the pressures exerted on Monteverdi by highly placed persons to have the opera performed in Venice. It also emphasizes the efforts of "private people" (that is, non-professionals) to help in the production, as well as the exceptional patronage accorded it.[22] Apparently, all these exceptional circumstances were enough to induce Monteverdi to yield gladly to external pressure, which coincided with the internal urge of his dramatic talent.

APPENDIX

CONTENTS OF VOLUMES 1–4 OF THE LOS ANGELES COLLECTION

In the following list each libretto is identified by its title, printer, and date. (The place of printing, unless otherwise stated, is Venice.) To these elements any other information is added that may help to distinguish between prints having the same title. Whenever possible, reference is made (by the abbreviation LC) to an entry in the Library of Congress *Catalogue of Opera Librettos Printed before 1800,* prepared by O. G. T. Sonneck (Washington, 1914).

Volume 1 ("1637–38–39").

1. *La Deianira,* Salvadori, 1635; 66, [2] pp. (see the text of the article).

2. *L'Andromeda,* Bariletti, 1637 (LC).

3. *La Maga fulminata,* Bariletti, 1638; 2nd printing, 94 pp.; p. 28, on which other copies are reported to have Ferrari's portrait, is blank.

4. *La Delia O Sia La Sera sposa del Sole,* Pinelli, 1639 (LC).

5. *Le Nozze di Teti, e di Peleo,* Sarzina, 1639 (LC).

22. "Gl'habiti ben intesi, le numerose comparse studiosamente elaborate dall'Illmo Malipiero han condotto col maggior segno il possibile di private persone, cosiche per l'avvenire s'affaticherà forse in darno, chi sanza le Protettioni havute dal mio Ulisse cercherà d'uguagliarlo." The full text of the letter is given by Osthoff, "Zu den Quellen. . . ." (pp. 73-74).

6. *Breve espositione . . .* (scenario of No. 5), n.i. [Sarzina, 1639]; 23 pp. (see the text of the article).

7. *L'Armida,* Bariletti, n.d.; 1 p.l., 58 pp. (LC copy lacks the finely engraved frontispiece).

8. *L'Adone,* Sarzina, 1640 (LC).

9. *L'Arianna,* Salvadori, 1639; 45 pp.

Volume 2 ("1640–41").

10. *Gli Amori d'Apollo, e di Dafne,* Giuliani, 1656 (LC).

11. *La Didone,* Giuliani, 1656 (LC).

12. *Il Pastor regio,* Bariletti, 1640 (LC).

13. *L'Arianna,* Bariletti, 1640; 1 p.l., 64 pp. (LC).

14. *La Didone,* Giuliani, 1656 (=No. 11, except for one additional engraved p.l.).

15. *La Finta pazza,* Surian, 1641; 108 pp.

16. *La Ninfa avara,* n.i., n.d.; pp. 177–205 of *Poesie drammatiche di Benedetto Ferrari* (Milan, 1644), preceded and followed by respectively 10 and 9 unnumbered manuscript pp., reproducing the missing parts of an earlier libretto (Salis, 1662, but 1642), and including *Proserpina rapita,* an "Intermedio per Musica."

17. *Il Ritorno d'Ulisse in Patria,* MS., 1641 (?); 116 unnumbered pp., plus blank flyleaves (see the text of the article).

18. *Le Nozze d'Enea con Lavinia,* MS., 1641 (?); 68 pp., plus blank flyleaves (see the text of the article).

19. *La Finta pazza,* Surian, 1641; 96, [4] pp. ("Seconda impressione").

20. *La Finta pazza,* Surian, 1644; 96 pp. ("Terza impressione").

Volume 3 ("1642").

21. *Amore innamorato,* Surian, 1642 (LC).

22. *La Virtù de' strali d'Amore,* Miloco, 1642 (LC).

23. *Il Bellerofonte,* Surian, 1642 (LC).

24. *Argomento et scenario del Bellerofonte,* Surian, 1642; 19 pp.

25. *Narciso, et Ecco immortalati,* Bariletti, 1642 (LC).

26. *Argomento et scenario di Narciso, et Ecco immortalati,* n.i., n.d.; 18 pp.

27. *L'Alcate,* Surian, 1642 (LC).

28. *Sidonio, e Dorisbe,* Surian, 1642 (LC indicates a mounted notice on p. 106, which is missing here).

29. *Gli Amori di Giasone, e d'Isifile,* Bariletti, 1642 (LC).

30. *L'Incoronatione di Poppea,* Giuliani, 1656 (includes an engraved p.l. not indicated in LC).

Volume 4 ("1643").

31. *La Finta savia,* Leni & Vecellio, 1643 (L.C).

32. *La Venere gelosa,* Surian, 1643; 6 p.l., 92 pp.

33. *La Venere gelosa,* Padova, P. Framo, 1643 (LC. The copy at Los Angeles has only 6 p.l.).

34. *L'Egisto,* Miloco, 1643 (LC).

35. *L'Egisto,* Surian, 1644; 93 pp. ("Seconda impressione"; pp. 25–48 missing.)

16 / Text Underlay in Early Fifteenth-Century Musical Manuscripts

GILBERT REANEY
University of California, Los Angeles

ONE of the most striking features of musical manuscripts written after 1400 is the gradual increase in compositions which have a text or partial text in their lower voices. At first, this is particularly true of Latin texts, and a glance at Volume IV (*Fragmenta Missarum*) of the complete Dufay edition will show how important this development has become by the mid-fifteenth century. In the fourteenth century, motets, Mass movements, and polyphonic songs nearly always have no text in the tenor and contratenor parts. The reason is not immediately obvious. Traditionally, the historian has assumed that these lower parts—which don't look very vocal, particularly in some of the polyphonic songs—were intended for instruments. He may be right, but let us consider why tenors and contratenors have no text. Those compositions from the fourteenth century that do have a text usually involve polytextual writing. An example is Machaut's *De triste cuer—Certes, je di—Quant vrais amans*, Ballade 29 in the editions of both Ludwig and Schrade. Could the reason for the omission of a text in lower parts be that it was identical with the upper voice, and hence could be easily inserted? Parchment was expensive in the Middle Ages, and every little space was used. If a previous copyist had left a space, a later one would enter a new composition there. Examples of this are legion, and include the added secular compositions in Codex Bologna, Biblioteca del Conservatorio G. B. Martini, Q.15 (BL). Notation, too, was a means of conserving space, and ligatures rather than single notes were used wherever possible.

Needless to say, I am not trying to suggest that instruments did not perform the lower parts of late medieval polyphonic music. On the other hand, we do tend to assume that all textless parts are not vocal, when perhaps we should add the upper voice text to the lower parts. This situation becomes particularly clear in early fifteenth-century music, where a piece may appear in one source with a text in the tenor and in another without it. Moreover, the process is continued, though less frequently, in the contratenor. For instance, a two-part composition which has text in both parts in MSS. BL and O (Oxford, Bodleian Library, Canonici misc. 213) has a textless tenor in Codex Pz (Paris, Bibliothèque Nationale, nouv. acq. fr., 4917). This is the Rondeau refrain by Briquet, *Ma seul amour*, published in my *Early Fifteenth-Century Music*, Volume II (1959), p. 13. Yet this piece also has clearly instrumental interludes in both parts at the end of each half of the composition.

A particularly interesting piece from the same point of view is Grossin's *Imera dat hodierno*, No. 15 in *Early Fifteenth-Century Music*, Volume III (1966), and also published in the *Denkmäler der Tonkunst in Österreich*, Jahrgang VII (1900), p. 209. It occurs in no less than six sources, though in one of these only the tenor part is given. It might be expected that a work as thoroughly homophonic as this one would have the text in all three parts, but not one manuscript gives such a version. However, both BL and BU (Bologna, Biblioteca Universitaria, 2216) have the text in the tenor as well as in the *cantus*, whereas Em (Munich, Staatsbibliothek, Mus. 3232a) is so exceptional as to have the text in the contratenor but not in the tenor. Since this source is a little peripheral, it is possible that the copyist intended to place the text in the tenor and put it in the contratenor by accident—that is, he may have mistaken the contratenor for the tenor, quite an easy error to make, since the two voices are much alike. It would seem, however, that all three voices should have had the text—an assumption already made by the editors of the *Denkmäler* volume, although O and Tr have the text only in the *cantus*, and the notation of the textless lower voices often makes use of ligatures and frequently replaces groups of three unison eighth-notes with dotted quarters. The presence of many text cues in the contratenor of BL supports the use of text in all voices. Of course, it may be alleged, though I believe there is no foundation for such an assumption, that the application of text to lower parts is a peculiarly Italian custom; and it does seem true that Italian scribes were fond of indicating the presence of text in lower parts. But we should not forget that it is partly a matter of chance that we have so many Italian manuscripts from the first half of the fifteenth century.

It does at any rate seem clear that the Italian MSS. BL and BU show us the way performers applied text to voices that were often notated without a text. A good example is Reson's *Salve regina,* published in my *Early Fifteenth-Century Music,* Volume II, p. 111. The tenor given in the transcription is the textless version of BL, but the tenor of BU with the full text appears in the Critical Notes on page lv. The process of applying a text to a textless voice, although it may involve musical variants, is usually simple. A dotted half-note in 6/8 may be split into two dotted quarters to accommodate two syllables. Often, however, it is clear that in order to preserve the trochaic rhythms, a dotted quarter-note is divided into a quarter plus an eighth, and a dotted half-note may be unequally divided into a dotted quarter-note tied to a normal quarter and followed by an eighth-note. Usually, the division into smaller values produces unisons, but in a comparison with the original an occasional second or third may be expected to appear.

The presence in BL and other sources of many partial texts in tenors and contratenors is perhaps even more interesting. I find that I cannot follow Professor Besseler's opinion, that text incipits indicate instrumental performance (Dufay edition, Volume II, p. xv). Surely these incipits are more likely to indicate what the voice should be singing, as compared with the *cantus,* even though the complete text is not given. I am convinced that the use of partially complete texts confirms a vocal performance, though I am inclined to agree with Professor Besseler that instruments may often have been used as well. Perhaps I shall be accused here of lack of consistency—a doubtful virtue anyhow—since in my edition of Cesaris' *A l'aventure va Gauvain,* published in *Early Fifteenth-Century Music,* Volume I, p. 21, I included a line of text in the tenor and contratenor, which are otherwise textless. Now it is curious that such snatches of text do appear in the lower parts of polyphonic songs, usually in connection with imitation, as in *A l'aventure*. On the face of it, there would seem to be little necessity for indicating this text-line in tenor and contratenor, since the *cantus* has the same notes. However, the use of imitation tends to displace the text, so that, if voices do sing the full text in tenor and contratenor, the *cantus* will be differently placed when there is imitation. Otherwise, all voices presumably are to sing the same words at the same time. And I must say that I have never felt drawn toward the theory that an instrumentalist might suddenly start to sing and as suddenly stop again—a possibility for the player of a stringed but hardly of a wind instrument! I should like to think, therefore, either that this piece was performed by three voices, with the tenor and contratenor arranging the text much as I proposed in the Reson *Salve regina*, or that the same two parts were performed on instruments. It may be that the *cantus* too had an instrumental doubling, since there seems to be a textless prelude and postlude to the work.

A composition that seems clearly to confirm the idea that a tenor or contratenor may be fully vocal, even when only a partial text occurs in the manuscript, is the *Patrem Scabroso* by Zacar (BL, folios 68v–71). Presumably this work should be attributed to Antonio Zachara, rather than to Zacharias since it is evidently a parody work based on one of the composer's polyphonic songs, probably a lost ballata. It is of course another matter to decide whether Zachara wrote the Mass movement as well as the song on which it is based. It may be that the name Zacar in the BL codex simply refers to the composer of the original song, and that a different composer wrote a parody Mass on it. Still, so long as we have no further information on this matter, we probably must continue to regard Zachara as the composer of both the original and the parody. But to return to the question of the text underlay: it is striking that the contratenor of the *Patrem* has the complete text on two pages, whereas the third or middle page lacks it almost entirely. Surely this lack can be explained only by the scribe's casual attitude to the text: he didn't want the bother of writing it on the middle page.

Turning now to Besseler's *Fragmenta Missarum*, Volume IV of the Dufay edition, we find partially complete texts in a striking number of Mass movements. The Credo on page 25 is again from BL. The tenor text is fairly complete up to the "Crucifixus." A glance at the manuscript confirms our immediate suspicion. The "Crucifixus" begins on the following double page. Again the copyist didn't want the bother of writing more text. And we can probably assume that the omission of the word "omnipotentem" after "Patrem" was due to being crowded out by the preceding word "Tenor." Moreover, the missing words "Et in unum dominum" could easily be accommodated in bar 20 by splitting the preceding long into a dotted half-note plus six eighths in unison with it.

Up to now this article has been concerned with underlaying texts that are missing or partly missing from the manuscripts. In the upper parts, the text is usually present, but unfortunately it is never placed exactly as it should be: in other words, even very accurate manuscripts do not place all the syllables exactly under the notes to which they must be sung. Leaving out of consideration sources in which the text underlay is very casual, such as Em and the Trent codices, it is possible to say that syllabic passages in which there are as many notes as syllables are in general correctly underlaid. Those few exceptions in which the alignment is *not* good are in themselves no problem. A different matter, however, is the long melisma ending a section of music. Generally the copyist has simply placed the final syllable approximately under the last note of the section. Where BL, as often happens, places this syllable beneath the penultimate note, it seems reasonable to apply it to the final note; but for some pieces such a procedure is almost impossible, and the position of the text and ligatures suggests rather that the final syllable should be sung to the penultimate note. This is often true of sections employing long notes, such as the passages at "miserere nobis" and "Iesu Christe" in Grossin's *Et in terra*, No. 9 in *Early Fifteenth-Century Music*, Volume III (also in *Denkmäler der Tonkunst in Österreich*, Volume 61, p. 7). More commonly the copyist did not bother to align the syllables under an extended final series of notes. He would arrange the preceding syllables correctly; but, when he saw there were too many notes for the final word or words, he merely wrote down the word, assuming that the performer would make the correct alignment. This surely does not mean, as we in the mid-twentieth century are too prone to believe, that there was a prescribed way of making the alignment. It is much more likely that the performers lined up final notes and syllables in whatever way suited them best, though it seems clear that where the syllables fall on main beats, they were intended to do so. Often enough, a group can be divided so that each syllable falls on the first note of a bar. The most difficult type of underlay consists of a moderately large group of notes with rather fewer syllables; and I cannot see how rules could be given for such an underlay. However, it is possible to find at times some *point de repère* in the tenor text—when there is one—since the tenor usually consists of slower notes than the upper parts and is thus more simply underlaid.

For the modern editor textual underlaying in the polyphonic Kyrie is particularly difficult. In the manuscripts the word "Kyrie" or "Christe" usually appears at the very beginning, and the word "[e]leyson" at the end, of the principal musical sections. Perhaps we are only making the situation more difficult for ourselves than it really is. We would like to see various words beneath most of the notes, when all that we have is a word at the beginning and one at the end, with a huge gap in between. Like other editors, I have sometimes tried to introduce the triple invocation Kyrie—Kyrie—Kyrie, Christe—Christe—Christe, Kyrie—Kyrie—Kyrie into fourteenth- and early fifteenth-century works. But the truth seems to be that we are well provided for already. We hate to acknowledge that medieval composers and performers, not to mention their audiences, did not mind the multiple musical repetitions often indicated in the manuscripts. Machaut's Mass clearly indicates triple statements of the first Kyrie and of the Christe, just as these repetitions occur in the plainsong he used. Similarly, many of Dufay's Kyries are marked plainly with signs that show the correct repetition, usually three statements. To be sure, there are passages like the "Kyrie cum iubilo," No. 14 of the modern edition, which alternate plainsong with polyphony. In such passages, repetition of the polyphony does not occur in the Kyrie sections, because the triple invocation consists of plainsong—polyphony—plainsong. In the Christe, however, where a similar procedure would have avoided repetition, the polyphony begins and the plainsong follows, so that we have polyphony—plainsong—polyphony. The composer again did not wish to avoid repetition, and still he got his triple invocations. The question seems to be: why introduce further invocations and syllable arrangements into the texts? They are not necessary, and the text form "Kyrie leison" clearly indicates that early polyphonic Kyries were mainly vocalized to the vowel *e*.

The correct positioning of texts in late medieval compositions, and the problem of how to employ voices and instruments, are questions that still need much study. An examination of textual planning as it occurs in individual manuscripts can help to clear up some difficulties. At all events, it is to be hoped that the few points I have brought up will be of use and stimulate further thought. Textless or partially textless works may form a useful point of departure.

17 / An Early Seventeenth-Century Italian Lute Manuscript at San Francisco

GUSTAVE REESE
New York University

THE Frank V. de Bellis Collection, given by the late Mr. de Bellis to San Francisco State College, contains a rich group of works representing the fields of Italian literature, art, and music.[1] Among the most interesting musical items in the collection is an Italian lute manuscript dating from the early seventeenth century. This source, previously unknown to musicological literature, will be the subject of the present study.

Excluding the flyleaves added in binding, the manuscript contains eighty-four pages (forty-two leaves) in oblong format, each page being 10 3/8 by 7 7/8 inches in size. The manuscript begins with four pages that do not contain music, these being followed by seventy-nine pages of music notated in Italian lute tablature. The final page of the volume, although it is ruled with six six-line "staves" like the body of the manuscript, does not contain music (unless seven rhythmic signs written near the upper left-hand margin are to be interpreted as the beginning of a piece). Not all pages are numbered. The first one that is bears the numeral 20; but, since this is the fourth page of tablature, the first page bearing music must be assigned the number 17. Some earlier pages of the manuscript are

1. See *The Frank V. de Bellis Collection in the Library of San Francisco State College* (San Francisco, 1964). I recall with special gratitude the kindness of Mr. de Bellis. In addition to receiving me graciously when I visited the collection and providing me with a microfilm of the source described in this essay, he promptly answered by mail various questions directed to him in writing.

now missing, but it is unlikely that they contained musical compositions, since the following inscription, which seems to apply only to the tablature itself, appears in the right-hand margin on page 17: "Cominciato al 5 Agosto 1615." This remark conveniently provides a *terminus a quo* for the preparation of the music.[2]

The four pages that today still precede the music are not ruled with tablature "staves." The recto of the first leaf bears the name of Ascanio Bentivoglio, preceded by either an indecipherable word or, possibly, a scrawl produced by a scribe trying out his pen. The famous Bentivoglio family, which had branches in many parts of Italy, is well known to the historian as having produced many patrons of the arts. If the Ascanio Bentivoglio mentioned in the present source was contemporaneous with the apparent date of the manuscript, he is likely the Ascanio described by Litta as "Del Magistrato degli Anziani nel 1631," but about whom nothing further seems to be known.[3] The final page of the manuscript bears another inscription: "Al Molto Ill^{o} Sig^{e} Erchole Corio mio Oss^{mo} Milano." The Corio family of which information is available, and which apparently included the fifteenth-century historian Bernardino Corio, was one of the less illustrious Milanese houses of the period;[4] it has not been possible to track down our Erchole. If there was any relationship between Corio and Bentivoglio, its nature seems now to be beyond discovery. The Bentivoglio family had a branch in Milan,[5] but whether it had any links with the Corio family is unknown. Until further biographical material is discovered, we must be satisfied with the deduction that Ascanio and Erchole owned the manuscript at different times, though we might conjecture that Ascanio was the earlier owner, and that he *may* have presented the manuscript to Corio.

2. The same margin also contains an inked-out inscription that, on close inspection, turns out to read, "Al 6 Agosto 16." The scribe presumably entered this date first, then crossed it out when he realized it was incorrect.

3. Pompeo Litta, *Famiglie celebri italiane* (Milan, 1830), III, Pt. 1 (facs. XXXI/1), Tab. IX. According to Tab. VII, a later Ascanio was born in 1673. The term "Anziano" is perhaps best translated as "Alderman."

4. Giovanni Battista Crollalanza, *Dizionario storico-blasonico delle famiglie nobili italiane* (Pisa, 1886-1890), I, 322.

5. Silvio Manucci, *Nobiliario e blasonario del Regno d'Italia* (Rome, 1929?), I, 156.

To whom the manuscript belonged between the time it was Corio's and the recent past, it has proved impossible to determine. Mr. de Bellis bought it from the music dealer, Kenneth Mummery of Bournemouth, England, in March, 1954. Mr. Mummery, in a letter to Mr. de Bellis dated 28 July, 1960, stated: "I have no record of where this lute book came from, nor was there any record of this at the time when I bought it, as I remember the item, so I cannot help . . . in that direction."

The possibility that it is of Milanese origin is strengthened by the fact that its paper bears a watermark generally characteristic of Lombardian, and hence of Milanese, papers—a small flower with five petals around a central circle.[6]

The verso of the leaf that bears Bentivoglio's name on the recto is blank. The second leaf has numerical computations on both sides; these are evidently the work of a person with a poor command of arithmetic, if one may judge from the sometimes faulty totals.

The seventy-nine pages of music are the work of three different scribes. The work of the first scribe makes a brief initial appearance; his copying in the earlier part of the tablature is limited to page 17. The work of the second scribe extends from page 18 through page 55. Hands One and Two show many common stylistic features, but they can readily be distinguished by the first scribe's tendency to slant the barlines downward from right to left (see Plate I), whereas the second scribe reverses the direction (see Plate II). The work of the third scribe begins on page 56 and continues through page 69 (for a sample, see Plate III). His handwriting is characterized by bold, coarse strokes and a tendency to omit the lute fingerings abundantly added by the other copyists. Scribe One returns, writing out pages 70 through 84, after which the third scribe completes the manuscript.

The majority of the compositions bear titles. Like the music, these were written down by several scribes, but the changes in the

6. Actually, two different watermarks are found scattered throughout the manuscript. Both are consistently centered at the top of the page, crossing the central "chain line" (there are 7 "chain lines" on each page, spaced 1⅜ inches apart). The first design is a square, approximately ⅓ inch in width; this seems to be part of an incomplete, unidentified watermark. The second, the small flower, appears most clearly on pp. 21, 29, 37, 73, 85, and 93. For some early examples of this watermark, see Charles M. Briquet, *Les Filigranes, Dictionnaire historique des marques du papier* (Geneva, 1907), II, 365 and Nos. 6392–97.

PLATE I. Page 17 of the De Bellis Lute Tablature.

PLATE II. Page 30 of the De Bellis Lute Tablature.

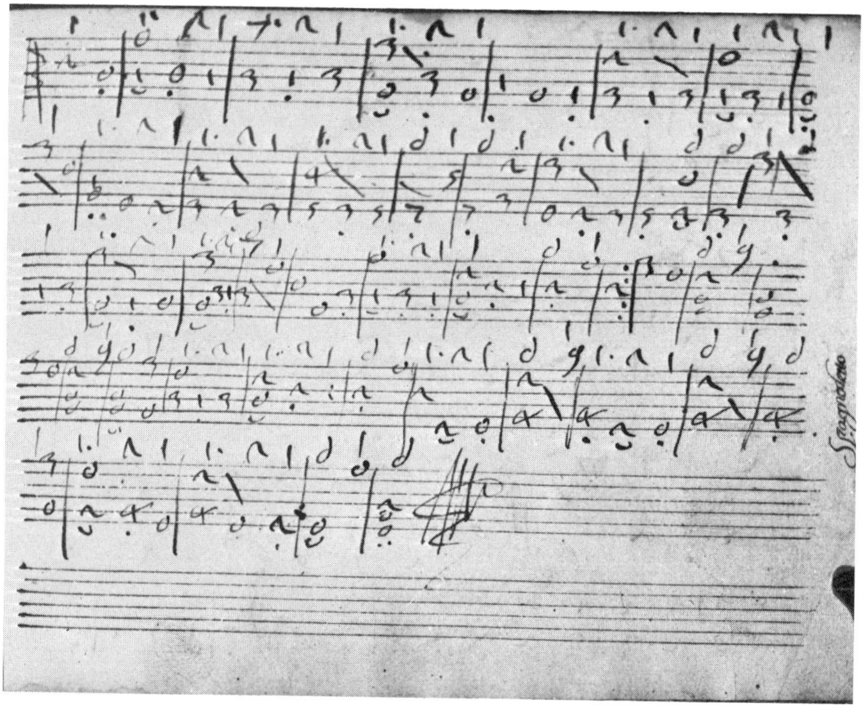

PLATE III. Page 59 of the De Bellis Lute Tablature.

hands responsible for the titles do not always conform to the changes in the hands responsible for the music. At least some of the titles were certainly entered after the music was written out, since they are crowded into the margin or at the bottom of the page.

The tablature was probably intended not as a presentation copy for some person of consequence, but rather for the use of a practical musician. This is suggested not only by the inelegant appearance of the source, but also by the extensive and practical inclusion of lute fingerings.

The manuscript is notated in the basically conventional system of Italian lute tablature. A six-line "staff" represents the six normal courses of the lute, which are tuned at the intervallic distances of a fourth, a fourth, a major third, a fourth, and again a fourth. But, in addition, some pieces call for extra bass courses, so that the repertoire as a whole requires a multi-course instrument—perhaps a theorbo or chittarone rather than a lute in the more specific sense (see No. 48

in the thematic index). In keeping with the Italian method of having the figures that correspond to the high pitches written on the low lines of the "staff," and the figures that correspond to the low pitches on the upper lines, the signs calling for the use of the bass courses are written above the "staff." Rhythmic signs are also written above it. Barlines are consistently included, and are used in the conventional fashion. The fingerings mentioned earlier in this study consist of series of dots, three dots calling for the use of the third finger, four for the fourth finger, etc.

The manuscript includes about eighty compositions and one page (which contains No. 48, mentioned above) concerning lute tuning. The contents are listed in the following index.

THEMATIC INDEX

No.	*Page*	*Title*
1	17	No title.

2	18–19	Corente deta la vitale.

3	20	Aria del gr: ducha di toschana in dialogo.

4	21	Galiarda del Sig. Conte Fabio Visconti.

No. *Page* *Title*

5 22 Romanescha.

6 23 Corente in semitone.

7 23 No title.

8 24 Baletto in soprano di gcc.

9 25 Corente in basso.

10 26–27 Galiarda detta la mezza pace.

No.	*Page*	*Title*
11	28–29	No title.

12	30–31	Pevanilia in soprano.

13	32–33	Matacino in tenore.

14	34–35	Corente in soprano.

15	36–37	Galiarda del re de franzza.

*Bass of this measure is defective in source.

16	38	Passo e mezzo in tenore per bemolle.

No.	*Page*	*Title*
17	39	Corente in basso.

18	40–41	Corente in semitone.

19	42	No title.

20a	43	Passo e mezzo in soprano.

20b	44	Parte seconda in tripolla.

21	45	Piva in soprano.

(See the erratum at the end of this Index.)

No.	*Page*	*Title*
22	47	Gagliarda in tenore.

23	48–49	Repeggiata in soprano.

24	49	Corente in soprano.

25	50	No title.

26	51	No title.

27	52–53	No title.

No.	*Page*	*Title*
28	54	Galiarda dele cinque mentitte.

29	55	Alemana in soprano baletto.

30	56	Baletto Franse.

31	57	Baletto Franse.

32	57	Baletto Franse.

33	58	Sarabanda Fransa.

No. *Page* *Title*

34 58 Sarabanda Fran[sa].

35 59 Spagnoletto.

36 60–61 Ballo Gagliarda.

37 62 Ballo detto del Distolese.

38 63 Marinetta.

39 63 Corrente della Berggera.

No.	*Page*	*Title*
40	64	Sogno della Regina di Francia.

No.	*Page*	*Title*
41a	65	Aria del Prencipe Tomaso.

No.	*Page*	*Title*
41b	65	Aria del Prencipe Tomaso (possibly part 2 of above).

No.	*Page*	*Title*
42	66–67	Corrente di Gilidasso.

No.	*Page*	*Title*
43	67	Sarabanda Fran[sa].

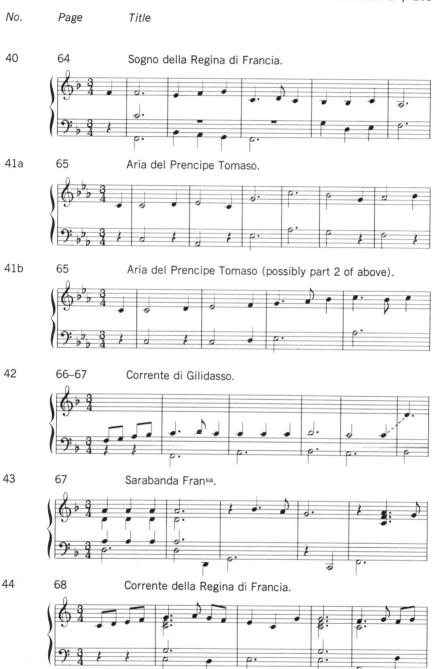

No.	*Page*	*Title*
44	68	Corrente della Regina di Francia.

No.	Page	Title
45	69	Và pur superba và.

No.	Page	Title
46	69–70	Ballo de Cavalli.

No.	Page	Title
47	70	Montannara.

No.	Page	Title
48	71	Regola d'accordare il Leutto.

This page contains directions for the tuning of a 13-course instrument. The tuning of the bass courses indicated in the directions is:

No.	Page	Title
49a	72	Passo e mezo in soprano.

No.	Page	Title
49b	73	Seconda parte.

No. *Page* *Title*

50 74 Galiarda.

51 74 Baletto in soprano.

52 75 Passo e mezzo in tenore.

53 76–77 Pavaniglia.

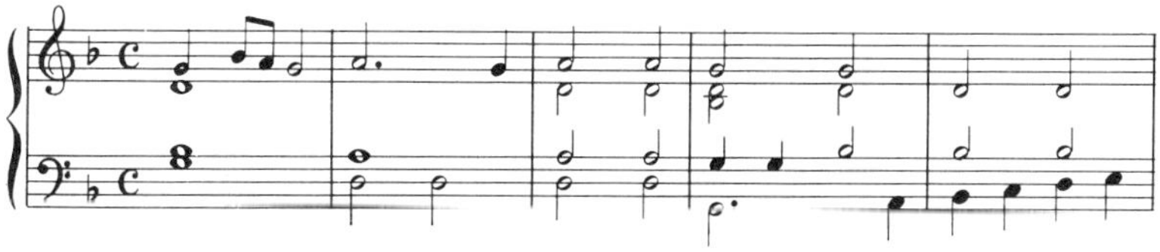

54 77 Corente.

55 77 Ballo da Colla.

No. *Page* *Title*

56 78 Passo e mezzo in soprano.

57 79 Gagliarda.

58 80 Corente.

59 80 Corente.

60 81 Aria del gran Duca in Tenore.

61 82 Passo e mezo in sop.º per B. M. parte pª.

No.	*Page*	*Title*
62	83	Spagnoletta in sop.º

63	83	Spagnoletta in Basso.

64	84	Saltarello in sop.º per B. q.

65	84	La sua represa con la zoppa.

66	85	Vilan. di spagna.

67	85	Bergamasca.

No. *Page* *Title*

68 86 Ruggiero.

69 87 Ruggiero in trippola.

70 88 Sarabanda Francesa.

71 89 Altra Sarabanda.

72 90 Aria Millanesa.

73 90 Aria della girometta.

No.	*Page*	*Title*
74	91	Pavaniglia in sop.no

75	91	In Basso.

76	92	Pavaniglia in trippola.

77	93	Sarabanda Fransa.

78	93	Sarabanda Fransa.

79	94	Corrente Fransa.

No. *Page* *Title*

80 95 Gian de nivello.

81 95 Aria Frans.[a]

Erratum: Between Nos. 21 and 22 in the above list, there is, on p. 46, a short, untitled piece. The top part begins c^2, b^1-flat, a^1, f^1, bar, g^1, a^1, b^1-flat, e^1, a^1, g^1, e^1, bar, all eighth-notes except Nos. 1 and 3 (dotted quarters) and 9 (quarter). The bottom part begins F, c, f, G, F, c, f, F, bar, dotted-quarter rest, G, F, c, bar, all notes being eighths, except the last, which is a quarter.

A thorough discussion of the contents of the San Francisco tablature is beyond the scope of the present article, in which it will be possible to consider only a few aspects of the collection. As the Thematic Index shows, the repertoire consists largely of dance pieces and of compositions based on the numerous "stock" formulas of the period. One unusual feature of the dance repertoire is the inclusion of a piece entitled *Piva in soprano* (No. 21 in the Thematic Index). As is well known, the *piva* was a popular dance form of the early sixteenth century, but one hitherto believed to have disappeared from the repertoire about the middle of the century.[7] The composition in our tablature retains some of the stylistic features of the earlier repertoire—compound meter and a drone-like bass reminiscent of the original meaning of *piva* (= bagpipe).

Another interesting feature of the repertoire is the inclusion of no fewer than four pieces designated *pavaniglia* (or a variant thereof; see Nos. 12, 53, 74, and 76 in the Thematic Index; the last of these is presented in full in the Appendix). Diana Poulton has pointed out

7. See the article by L. Moe in *Die Musik in Geschichte und Gegenwart,* IX, cols. 1315 ff. The latest listing of a *piva* in Howard M. Brown, *Instrumental Music Printed Before 1600* (Cambridge, 1965) is in 1564^8, a collection by Vincenzo Ruffo.

in her helpful article, "Notes on the Spanish Pavan," that "a number of pieces called 'Pavaniglia,' though bearing a certain family likeness [to the Spanish Pavan] . . . , are not, in fact, identical" with it.[8] The four pieces just referred to, however, all contain characteristics of the standard Spanish Pavan which, as it happens, Cabezón, although himself a Spaniard, called "Pavana Italiana." Example 1 gives the first six measures of one of his two pieces bearing that title.[9] By

EX. 1. Cabezón, "Pavana Italiana."

comparing the incipits in the Thematic Index with this example, one can easily see the relation between the basses of our four pieces, or between both their bass and superius parts, and the work of Cabezón.

Besides the four pieces having the designation *pavaniglia* in the de Bellis tablature, another, as has been pointed out to me by Professor John Ward (who has likewise studied the source), should probably be included in the same category. This is No. 75, *In Basso.* The tune is missing, but the harmonic pattern is present. Example 2, which has very kindly been provided by Professor Ward, gives the

8. *Lute Society Journal,* III (1961), 6. Miss Poulton tries to show that "pavaniglia" was, strictly speaking, the name of a dance and that the term "Spanish Pavan" "was reserved almost exclusively for recognizable versions of the original tune." However, she may well be imputing more orderliness to the users of the nomenclature than they actually applied. Professor John Ward has called my attention to a passage on p. 55 of Fuhrmann's *Testudo Gallo-Germanica* (1615) that illustrates strikingly the free and easy manner in which terminology such as that under discussion was used: "The 'Pavana Spagnolet 1' [in the *Testudo*] is a setting of the 'Spagnoletta,' and the 'Pavana Spagnolet 2' is a setting of the 'Spanish Pavan.' "

9. For the complete piece see Higinio Anglès, ed., *Antonio de Cabezón . . . Obras de Música . . .*, III, Monumentos de la música española, XXIX, 53, or M. S. Kastner, ed., *Antonio de Cabezón, Claviermusik* (Edition Schott 4286), pp. 4 ff, or Felipe Pedrell, ed., *Hispaniae schola musica sacra,* VII, 73. Cabezón's other composition entitled *Pavana Italiana* is printed in Anglès, *Cabezón,* III, 63; Willi Apel, *Masters of the Keyboard* (Cambridge, 1947), pp. 46 ff; Pedrell, *Hispaniae,* VIII, 6. Although both compositions have the *folia* pattern in the bass, they are constructed on different melodies, the one underlying the second piece being the tune that is found in the charming *Belle qui tient ma vie,* included by Arbeau in his *Orchésographie* (cf. Apel, *Masters of the Keyboard,* p. 45, *n.* 17). Further regarding the Spanish Pavan, see Claude M. Simpson, *The British Broadside Ballad and Its Music* (New Brunswick, 1966), pp. 678 ff; John Ward, "Apropos *The British Broadside Ballad and its Music,*" *Journal, American Musicological Society,* XX (1967), 75.

first seven measures of *In Basso* together with the parallel measures of four Spanish Pavan settings.

On page 6 of her article, Miss Poulton calls attention to the

EX. 2.

De Bellis MS., "In Basso."

Francisque, *Trésor,* "Pavane Espagnolle."

John Bull, "The Spanish Pavan."

Thysius MS., fol. 140: "Pavane d'Espaigne."

Alfonsus [Ferrabosco], "The treble to the Spanish Pavan."

The same, "The ground to the treble."

variety and freedom of treatment with which composers handled the Spanish Pavan; such treatment is found in each of the five compositions just discussed. The San Francisco tablature is an important addition to the comprehensive list of "Sources of the Spanish Pavan so far traced" given by Miss Poulton on pages 9 ff. of her essay.

At the 1941 annual meeting of the American Musicological Society, Professor Dragan Plamenac read a paper entitled "An Unknown Violin Tablature of the Early 17th Century."[10] Among the pieces contained in the source mentioned in the title, a manuscript at Zagreb, are examples based on the *Spagnoletta, Bergamasca, Passamezzo,* and *Ruggiero* formulas. In view of the special circumstances for which the present report is written, it would seem especially appropriate to include a few comments on the compositions that are written on the same formulas and that appear in the San Francisco tablature.

Professor Plamenac, on the basis of the violin tablature he was discussing, and of Coferati's *Corona di Sacre Canzoni* (1575, 1589), reconstructed the Spagnoletta tune as presented in Example 3.[11] The

EX. 3. "Spagnoletta."

*Repetition optional; cf. Praetorius, *Terpsichore* No. 28.

three compositions designated *spagnoletta* or *spagnoletto* in our MS. (Nos. 35, 62, and 63) are all based on this reconstructed tune. No. 35 is given complete in the Appendix.

No. 67 consists of variations over the *Bergamasca* ground—GCDG—which is here simply transposed. No. 13, *Matacino in tenore,*

10. Printed in *Papers of the American Musicological Society, 1941* (New York, 1946), pp. 144 ff.

11. *Ibid.*, p. 155. To the examples of the *spagnoletta* mentioned by him in 1941 Professor Plamenac would undoubtedly wish to add (besides those in the de Bellis tablature) *The Old Spagnoletta* by Giles Farnaby (*The Fitzwilliam Virginal Book*, ed. J. A. Fuller Maitland and W. Barclay Squire, II [Leipzig, 1899], 471).

consists of a longer set of variations over the same ground. The term "matacino" is the Italian equivalent of "mattachins," one of the names of a sword dance of the type described by Arbeau near the end of his *Orchésographie.*[12] This dance often makes use of the *Bergamasca* bass pattern—though not always throughout[13]—as does No. 13.

The six pieces in our tablature whose titles indicate that they are *passamezzi* are equally divided between examples of the *passamezzo antico* (Nos. 16, 52, and 61) and the *passamezzo moderno* (Nos. 20, 49, and 56). No. 16 is much more faithful to the harmonies of the formula than are the other pieces, which make use of embellishing harmonies in a way that is not uncommon among contemporaneous treatments of both formulas.

Of the two settings of the *Ruggiero* formula, No. 69 has a bass that is close to the fifth variant given in John Ward's article, "Ruggiero," in *Die Musik in Geschichte und Gegenwart.*[14] The top part, decorated to produce the ternary figures referred to in the title, *Ruggiero in trippola,* is still close to Ward's second melody variant.[15] The other setting, No. 68, provides evidence in support of Claude Palisca's observation that "while the *arie di Romanesca* and *Ruggiero* must have been discant formulas, this did not prevent composers from writing pieces on the harmonic patterns derived from them and ignoring the melodies themselves."[16] In this setting, to be sure, fragments of the melodic patterns may be found in the superius and middle parts, but the principal constructive element is found in the bass, which outlines the fundamental harmonic pattern of the *Ruggiero* formula.

The *Aria del Gran Duca,* which underlies Nos. 3 and 60, is also the basis of a composition by Santino Garsi da Parma in the Dusiacki Lute Book,[17] and of a set of variations by Sweelinck.[18]

12. Beginning on fol. 97v of the 1596 edition (p. 153 of the Beaumont translation; p. 182 of the Evans translation in the Sutton edition).

13. I am indebted to Professor Ward for this information.

14. Vol. IX, col. 1086.

15. *Ibid.*

16. Claude V. Palisca, "Vincenzo Galilei and Some Links Between 'Pseudo-Monody' and Monody," *Musical Quarterly,* XLVI (1960) 350.

17. Printed in Helmuth Osthoff, *Der Lautenist Santino Garsi da Parma* (Leipzig, 1926), p. 162.

18. Printed in Max Seiffert, ed., *Werken van Jan Pieterszoon Sweelinck,* I (2d ed.; Amsterdam, 1943), 237.

No. 10 provides a third Italian version for lute of material contained in the piece entitled *Balletto di me Donino Garsi, fatto per il S. Duca di Mantua* in the Dusiacki manuscript,[19] and *Pezzo italiano* in the lute manuscript that belonged to Oscar Chilesotti when he published its contents in 1890,[20] but which seems now to be lost. No. 57 in the de Bellis tablature, which is clearly related to No. 10, as was pointed out to me by Mr. Joel Cohen, may be considered a fourth Italian version of this material for lute. Brian Richardson has called attention[21] to the fact that the Dusiacki version and the one transcribed by Chilesotti are closely related to the piece by Dowland that is preserved under the varying titles *My Lady Hunsdon's Puffe* and *My Lady Hunsdon's Allmande* in four English sources.[22] Richardson goes so far as to regard the Dusiacki and Chilesotti versions as being paraphrases of the work by Dowland. Mr. Cohen, however, who points out that Campion's *Fair, if you expect admiring*[23] belongs to the same family, asks whether the European versions of the tune may not antedate those of both Dowland and Campion, and if the two Englishmen may not simply have helped themselves to an already existing popular melody.

The *alemana* that constitutes No. 29 in the de Bellis MS. turns out to be another setting of the widely disseminated tune known as *Une jeune fillette* and by a variety of other titles—*Aria della Monaca, The Queen's Almaine, Almand Nonette, Ich ging einmal spazieren, Von Gott will ich nicht lassen,* etc.[23a] The full text of *Une jeune fillette* was published in 1557, and a sacred text, *Une jeune Pucelle,*

19. Osthoff, *Santino Garsi,* p. 171.

20. In *Da un codice Lautenbuch* (Leipzig), p. 78.

21. In "New Light on Dowland's Continental Movements," *Monthly Musical Record,* XC (1960), 3 ff.

22. The composition is printed in David Lumsden, *An Anthology of English Lute Music* (London, 1954), p. 29. A facsimile of it, as it appears in the manuscript in the Folger Library that is believed to be in Dowland's handwriting, is printed in G. Reese, *Music in the Renaissance* (New York, 1954), opposite p. 846.

23. Printed by Edmund H. Fellowes, ed., *The English School of Lutenist Song Writers,* Series I, XIII (1924), 40.

23a. See John Ward, "Music for A Handeful of Pleasant Delites," *Journal, American Musicological Society,* X (1957), 175, *n.* 85. A lute setting by Terzi, under the title *Ballo Tedesco, et Francese,* and another setting by Besard, under the title *Allemande "Une jeune fille"* are printed in Chilesotti, *Lautenspieler des 16. Jahrhunderts* (Leipzig, 1891), pp. 116, 200. The Besard example is taken from his *Thesaurus harmonicus* (1603), which contains still another setting of the tune, as does his *Novus partus* of 1617. For details, see Julia Sutton, "J. B. Besard's Novus partus, 1617" (diss., Eastman School of Music, 1962), p. 166. See also Simpson, *British Broadside Ballad,* pp. 590 f; Ward, "Apropos *The British Broadside Ballad,*" pp. 66 f.

that may have been sung to the same tune, appeared in 1520.[24]

No. 46 incorporates the tune that Giles Farnaby treats in *The New Sa-Hoo*,[25] and upon which Sweelinck and Scheidt each wrote a set of variations for keyboard under the title *Est-ce Mars*.[26] The tune has been known also in England as *Slaves to the world should be toss'd in a blanket;* in the Low Countries as *Geluckig is hy die leert sterven* (in the *Gedenckclanck* of Valerius), as *Wie gaat mee, gaat mee over zee,* as the *Van Arteveldlied,* and as *Isser ijemant uijt Oost-Indien gekomen;* and in Germany as *Lustig seid ihr, lieben Brüder* and *Ehrlich, freundlich und schön dabei.* Nicolas Vallet reworked the melody for four lutes, and Nikolaus Bleyer wrote variations on it for viol and continuo.[27]

The tune of No. 73, entitled *Aria della girometta,* has been described by Professor Palisca as "one of the most popular melodies in the late sixteenth and early seventeenth centuries."[28] Our example is squarely based on the apparently standard version of the tune.[29] Another favorite tune, used, for example, by Praetorius as *La Bouree*,[30] provides the basis for No. 80.

No. 43 incorporates the same tune as does the tenth of the twelve *courantes* in the *Courante de la Reyne* in Ballard's *Premier livre* of 1611.[31]

No. 19, which has no title in the source, is an "echo" piece, and echo effects are marked as such in the manuscript. This would seem to make the piece a rarity in the lute repertoire. No. 23 is a kind of *moto perpetuo* étude.

Even without discussion of additional types represented in the

24. Sutton, "Besard's Novus partus," p. 166.

25. *The Fitzwilliam Virginal Book,* II, 161.

26. *Werken van . . . Sweelinck,* I, 211; Christhard Mahrenholz, ed. *Samuel Scheidt: Werke,* VI, (Hamburg, 1953), 93.

27. For details concerning these titles and versions, see Bernard van den Sigtenhorst Meyer, *Jan P. Sweelinck en zijn instrumentale muziek,* (2d ed.; The Hague, 1946), pp. 181 ff; *Werken van . . . Sweelinck,* I, p. lxi; Max Seiffert, "J. P. Sweelinck und seine direkten deutschen Schüler," *Vierteljahrsschrift für Musikwissenschaft,* VII (1891), 202 f.

28. Palisca, *loc. cit.,* p. 355.

29. Printed by Palisca, *ibid.,* p. 351.

30. *Gesamtausgabe der musikalischen Werke von Michael Praetorius,* XV (1929; this vol. ed. by Günther Oberst), 41.

31. *Cf.* the edition of André Souris and Sylvie Spycket (Paris, 1963), pp. 57 ff. See also the relevant entry in Monique Rollin's *Étude des concordances, ibid.,* p. xviii.

tablature, it should, we hope, be apparent that the San Francisco MS. is in most respects a typical Italian lute-book of its time, containing as it does a repertoire of dances and other pieces, many of which are based on the "stock" patterns that the Baroque inherited from the Renaissance.

NO. 35. SPAGNOLETTO, P. 59.

NO. 76. PAVANIGLIA IN TRIPOLLA, P. 92.

18 / Cherubini's *Médée* and the Spirit of French Revolutionary Opera

ALEXANDER L. RINGER
University of Illinois

IN THE spring of 1786 Luigi Cherubini, who had made his way to London two years earlier, suffered his first real operatic defeat. As Charles Burney so graphically put it, his *Giulio Sabino* was "murdered in its birth for want of the necessary support of capital singers in the principal parts."[1] Understandably disappointed, the twenty-six-year-old composer resolved to leave London at least temporarily for the promise and challenge of Paris, the operatic capital of eighteenth-century Europe. Although he had enjoyed the personal interest of the Prince of Wales virtually since his arrival, he departed with few regrets. For his original high hopes engendered by a number of earlier operatic successes in his native Italy had gradually given way to the frustrations and despair of "a young man of genius, who had no opportunity while he was here of displaying his abilities."[2]

A previous trip to Paris in the summer of 1785 had led to friendly relations with Viotti, who introduced him at Court and promoted his music at the *concerts spirituels*. Later, when Viotti became musical director of the Théâtre de Monsieur, the Italian repertory house founded by Marie-Antoinette's coiffeur, Cherubini joined his staff and quickly gained recognition as a composer of *arie aggiunte* for the popular works of Paisiello, Cimarosa, Anfossi, and countless others.

1. Charles Burney, *A General History of Music*, II, (London, 1776–1789), 899.
2. *Ibid.*

But in 1786, even though he had been commissioned to write a cantata for the Loge Olympique and had been generally well received in artistic circles, the ambitious young man, still stymied in his bid for operatic honors, decided to try his luck once more in London. Inevitably, viewed from London Bridge, Paris regained much of its attraction. By the end of spring 1787, Cherubini's mind was made up. Taking to heart Viotti's urgent advice, he put an end to his peregrinations and settled in France for good.

Soon thereafter, he composed his last *opera seria*, an *Ifigenia in Aulide* that reflects the budding influence of Gluck, even though it appears in the traditional Italian garb. The success of its first performances in Turin early in 1788, under Cherubini's personal direction, led to a string of Italian productions. Still, the composer was eager to get back to Paris where conditions had drastically changed since the days, not so long before, when the Piccinnists had almost succeeded in hissing Gluck's *Alceste* off the stage. The once hotly debated Gluck-Piccinni feud was certainly no longer a living issue, if only because the crushing Gluckist victory had left little room for artistic dissenters. When the Gluck-follower Sacchini died, shortly after Cherubini's arrival in 1786, it was Piccinni who wrote a eulogy in which he praised "the richness of his accompaniments" and "his well-wrought choruses."[3] Within less than a year, Gluck himself passed away in distant Vienna, and this time Piccinni went out of his way to secure financial support from the Parisian aristocracy for an annual memorial concert of works by "the man to whom your lyrical theater owes as much as the French stage to the great Corneille."[4] Piccinni's generous effort came to nought, but it typifies the French musical atmosphere of the late 1780's.

That the newcomer Cherubini proved able to adjust as rapidly as he did was by no means the result of some sinister, chameleon-like capacity for change in accordance with the requirements of any given situation. On the contrary, it was in Paris that he encountered for the first time musico-dramatic conditions ideally suited to his peculiar talent, training, and esthetic outlook. Back home in Italy, the intricacies of his "learned" style had often baffled singers and

3. Cf. P. L. Ginguené, *Notice sur la vie et les ouvrages de Nicolas Piccinni* (Paris, an IX [1801]), pp. 132–33.
4. *Ibid.*, p. 134.

large segments of the public alike. Indeed, his best early work had been in church music, and it was hardly by accident that his father apprenticed him to Giuseppe Sarti, a composer renowned for his contrapuntal skill. An early concern with prosody and textual expression, too, predestined him for the kind of compositional procedures expected of anyone staking his claim on the French operatic stage in the wake of the Italian debacle.[5]

Thus it was with some confidence that Cherubini made his first French bid with Marmontel's *Démophon* on December 5, 1788. But this *tragédie lyrique,* though ostensibly in the classical tradition of Gluck, literally seethed with the passions that animated the emotionally supercharged period immediately preceding the storming of the Bastille. The conservative audiences of the Royal Academy were utterly perplexed by what they heard and saw, and Cherubini's remarkable if somewhat premature work, one of the very first to apply symphonic development techniques to large-scale operatic scenes, failed to survive more than a few only moderately successful performances.[6]

Although Cherubini's was not the only *Démophon* to see completion in 1788 employing a different libretto, Johann Christoph Vogel, a young Gluckist from Nuremberg who had come to Paris a dozen years earlier, composed an opera by the same title just before his untimely death at the age of thirty-two. It was staged posthumously the following year.[7] As far as chromatic harmonies, sudden dynamic contrasts and novel orchestral effects were concerned, few eighteenth-century works, if any, anticipated the musical ideals of the Revolution more directly. Vogel's masterpiece, too, failed to

5. For a translation of Cherubini's rules for vocal settings, first noted by Pougin, see Margery Stomne Selden, "Cherubini, the Italian 'Image,'" *Journal, American Musicological Society,* XVII (1964), 381.

6. The stylistic innovations of this work have recently been examined by Georg Knepler in "Die Technik der sinfonischen Durchführung in der französischen Revolutionsoper," *Beiträge zur Musikwissenschaft,* I (1959), 4–22. Unfortunately, Knepler singles out Cherubini's opera without regard for the contemporaneous compositions of men like Vogel, whose contributions deserve more thorough examination than is possible here if historical truth is to be served. Cf. also Georg Knepler, *Die Musik des 19. Jahrhunderts,* I (Berlin, 1961), 144–59.

7. Roger Cotte, in *Die Musik in Geschichte und Gegenwart,* II, col. 1171, perpetuates the confusion with regard to the two *Démophons,* originated by Fétis more than a century ago. Vogel did not use the Marmontel libretto but remained faithful to his earlier collaborator, P. Desriaux. As for the myth that Vogel died before he could complete his opera, even Fétis says no such thing.

hold the stage, but its somber overture in F minor, first given at the Loge Olympique early in 1789, remained a concert favorite throughout the Revolutionary decade. In 1791 it was selected for performance by a band of 1200 instruments (including a dozen tam-tams) at the Champ-de-Mars ceremonies honoring the victims of the Nancy massacre. The opera's dramatic qualities continued to attract attention for some time. E. T. A. Hoffmann called it "a truly magnificent tragic opera,"[8] and G. L. P. Sievers, the Paris correspondent of the *Allgemeine Musikalische Zeitung*, referred to Vogel as "that young giant, who demonstrated in his last work (*La Toison d'Or* remained unfinished) what a colossal strength he would have developed had he been able to reach full maturity."[9] Even Berlioz, who devoted a whole article to Vogel and his operas, had words of praise for *Démophon.*[10]

Sievers' belief to the contrary, *La Toison d'Or*, better known as *Médée à Colchos*, was completed and staged two full years before *Démophon*. As Berlioz was quick to perceive, in this, his first dramatic attempt, Vogel had taken his cues directly from Gluck's two *Iphigénies*. That aging master, the "legislator of music," to whom the printed score is respectfully dedicated, appears to have been duly impressed,[11] even though his youthful disciple showed notably little regard for his classic injunction against novelty of invention "not naturally suggested by the situation and the expression."[12] Vogel favored minor keys regardless of whether or not a number began and ended in major; he treated the diminished seventh chord as an idiomatic fixture and elevated chromaticism to well-nigh leitmotivic importance. Above all, he managed to generate a rhythmic restlessness that points directly to the *élan terrible* of Revolutionary opera.[13] In short, like his subsequent *Démophon*, his Medea score bears all the earmarks of a post-Gluckian rather than a

8. E. T. A. Hoffmann, *Betrachtungen über Musik*, ed. Walter Florian (Stuttgart, 1947), p. 86.

9. G. L. P. Sievers, "Bemerkungen veranlasst durch die Schrift: Über Reinheit der Tonkunst," *Caecilia*, IX (1828), 18.

10. H. Berlioz, "Vogel et ses opéras," *Revue et Gazette Musicale*, V (1838), 465.

11. Alfred Loewenberg, *Annals of Opera* (2d ed.; Geneva, 1955), I, 431.

12. Cf. Gluck's preface to *Alceste* (1769), translated in Alfred Einstein, *Gluck* (London, 1936), p. 99.

13. The dedication of the score to a fellow composer, instead of to some high-ranking patron, anticipates the fraternal ideals of the Revolution. Similarly, in referring to Gluck as a "legislator," Vogel identified himself with a favorite Revolutionary theme.

Gluckist work; and this may account at least in part for its lack of success at the very time when the ideals of Gluck found such faithful expression in Sacchini's *Oedipe à Colone* or, for that matter, in Lemoyne's *Phèdre*.

French opera has always been an extraordinarily sensitive reflection of socio-cultural problems and attitudes. Lully is often cited as a case in point. In the light of subsequent events, the successive crises that periodically upset French operatic life in the eighteenth century stand out as a series of landmarks, symptomatic convulsions, as it were, in the continuous and organic process of sociological regeneration that reached its dramatic apogee with the fall of the *ancien régime* in 1789. D'Alembert observed as early as 1760 that there were people in France who saw a dangerous republican behind every adherent of *opera buffa*.[14] Fourteen years later, none other than Gluck found it necessary to remind the new king, Louis XVI, that "when Augustus, the Medici, and Louis XIV emulated the example of the Greeks by welcoming and furthering the arts, they did so in the interest of matters more important than to add to the forms of pleasure and entertainment; they considered this branch of human knowledge one of the most precious links in the chain of politics." These words, it may be worth noting, appear in the dedicatory preface to his *Iphigénie en Aulide*, the very work which according to Grimm converted Rousseau, once the most eloquent spokesman of the buffoon party, to the Gluckist cause.[15]

The political leaders of the Revolution, practical-minded disciples of Plato as well as of Rousseau, logically enough decreed the cultivation of opera à la Gluck as an infallible means of large-scale public education. Except for this officially sanctioned Gluck cult, however, classical subject matter virtually vanished from the French operatic stage during the Revolutionary decade. The freedom of the stage, proclaimed in 1790, favored countless theatrical entrepreneurs ill equipped artistically or, for that matter, financially to cope with the demands of serious opera. Such men readily catered to the ever growing quest for popular shows in which the circus element often

14. Cf. Romain Rolland, *Musiciens d'autrefois* (3d rev. ed.; Paris, 1912), p. 213.
15. F. W. von Grimm, *Correspondance littéraire*, VIII, 321, quoted by Lionel de la Laurencie in Lavignac, *Encyclopédie de la musique et dictionnaire du Conservatoire, première partie* (Paris, 1931), p. 1437.

outweighed the feeble remnants of operatic tradition. Then, too, increasingly large segments of the established repertory fell victim to a merciless censorship that regarded most pre-revolutionary librettos as subversive by definition. Fortunately, a handful of younger composers, foremost among them Cherubini and his friend Méhul, managed both to preserve their artistic integrity and to uphold the much advertised Platonic ideal of music as a character-building force. But, instead of continuing to rely on the heroic lore of antiquity, they drew inspiration from the daily acts of personal courage and civic devotion that were far more typical of French society in the clutches of total war than the isolated examples of selfishness and injustice, so highly publicized abroad. Their "bandit" operas extolled the basic virtues of men whom a viciously ruled society had forced to live as outlaws, and their "rescue" plots offered up-to-date versions of the classic *deus-ex-machina* ending, replacing supernatural intervention with a last-minute act of justice on the part of some incorruptible human being, preferably an official of the state.[16]

Meanwhile, the image of antiquity did inspire a rapidly growing number of monumental public ceremonies, until the whole Revolution struck at least one facetious observer as "a lyrical drama, text by M. J. Chénier, music by Gossec, décor by David."[17] The painter David, under whose general direction these elaborate outdoor rituals were staged, enlisted the services of virtually every prominent composer in Paris, with the result that new techniques and procedures prompted originally by the sonorous potential of massed choirs and wind bands soon affected all of music. Hence the unprecedented importance and novel treatment of the chorus in Revolutionary opera; hence, too, the conspicuous growth and changing role of the orchestra. Captain Sarrette, the founder of the National Guard band and its Institute of Music (later the Conservatoire), eventually issued the official slogan: "Let us revolutionize opera." And the same musicians who had sworn eternal allegiance to Gluck responded

16. For a recent summary of the musico-dramatic characteristics of this particular genre, see R. Morgan Longyear, "Notes on the Rescue Opera," *Musical Quarterly*, XLV (1959), 49–66. A comprehensive study has been published by György Kroó, *A "szabadito" opera* (Budapest, 1966).

17. See Henri Radiguier, "La musique française de 1789 à 1815," in Lavignac, *Encyclopédie*, p. 1562.

enthusiastically with a style that made the most of wide melodic skips, obsessive repetitions of a single motif, irregular metrical patterns, and startling juxtapositions of but distantly related chords. The violent temper that dominated the operatic stage even before the apocalyptic final days of the Terror is exemplified by Jean-François Lesueur's first dramatic work, the bandit opera *La Caverne* presented at the Théâtre Feydeau in 1793. After reaching an unprecedented climax of sustained violence, with the sound and fury of the worst massacre ever to shock a theater audience, this monument to Revolutionary realism ends with a huge chorus glorifying virtue as the one and only goal of human existence.

The Royal Academy, laboring under the weight of time-honored tradition, found it understandably difficult to adjust to this "new look" in opera. The Academy's artistic prestige soon reached an all-time low, as did its attendance once the royalist activities carried on within its walls became public knowledge. Fortunately, the composers of the Revolution could count on two excellent progressive houses, the Feydeau and its principal competitor, the Théâtre Favart. The Feydeau was actually the renamed Théâtre de Monsieur where Cherubini had previously served as an important supplier of added numbers. The house had been moved from the Tuileries to the Rue Feydeau, and now produced the very best in Revolutionary *opéra-comique.* And it was here that Cherubini made his triumphant debut in July 1791 with a rescue opera, *Lodoïska,* which turned him into a hero of the Revolution virtually overnight. Unlike Méhul, however, Cherubini cared little for politics or social philosophy. When the ensuing public power struggle threatened to disrupt his personal and artistic life, he quietly retreated to Rouen, where he courted his future wife and enjoyed life as a celebrity in provincial salons. As soon as things quieted down a bit, he slipped back into a Paris awaiting the fall of Robespierre, and prepared to reconquer his public with an even more spectacular spellbinder, *Élisa.* In much the same fashion he sat out the Thermidorean reaction, concentrating for a while on his official duties as a ceremonial composer in the service of the Republic and attending conscientiously to his assigned tasks as one of the five newly appointed national inspectors of music. Two and a half years were to pass before he came forth with his fourth French opera, his dramatic masterpiece, *Médée.*

As de Longepierre, the seventeenth-century author of a spoken *Médée,* once remarked, most people react rather negatively to Euripides' explosive story of the spurned foreign princess who did not shrink from murdering her own children in her frenzied search for revenge. The few composers who, like Cavalli in 1649, had dared take up the subject in the past, therefore, tended to favor Jason, the weak but handsome young warrior, while relegating Medea to the more or less stereotyped role of a sorceress. Cherubini, on the other hand, writing at the very crossroads of European history, resolved to treat this frightful tragedy as a cathartic object lesson of the fateful truth that pain and frustration, unjustly suffered, uncover the very worst in the soul of man. Like Euripides, Cherubini hated "the revenge of the oppressed almost as much as the original cruelty of the oppressor."[18] And so Medea, humiliated by a Greek prince who had been brought up with little regard for promises made to a barbarian, became the terrifying symbol of the raging *sans-culotte* taking cruel, senseless revenge on anyone and anything however remotely related to, or cherished by, the subject of his boundless hatred.

The newly risen bourgeoisie that dictated public taste in 1797 was completely unprepared for such a violent plea on behalf of non-violence. Addicted to moralizing pronouncements dripping with self-satisfaction, the *incroyables* and *merveilleuses,* the precious "golden youth" of the Directory, found Jason's unscrupulous desertion of his wife and children for Dircé, the daughter of Creon, ruler of Corinth, hardly less offensive than the heroine's inhuman final triumph. Incapable of sympathy with any major figure in the drama, they reacted with a typical sense of moral outrage at so much passion and bloodthirstiness, and thus missed the point entirely.

Cherubini's collaborator, the feuilletonist of the influential *Journal des débats,* F. B. Hoffman, who had previously served Méhul with some distinction, was certainly no Euripides. Even so, Fétis surely went too far when he condemned the libretto outright as "written in a ridiculous style."[19] For, if Hoffman lacked the power to develop all the possibilities of his story and admittedly produced some rather awkward lines, he succeeded nevertheless in tightening

18. *The Medea of Euripides,* trans. and ed. Gilbert Murray (New York, 1912), Introd., p. x.

19. F. J. Fétis, *Biographie universelle des musiciens,* II (2d ed.; Paris 1866), 266.

the plot by dropping the secondary figure of Aegeus while adding romantic interest in the person of Dircé, the unfortunate bride who does not appear in the original play at all. Facing a sophisticated audience nursed at the bosom of Reason, Hoffman actually had little choice except to produce what amounted in essence to a new version of the classical story. Playing down the traditional emphasis on sorcery and supernatural intervention, he focused on the rapid mental deterioration caused in a passionate human being by repeated acts of injustice, both real and imagined. At the end, the murderous heroine characteristically rushes into the flaming temple to perish at the side of her two lifeless children instead of prophesying the doom of Jason and Corinth from a chariot pulled aloft by winged dragons, as in Euripides or, for that matter, in Marc-Antoine Charpentier's opera of 1693. Forced to move within the framework of Revolutionary dialogue opera, Hoffman conceived *Médée* in the heroic manner of Gluck's *Armide,* a manner little appreciated by romantic audiences at the turn of the century. By the same token, his analytical concern with Medea as a thoroughly frustrated woman of great psychological complexity initiated a musico-dramatic genre that was to find historical fulfillment only a hundred years later in the cathartic stage works of Strauss, Schoenberg, and Alban Berg.

If Hoffman's valiant attempt to rehabilitate classical subject matter, following its virtual disappearance during and immediately after the Terror put a severe strain on his modest resources, Cherubini proved more than equal to the challenge. At the very height of his creative powers, and compassionately sensitive to human tragedy, he managed to bypass most of the obvious structural and emotional limitations of Revolutionary dialogue opera, imbuing it with a sense of dramatic continuity such as even Mozart had produced only once, in *Don Giovanni.* Whether or not Hoffman was altogether successful in evoking the spirit of classical tragedy, the atmosphere of inescapable doom and destruction suggested by the very first strains of the F minor overture haunts the listener long after the final D minor chords of the climactic holocaust have died away. Some purists have been critical of apparent stylistic inconsistencies in Cherubini's score.[20] And yet, its undeniable idiomatic variety is also one of its

20. A report on the Viennese performances of 1803 observes that "the music of the first act is entirely different from the rest." *Allgemeine Musikalische Zeitung,* V (1803), 354.

greatest assets. For, like Mozart, Cherubini makes musical distinctions between different characters and situations without impinging upon the essential unity of the whole.[21]

The Revolutionary era that plowed the virgin soil in which Beethoven's heroic art was soon to take root, and which conditioned so many aspects of nineteenth-century romanticism, drew freely upon its eighteenth-century heritage in music no less than in literature or philosophy. Cherubini, for his part, took full advantage of the stylistic opportunities inherent in his "transitional" position, turning to Italian *opera seria* specifically in those rare moments when passion takes a brief leave or attention shifts to conventional figures of exalted social rank. This is why Jason reminds ears familiar with *Don Giovanni* of Don Ottavio, and why Creon recalls the Commendatore. The possibility of any direct influence may be safely discounted, since Mozart's mature works were virtually unknown in France until well after the turn of the century. A mutilated version of *The Marriage of Figaro* with spoken dialogue from the original play of Beaumarchais had been presented briefly in 1793. But just then Cherubini was in Rouen, and it seems most unlikely that he would have taken the trouble, upon his return, to track down a manuscript copy of this poorly received work by a virtually forgotten Austrian composer. One rather suspects that the apparent stylistic affinities are the result of similarities in expressive intent on the part of two musical dramatists born only four years apart, each brought up on Italian opera and each conversant with the French classical style as transformed by Gluck. Both were, moreover, masters of the traditional counterpoint that Cherubini had studied with Giuseppe Sarti, the very composer whom Mozart honored with both a set of keyboard variations and a brief quotation in the dinner scene of *Don Giovanni.* The indebtedness of Mozart's patriarchal heroes—the Commendatore no less than Sarastro—to Gluck, the musical oracle of the Revolution, is of course well known. But in addition, the com-

21. Needless to say, Gluck had paved the way in this respect, too. As he wrote to du Roullet in the summer of 1776: "The public, indeed, will take as long to understand *Armide* as they did to understand *Alceste*. There is a kind of refinement in the former that is not in the latter; for I have managed to make the difference personages express themselves in such a way that you will be able to tell at once whether Armide or another is singing." Cf. H. and E. H. Mueller Von Asow, eds., *The Collected Correspondence and Papers of Christoph Willibald Gluck* (London, 1962).

poser of Beaumarchais and the rites of Freemasonry, who had a Spanish nobleman render a toast to the cause of freedom in the presence of members of the most diverse social classes clearly identified in turn by distinct types of dance music—this Mozart, whom Cherubini was to idolize in his later years, may well prove in the long run to have been a far more willing agent of "the revolution that was accomplished before it occurred" (in the words of Chateaubriand) than has usually been acknowledged.

In *Médée*, at any rate, the conventions of Italian opera have undergone drastic modification. For one, the orchestra never relinquishes its prominent role. Moreover, as the action unfolds, and as Medea becomes more and more the magnetic center of everything that happens, the last vestiges of *opera seria* yield to the powerful sweep of the new revolutionary style forged by the collective efforts of Méhul and Lesueur, as well as of Cherubini himself. The last act in particular combines aspects of the pathos of Méhul's *Stratonice* (1792) and *Mélidore et Phrosine* (1794) with the naked violence of Lesueur's *La Caverne*. Cherubini, to be sure, was careful not to succumb to the kind of hair-raising musico-dramatic antics exemplified by Lesueur's incredible finale. *Médée*, instead, incorporates some of the more viable structural and coloristic features of its predecessors. Such an influence, fully absorbed and put to genuinely new use, is found in the second-act duet between Jason and Medea, which owes much of its overpowering effect to the judicious exploitation of a persistent bass pattern. This essentially symphonic procedure, subsequently taken over by Beethoven with such singular success, had first been put to dramatic use by Méhul in the very similar "Gardez-vous de la jalousie" from *Euphrosine* (1790), a famous duet that was singled out by Berlioz as "the most formidable example of what the union of musical art and dramatic action can accomplish in the expression of human passion."[21a]

Cherubini's contemporaries were by no means unaware of what one critic called "reminiscences and imitation of Méhul's manner" in *Médée*.[22] Structural affinities of the type noted in the two duets are, of course, easily explained in general historical terms. A number of striking motivic parallels, on the other hand, pose a slightly different

21a. H. Berlioz, *Les soirées de l'orchestre* (Paris, 1854), p. 394.
22. Quoted in Arthur Pougin, *Méhul* (2d ed.; Paris, 1893), p. 138.

problem. The beginning of the overture, for example, bears a striking resemblance to the principal theme of Méhul's First Symphony in G minor. According to such knowledgeable scholars as Pougin and Brancour, the Méhul symphony was performed at the Théâtre Feydeau as early as in February 1797. If so, the charge of plagiarism is not easily dismissed. By the same token, one wonders whether Cherubini could have been either so cold-blooded or so naïve as to offer his overture to the very same audience that had heard its basic material only a few weeks previous in the work of a leading composer like Méhul. Actually, the best evidence available today suggests that Méhul wrote his symphony a full ten years later.[23] It was, therefore, not mere modesty but a characteristic sense of justice which caused Méhul to protest the indiscriminate charges of piracy leveled against his friend. "The inimitable author of *Démophon*, *Lodoïska*, *Elisé*, and *Médée*," he declared in reply to the critic's attack, "never required to imitate in order to be successively elegant or tender, graceful or tragic—to be, in a word, that Cherubini whom some few may accuse of imitating others, but whom they themselves will unfortunately not fail to imitate at the first opportunity."[24] Cherubini, deeply touched by his friend's gallant defense, if perhaps not entirely free of pangs of conscience, returned the compliment when he dedicated the printed score of *Médée* to him with these fraternal words: "Your name placed at the head of this work will lend it merit it did not possess—namely that of appearing worthy of dedication to you, and this will serve it as a support. May the union of our two names everywhere attest to the tender sentiments which bind us to each other, and the respect I entertain for real talent." Méhul promptly offered his next opera, *Ariodant*, to Cherubini with similar affirmations of friendship and respect. Both men were entirely sincere, realizing as they did that the stylistic revolution wrought in such an amazingly brief period of time was not so much the achievement of any single artistic mind as it was the collective product of a group of fully committed young composers.

In keeping with the "new look," *Médée* contains no more than five independent solo arias, sung successively by Dircé, Jason, Medea,

23. See Alexander L. Ringer, "A French Symphonist at the Time of Beethoven: Étienne Nicolas Méhul," *Musical Quarterly*, XXXVII (1951), 547–48.

24. Pougin, *loc. cit.*

Medea's nurse Neris, and once again by Medea. Characteristically, three of the five arias belong to Act I and hence precede the full maturation of Medea's hateful designs. There are other extended solo passages, of course. But instead of forming self-contained units, they all end as duets or ensemble pieces of some sort. A few, like Creon's first-act aria, turn into full-fledged choral scenes. On the whole, Cherubini favored the type of compound number that was to reach such prominence in early nineteenth-century German opera, beginning with Pizzarro's revenge aria in the first act of *Fidelio.* The latter, by the way, may have been written under the direct influence of *Médée.* For Beethoven, who by his own admission valued Cherubini's works "more than all others written for the stage," no doubt attended the Vienna performances of 1803 just as he was about to embark on his first and only operatic venture.

Dircé sings her aria at the conclusion of a carefully wrought scene in the course of which her ladies-in-waiting attempt to dispel their mistress' dark premonitions. This scene, cast in the form of strophic variations for solo and chorus, affords a first glimpse of the novel complementary role of the orchestra, which subsequently puts its characteristic stamp on the bridal march at the end of Act II, where the contrapuntally and antiphonally treated chorus is pitted against a large offstage band. The association of emotional with physical distance, though embryonically present in an occasional earlier example such as the ballroom scene in *Don Giovanni,* was clearly inspired by the gigantic outdoor ceremonies of the Revolution, just as the increased participation of the orchestra in vocal scenes owed much to the dilemma of composers who, when writing rather simply for masses of untrained singers, had to find some effective means of sustaining musical interest.

The beautiful aria in G minor sung by Neris in Act II deserves very special attention, not only because in it Medea's devoted nurse, the one person who truly loves her, expresses her suppressed fears with heart-rending pathos, but also because of its structurally pivotal position between two dramatically decisive ensemble pieces: the great trio with chorus, in the course of which Medea obtains the fatal day's delay in her banishment, and her duet with Jason, a last desperate attempt to win her husband back. Harmonically, too, Neris' aria marks the point of no return, since it provides the transition from the

E-flat major of the trio to the D minor of the duet, which is also the central tonality of the final act. Like Mozart, Cherubini employed D minor as the key of revenge.[25] Following its first appearance here in Act II, symbolic of Medea's true intentions while she feigns tenderness for her children in order to arouse Jason's pity, D minor returns with the powerful storm prelude that sets the general mood for Act III. Finally, after Medea has made the decision that seals the fate of her children, it dominates the proceedings all the way to their gruesome conclusion. Since the second act ends with a final return to the initial key of F minor, the opera as a whole divides harmonically into two balanced components, following an AAB or *Bar* pattern. The AA section in F minor stretches from the overture to the conclusion of the bridal march scene at the end of the second act; the mediant-related B section in D minor comprises the entire third act. In the eighteenth century, it should be remembered, the key of F minor was generally associated with "profound melancholy, funereal lament, lamentation, and longing for the grave."[26] Haydn had employed it in this fashion in the Quartet Op. 20, 5 and the Symphony No. 49, *La Passione*, and so had Benda in his melodrama *Medea*. In Vogel's *Démophon*, F minor, the key of the overture, returns dramatically near the middle of the second act, as the priests implore Mars with the characteristic words: "Have you not seen enough blood, enough graves?"

Symbolic conventions, so important in the matter of key, also explain the use of the solo bassoon in Neris' aria (Example 1). "The bassoon is somber and must be employed for pathetic passages," wrote Grétry in 1797, the year of *Médée*.[27] Benda, too, in his melodrama *Ariadne*, had used the bassoon in accordance with this precept (Example 2). The first aria in Vogel's *La Toison d'Or*, on the other hand, shares the key of G minor with Cherubini's number, as well as a similar pizzicato string accompaniment. Although the obbligato part is here assigned to an oboe instead of a bassoon, this striking

25. Cf. Eugen Schmitz, "Formgesetze in Mozarts 'Zauberflöte,'" *Festschrift Max Schneider* (Leipzig, 1955), p. 211.

26. Christian Friedrich Daniel Schubart, *Ideen zu einer Ästhetik der Tonkunst*, ed. Ludwig Schubart (Vienna, 1806), p. 378. Grétry, too, considered F minor "the most pathetic" key. M. J. Grétry, *Mémoires ou Essais sur la musique* (Paris, an V [1797]), II, 357. See also J. Ph. Rameau, *Traité de l'harmonie réduite à ses principes naturels* (Paris, 1722), II, 24.

27. Grétry, *Mémoires*, I, 237.

aria, which begins with the outcry, "Alas, not a shred of hope," may well have served as Cherubini's basic model (Example 3).

Neris' crucial aria also illustrates the uncanny manner in which Cherubini responded to the most subtle suggestion of emotional change. As the nurse expresses her ultimate resignation in the face of the inevitable, the orchestra produces a prophetically novel effect. At first the high strings descend with the voice in parallel sixth chords; then, as they rise again, the lower instruments continue the descent in contrary motion (Example 4). Again, the original stimulus may have come from Vogel (Example 5). But to modern ears this passage

EX. 1. Beginning of Neris' aria, Act II of *Médée*—Cherubini.

EX. 2. Extract from *Ariadne auf Naxos* (after A. Einstein)—G. Benda.

EX. 3. Beginning of Hisiphile's aria, Act I of *La Toison d'Or*—J. C. Vogel.

sounds amazingly like the mature Verdi of *Otello* (Example 6).

The bridal march in F, with which the final portion of Act II opens, derives its very special flavor from an ingenious mixture of three distinct elements: the march proper played by the offstage wind band, repeated choral invocations in a curiously pentatonic vein, and Medea's furious punctuations in a style reminiscent once again of melodrama à la Benda. In order to convey the hidden anxiety of the celebrants, moreover, Cherubini revels in unadulterated chromatic progressions and employs mediant-related chords as though they were readily interchangeable (Example 7). In so doing,

EX. 4. Extract from Neris' aria, Act II of *Médée*—Cherubini.

EX. 5. Extract from Calciope's aria, Act II of *La Toison d'Or*—J. C. Vogel.

EX. 6. Extract from Desdemona (Otello duet), Act I of *Otello*—Verdi.

EX. 7. Extract from bridal march, Act II of *Médée*—Cherubini.

he goes even beyond Beethoven, presaging subsequent ninteenth-century usage.

The importance of the final act as a fountainhead of romantic music can hardly be overestimated. For here Cherubini succeeded admirably in transforming the time-bound peculiarities of the Revolutionary style into a new musical expressiveness that speaks of, and to, all mankind. The instrumental introduction left its traces not only in the piccolo shrieks of the storm movement in Beethoven's Pastoral Symphony, but also in the Wolf's Glen scene of Weber's *Freischütz* and the opening strains of the Scene in the Country in Berlioz' *Symphonie Fantastique.* Medea's final solo appearance, in turn, sheds the last pretense of traditional aria structure. Succumbing to a ruthless dramatic force that exceeds even the melodramatic passages of the second act, it points straight to Spontini, Weber, and Meyerbeer. Finally, the frantic conclusion in D minor, which sends the horrified citizens of Corinth scattering in panic, as the raging flames devour the cruelly avenged heroine, destroyed once and for all the eighteenth-century taboo that prompted even a Mozart to reassemble his cast at the end of *Don Giovanni* in order to assure the audience that divine justice had triumphed after all. Once more the pattern may have been set by Benda, whose *Ariadne* of 1774 ends also in D minor, as does indeed Vogel's *La Toison d'Or.* Salieri's *Les Danaides* (1784) concludes in a somber C minor. But no earlier composer had left his audience in such a state of utter terror. Both Gluck and Mozart composed comparable finales, the former at the end of *Armide,* the latter in *Idomeneo.* Yet, if anything, Mozart's second-act finale reflects the basic difference in attitude that separates him from Cherubini. Here, too, a horrified populace takes flight, and D minor serves as the principal key. However, just as the curtain falls, Mozart, like Gluck, yields to the brilliant sounds of the parallel major. On the other hand, in *Médée,* which eliminates even the human *deus ex machina* of Revolutionary rescue-opera, all main subdivisions, including the overture and the three acts, end in minor keys: the triumph of man's inhumanity to man has become complete.

Considering the many forward-looking aspects of *Médée,* one is hardly surprised to find that more than fifty years later Franz Lachner managed to replace the spoken portions with remarkably fitting recitatives. Characteristically, his additions do not quite match the largely eighteenth-century style of the opera's first half. Beginning with the simple but effective recitative that introduces Neris' aria, however, Lachner—who had enjoyed recognition in the circles of Beethoven and Schubert—moved in a musical world that was eminently his own. In Act III, to be sure, Cherubini himself put musico-dramatic necessity before the conventions of a genre that did not suit his tragic subject to begin with and inserted recitative-like passages of his own. Occasionally, as in Medea's opening solo, he abandoned the traditional separation of aria and recitative altogether and wrote extended "through-composed" ariosos. The systematically increasing duration of these final scenes produces a driving structural and dramatic climax rarely equaled in operatic history. As Brahms put it generations later: "We never stop blabbering about Tristan; yet this magnificent work we accept in perfect silence without giving it a second thought."[28]

No doubt Brahms was thinking primarily of the orchestra which none of the earlier masters of French opera, let alone their Italian contemporaries, had endowed, individually or collectively, with similar powers of expression. Freed of the necessity to compose lengthy ballet scenes, since he operated within the formal framework of dialogue opera, Cherubini assigned to the orchestra psychological functions which assimilated its dramatic role to that of the chorus in ancient tragedy. Thus it punctuates, underscores and illuminates in a manner that has few parallels even in Mozart. In short, vocal and instrumental forces collaborate in Médée in a nearly equal partnership. That in this respect, too, Cherubini helped lay the foundations of nineteenth-century music-drama is self-evident.

Its unquestioned artistic virtues notwithstanding, *Médée* has had a rather checkered performance history—and not entirely without reason. Its success certainly depends in large measure upon the vocal stamina and histrionic versatility of the soprano cast in the title role. Ever since the creation of the role by Madame Scio, one of the Revolution's favorite heroic sopranos, her name has been linked with that of Medea as an unsurpassable combination. Then, too, the spirit of the Empire, exemplified in the glamorous theatrical manifestations of a nation drunk with power, went directly counter to the profound

28. Cf. Leopold Schmidt, ed., *Briefwechsel mit Hermann Levi, Friedr. Gernsheim . . .* (Berlin, 1910), p. 83.

sense of humanity that speaks from Cherubini's interpretation of the ancient legend. In competition with an opera like Spontini's *La Vestale,* which exploits its superficial aspects while ignoring its essence, *Médée* faced inevitable if temporary defeat.

A typical product of the spiritual and socio-political ferment that changed the very foundations of modern thought and behavior, straddling eighteenth-century Classicism and nineteenth-century Romanticism within the dramatically inadequate framework of *opéra comique*—and thus handicapped from the outset in a manner that no later patchwork could remedy—*Médée* remains in many respects a magnificent torso not unlike the double-edged story it deals with. That Cherubini was not unaware of certain flaws is attested by the numerous cuts he authorized for the production at Vienna. Then, too, his next major work, *Les deux journées,* based on what both Goethe and Beethoven considered the best libretto ever written, became the well-nigh perfect prototype of nineteenth-century romantic opera. Unfortunately, the bourgeoisie's gain proved to be dramatic music's loss. With its carefully balanced characters and smooth formal patterns *Les deux journées* indeed inaugurated a new genre. But by the same token, the elementary powers of *Médée,* its Revolutionary *élan,* its ruthless honesty and emotional realism, went begging. At least three generations and an equal number of additional revolutions were needed to fuse these esthetic attributes into the very essence of modern opera.

19 / The Mass-Motet Cycle: A Mid-Fifteenth-Century Experiment

ROBERT J. SNOW
University of Pittsburgh

ONE of the more significant musical events of the middle of the fifteenth century was the development of the cyclic Mass Ordinary and its establishment as one of the principal forms of Renaissance music. The main outlines of this development are well known; but one experiment that took place, the expansion of the cycle through the addition of a motet to the items of the Ordinary, has escaped notice until now. Two cycles expanded in this manner exist in manuscripts long known to musicologists, but the recognition of them was dependent upon the discovery of other examples in a source that still remains generally unknown.

The manuscript in question is preserved in the library of what was formerly the Praemonstratensian abbey of Strahov in Prague, and is now a museum administered by the Czech Academy of Sciences.[1] It is assigned the call number D.G.IV.47, and was first brought to the attention of the musicological world, well over fifty years ago, by Dobroslav Orel, who examined it during his study of the so-called Speciálník Codex, MS. II.A.7 of the Museum at Hradec Králové.[2] This same author mentioned it again a few years later in

A preliminary report on the findings presented here was given at the Spring meeting of the Midwest Chapter of the American Musicological Society, held in May 1959.

1. Památník Národního Písemnictví.
2. "Der Mensuralkodex Specialnik" (diss., University of Vienna, 1914).

an article published in the Czech language[3] and still later, in a very cursory manner, in an article printed in German.[4] The manuscript received no further attention, however, until Dragan Plamenac, in a paper delivered at the International Musicological Congress at Cologne in 1958, dealt with the German songs in it,[5] and with certain other aspects in an article published in 1960.[6]

The manuscript probably was written about 1480 in Bohemia or Silesia. It consists of 306 folios and contains 330 entries. A large number of the items are *unica,* and most of the concordances to those that are not occur in one or another of six of the Trent manuscripts. The music is almost exclusively liturgical in character, with the exception of a few secular songs in German, a setting of the well-known Italian text *O rosa bella,* and a small number of textless items. The contents are systematically grouped into five categories: (1) introits; (2) Mass Ordinary items; (3) responsories, antiphons, sequences, miscellaneous minor liturgical forms, and paraliturgical items such as motets and *cantiones;* (4) Office hymns; and (5) Magnificat settings.[7]

No single category is without interest, but the Mass Ordinary group is of particular importance because it contains several cyclic Ordinaries that are unknown from other sources. Even more important, it contains two cycles, each of which includes, in addition to the usual Ordinary items, a motet based on the same musical material. In both instances the motet occurs as the final item of the cycle. At first glance it would appear that these were simply two early examples of parody Masses, each Mass being followed by the motet on which it was based. As will be seen, however, a closer examination suggests that this probably is not the case at all; rather, the motets would appear to have been conceived simultaneously with

3. "Počátky umělého vícehlasu v Čechách" (The Origins of Polyphonic Art-Music in Bohemia), in *Sbornik filozofickej fakulty university Komenského v Bratislave* (Miscellany of the Faculty of Philosophy of the University of Bratislava), I (Bratislava, 1922), 143–214.

4. "Stilarten der Mehrstimmigkeit des 15. und 16. Jahrhunderts in Böhmen," *Guido Adler-Festschrift* (1930), pp. 87–91.

5. "German Polyphonic Lieder of the 15th Century in a Little-Known Manuscript," *Bericht über den Siebenten Internationalen Musikwissenschaftlichen Kongress Köln 1958* (Kassel, 1959), pp. 214–15.

6. "Browsing Through a Little-Known Manuscript," *Journal, American Musicological Society,* XIII (1960), 102–11.

7. A complete description of the manuscript and an inventory of its contents have been prepared by the present writer and will appear in a future issue of *Musica Disciplina.*

the Mass Ordinary items and thus to be integral parts of the two cycles.

One of these cycles is anonymous and consists of a Kyrie using the *Rex virginum* trope, the Gloria, Credo, Sanctus, and Agnus Dei, and the motet *O pater eterne*. Each movement is set for four voices. The motet of the cycle seems to be an *unicum*,[8] but the Ordinary items are to be found in two other sources, Trent MS. 89 and Modena MS. 456 (V.H.10). They constitute, in fact, the well-known *Missa O rosa bella*, a modern edition of which appears in *Denkmäler der Tonkunst in Österreich* (Band 22, pages 28–69).

Cyclic unity is achieved primarily through the use of a tenor and a motto, both of which are easily identifiable as being based, respectively, on the tenor and superius of Dunstable's setting of *O rosa bella*. A comparison of the tenors of the various items of the Mass-motet cycle with the original Dunstable tenor reveals that a complete melodic statement of the *O rosa bella* tenor occurs once in each item of the cycle. Since, however, Dunstable's tenor is subjected to a free treatment of durational values and a certain amount of melodic modification, the melody appears in a somewhat different guise in each of the different movements. Also, in the Mass items, the tenor is always divided into two parts, the first part cast in *tempus perfectum*, the second part in *tempus imperfectum diminutum*. Example 1 illustrates the nature of the tenor treatment.

The opening notes of the superius of *O rosa bella* serve as the source for the rather loosely shaped motto that appears at the beginning of each item of the Mass-motet cycle. It is interesting to note the great degree of similarity between the mottos of the Gloria and Credo and of the Sanctus and Agnus Dei. This similarity is undoubtedly a vestige of the earlier, pre-cyclic practice of pairing these particular movements. The mottos of the Kyrie and motet are also closely related, the opening of the motet motto being identical with the beginning of Dunstable's superius, as can be seen in Example 2.

From a comparison of the tenors of the Mass items and the motet one with another and with the tenor of Dunstable's *O rosa bella*, it is obvious that the tenors of the entire cycle must have been derived

8. A transcription of this motet is given on pp. 315–20. After writing the article, I identified a concordance in Milan MS. 2269 (Librone I), fols. 123v–124r. In this source it has the text *O admirabile comertium*, the first antiphon for Vespers of the feast of the Circumision.

EX. 1. Tenors of *O rosa bella* cycle.

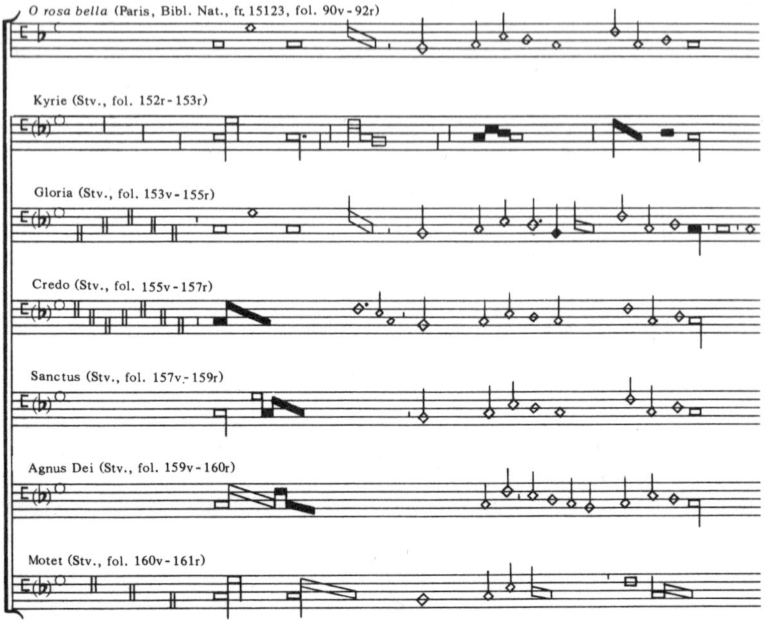

EX. 2. Mottos of *O rosa bella* cycle.

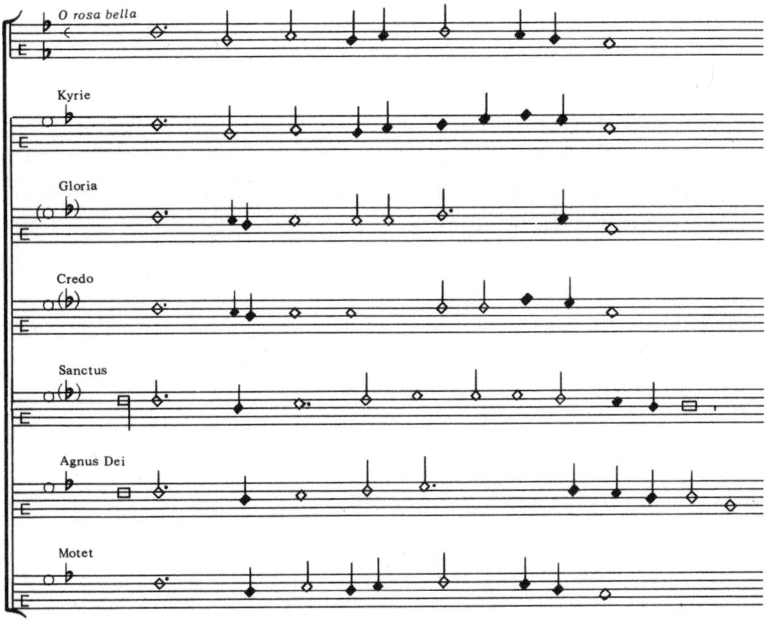

directly from Dunstable's composition. If the tenors of the Mass Ordinary items had been based on the *O rosa bella* tenor as it appears in the motet, certain distinctive features characteristic of the treatment of the durational values and of the melodic modifications proper to the tenor as used in the motet surely would have manifested themselves in the tenor of the Mass Ordinary items. This does not happen, however, and consequently there is a considerable degree of certitude that the motet is a constituent member of the cycle and not a pre-existent work that served as a model for the Mass Ordinary items.

The other Mass-motet cycle found in the Strahov manuscript is attributed to a certain Philipus, a composer to whom several other compositions in the same source are ascribed. He is perhaps identical with the Philippon of the Speciálník Codex, a related but somewhat later manuscript of Bohemian origin. This cycle lacks the Kyrie and thus consists of the Gloria, Credo, Sanctus, and Agnus Dei, and the motet *O gloriosa mater cristi maria.* The Mass Ordinary items are all set for four voices, and the motet has an optional fifth part, a contratenor concordans cum omnibus. The Mass items seem to be *unica,* but the motet, without the optional contratenor, also occurs in Trent MS. 89. In Trent, however, the motet has two texts, each different from the one found in Strahov. One of these is the well-known Marian antiphon *Salve regina;* the other begins *Gaude rosa spetiosa* and is a slightly later addition to the manuscript.

Here, as in the *O rosa bella* cycle, the various items are unified by means of a tenor and a motto. The tenor is not identified in any of the Mass items, but in both of the sources for the motet it is accompanied by the inscription *Hilf und gib rat.* Certain of its features suggest that it is derived from a monophonic rather than a polyphonic source. It is stated twice in each item of the cycle, with the first statement always notated in *tempus perfectum,* the second in *tempus imperfectum diminutum.* Furthermore, since the durational treatment applied to the tenor melody is completely free, the melody appears in a different guise not only in each movement but also in each statement of each movement. Example 3 contains the beginning of the tenor of each item of the cycle.

The opening motto, the superius of which seems to be based on the material used in the tenor, is cast in the form of a duet between the superius and contratenor primus, or in the motet, as a trio, if the

EX. 3. Tenors of *Hilf und gib rat* cycle.

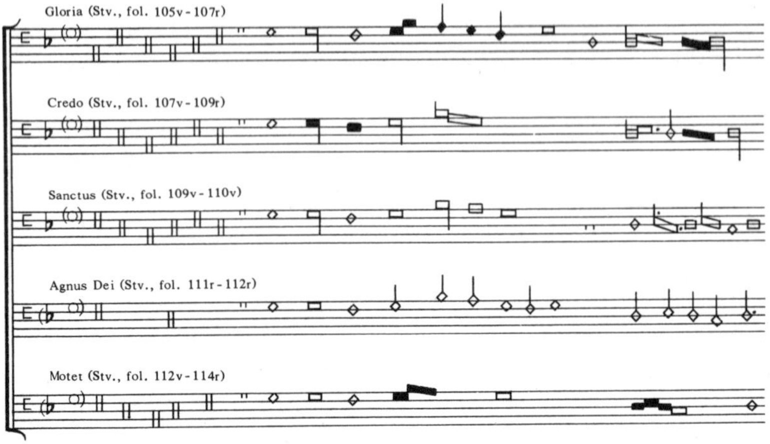

EX. 4. Mottos of *Hilf und gib rat* cycle.

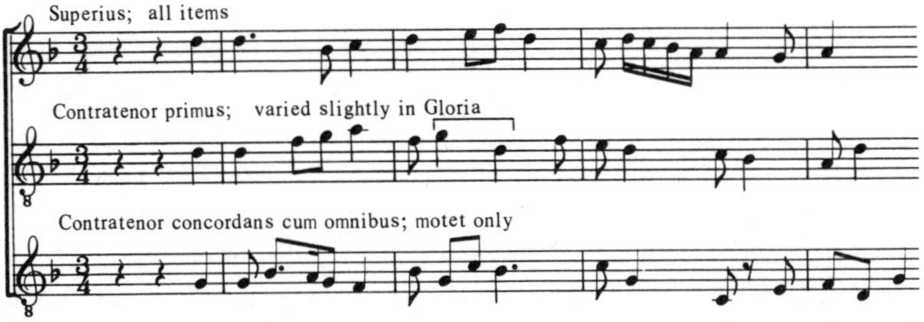

contratenor concordans cum omnibus is used. The beginning of the motto is essentially the same in each of the items. See Example 4.

Even though the source of the tenor is unknown, a comparison of the tenor of each of the Mass Ordinary items with that of the motet indicates that here again we probably have a Mass-motet cycle rather than a parody Mass and its model. The reasons for this conclusion are the same as for the *O rosa bella* cycle: not one of the features characteristic of the treatment of the durational values, or of the melodic modifications of the tenor as it occurs in the motet, manifests itself in the tenors of the Mass Ordinary items. Therefore, one may conclude that all of the tenors, including that of the motet, were based directly on the unidentified original melody.[8a]

8a. After the completion of this article the opening phrase of the melody, with the words "Hilf und gib rat," was discovered to be identical, both musically and textually, with the fourth phrase of the tenor of a quodlibet in the Glogau Songbook. The quodlibet in question is No. 119 of the inventory of this source given in Heribert Ringmann, ed., *Das Glogauer Liederbuch,* I, Das Erbe deutscher Musik, Band 4 (Kassel, 1954), 102–19. A transcription of the quodlibet occurs on pp. 40–41 of the same volume.

The discovery of these two Mass-motet cycles in the Strahov manuscript raises several questions. Are the two Strahov cycles the only examples of the Mass-motet cycle? Is it a type peculiar to the immediate locale in which the manuscript was compiled, or was it employed throughout a wide area? When did it come into existence, and how long did it remain in use? Which, if any, group or school of composers wrote Mass-motet cycles? What were the considerations that prompted the addition of a motet to the cyclic Mass Ordinary?

The first of these questions can be answered in the negative, since an investigation of the principal sources contemporary with the Strahov manuscript has led to the discovery of other examples. One of these is preserved in Trent MS. 88, Nos. 490–496, and consists of all five Mass Ordinary items and a motet entitled *Gaude maria virgo.*[9] The Mass movements are *a 3*, whereas the motet is *a 4*. As in the *O rosa bella* and *Hilf und gib rat* cycles, the items have in common a tenor and a motto. In this instance these are derived from a chanson by Binchois, *Esclave puist yl.*[10]

Here again there is a free treatment of the durational values of the original tenor, which is stated twice in each of the movements except the Agnus Dei. In the Gloria, Credo and motet the first statement is notated in *tempus perfectum,* the second in *tempus imperfectum diminutum.* In the Kyrie and Sanctus the first half of the first statement is notated in *tempus perfectum,* the second half in *tempus imperfectum diminutum,* whereas all of the second statement is notated under the sign for *tempus perfectum* in the Kyrie and *tempus perfectum diminutum* in the Sanctus. The first and third invocations of the Agnus Dei, which are musically identical, use the first half of the tenor notated in *tempus perfectum;* the second invocation, notated in *tempus imperfectum diminutum,* makes no use of the tenor material. The incipits of the tenors of these items are given in Example 5.

9. The text of this bipartite motet is that of one of the Responsories sung at Matins on the feast of the Assumption. See Peter Wagner, *Einführung in die gregorianischen Melodien, II: Neumenkunde* (Freiburg, 1905), pp. 80–81. This suggests that the cycle was intended for use on this feast and throughout its octave. Because the text of the respond is used for the *prima pars* of the motet and that of the verse for the *secunda pars,* it might perhaps be argued that the setting is a polyphonic Responsory instead of a motet. That this is not the case is evident from the fact that none of the musical material of the original Responsory is utilized in the setting.

10. Modern edition in Wolfgang Rehm, ed., *Die Chansons von Gilles Binchois,* Musikalische Denkmäler, Band II (Mainz, 1957), p. 13.

EX. 5. Tenors of *Esclave puist yl* cycle.

EX. 6. Mottos of *Esclave puist yl* cycle.

The relation of the mottos of the cycle to the opening of the superius of the chanson is a particularly interesting one. Here the borrowed material is not only accorded free treatment but is also transposed up a fourth, although the tenor material remains at the original pitch level (Example 6). Once again, a comparison of the tenors and the mottos of the cycle one with another, and with Binchois' chanson, suggests that the motet is not a model for the Ordinary items but rather an integral part of the cycle.

The members of another cycle occur in two different Trent manuscripts. The five Ordinary items, *a 3* and attributed to W. de Rouge, appear in Trent MS. 90, Nos. 1031–1035; the four-part motet, *Stella coeli extirpavit,* is preserved anonymously in Trent MS. 88, No. 204. The Ordinary items also occur anonymously in San Pietro MS. B.80, where the tenor part has the inscription *Soyez aprantiz,* one of the texts that, in continental sources, often replace the original text of Walter Frye's ballade *So ys emprentid.*[11] The cycle has no motto, even though the tenor is derived from this polyphonic work. A single full statement of the original tenor, the durational values of which are treated freely, appears in the Kyrie, Sanctus and Agnus Dei; in the Gloria, Credo and motet the first half is repeated after a complete statement in order to accommodate the longer texts of these three items. See Example 7 for the beginnings of the tenors of the various items.

The Gloria, Credo, Sanctus and Agnus Dei of still another cycle are to be found in the Strahov manuscript; the motet, *Gaude maria virgo,* is preserved in Trent MS. 88, Nos. 416–417.[12] All items of the cycle are *a 4,* and there is no motto. The tenor is based on the Gregorian introit *Meditatio cordis,* used on the Friday after the Fourth Sunday of Lent. A comparison of the manner in which the tenor is derived from the original and is employed in the various movements leaves little doubt that the motet belongs with the Mass items, a conclusion that is strengthened by general stylistic relation-

11. Modern ed. in Sylvia W. Kenney, ed., *Walter Frye: Collected Works* (New Haven, 1960), pp. 5–6. Other texts which replaced the original were *Pour une suis desconforté* and *Sancta maria succurre.* It is interesting to note that the ballade also appears in Tr. 90 in a textless state on fol. 308v–309r, only three folios before the appearance of the Mass items that utilize its tenor.

12. The text of this motet is identical with that of the motet of the *Esclave puist yl* cycle. See Note 9.

EX. 7. Tenors of *Soyez aprantiz* cycle.

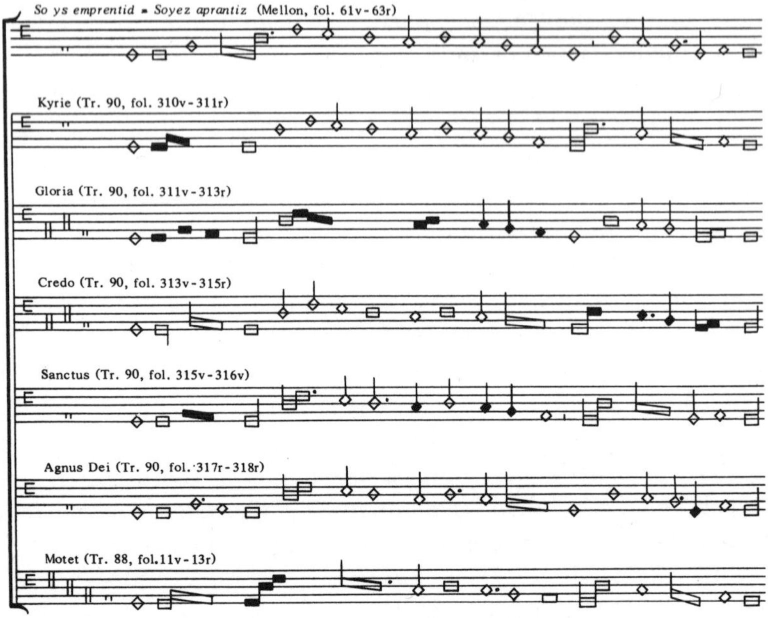

ships. The incipits of the tenors of the various movements are given in Example 8.

One other cyclic Mass and a motet that probably constitute a Mass-motet cycle are the *Missa Summe trinitati* of Walter Frye, preserved in Brussels MS. 5557, and the anonymous motet *Salve virgo mater pia*, found in Trent MS. 88, No. 240.[13] The Mass items and the motet all utilize a tenor that is derived from the responsory *Summae trinitati*, and which occurs with the same durational values in each item. All of the items also open with the same motto.

Bukofzer, in his article on Frye in *Die Musik in Geschichte und Gegenwart*, first called attention to the relation between this Mass cycle and motet.[14] He assigned the motet to Frye because its tenor and motto were identical with those of the Mass items, and for stylistic reasons. He also asserted that the motet undoubtedly served as a model for the Mass and that consequently this was one of the

13. Modern ed. of the Mass items and the motet in Kenney, *Walter Frye: Works*, pp. 25–39 and 21–24. For a discussion of the handling of the cantus firmus material see Kenney, *Walter Frye and the "Contenance Angloise"* (New Haven, 1965), pp. 141–42.

14. Vol. IV (1955), cols. 1069–71. He also deals with it in "English Church Music of the Fifteenth Century," *Vol. 3: New Oxford History of Music* (Oxford, 1960), 212.

EX. 8. Tenors of *Meditatio cordis* cycle.

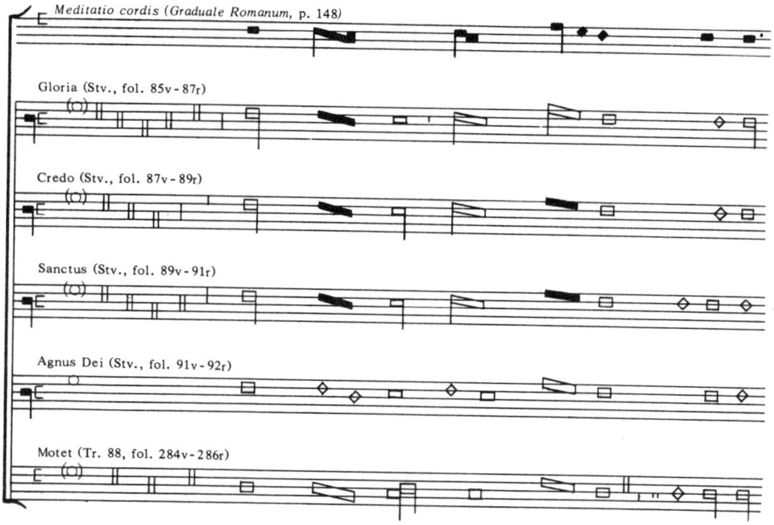

earliest examples of the parody Mass. Sylvia Kenney, on the other hand, has suggested that the situation is just the reverse and that the motet is based on the Mass.[15] In view of the discovery of the Mass-motet cycle, however, it seems more probable that here we have another example of this form rather than either an early parody Mass or a parody motet.

Further investigations of sources contemporary with Strahov may well yield other examples of the Mass-motet cycle and perhaps even information as to the origin and development of the form. Solely from a consideration of the cycles so far identified, however, we may deduce certain facts and tentatively answer some of the questions raised by its discovery.

Since the six cycles thus far discovered occur in the Strahov and Trent manuscripts, it is obvious that the Mass-motet cycle was used in the south-Germanic areas. Furthermore, we can assume that it probably was not used in other parts of Europe, since only the Mass Ordinary items of Mass-motet cycles thus far identified are to be found in manuscripts written anywhere other than in the south-Germanic areas. Only the Mass items of the *O rosa bella* cycle appear in Modena 456, a manuscript of central Italian origin; only

15. Kenney, *Walter Frye: Works*, p. iii.

the Mass items of the *Summe trinitati* cycle were copied into Brussels 5557, a manuscript of Burgundian origin; and only the Mass items of the de Rouge cycle are to be found in San Pietro B.80, a manuscript of Italian provenance.

In regard to the date of origin, an analysis of the six Mass-motet cycles suggests that the earliest of these were W. de Rouge's cycle on the contrafactum of Frye's ballade, the anonymous cycle based on Binchois' *Esclave puist yl* and the *Summe trinitati* cycle of Frye. Except for the motets of two of these cycles, the items are *a 3* and all have stylistic features characteristic of the Mass cycles known to have been produced by the continental school of English composers about 1435–1445. The use of a motto as well as a tenor in two of the cycles, and of cantus firmi drawn from polyphonic sources in two instances, suggests a date around 1440.

The other three Mass-motet cycles, all written for four voices, are closely related stylistically to the Masses of Dufay's middle period, about 1440–1455. Certain technical features also indicate that they date from this time. The *Meditatio cordis* cycle, for example, lacks a motto, a unifying feature rarely absent from cycles written after about 1450. The tenors of all of the Mass items of the *O rosa bella* and *Hilf und gib rat* cycles are cast in an essentially bipartite form. This kind of treatment, with each of the two parts in a different mensuration, is frequently used in the paired items of the Dunstable generation for unifying purposes. It was used only once by Dufay, however, in his *Missa Caput*, of about 1440, and falls into disuse shortly after this. Consequently, these two cycles must date from not much later than the middle of the century. Also, the vestigial Gloria–Credo and Sanctus–Agnus Dei pairing to be found in the mottos of the *O rosa bella* cycle indicates that this particular cycle cannot be very far removed from the earlier, pre-cyclic period in which this kind of pairing was practiced.

Turning to the question of who created the Mass-motet cycle, we find much evidence that points to members of the continental English school. For example, two of the cycles, *Summe trinitati* and *O rosa bella*, have troped Kyrie settings; and two cycles, *Hilf und gib rat* and *Meditatio cordis*, lack the Kyrie. The three basically three-part cycles, *Soyez aprantiz, Esclave puist yl* and *Summe trinitati*, are stylistically related to the continental English school of the late

1430's. Two of the cycles, *Summe trinitati* and *Meditatio cordis,* derive their tenors from monophonic sacred chants; two others, *O rosa bella* and *Hilf und gib rat,* use a bipartite type of tenor structure favored by the English school. Finally, it should not be forgotten that Walter Frye, the composer of *Summe trinitati,* presumably was English.

Although it is true that none of these features is exclusively English, they are found primarily in the works of members of the continental English school. Therefore, it seems that at least some of the Mass-motet cycles can be attributed to English composers working in the south-Germanic area.

One important question remains to be discussed: What prompted the creation of the Mass-motet cycle, and what led to its dissolution? In order to answer this question it is first necessary to determine the liturgical purpose of the motet. The placing of the motet after the Mass items in the two complete cycles in Strahov, and in the cycle that is found in its entirety in Trent MS. 88, suggests that it was intended for use at the conclusion of Mass. The supposition is borne out by various fifteenth- and early sixteenth-century references to the use of a motet at this point in the liturgy. Houdoy, for example, in his history of the cathedral of Cambrai, quotes a note found in one of the manuscripts in the library of Cambrai to the effect that Charles, count of Charolais, son of Philip of Burgundy, composed a motet that was sung by the choirboys and their master in the church of Cambrai after a Mass at which Charles was present on the twenty-third of October, 1460.[16] It is also known that at the meeting of Henry VIII and Francis I at the Field of the Cloth of Gold in 1520, Mass was concluded with the singing of several motets.[17] From these and similar statements it is evident that motets were often used at the end of Mass during the early and middle Renaissance. Motets were, of course, also used during the course of the Mass at this period, particularly during the Canon, either at the elevation or immediately after it, and as substitutes for sequences.[18] The length of most of those that are part of a Mass-motet cycle, however, seems

16. Jules Houdoy, *Histoire artistique de la cathédrale de Cambrai* (Paris, 1880), p. 87.

17. Frank Ll. Harrison, *Music in Medieval Britain* (London, 1958), p. 228.

18. Joseph A. Jungmann, *The Mass of the Roman Rite,* trans. Francis A. Brunner (New York, 1951), I, 133–34; II (1955), 214–16.

to preclude their use at least during the Canon and suggests that they were intended to be sung at the end of the service as a sort of recessional or even as substitutes for the "Deo gratias."[19]

Once we know that a motet was used at the conclusion of Mass, it becomes possible to determine what may have prompted the creation of the Mass-motet cycle. First, though, a few words about the background of the cyclic Mass are necessary. Essentially, the principle of the cyclic Mass Ordinary is the incorporation of some common musical material into each of the sung items of the Ordinary—material which in the fifteenth century was more often than not chosen more for the possible symbolic import of its text than for its purely musical aspects. The result is the creation of a set of coherent musical compositions out of what liturgically are separate and unrelated, even disparate items. Here the "absolute" work of art begins to encroach on liturgical function, and purely aesthetic conceptions begin to supersede liturgical considerations. Here is manifested one aspect of the emerging Renaissance philosophy of art.

After the development of the cyclic Mass, only a single act was needed to create the Mass-motet cycle. Under the influence of Renaissance aesthetic concepts the material common to the Mass Ordinary items was simply extended to the motet intended for use on special occasions at the conclusion of Mass. In the Mass-motet cycle, however, there exists a conflict between practical liturgical considerations and aesthetic principle that is not found in the cyclic Mass Ordinary. From the liturgical point of view the superimposition of a unifying aesthetic device upon the Mass Ordinary items is superfluous but not necessarily contradictory or impractical, even though the symbolic import of the pre-existent material would limit the use of a cycle to certain feasts or votive Masses. Even though the liturgical purpose of each of the Ordinary items is different, they all share the characteristic of being "ordinary"—that is, the text of each item is invariable, and each item is used in the normal form of the Mass rite. Thus, they could be related musically without any real violation of the liturgical principles of that period.

The motet, however, was not liturgical in nature and its use was optional, as was the choice of text when one was used. Thus, the Mass-motet cycle was an attempt to unite by common material items

19. Harrison, *Medieval Britain,* p. 227.

that were strictly liturgical, always required, and invariable with an item that was optional in every regard. That the attempt was soon abandoned, undoubtedly because of practical liturgical considerations, can be seen from the scarcity of examples of the form that have been preserved.

O PATER AETERNE

Anonymous
(Strahov, fol. 160v - 161r)

bis, O Fi –
li Pa –
20
tris, O Mu –

(1) d in ms.

nos
gra
te
per
me
ri
tum
vir
gi
nis
50
al
mae

(2) The contratenor primus and contratenor bassus each have one semibreve less than demanded by the rests in the other two parts.

(3) Sic.

The version of this motet in Milan MS. 2269 (see above, note 8) has a considerably different reading for measures 57–59, which is probably the correct one:

20 / New Data About the Serbian Chant

DIMITRIJE STEFANOVIĆ
Belgrade Musicological Institute

THE use of various languages in the Eastern Orthodox Churches has led to the establishment of several bodies of liturgical chant, including, for example, the Byzantine, Armenian, and Russian repertories. Also included in this group is the ecclesiastical music of the Serbs, a music which, although sung in Church Slavonic and used by the Russians and Bulgarians as well as the Serbs during the Middle Ages, is referred to as the Serbian Chant. The use of the Serbian Chant is not restricted to the boundaries of the Serbian state, but is sung by Serbian ethnic groups wherever they live.

The history of the Serbian Chant is still insufficiently known. The first collection of melodies in modern notation in use in the Serbian Orthodox Church dates only from 1862.[1] So far as is known, there are no Serbian musical manuscripts prior to the eighteenth century that contain ecclesiastical tunes written in neumatic notation. A collection of twenty-odd manuscripts of the eighteenth and nineteenth centuries, written in late Byzantine neumatic notation, may be found in the Serbian monastery of Chilandar on Mount Athos in Greece. Recently, however, a few fragments of an earlier date—sixteenth and seventeenth century—were discovered, and these may

1. *Božestvennaja služba vo svjatago otca našego Ioanna Zlatoustago,* u note napisao, za četiri glasa i klavir udesio Kornilie Stanković (The Divine Liturgy of St. John Chrysostom, for four voices and piano arranged by Kornelije Stanković), (Vienna, 1862).

serve as specific examples to demonstrate the intertwining of the Byzantine elements with the Serbian Chant, and the extent of the potent Greek influence on singing in the Serbian Church.

This writer, working jointly with Mr. Nigel Wilson, now a fellow of Lincoln College, Oxford, was fortunate enough to discover in the Bodleian Library the oldest dated document on record implying a specifically Serbian manner of chanting.[2] On the last folio, 409v, of a Greek musical manuscript with neumatic notation,[3] there is a sticheron preceded by the following inscription:

Δόξα εἰς τὴν εἴσοδον τῆς ὑπεραγίας θεοτόκου : σέρβικον.

Its text is written in the Church Slavonic language but with Greek letters.[4] The manuscript is dated A.D. 1553.

A comparison with the corresponding Middle Byzantine version of the same sticheron[5] reveals that the differences are negligible. In other words, the *servikon* (this writer is assuming that it may have been written down in the Chilandar monastery) does not differ essentially from the Byzantine melody that served as its model. For the history of the Serbian Chant this is an indication, if not a direct proof, that in the sixteenth century it was dominated by Greek influence.

The oldest known inscription concerning a Serbian composer was also found in a Greek musical manuscript with neumatic notation. This manuscript, formerly in the Belgrade Public Library, was

2. See this writer's study, "The Earliest Dated and Notated Document of the Serbian Chant," Zbornik Radova Vizantološkog Instituta (Publications of the Byzantological Institute of the Serbian Academy of Sciences and Arts), VII (Belgrade, 1961), 187–96; N. G. Wilson and D. I. Stefanović, *Manuscripts of Byzantine Chant in Oxford* (Bodleian Library, 1963), pp. 24–25; 30. For the oldest reference to Serbia in a musical manuscript, cf. M. Velimirović, " Ἰωακεὶμ μοναχὸς τοῦ Χαρσι ανίτου καὶ δομέστικος Σερβίας," in English, in *Recueil des travaux de l'Institut d' Études byzantines,* VIII, Mélanges G. Ostrogorsky, II (Belgrade, 1964), 451–58.

3. MS. E. D. Clarke 14 (Summary Catalogue No. 18376).

4. This is an interesting reversal of the procedure in the early centuries of Christianity in Russia, a period from which Greek words are to be found written in Cyrillic characters. A reproduction of one page with such a text in the *Blagoveščenskii kondakar* may be seen in Carsten Hoeg's "The Oldest Slavonic Tradition of Byzantine Music," *Proceedings of the British Academy,* XXXIX (1953), Plate IV, following p. 66.

5. H. J. W. Tillyard, *The Hymns of the Sticherarium for November,* Monumenta musicae Byzantinae, series *Transcripta,* II (Copenhagen, 1938), p. 126, hymn No. 71. See also the facs. of Cod. Dalasseni in *Monumenta,* the main series of the same collection, I (Copenhagen, 1935), fol. 64v.

destroyed during the German bombing of that city in the last war. All that remains are twelve photostats of various pages, thanks to the endeavors of the late composer and historian of music, Kosta P. Manojlović.[6] In one of these photostats (see Plate I) may be seen the inscription: "Tvorenie domestika kir Stefana Srbina" (Work [composition] of domestikos Kir Stefan the Serb.)[7]

The neumatic notation is late Byzantine, and although the date of the manuscript is unknown, it is believed to date from the fifteenth century.[8] In this specific example one finds a bilingual version of a hymn that was used in place of the Cherubic Hymn at the Mass of the Presanctified. What makes it important is that the Greek text is written beneath the text in Church Slavonic, a language that discloses distinct features of the Serbian dialect.

From a partial description of this manuscript published in 1932, it is known that on folio 86 there was also a bilingual version of the Cherubic Hymn.[9] It was further noted that in one instance (folio

6. The original plates for the photographs are now in the archives of the Serbian Academy of Sciences and Arts in Belgrade, where they are catalogued as VII/433.

7. The first transcription of the fragment is published in J. Andreis, D. Cvetko, and S. Djurić-Klajn, *Historijski razvoj muzičke kulture u Jugoslaviji* (Historical Development of the Musical Culture in Yugoslavia), (Zagreb, 1962), p. 564. Additional information on the manuscript may be found in J. Milojković-Djurić, "A Papadike from Skoplje," *Studies in Eastern Chant,* ed. M. Velimirović, I (London, 1966), 50–56.

8. The first mention of this manuscript appears in the catalogue of the Belgrade Public Library: Ljubomir Stojanović, *Katalog Narodne biblioteke u Beogradu,* IV (Belgrade, 1903), xiv, 100–01. Its call number was 369(93) and it had 307 folios. Stojanović thought it to be "perhaps of the 16th c." In his description of the holdings of the Belgrade Public Library, Svetozar Matić, *Opis rukopisa Narodne biblioteke,* Srpska Akademija Nauka, Posebna izdanja, CXCI, (Belgrade, 1952), pp. 253–54, notes that the inscription about "Kir Stefan the Serb" is "perhaps a contemporary note (15th c.)."

Recently, Djordje Sp. Radojičić expressed the opinion that the "domestikos Stefan" may be identical with the scribe of the same name who was known to have lived in the city of Smederevo on the Danube about the middle of the 15th century. See his "Arhidjakon Jovan, pisac stihova XVIII veka," *Godišnjak Filozofskog Fakulteta* (Novi Sad), IV (1959), 258–73, esp. 260. Should this assumption be correct, there is a likelihood that the manuscript may have originated in the mid-fifteenth century.

The history of this manuscript, on the basis of two later inscriptions, appears to be as follows: In 1710 the manuscript was in the possession of the bishop of Skoplje. When a monk from Mount Athos came to Skoplje in 1735, he was the first in a long time to know how to sing tunes from this manuscript. This implies that a good deal of singing must have been transmitted exclusively orally. See Kosta P. Manojlović's preface to Stevan Mokranjac, *Pravoslavno srpsko narodno crkveno pojanje* (Serbian Orthodox Church Chanting), (Belgrade, 1935), p. 10 of the preface.

9. Svetozar Matić, "Jedan spomenik stare muzičke kulture srpske" (A document of the old Serbian musical culture), *Muzički glasnik,* V (1932), 277–80.

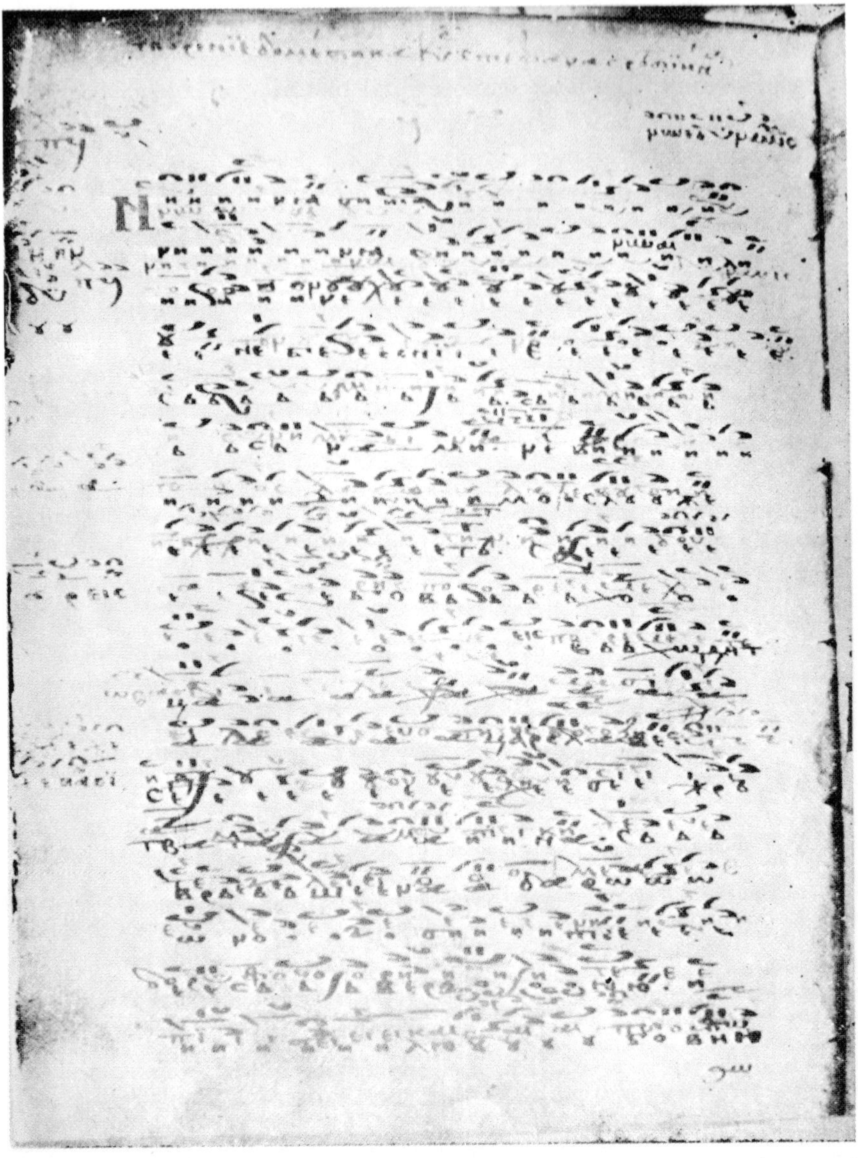

PLATE I. The earliest known record of a Serbian composer. The inscription in the upper margin reads "Tvorenie domestika kir Stefana Srbina" ("The work of domestikos Kir Stefan the Serb"). From MS. 369(93), formerly in the Belgrade Public Library, p. 287.

288r) the name of Stefan the Serb was listed as author of a hymn of which only the Greek version was written. Since in the manuscript numerous incipits in the Serbian language had been written above the Greek text, it was tentatively assumed that a substantial part of the Serbian texts may have been a later addition. Regardless of the possible variance in the date of these incipits in the Serbian language, it would seem clear that the incipits were inserted to remind singers to sing the Slavic text, utilizing the melodic outlines of the Greek tunes.

Among available materials a special place belongs to MS. 421 in the Archives of the Serbian Academy of Sciences and Arts in Belgrade, dated A.D. 1668. This interesting manuscript of sixty-one folios consists of two distinct parts. The first part, folios 1–47, contains only texts of troparia, kathismata, kontakia, hirmoi, and some other chants, all written in Church Slavonic. Despite the lack of neumatic notation in this part of the manuscript, it seems almost certain that it was intended for use by singers. That this is true may be inferred from a number of words on folios 42–45 in which the scribe repeated the vowels many times. Since the scribe did not leave room enough for the insertion of neumes, it would appear that he desired to indicate those parts of the text that were to be performed melismatically.

The second part of this manuscript, folios 48–61, contains notated Greek texts of chants from the standard repertory to be found in a typical Anthologion: trisagia, alleluiaria, the Cherubic Hymn, Communion songs (koinonika), and hymns of a few other kinds. It is in this part of the manuscript that two of the most unusual examples of the substitution of texts may be found. Whereas in former examples bilingual versions of the *same* text were encountered, on folios 51r and 54r instances may be found of a Greek text under which a completely *different* text appears in the Church Slavonic language. Both texts are of Communion songs whose melodies may easily be transcribed. On folio 51r may be found one of the most frequently sung Communion hymns, Αἰνεῖτε τὸν Κύριον (Psalm 148:1). Instead of the expected translation of this text (which would have read "Hvalite Gospoda s nebes") one finds in red ink the Church Slavonic text of a different Communion hymn, whose text is from Psalm 111:9, sung on the feast of Christmas. The scribe did not insert any Slavic text underneath the word "Alleluia." On the right-hand margin another text has been added in red ink, a hymn sung during the Communion of the faithful. On folio 54r may be found Chrysaphes' composition for the Communion hymn Εἰς μνημόσυνον αἰώνιον (Psalm 111:6); and underneath may be found the Slavic text of a different Communion hymn, based on Psalm 115:4. For the word "Alleluia," as in the previous example, no Slavic text was added. The appended transcriptions of these examples demonstrate the procedures used by the Serbian scribe who added those texts. Although the Church Slavonic text was inserted with relative freedom, it is important to stress that in each instance the scribe did take the accents into account and tried to bring them into accord with the melodic stresses. The inclusion of the intonation signs (μαρτυρίαι) that served as checks for correct pitch was of great help. It will be noted that great attention was paid to these in the disposition of syllables of the subscribed Slavic text. These two examples may indicate some of the ways in which the Greek tunes were combined with the Slavic text. (See Plates II, III, and Music Examples 1, 2.)

In addition to the direct evidence found in musical manuscripts, there is some indirect evidence concerning the Greek influence on church music in Serbia. In 1727, for instance, Mojsije Petrović, Metropolitan of Belgrade, opened a school there. About half a century later it was recorded that a monk from Mount Athos by the name of Anatol came to Belgrade. Children with good voices were selected from the school and assigned as pupils to the monk, who was an experienced singer. He taught them how to sing in Greek. Thus the Greek Chant spread "everywhere," records the chronicler, and the Serbian Chant (by which obviously is meant not only "in the Serbian manner" but more specifically "singing *in Serbian*") ceased so that one seldom heard it any more.[10]

In a report dated 1733, it is said that some priests sing the Cherubic Hymn in Greek while the communion song of the First Mode is sung "in the simple way." It is also reported that some

10. Jovan Rajić, *Istorija katihizma pravoslavnih Srbalja u cesarskim državama,* Narodna biblioteka braće Jovanovića, Sveska 95 (Pančevo, n.d.), p. 22. (History of the catechism of the Serbian Orthodox in the Imperial [i.e., Austrian] Domain, a late 18th century work).

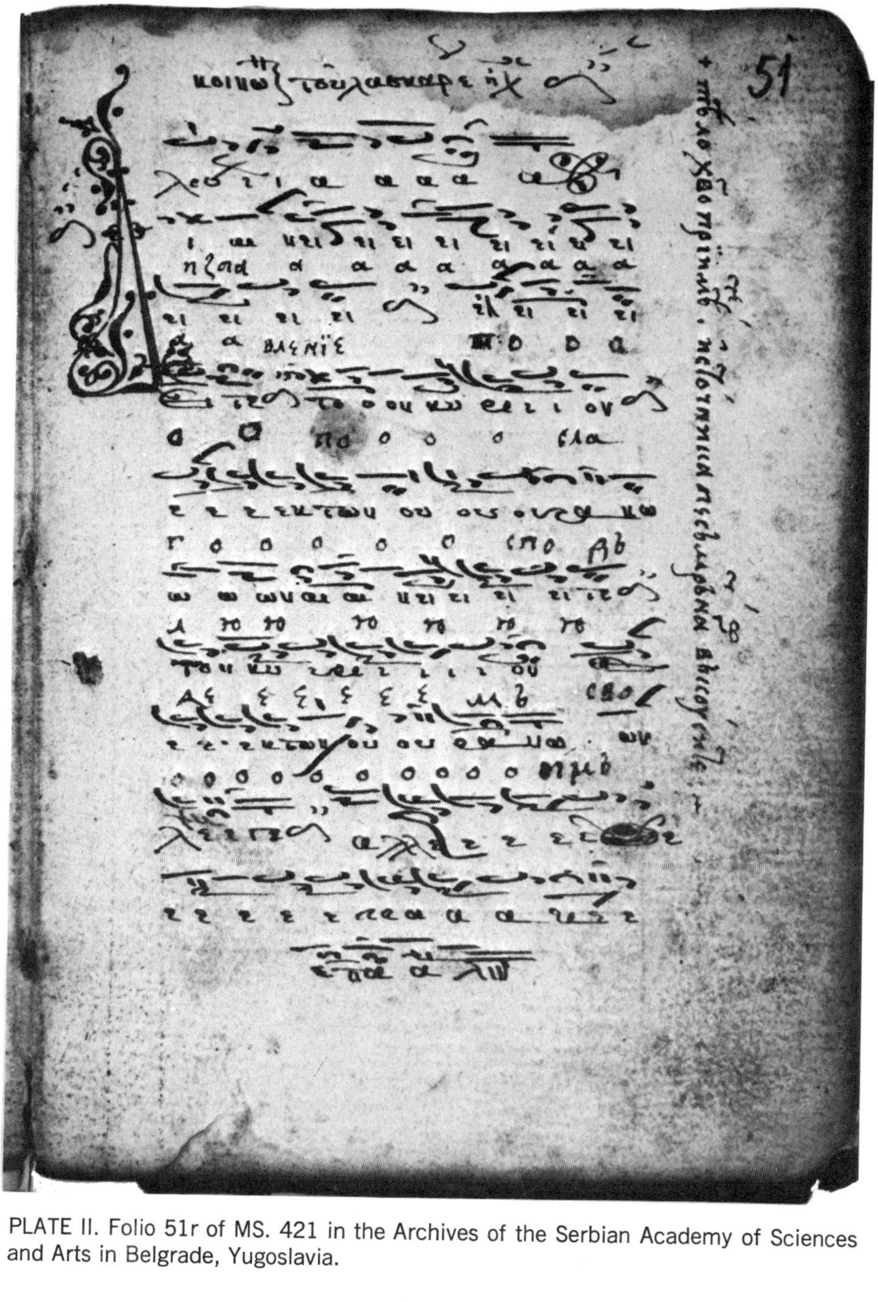

PLATE II. Folio 51r of MS. 421 in the Archives of the Serbian Academy of Sciences and Arts in Belgrade, Yugoslavia.

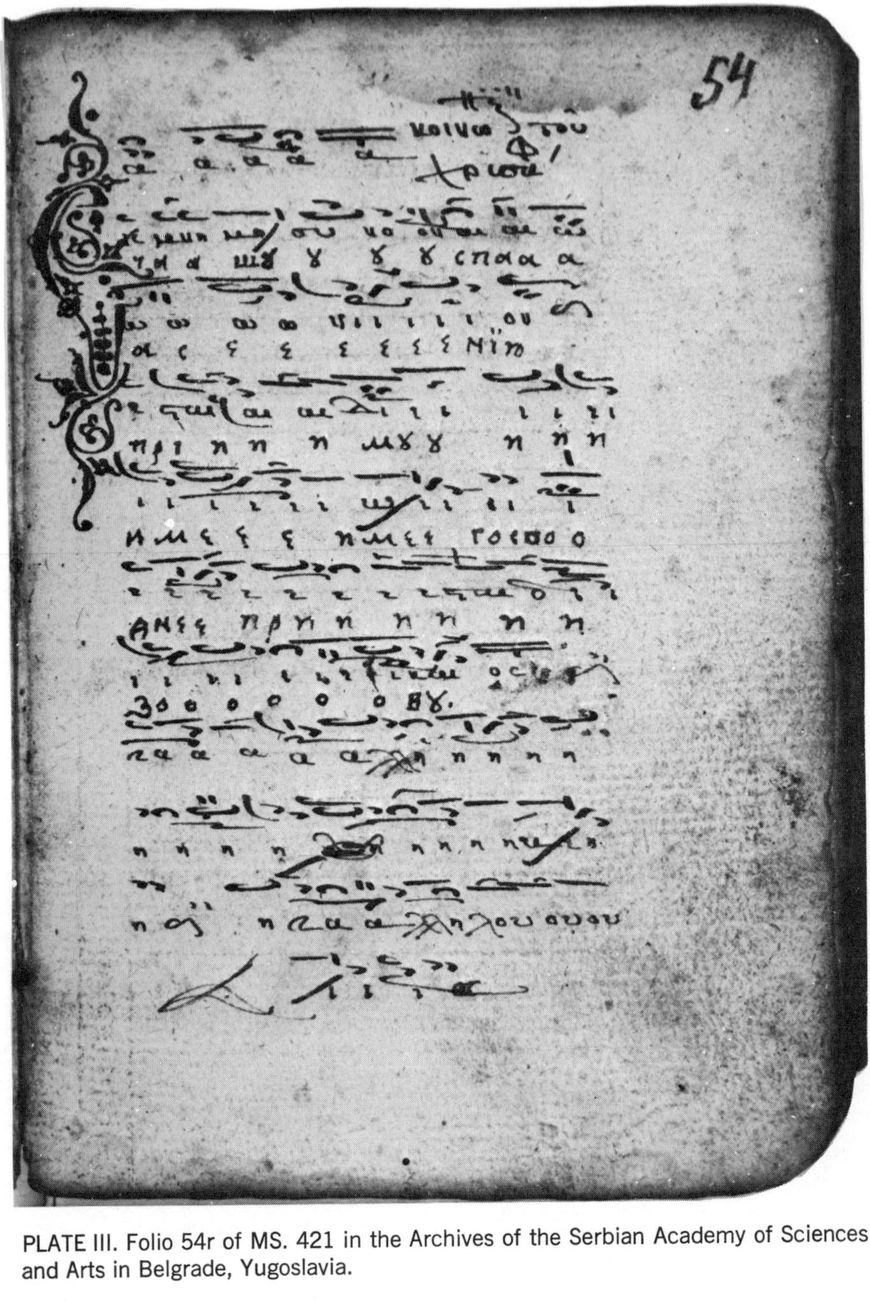

PLATE III. Folio 54r of MS. 421 in the Archives of the Serbian Academy of Sciences and Arts in Belgrade, Yugoslavia.

EX. 1. MS. 421, fol. 51r (partial transcription of the example on Plate II).

EX. 2. MS. 421, fol. 54r (partial transcription of the example on Plate III).

priests had learned *kanerati,* a term interpreted to mean singing "after the Greek pattern."[11]

The Greek singing was practiced not only in Serbia but in Valachia and Moldavia, as may be inferred from a statement in a Spanish diplomatic report of 1809: "It would seem that the Russians have decided to keep Valachia and Moldavia for themselves. They assembled priests and ordered that henceforth the liturgy must be performed only in Russian, instead of in Greek as heretofore."[12]

All these data substantiate the conclusion that the Serbian Chant as well as the Russian and Bulgarian chants originated as offshoots of the Byzantine Chant.[13] The Greek influence was to be felt even in the nineteenth century. In our day in the Slavic Eastern Orthodox Churches may still be heard two hymns that are sung in Greek during the liturgy in which the bishop officiates. These are *Ispolaeti Despota,* derived from Εἰς πολλὰ ἔτη, and *Ton Despotin.*

The current research work and studies of the manuscripts of the eighteenth and nineteenth centuries in the Chilandar monastery may clarify and illuminate a part of this hitherto neglected field—the history of church music in Serbia.[14]

11. "Izveštaj napisao 1733 Maksim Ratković, eksarh beogradskog mitropolita," ed. Gavrilo Vitković, *Glasnik Srpskog Učenog Društva,* LVI (Belgrade, 1884), 117–360, esp. 236 and 266.

12. See Bogoljub Petković's review of Dragomir Janković, *Ispisi iz španskih arhiva* in *Arhivist* (Belgrade), VII (1957), 63.

13. See this writer's "Einige Probleme zur Erforschung der slavischen Kirchenmusik," *Kirchenmusikalisches Jahrbuch,* XLIII (1959), 1–7; cf. also the conclusions of Miloš Velimirović, *Byzantine Elements in Early Slavic Chant,* Monumenta musicae Byzantinae, series *Subsidia,* IV—Pars principalis (Copenhagen, 1960), p. 127; also Myroslaw Antonowytsch, "Die byzantinischen Elemente in den Antiphonen der Ukrainischen Kirche," *Kirchenmusikalisches Jahrbuch,* XLIII (1959), 8–26.

14. Cf. J. Milojković-Djurić, "Some Aspects of the Byzantine Origin of the Serbian Chant," *Byzantinoslavica,* XXIII:1 (Prague, 1962), 45–51. D. Stefanović, "The Serbian Chant from the 15th to the 18th Centuries," *Musica Antiqua Europae Orientalis* (Warsaw, 1966), pp. 140–63; in collaboration with M. Velimirović "Peter Lampadarios and Metropolitan Serafim of Bosnia," *Studies in Eastern Chant,* I, 67–88.

21 / John Taverner

DENIS STEVENS
Columbia University

JOHN TAVERNER was born about 1490, probably at Tattershall (Lincolnshire), and died October 25, 1545, at Boston (Lincolnshire). The surname Taverner occurs frequently in records at Boston and Tattershall from the early fourteenth century. At the time John Taverner was born, the collegiate church at Tattershall could look back on half a century of service to the community and castle, and its warden, six chaplains, and choir of twelve (six men, six boys) encouraged the growth of interest in liturgical polyphony. As one of the choirboys, Taverner would have received a thorough schooling in music as well as in Latin and English grammar, and since it was the custom to teach choirboys to play the clavichord in preparation for later studies on the organ, he may well have received his first instruction in instrumental techniques at this time. In 1514 Taverner became a member of the Fraternity of St. Nicholas (a guild of parish clerks) in London, and in order to obtain this membership he must have traveled to London and stayed there for some time, although no reference to his musical career there has so far come to light. His approximate date of birth is usually given as 1495; but it is unlikely that he would have gained admittance to the guild at less than twenty years of age. The earlier date of 1490 is therefore more

This article is a fuller version of the entry on Taverner prepared for *Die Musik in Geschichte und Gegenwart*. The original and complete form of the article is printed here by permission of the editor of *MGG*.

plausible in view of the recently discovered reference to his presence in London. He seems, however, to have returned to Tattershall, for he is listed as a "clericus socius" in the record of a visitation by the chancellor of John Longland, Bishop of Lincoln, in May 1525.

In October of the following year the Bishop, who had been in correspondence with Cardinal Wolsey, tried to persuade Taverner to leave Tattershall and go to Oxford as "informator choristarum" at Cardinal College (now Christ Church College), Oxford. Then a new foundation, the College consisted of a dean, one hundred canons, thirteen priests, and a choir of twenty-eight (twelve men, sixteen boys) to be directed by a skilled musician. At first Taverner resisted the temptation of this important post; he told the Bishop that he was reluctant to give up his duties at Tattershall, and unwilling to forgo the financial benefits of a dowry resulting from a good marriage. Within a week or so Taverner was offered a salary and other expenses amounting to a greater sum than the annual salary of any member of the college except the Dean and the Sub-Dean, and by November 1526 he had accepted the post and removed to Oxford.

The college chapel, which retained its dedication to St. Frideswide until it became the Cathedral Church of Christ (foundation of the See of Oxford, 1546), is mentioned in an account by Anthony Delaber: "Then went I straight to Friswides, and Evensong was begun, and the Deane and the other Canons were there in their gray Amices; they were almost at Magnificat before I came thether. I stood at the quier door and heard Master Taverner play, and others of the chappell there sing." This account first appeared in Foxe's *Acts and Monuments*, the various editions of which refer to Taverner as "a man very singular in musick," "a good musician," and as one who "repented him very much that he had made Songes to Popish Ditties in the time of his blindness." Since Taverner became seriously involved in Lutheran controversies that shook the very foundations of the college in 1527 and came to a head in 1528, it must be assumed that he composed the greater part of his Latin church music before he moved to Oxford. On the other hand, the statutes of the new college specifically mention certain texts that were to be sung daily in chapel, among them antiphons to the Trinity, to St. William of York, and to the Virgin, also *Salve regina, Ave Maria,* and *Sancte Deus.* Five of the six items have come down to us in settings by

Taverner: *O splendor gloriae* (Trinity), *Christe Jesu pastor bone* (originally *O Wilhelme pastor bone*), *Gaude plurimum* (and several other antiphons in honor of the Virgin), *Ave Maria*, and *Sancte Deus*. From this same period comes the Mass derived from *Christe Jesu / O Wilhelme*, and designated in the earliest sources as *Small Devotion*. The word "small" is undoubtedly a misreading of the normal scribal contraction for "S. willi" = "S. Wilhelmi devocio." Both motet and Mass are thus connected with St. William, Archbishop of York (died 1154, canonized 1226).

Together with several of his colleagues, Taverner was imprisoned after being accused of heresy, yet (to quote Fox once again) "the Cardinal for his musick excused him, saying, that he was but a Musitian, and so he escaped." In March 1530, Taverner received his final salary payment at Cardinal College, and his place was taken by John Benbow of Manchester. Nothing is known of Taverner's life for the next seven years, although he undoubtedly returned to Lincolnshire and may at this time have married Rose Parrowe, by whom he had two daughters. He was elected a member of the Guild of Corpus Christi at Boston in 1537, and acted as steward from 1541 to 1543. Between 1538 and 1540 he served as the chief local agent of Thomas Cromwell, Lord Privy Seal, in bringing about the dissolution of friaries and monasteries. No longer much concerned with music, Taverner turned to this office of destruction with a zeal that amounted almost to fanaticism. He nevertheless did his best to help some of the displaced friars, and wrote to Cromwell about their dire poverty and need. He dissuaded them from taking down and selling the lead from the priory roof, offering to help them personally "in mean while at all times when they lacked anything." Another eloquent plea for assistance from the Lord Privy Seal concerns a dispute over property, which involved a friend and relative named Charles Yerburgh, then elderly, blind, and infirm. Although Taverner lived to see many of the changes in religion resulting from Henry VIII's break with Rome, he did not apparently make any contribution to the musical repertory of the new services. A section of his Mass *Gloria tibi Trinitas* was adapted to two different sets of English words, almost certainly after his death, and similar adaptations (though much less skillful) were made from the Mass *Sine nomine* (=*Meane Mass*) and the Mass *Sancti Wilhelmi*. Taverner died in

1545, and was buried under the bell-tower of Boston Parish Church. His wife survived him by eight years, and her will specifies certain lands owned by her late husband, indicating that they were a fairly prosperous family. Taverner's church music appears in Volumes I and III of *Tudor Church Music*, the former giving transcriptions of relevant documents, as well as a facsimile of his handwriting and a series of alleged portraits in a set of part-books at Oxford. Page references in the following list of works are to these volumes.

WORKS

Church Music

(A) Latin.

(1) Masses: *Gloria tibi Trinitas,* 6 voices (I, 126–56); *Corona spinea,* 6 v. (I, 157–93); *O Michaell,* 6 v. (I, 194–225); *Meane Mass* (wrongly entitled *Sine nomine*), 5 v. (I, 50–69); *Sancti Wilhelmi* (wrongly entitled *Small Devotion* or *In all devotion*), 5 v. (I, 70–98); *Mater Christi,* 5 v. (I, 99–125); *The Western Wynde,* 4 v. (I, 3–29); *Playn Song Mass,* 4 v. (I, 30–49).

(2) Magnificats: 6 v. (III, 17–25); 5 v. (III, 9–16); 4 v. (III, 3–8).

(3) Te Deum: 5 v. (III, 26–34).

(4) Responsories: *Audivi vocem de caelo. . . . Media nocte,* 4 v. (III, 35–36); *Dum transisset sabbatum,* No. 1, 5 v. (III, 37–40; alternative version, 4 v., III, 40–42); *Dum transisset sabbatum,* No. 2, 5 v. (III, 43–45); [*Hodie nobis caelorum rex*]. . . . *Gloria in excelsis,* 4 v. (III, 46–47); *In pace in idipsum. . . . Si dedero,* 4 v. (III, 48–51); [*Ex ejus tumba*] . . . *Sospitati dedit,* 5 v. (III, 110–16).

(5) Alleluias: *Salve virgo,* 4 v. (III, 52); *Veni electa mea,* 4 v (III, 53).

(6) Antiphons: *Sub tuum praesidium,* 5 v. (III, 141–42); *Fac nobis secundum hoc nomen suave,* 5 v. (III, 135–38); *Ave Maria,* 5 v. (III, 134); *Sancte Deus,* 5 v. (III, 139–40).

(7) Psalm: *Quemadmodum desiderat cervus,* 6 v. (III, 117–121).

(8) Motets: *Ave Dei Patris Filia,* 5 v. (III, 61–72); *Christe Jesu pastor bone,* 5 v. (III, 73–77); *Gaude plurimum,* 5 v. (III, 78–91); *Mater Christi,* 5 v. (III, 92–98); *O splendor gloriae,* 5 v. (III, 99–109).

(9) Isolated sections of the *Ordinarium Missae:* Kyrie "Le roy," 4 v. (III, 54–55); Christe eleison, i, ii, iii, 3 v. (III, 56–57); Sanctus, 3 v. (III, 58); Benedictus 3 v. (III, 59); Agnus Dei, 3 v. (III, 60).

(10) Fragments: *Ecce mater,* 2 v. (III, 122); *Jesu spes poenitentibus* (from Sequence *Dulcis Jesu memoria*), 3 v. (III, 123); *Prudens virgo,* 3 v. (III, 124); *Tam peccatum* (from Tract, *Dulce nomen Jesu Christi*), 3 v. (III, 126); *Traditur militibus* (from Sequence *Coenam cum discipulis*), 3 v. (III, 132); *Virgo pura,* 3 v. (III, 131).

(N.B. The other four short compositions in Vol. III are by Fayrfax, Tallis, and Aston.)

(B) English.

(1) Masses: *Meane Mass,* 5 v. (III, 143–68); *Sancti Wilhelmi,* 5 v. (III, 169–98).

(2) Anthems: *In trouble and adversity,* 4 v. (III, 199–200); *O give thanks unto the Lord,* 4 v. (N.B. Both these anthems are English adaptations of the "in nomine" section of the Benedictus from *Missa Gloria tibi Trinitas*).

Secular Music

(A) Vocal.

My heart, my mind; Love will I; The bella (in *XX Songes,* 1530); *For women no season is rest* (in British Museum, Baldwin's MS.).

(B) Instrumental.

Many arrangements of Taverner's original *In nomine* for viols (*a 4* and *a 5*), lute, organ, and harpsichord.

Unlike Tallis and Byrd, who had to contend with conflicting religious practices and widely divergent musical styles for the Roman and English rites, Taverner spent his entire musical career (less than thirty-five years) in singing and composing Latin church music. At length disenchanted with it, he retired from the musical scene while his technique was at its height, and spent the remainder of his days as a paid agent of the Crown. Although evidently a capable organist, he left no organ music to posterity, apart from a keyboard arrangement of his famous *In nomine,* and even that may have been the work of an admiring colleague. In refining his vocal writing to the point at which it seemed to suggest the suave sonorities and soft textures of the consort of viols, Taverner unintentionally brought into being not only the *In nomine* which was in essence a fantasia on a *cantus firmus*, but also the later fantasia proper, in which the composer was able to invent his own points of imitation and to proceed with relative freedom from structural or modal considerations. Both these forms, *In nomine* and fantasia, lived on until Purcell's day, giving to English chamber music a continuity of tradition that it was never again to enjoy. But it was in his church music that Taverner displayed his uncanny sense of total planning, his remarkable ability to weave a contrapuntal texture at the same time strong yet pliable, and his unerring instinct for the development of melodic phrases rich in both beauty and personality. Nowhere are these qualities more clearly set forth than in the five- and six-voice Masses and in the great Marian motets or votive antiphons.

The reason why such excellence should emerge from a flourishing but relatively obscure district many miles from city and court is best explained by a hitherto unnoticed estimate of English music written by a Scottish theologian shortly before 1521, when the volume in question was published in Paris. At a time when Taverner was not yet thirty, though already a highly skilled musician, John Major stated in his *Historia Majoris Britanniae tam Angliae quam Scotiae:* "In England every village, be it only of twelve or thirteen houses, has a parish church; their places of worship are most richly adorned, and in the art of music they stand, in my opinion, first in all Europe. For though in France or in Scotland you may meet with some musicians of such absolute accomplishment as in England, yet 'tis not in such numbers."

Among Taverner's more subtle accomplishments was his close and careful integration of the polyphonic texture by frequent use of imitative points based on the outstanding melodic features of his chosen plainsong. Instead of inventing points or themes of his own, he would contrive to have them echo or anticipate the chant, with the result that the gulf between the slow-moving cantus firmus and the more rapid and flexible surroundings lessened to a noticeable degree. Yet his polyphonic lines, considered as entities, do not resemble plainsong except at their beginnings: assimilated into the texture at an early stage, they later become independent and often quasi-instrumental in their use of wide leaps and bold sequential patterns. The "Qui tollis" from the Gloria of the *Missa Gloria tibi*

Trinitas and the opening of the Sanctus of the *Missa Corona spinea* offer classical examples of these procedures, in which the restricted number of voice-parts contributes to the effect of personal eloquence. In both works the interplay of vocal timbres is managed with the utmost skill, and the maximum use is made of contrasting effects of light and shade.

In the stricter contrapuntal forms, especially canon, Taverner achieved delicate and memorable effects whose beauty almost disguises their complexity. The *Missa O Michaell* (based on a responsory for the Feast of St. Michael in Monte Tumba, *Archangeli Michaelis interventione*) contains three very near approximations to celestial harmony in canons for two treble voices and a free supporting part, at "Qui tollis" in the Gloria, at "Filium Dei unigenitum" in the Credo, and at the beginning of the Benedictus. His parody technique is, however, much looser than that of Tallis, and in the two derived Masses (*Missa Mater Christi* from the motet of the same name, and *Missa Sancti Wilhelmi* from the motet *Christe Jesu pastor bone*) there is much more new than borrowed material. The possibilities of variation on a single theme are fully and often magnificently exploited in the *Western Wynde* Mass, based on a secular melody also used in Masses by Tye and Shepherd. Taverner's Agnus Dei is especially rich in the flowing ornamentation of *proportio tripla,* which also appears briefly but effectively in the Sanctus. Even more florid and complex is the brilliant setting of "Sicut erat" in the Magnificat for six voices, whose execution presupposes a choir well endowed with highly competent solo boys and men.

The larger motets afford less opportunity for display since Taverner is clearly concerned with the projection of the more important phrases of the text. *Gaude plurimum* has no *cantus firmus* but makes the fullest possible use of imitative points as well as occasional antiphony; on the other hand, *Ave Dei Patris Filia* uses parts of the Te Deum chant as its *cantus firmus,* the final Amen drawing on the last verse of the canticle with its neuma. Taverner also composed Te Deum for alternating plainsong and polyphony, without hesitating to change cadential figures and the pitch of certain verses where such changes would be beneficial to the harmony.

In certain works Taverner made extensive use of a simpler and entirely different style, stressing homophony and textual declamation in a way that would have pleased Cranmer. The *Playn Song Mass* confines itself to only four note-values: the breve, dotted breve, semibreve, and dotted semibreve. Monotony is carefully avoided by the judicious introduction of imitative phrases and by varying the texture within the limits of the four voice-parts, and the syllabic nature of the Gloria and Credo settings is offset by the considerably more melismatic Sanctus and Agnus Dei. The motets *Mater Christi* and *Christe Jesu* also lean toward homophony, contrast being achieved here by the skillfully playing off one section of the choir against another.

The Alleluias and responsories, based on their respective plainsongs, contain some of Taverner's finest music. The first setting of *Dum transisset sabbatum,* with its highly expressive setting of the words "aromata" and "Alleluia," and the four-voice "In pace" (where the chant by the boys seems to float effortlessly above the other polyphonic strands) demonstrate the art of counterpoint almost devoid of artifice. *Audivi,* for Matins of All Saints Day, retains the old liturgical custom of using boys' voices and countertenors only; so too does the verse "Gloria in excelsis" of the Christmas responsory *Hodie nobis.* The prose *Sospitati dedit aegros,* for Matins of St. Nicholas, affords numerous opportunities for the display of different technical devices, including imitations of the *cantus firmus,* melodic development of the chant, and use of the chant as the basis of free canon. Non-liturgical *cantus firmi* of the type known as "squares" may be found in the Kyrie "Le roy" (Ludford also uses this melody) and in the three settings of "Christe eleison." It appears that these may all be early works, written during Taverner's first Lincolnshire period, since manuscripts containing "squares" were known at Boston in the late fifteenth century, and one of them "emptus de Boston" is mentioned in an inventory at King's College, Cambridge.

As a contrapuntal craftsman, Taverner is entitled to a lofty place among his fellows, of whatever school or nationality. His technique was of such a kind as to exult in self-imposed problems and difficulties, which were often solved in an artistic rather than merely brilliant manner. His music consequently gives an aural impression of rugged grandeur in the five- and six-voice sections of his larger motets and Masses, yet in the smaller and more intimate works there are countless examples of dexterous polyphony drawing upon the slenderest of resources. No court appointment ever came his way, and the Chapel Royal apparently did not attract him as much as his native Lincolnshire; but his musical abilities were at least equal to those of the greatest of his contemporaries who served Henry VIII, and he is no less worthy than they of an honorable place in the history of music in England.

EDITIONS

Latin Church Music

Tudor Church Music, Vols. I and III (Oxford University Press, 1923, 1924); Supplementary volume (Oxford University Press, 1948).

Separate items available include: Kyrie "Le roy" (Oxford University Press); *Missa Gloria tibi Trinitas* (Stainer & Bell); *Western Wynde* Mass (Stainer & Bell); *Christe Jesu pastor bone* (Oxford University Press); *Dum transisset sabbatum* (Stainer & Bell).

Instrumental Music

In nomine (version for strings: Hortus Musicus [Bärenreiter]); *In nomine* (two versions for organ in *The Mulliner Book* [Stainer & Bell] and in *Altenglische Orgelmusik* [Bärenreiter]).

BIBLIOGRAPHY

H. Baillie, "A London Gild of Musicians," *Proceedings of the Royal Musical Association,* 83 (1956/7), 15–28.

———"Squares," *Acta musicologica,* XXXII (1960), 178–93.

J. Bergsagel, "An Introduction to Ludford," *Musica disciplina,* XIV (1960), 105–34.

H. B. Collins, "John Taverner's Masses," *Music and Letters,* V/VI (1924/25).

W. H. G. Flood, *Early Tudor Composers* (Oxford, 1925).

F. Ll. Harrison, *Music in Medieval Britain* (London: Routledge, 1958).

D. S. Josephson, "John Taverner: An English Renaissance Master," *American Choral Review,* IX (1967), 6–15.

———"The Festal Masses of John Taverner," *American Choral Review,* IX (1967), 10–21.

———"John Taverner: Smaller Liturgical Works," *American Choral Review,* IX (1967), 26–41.

G. Reese, *Music in the Renaissance* (New York, 1954, 1959).

———"The Origin of the English *In Nomine,*" *Journal, American Musicological Society,* II (1949), 7–22.

D. W. Stevens, *The Mulliner Book: A Commentary* (London: Stainer & Bell, 1952).

———*Tudor Church Music* (London: Faber, 1961, 1966).

22 / The Pre-English Use of the Term "Virginal"

MILOŠ M. VELIMIROVIĆ
Yale University

In the history of music for keyboard instruments there occurs, at the end of the sixteenth century and the beginning of the seventeenth, a group of composers called the English Virginalists. It is common knowledge, however, that in actual practice these musicians used keyboard instruments of several types, only one of which was the true virginal. According to Praetorius, every stringed keyboard instrument, regardless of shape or size, was called a virginal in England: "In Engelland werden alle solche Instrumenta sie seyn klein oder gross Virginall genennet."[1]

The origin of the term "virginal" as the name for a stringed keyboard instrument has been much discussed, yet no satisfactory conclusion has been reached. In this essay an attempt will be made to trace the history of the term "virginal" prior to its appearance in England.

I

The general assumption is that the first reference to the term "virginal" appeared in Sebastian Virdung's *Musica getutscht*, published in 1511 at Basel.[2] A number of English writers accept this as a fact, and it is restated in the fifth edition of *Grove's Dictionary of*

1. M. Praetorius, *Syntagma musicum*, II, *De Organographia* (Wolfenbüttel, 1619), p. 62.
2. S. Virdung, *Musica getutscht und ausgezogen* (Basel, 1511), fol. Bi, recto and verso.

Music and Musicians.[3] However, as Curt Sachs has pointed out, there are two earlier references to the virginal, one in a poem from the epoch of Henry VII (1485–1509) and the other in a manuscript treatise by Paulus Paulirinus.[4] Unfortunately, Sachs did not identify the poem containing this reference. One must assume that he was referring to the so-called "Leckingfield Proverbs," at one time believed to date from the reign of Henry VII. In an article dealing with that poem, Canon Galpin demonstrated that this particular text dates from a slightly later period, from 1516 to 1523.[5] This discovery leaves Paulirinus' treatise as apparently the only source in which this term is used prior to its appearance in *Musica getutscht.*

Among modern scholars, Reese seems to have been the only music historian to remark on Paulirinus' treatise, and he gives the only English translation of the pertinent text concerning the virginal.[6] The full text of the sections of Paulirinus' manuscript dealing with musical forms and musical instruments was published in full in 1924–1925.[7] It is really remarkable, in view of its availability, that so little use has been made of this highly interesting and important listing of musical instruments known in Central Europe about 1460.

II

Since available data about Paulirinus in musicological literature are scattered and incomplete, and since he is the author of a treatise that contains the earliest known reference to the virginal, it is of interest to reconstruct the biography of this colorful personality.

In his commentary on the text of Paulirinus' treatise on music, its editor, J. Reiss, lists a few biographical facts, from which it is concluded that Paulirinus was born in 1413 at Prague.[8] He was of

3. *Grove's Dictionary of Music and Musicians* (5th ed.; London, 1954), IX, 2–3.

4. C. Sachs, *The History of Musical Instruments* (New York, 1940), p. 335.

5. F. W. Galpin, "Musical Proverbs at Lekingfelde Lodge," *Music and Letters,* VI (1925), 146–50.

6. G. Reese, *Music in the Renaissance* (New York, 1954), p. 667.

7. J. Reiss, "Pauli Paulirini de Praga Tractatus de Musica (etwa 1460)," *Zeitschrift für Musikwissenschaft,* VII (1924–1925), 259–64.

8. *Ibid.,* p. 259. Reiss obtained the basic information from Josef Muczkowski's Latin dissertation, *Pauli Paulirini olim Paulus de Praga vocitati XX. artium manuscriptus liber* (Cracow, 1835), which was unavailable to this writer. A review of Muczkowski's study, with a number of quotations, by Josef Jungmann, may be found in *Časopis Českého Museum,* XI (1837), 225–32.

PLATE I. Paulus Židek, also known as Paulus Paulirinus and Paulus de Praga. This portrait appears in Pelzel's book (see note 9), facing page 6. According to Pelzel (page 11) this portrait is reproduced from one "bey dem Domkapitel auf dem Prager Schlosse."

Jewish origin, a circumstance which led to the nickname "Židek." Under this name he is relatively well known in the history of Czech literature, and several biographies of Paulus Židek are available.[9] Although some of the earlier writings about Paulus Židek are considered unreliable, it has been assumed that Muczkowski's dissertation (the source of information for Reiss) weeded out most of the incorrect statements concerning Paulirinus.

According to the available information, Paulirinus appears to have been taken from his Jewish parents as a small child and to have been reared in the Roman Catholic faith. His biographers assert that Paulirinus studied philosophy in Vienna, and that he also studied medicine in Padua and Bologna. On his return from Italy he supposedly became a priest in Regensburg. Immediately one may ask why Paulirinus did not study in Prague. Although the religious controversies produced by the Hussite movement had made this a period of instability and brought about the partial closing of the University of Prague in the 1420's, the study of the liberal arts was resumed there in the next decade.[10] Whatever the reasons for his decision, Paulirinus did go abroad, although the statements of his biographers about where and what he studied do not always find documentary support.

Although the name of Paulus cannot be found in the available registers of the University in Vienna, it seems that he was there in 1442 as "magister regens."[11] No indication is now available, however, as to what part of that year he served in this capacity.[12] Since a "magister" is known to have taught only one course in a year,[13] Paulirinus' stay in Vienna may not have been a long one; a course on music (if he did teach that subject!) would have lasted only four

9. Those accessible to this writer are: F. M. Pelzel, *Abbildungen böhmischer und mährischer Gelehrter und Künstler,* III (Prague, 1777), 6–11; Jos. Jireček, *Rukověť k dějinám literatury české do konce XVIII věku,* II (Prague, 1876), 375–77; *Ottův Slovník Naučný,* XXVII (Prague, 1908), 834; J. Vlček, *Dějiny české literatury,* I (3d ed.; Prague, 1940), 240–45.

10. W. W. Tomek, *Geschichte der Prager Universität* (Prague, 1849), p. 126; cf. J. Krčmář, *The Prague Universities* (Prague, 1934), p. 18.

11. *Die Matrikel der Universität Wien,* 1377–1450, Vol. I/1 (Vienna, 1954) and Vol. I/2 (Vienna, 1956).

12. J. Aschbach, *Geschichte der Wiener Universität im ersten Jahrhundert ihres Bestehens* (Vienna, 1865), p. 619.

13. *Ibid.,* pp. 354–55.

weeks, with a total of sixteen lectures.[14] It is possible that Paulirinus did study in Vienna prior to that time, since it is stated in the records of the University of Padua for March 24, 1442 that a Paulus de Praga "scolaris vienensis studii" obtained his degree in liberal arts.[15]

As for Bologna, Paulirinus' name is not to be found in any of the available sources of information concerning students and recipients of degrees.[16] Neither has documentary evidence been found that Paulirinus went to Regensburg, or that he actually became a priest.

In October 1442 (a year rich in data about him) Paulirinus was in Prague, where he obtained the degree of "magister." On that occasion he presented his credentials to the University, and was listed as "Mag. Paulus de Praga, Paduanae, Bononiensis, Wyennensis universitatum magister . . . docuissetque literarum cum sigillis pendentibus dictarum universitatum, se esse earundem magistrum."[17] On January 28, 1443, Paulirinus became a member of the faculty at the University of Prague.[18] He made another trip to Padua in August 1445, apparently to attend the promotion of a friend. At this time Paulirinus is listed as doctor of arts.[19]

There is no proof that Paulirinus ever studied medicine. After some initial quarrels with the faculty in Prague in 1444, Paulirinus was accused in 1447 of speaking against the medical profession, even of stating that "omnis medicus est homicida"—a statement which he had to retract publicly.[20] After that year there are no further

14. R. Kink, *Geschichte der kaiserlichen Universität zu Wien* (Vienna, 1854), I, Pt. 2, p. 111: "Statutum facultatis Arcium circa tempus et horas legendi," of April 14, 1449: "musica per 4 ebd., 16 *l*."

15. *Acta Graduum Academicorum gymnasii Patavini ab anno MCCCCVI ad annum MCCCCL,* ed. C. Zonta and I. Brotto (Padua, 1922), p. 327, Nos. 1586 and 1588.

16. G. N. P. Alidosi, *I dottori bolognesi di Teologia, Filosofia, Medicina e d'Arti Liberali, dall'anno 1000 per tutto Marzo del 1623* (Bologna, 1623). Cf. by the same author, *I dottori forestieri che in Bologna hanno letto Teologia, Filosofia, Medicina & Arti Liberali, con li rettori dello studio dagli anni 1000 fino per tutto Maggio del 1623* (Bologna, 1623).

17. *Monumenta Universitatis Pragensis, I. Liber Decanorum facultatis philosophicae, Pars ii* (Prague, 1830), p. 18, quoted by Jungmann in *Časopis Čes. Mus.*, p. 228.

18. *Ibid.;* also mentioned by Pelzel, *Abbildungen . . . ,* p. 7, and cited in G. Pietzsch, "Die Pflege der Musik an den Universitäten bis sur Mitte des 16. Jahrhunderts—1. Die Universität Prag und ihre Vorbilder," *Mitteilungen des Vereines für Geschichte der Deutschen in Böhmen,* LXXIII (1935), 36.

19. *Acta Graduum Academicorum . . . ,* p. 387, No. 1958.

20. Cf. Jungmann in *Časopis Čes. Mus.*, p. 229; see also the article of Pietzsch quoted in note 18, and N. C. Carpenter, *Music in the Medieval and Renaissance Universities,* (Norman, Oklahoma, 1958), p. 98, *n.* 11.

records of his affiliation with the University in Prague. According to his biographers, he was expelled from Prague shortly thereafter and went to Pilsen, where he began writing his voluminous encyclopedia of twenty arts. In the fall of 1451 Paulirinus registered as a student at the University of Cracow, and it is here, for the first time, that he is listed as "doctor arcium et medecine totum."[21]

When the plague appeared in Cracow in the summer of 1452, Paulirinus fled to Breslau where he stayed until the spring of 1453. In February of the same year a famous preacher against the Hussites, John of Capistrano, arrived in Breslau and delivered a series of sermons attacking the Czechs. Paulirinus—who, so far as is known, never had particularly close associations with the followers of Huss—apparently felt an upsurge of patriotism and wrote to acquaintances in Prague as if to warn them about the potential danger in Breslau. His notes were intercepted and delivered to the mayor of Breslau, and Paulirinus was jailed. Through the intervention of friends in Prague, and even of George of Podiebrad himself, Paulirinus was released in May 1453, after he had submitted himself to Capistrano's chastisement and renounced his ties with the Hussites.[22] As soon as he was freed, Paulirinus fled to Prague, where he expected to be rewarded. Since his hopes were not fulfilled, he once more went to Cracow, arriving at the time of Capistrano's visit to that city, and again was jailed. In the same year Cardinal Olesnicki interceded for Paulirinus with Pope Nicholas V,[23] and in 1455, after his release from jail in Cracow, Paulirinus settled in Pilsen, where he continued the work on his treatise. According to Reiss, the manuscript containing the treatise was written between 1459 and 1463.

By 1466 Paulirinus had found refuge at the court of the King of Bohemia, George of Podiebrad, for whom he wrote several treatises in Czech, among them one devoted to advice on how to rule. George of Podiebrad died in 1471, and it is generally believed that Paulirinus died shortly afterward.[24]

21. *Album Studiosorum Universitatis Cracoviensis,* I (Cracow, 1877), 131.

22. For the date of the plague in Silesia, as well as for Capistrano's arrival in Breslau, see *Scriptores Rerum Silesiacarum,* XII (Breslau, 1883), 63. Paulirinus' notes, seven in Latin and two in Czech, are still extant and are preserved in the archives of Capestrano in Italy. Cf. J. Hofer, *Johannes von Capestrano* (Innsbruck, 1936), pp. 481–82, *n.* 185a, with indications of sources.

23. C. Morawski, *Histoire de l'Université de Cracovie,* II (Paris and Cracow, 1903), 200–01 *n;* J. Reiss, "Das Twardowski Buch," *Germanoslavica,* II (1932–1933), 90–101.

24. See note 9.

III

In Paulirinus' *Liber viginti artium,* music is discussed as the seventh of the twenty arts, and it is in this treatise that the term "virginal" first appears in a listing of musical instruments. The paragraph about the virginal, in Reese's translation, reads: "The virginal is an instrument with the form of a clavichord, having metal strings which make it sound like a *clavicembalo.* It has thirty-two courses of strings set in action by striking the fingers on projecting keys, sounding sweetly in both tones and semitones. It is called a virginal because, like a virgin, it sounds with a sweet and tranquil voice."[25]

It is immediately evident that Paulirinus was a careful observer and knew instruments well. His seeming lack of preciseness in referring to other instruments is compensated for by his descriptions of both the clavichord and the clavicymbalum. He states that the virginal is an instrument having the shape of a clavichord, and in the shape of a casket.[26] Paulirinus also states that the virginal has the sonority of the clavicymbalum and one learns from his description of this latter instrument that it has an extraordinary sweetness "in simfonisando," which may be translated as "when played in concert," that it is to be played in the same way as the clavichord, and that the clavicymbalum sounds sweeter and is more sonorous than the clavichord.[27] The "virginale" is, then, an oblong, presumably rectangular, instrument in the shape of a casket, and its sound is more sonorous than that of the clavichord. Furthermore, the special tonal quality of the virginal derives from the fact that its strings are plucked and its sound can be compared favorably with the sound of the female voice.

This description of the virginal is one of the most important statements from the period, and as far as can be ascertained, it contains reliable data for the history of stringed keyboard instruments. For example, Paulirinus states quite explicitly that metallic strings—"cordas metallinas"—are used in stringed keyboard instruments. As a matter of fact, in almost all instances he was careful to

25. *Music in Renaissance,* p. 667.

26. Reiss, "Pauli Paulirini de Praga," p. 262; "Clavicordium est instrumentum oblongum in modum cistule. . . ."

27. *Ibid.:* "Clavicimbalum est instrumentum mire suavitatis in simfonisando" and at the end of the description: "concordat in percussione cum clavicordio nisi quod dulcius & sonorosius sonat."

point out the kind of strings to be used.[28] About fifty years later, Virdung stated that the clavicytherium had gut strings,[29] but when Giovanni de Bardi wrote in 1580, he said once again that metal strings were used for "gravicembali," whereas gut strings were used for viols, harps, the lute, and such "other instruments as are similar to it."[30]

Another point in Paulirinus' description of the virginal is his mention of "choros chordarum," translated as "courses of strings," and implying the use of more than a single string for the production of sound by one key. This reference only confirms the statement in the treatise of Henri-Arnaut de Zwolle, written some twenty years earlier, that the doubling of strings was possible. The pertinent passage reads: "Similiter etiam posset fieri quod clavicordium sonaret ut clavisimbalum cum simplicibus cordis vel duplicibus."[31] In the chronological sequence of events it is not surprising, then, to find that in Virdung's time the use of three strings for each tone was already known.[32] It is difficult to generalize, and one must not assume that all stringed keyboard instruments conformed to this practice. An instrument made in 1533 by Dominicus Pisaurensis and having single strings is listed by Sachs as still existing today.[33]

Paulirinus is the first (to this writer's knowledge) to state explicitly the number of these "courses of strings," and thus indirectly the number of keys on a keyboard, which he gives as thirty-two. By way of pictorial evidence, a drawing in Arnaut's treatise shows a keyboard with thirty-five keys, and woodcuts in *Musica getutscht* make us believe that keyboards could have from thirty-eight to forty keys. Yet Virdung's text states that the clavichord has only thirty

28. Metal strings are mentioned as used in "clavicordium," "clavicymbalum," and "virginale"—all stringed keyboard instruments; metal strings are also mentioned for "dulce melos" and "ala"; gut strings are said to be used on "monocordum," "arfa," "cithara," "sistrum smiczocz" (Polish violin), "calcastrun," "ysis" and "tubalcana"; no description is given for "psalterium." The remaining instruments described by Paulirinus in his treatise are: "organum," "portatiwum," "cimbalum," "tintinabulum," "[?]nnportile" and "ormfa." Cf. *ZfMw,* VII, 262–64.

29. *Musica getutscht,* fol. B i verso.

30. Cf. "Discourse on Ancient Music and Good Singing," in *Source Readings in Music History,* ed. O. Strunk (New York, 1950), p. 297.

31. *Les Traités d' Henri-Arnaut de Zwolle et de divers anonymes* (MS. B.N. Latin 7295), ed. G. Le Cerf and E.-R. Labande (Paris, 1932), p. 21; Cf. Sachs, *Musical Instruments,* p. 338.

32. *Musica getutscht,* fol. E iii recto.

33. Sachs, p. 340. Presumably this is not the result of a "restoration."

keys, and then appears quite uncertain how many keys a keyboard should have: "Ich weiss dir kein gewis[s]e summ zu nennen die es haben müsse."[34] Since it is highly unlikely that Virdung was not informed about such details, it must be that he was unaware of a fixed number of keys simply because the custom varied.

Although Paulirinus does not specify the range of the virginal, or for that matter of any keyboard instrument, it very probably covered three octaves, the lowest being the "short octave" and the highest omitting b′-flat (i.e., C/E to c″).[35] This assumption is based on a comparison of pictorial representations of keyboards with known facts. Even though the drawing in Arnaut's treatise happens to have a few more keys than Paulirinus lists for the keyboard, it is known, as Schlick testifies, that the range of three octaves and a third may be encountered by the beginning of the sixteenth century. This is approximately the same range as that represented in Virdung's woodcuts. It is a reasonable assumption that a gradual development led to the enlargement of ranges of keyboards, and thus Paulirinus' testimony, although not explicit, implicitly supports this view.[36]

Concerning the mechanism for production of sound, the treatise of Paulirinus contains a reference in the description of the clavicymbalum to the use of quills, thus corroborating Arnaut's reference to the same thing. These references do not exclude the possibility of the use of metallic plectra, mentioned slightly later by Scaliger as having preceded the quills.[37]

Paulirinus' last sentence suggests the derivation of the term "virginal" from the quality of the sound of this instrument, which reminded listeners of the sweetness of a female voice. This, the problem of the origin of the term "virginal" as the name of a specific musical instrument, is the thorniest of all, and remains unsolved. Sachs appears almost certain that "the word probably is related to medieval Latin 'virga' (meaning rod, jack)."[38] Reese takes into consideration Paulirinus' explanation but follows Sachs with a

34. *Musica getutscht,* fols. B i recto and E ii verso; also *Les Traités . . .*, Plate VI.

35. Based on schemes in G. Kinsky, "Kurze Oktaven auf besaiteten Tasteninstrumenten, ein Beitrag zur Geschichte des Klaviers," *ZfMw,* II (1919–1920), 65–82.

36. Cf. Sachs, *Musical Instruments,* p. 306; also Sachs, *Handbuch der Musikinstrumentenkunde* (2d ed.; Leipzig, 1930), pp. 139–40; O. Kinkeldey, *Orgel und Klavier in der Musik des 16. Jahrhunderts* (Leipzig, 1910), pp. 61–66.

37. Sachs, *Musical Instruments,* pp. 338–39.

38. *Ibid.,* p. 335; also *Handbuch . . .*, p. 148.

cautious statement that "a derivation from *virga*, the Latin name for the jack seems more logical."[39] However, Galpin has forcefully proved (to this writer, at any rate) the impossibility of the derivation of "virginale" from "virga." This writer has consulted several classicists about the problem, and the consensus of these scholars is that Galpin was perfectly correct in stating that "no clerk would be likely to make an adjective 'virgin-alis' out of 'virga.' "[40] Galpin did go on to say: "Galilei calls the clavicymbalum the 'clavichordium matronale' because ladies used it, and we know that the spinet was used in the fifteenth and sixteenth century in the religious houses of women—hence 'clavichordium virginale.' " However, we cannot accept the latter statement as proof for or explanation of the origin of the term "virginal." It certainly is true that young ladies are most frequently represented as playing the instrument in the paintings of the period,[41] and that the majority of clavichords in the collection at Lucerne were assembled from nunneries.[42] This kind of information may appear to support the theory that the term "virginal" has been derived from the sex of the player. It would seem, however, that we are still lacking the necessary link in the chain of events that would help us to trace the exact provenance and meaning of the term "virginal." Paulirinus' remarks about the virginal, made around 1460, prove to be the earliest reference to this term, and the information about the instrument is quite clear except for the debatable origin of the name.

IV

Less than thirty-five years after the presumed date of the completion of the manuscript, Paulirinus' treatise found its way to the library of the University of Cracow. It is highly interesting to note that it was given to the library as a gift from Jan Welss, who was the personal physician of King Kazimir of Poland, and the man in charge of the education of Kazimir's sons.[43] Since Welss died in

39. *Music in Renaissance,* p. 667.

40. In a note added to W. G. H. Flood's article "The Eschequier Virginal: An English Invention," *Music and Letters,* VI (1925), 152.

41. P. James, *Early Keyboard Instruments from Their Beginnings to the Year 1820* (London, 1930), p. 24.

42. F. A. Goehlinger, *Geschichte des Klavichords* (Basel, 1910), p. 19.

43. Reiss, "Pauli Paulirini de Praga," p. 259. Concerning Jan Welss, some data may be found in Zofia Ameisenowa, *Rekopisy i pierwodruki iluminowane Biblioteki Jagiellońskiej* (Cracow, 1958), p. 210. A list of books which Welss possessed is listed in Wislocki's *Incunabula Typographica Bibliothecae Universitatis Jagellonicae Cracoviensis* (Cracow, 1900), p. 537.

1498, the manuscript must have been in his hands at an earlier date, quite likely at a time when he supervised the young princes. It is a reasonable assumption that most of the musical instruments mentioned by Paulirinus were known to his readers, whether in Bohemia or Poland.

Another interesting observation is that Paulirinus' patron, George of Podiebrad, was succeeded in 1471 as King of Bohemia by the fifteen-year-old Wladislav, oldest son of Kazimir. This same Wladislav became King of Hungary in 1490 and reigned in both lands until 1515.

It comes as no surprise to find that chronologically the next references to the virginal appear in Hungary,[44] and that the expenses incurred in the purchase of a new virginal as well as gratuities to players are listed in the expense accounts of Prince Sigismund (King of Poland from 1506 to 1548), the younger brother of King Wladislav; both were sons of Kazimir.[45] All these references are well dated, and cover the period from 1501 to 1505. The first of these, of January 1, 1501, records that the organist, Meister Grinpeck, "ludebat in virginali infra prandia ante dominum principem."[46] That the purchase of a *new* virginal for 24 guldens is recorded for November 21, 1502, suggests two distinct conclusions. On the one hand, the term may have been one of several synonyms for stringed keyboard instruments, as Praetorius recorded one century later. On the other hand, the term "virginal" may have been an accepted term for a specific instrument, even if it was not long in use on the Continent. It is significant that it was played by an organist in Hungary. Since the period was one of growing interest in keyboard music, the

44. The reference listed as appearing in 1500, in G. Schad's *Musik und Musikausdrücke in der mittelenglischen Literatur* (Frankfurt a. M., 1911), p. 117, must be discarded, for in a single line it contains three misprints: the date should read 1550–1560; the name of the author of the play is L. Wager (not Wagner) and the verse number is 735, not 753. See the modern ed. of Wager's play edited by Carpenter F. Ives (Chicago, 1904), p. xv. The same play has been published in *The Tudor Facsimile Texts* (London, 1908), where the line in question may be found on fol. D iii recto, as line 21.

45. O. Gombosi, "Der Organist als Tafelmusiker," *Acta Musicologica,* IX (1937), 54–55, quoting from Divéky, "Zsigmond lengyel herceg budai számadásai," *Magyar. Történélmi,* Tár XXVI (Budapest, 1914; inaccessible to this writer). The work by A. Pawiński, *Młode łata Zygmunta Starego* (Warsaw, 1893), presumably containing excerpts from Sigismund's books of expenses, was not available for this study.

46. Concerning this musician see G. Pietzsch, "Zur Pflege der Musik an den deutschen Universitäten bis zur Mitte des 16. Jahrhunderts," *Archiv für Musikforschung,* I (1936), 286; VI (1941), 45.

existence of a variety of instruments with keyboards could easily be presupposed.

Between the time of the references in Hungary and of that in Virdung's book, the term "virginal" could have easily traveled the distance between the two localities. It is curious, however, not to find one single reference to this term in any of the available Italian sources, especially at a time when Italians seem to have been the most frequently cited makers of keyboard instruments.

V

The fact that the term "virginal" appeared and was disseminated throughout Central Europe before it became popular in England emerges as the most significant result of this confrontation of data. The first authenticated reference to the virginal in England appears to be that of March 22–28, 1517, when it was recorded in the King's book of payments that John Dingley received payment for "a pair of virginals."[47] After that date the number of references increases constantly, so that one hundred years later Praetorius was able to record that nearly all stringed keyboard instruments in England "sie seyn klein oder gross [werden] virginall genennet."

47. *Letters and Papers, Foreign and Domestic, of the Reign of Henry VIII*, ed. J. S. Brewer, II, Pt. 2 (London, 1864), p. 986, No. 3065.

Fall 1961

23 / Spanish Musicians in Sixteenth-Century England

JOHN M. WARD
Harvard University

In the summer of 1554 Philip, Prince of Spain, sailed with extraordinary pomp from La Coruña to southern England, where, in Winchester Cathedral, before a great company of English and Spanish nobles, he was married to the Queen of England, Mary Tudor. For Philip and even more for his father, the Emperor Charles, whose diplomacy and fatherly suasion were mainly responsible for the marriage, and who hoped through this alliance to win England to his side in the long quarrel with France, the match was political; Philip reluctantly put aside personal feelings in the interest of the state, though he must be credited with appearing happy enough and even in love with a bride nine years his senior, whom none of the Spaniards described as fair. For Mary, the union with Philip was another assurance that the old faith had indeed returned to England; more than this, it was for her a love match, and the quick disintegration of the marriage, with the husband more often abroad than at home, is thought to have hastened her death. Philip remained in England for a little more than thirteen months (July 20, 1554 to September 4, 1555) and then left for the wars in France and the Lowlands. Two years later he returned for not quite four months (March 19 to July 6, 1557). Sixteen months later his queen was dead.

Our concern is not with the principal actors in this history, but with those scarcely mentioned in the contemporary accounts, with the servants of the prince, and in particular with the musicians. From documents preserved in the Casa Real at Simancas we know that Philip took a great number of musicians to England.[1] In addition to the Chapel, which consisted of a bishop, a Franciscan and a Dominican friar, and six chaplains, there were twenty-one singers—four "cantorcicos tiples," three "tiples," four "contraltos," six "tenores," and four "contrabaxos"—plus two "Moços de capilla." The instrumentalists included fifteen of the Emperor's "menestriles," one described as a flute player,[2] and the others, though nowhere identified as such, probably the ten trumpeters and four drummers ("atabaleros") mentioned in one of the documents;[3] a viol player; two organists; and an "oficial organista" who was in charge of the instruments. In total: forty-two musicians. Of these the best known to us are Antonio de Cabezón, the blind keyboard player, and Philippe de Monte, an unhappy member of the Prince's chapel choir, the only non-Spaniard in it.[4]

1. The Simancas documents have been published by H. Anglés, *Monumentos de la música española,* II (1944), 124–36.

2. Who probably performed more often outdoors than in; see, e.g., the description of the December 18 "tryhumph at the court gatte, by the Kyng and dyvers lordes boyth English-men and Spaneards, the wyche the Kyng and his compene [were] in goodly harnes, and a-pon ther armes goodly jerkyns of bluw velvett, and hosse in-brodered with sylver and bluw sarsenett; and so they rane on fott with spayrers and swerds at the tornay, and with dromes and flutes in whyt velvet [drawn] owt with blu sarsenett, and ther wer x aganst [the king] and ys compene, the wer xviij in odur colers." J. G. Nichols, ed., *The Diary of Henry Machyn,* Camden Society, XLII (1848), p. 79.

3. Trumpeters and drummers formed part of the panoply of 16th-century court and military life but almost never took part in the performance of "music," for which reason their activities are not taken into account in this paper. Typical is their participation at the exhibition of cane-play the Spanish gave for the English, "the wyche was Sonday, at after-non, the Kyngs grace and my lord Fuwater [=Fitzwater] and dyvers Spaneards dyd ryd in dyvers colars, the Kyng in red, and som [in] yellow, sum in gren, sum in whyt, sum in bluw, and with targets and canes in ther hand, herlyng of rods on at a-nodur, and thrumpets in the sam colars, and drumes mad of ketylles, and banars in the sam colars." Nichols, *The Diary of Henry Machyn,* p. 76.

4. In his well-known letter of September 22, 1555, Dr. Seld noted that Philippe "in des Königs Capell nit wol zu pleiben hat, dieweil die andern singen all Spanier und er allain ain Niderlander." G. van Doorslaer, *La Vie et les oeuvres de Philippe de Monte* (1921), pp. 217–18.

During the same 1554 summer Lassus is supposed to have visited England in company with a Neapolitan intriguer named Giulio Cesare Brancazzo; most scholars have been reluctant to credit the story, evidence for which is found only in Quickelberg's account of the composer's life; see, e.g., Van den Borren, *Orlande de Lassus* (1930), pp. 7–9. We do know that Brancazzo, who was described by Charles V's ambassador in London as "a most resolute and scandalous man," came to England against the Emperor's command with the declared intention "to present to the Queen a page who played very well upon the lute"; see the *Calendar of State Papers: Spanish,* XII

The chroniclers, both Spanish and English, who viewed the wedding solemnities and subsequent festivities at Winchester mention the important role of musicians. For example, on his arrival in the city, Philip went immediately to the cathedral, where he was met by six bishops, "mitred, coped, and staved," who led him through the church, the procession singing *Laus, honor et virtus.* When he had knelt in the choir of the church, the Lord Chancellor, Bishop Gardiner, "began *Te Deum Laudamus,* and the quere, together with the organs, song and plaied the rest."[5] Two days later, during the celebration of the Mass that followed immediately on the marriage ceremony, "the quenes chapell matched with the quire [of the cathedral?], and the organs, used suche swete proporcyon of musicke and harmonye, as," according to one English witness, "the like . . . was never beefore invented or harde."[6] The Spaniards were surprised to discover the Mass as solemnly sung as at Toledo.[7]

At the wedding banquet, though no particulars are recorded, "there was store of music," and, that evening, dancing. Since, according to one source, Philip did not know the dances of England nor Mary those of Spain, they danced the *alemana,* which was simple enough for the Queen to learn at one viewing.[8] One of the Englishmen present declared that "to behold the dukes and noblemen of Spain daunse with the faire ladyes and the moste beutifull nimphes of England, it should seme to him that never see suche, to be an other worlde."[9] His enthusiasm was not shared by one of the Spaniards, who wrote to his friends in Spain that Mary's ladies were

(1949), 300. It is unlikely that the page was Lassus, who was about 22 years old at the time. He did, however, compose a motet, *Te spectant, Reginalde,* in honor of Cardinal Pole, whose long-sought return to England occurred at the end of November 1554.

5. From a letter, published in 1555, by John Elder, tutor of Henry Stuart, Lord Darnley, to his pupil's uncle, the Bishop of Caithness, ed. J. G. Nichols, Camden Society, XLVIII (1849), 139–40.

6. *Ibid.,* p. 142.

7. Anglés, *Monumentos,* II, 128. ". . . le cantaron sus oraciones con tanta solenidad como lo podian hacer en la iglesia mayor de Toledo."

8. C. V. Malfatti, *The Accession, Coronation and Marriage of Mary Tudor* (1956), p. 144.

9. John Elder's letter, p. 143. Another Englishman, Edward Underhill, wrote: "I wyll not take vppon me to wryte the maner off the maryage, off the feaste, nor off the daunssyngs of the Spanyards thatt daye, who weare greately owte off countenaunce, specyally kynge Phelip dauncesynge, when they dide se me lorde Braye, Mr. Carowe, and others so farre excede them. . . . " *Ibid.,* p. 170.

"not at all handsome, nor do they dance gracefully, as all of their dances only consist of ambling and trotting."[10]

If the Spanish musicians participated in these events, the chroniclers and letter writers fail to record the fact. Certainly they were inactive if they shared in the treatment accorded Philip's companions, for the English nobles usurped most of the privileged tasks of waiting on the Prince, much to the anger of the Spaniards, one of whom wrote: "As for any of the Prince's own stewards doing anything, such a thing was never thought of, and not one of us took a wand [the symbol of office] in our hands, nor does it seem likely we ever shall, neither the controller nor any one else, and they had better turn us all out as vagabonds."[11]

A month after their marriage, Philip and Mary made a triumphal entry into London, where the Prince, with his unhappy entourage, was to wait out the next eleven months, hoping for an issue to the royal union and an opportunity to bring English arms actively into the quarrel between Charles V and Henry II. In the dreary months that followed, the Spanish lords who remained with the Prince found their position difficult. They were accorded scant courtesy at court and found life in an English palace dull and unpalatable; "all the rejoicings here," wrote one wretched courtier, "consist only of eating and drinking, as they understand nothing else."[12] At first the London innkeepers would take none of the Spaniards in, so that many had to be quartered in the halls of the City guilds. They were overcharged in the taverns and openly robbed on the highways—though this could happen to anyone who ventured on them unattended, it should be added; when they appeared on the street they were ridiculed; quarrels broke out and often led to bloodshed; worse yet, they were "ordered by the King to avoid dispute and put up with everything . . . enduring all their attacks in silence."[13]

10. M. Hume, *The Year After the Armada* (1896), p. 158. See also Anglés, *Monumentos*, II, 129 *n:* ". . . no son nada hermosas, ni airosas en danzar; todas sus danzas son andar de portante y al trote." The Spanish accounts leave one with the impression that Mary's court was rather dowdy, particularly as compared with her father's.

11. Hume, *Year After Armada*, p. 162; also *C.S.P., Span.*, XIII (1954), 11.

12. Hume, *Year After Armada*, p. 167; also *C.S.P., Span.*, XIII, 31.

13. *C.S.P., Span.* XIII, 32.

Matters mended somewhat with the passing of time. Simon Renard, the Emperor's ambassador in London, could write his master in October that "things are going rather better with the help of winter's approach and the fact that there is often dancing at Court where Spaniards and Englishmen are beginning to mingle."[14] Eventually the foreigners became for the townspeople little more than the companions of the Queen's husband; and while all England awaited the birth of a royal child, a kind of wary tolerance of the Spanish visitors settled on the land, troubled only by popular indignation over the first burning of Protestants.

Despite the initial hostility of Londoners, due in part to a general distrust of all foreigners and in part to gross exaggerations often circulated by agents of the French ambassador and enemies of the Catholic Queen as to the actual number of Spaniards in England, performances by Spanish musicians were heard in London, not only by the court but also by townspeople. Though the evidence is far from lavish and not detailed, references to such performances do occur in the diary of a citizen, supposedly a merchant-tailor, Henry Machyn, about whom no more is known than what his diary reveals. The pertinent entries are here reprinted in full.[15]

The vi day of October [1554] was bered at Westmynster a grett man a Spaneard, with syngyng, boyth Englys and Spaneards, with a hand-belle, a-for ryngyng, and ever[y] Spaneard havying gren torchys, and gren tapurs to the nombur of a C. bornyng, and ther bered in the Abbay.[16]

[The xviij day of October king Philip came down on horseback from Westminster unto Paul's, with many lords, being received under a canopy,

14. *Ibid.*, p. 64.

15. Pages 71, 72, 75, 77, 78, 107 of the Nichols edition. The manuscript was damaged in the Cotton Library fire; most of the words and passages enclosed in square brackets were supplied by the editor from Machyn extracts published in various of the writings of John Strype, who consulted the manuscript before the fire.

16. I have been able to identify neither this gentleman nor the one buried November 19. Both may have died of natural causes, or have been involved in the sort of fracas described by one of Philip's companions in a letter of October 2, 1554 to a friend in Salamanca. "The English hate us Spaniards, which comes out in violent quarrels between them and us, and not a day passes without some knife-work in the palace between the two nations. There have already been some deaths, and last week three Englishmen and a Spaniard were hanged on account of a broil." *C.S.P., Span.*, XIII, 60–61. Machyn records the burial of other Spaniards, e.g., on December 21, 1554, without, however, mentioning singing.

at the west end: and the lord Montagu bare the sword afore the king. There he heard mass, and] Spaneards song mase; and after masse [he went back to] Westmynster to dener.[17]

The xix day of November was bered at sant Martens at Charyng-crosse with ij crosses a gentyllman a Spaneard, and a iij^{xx} torchys and tapurs in ther handes, and with syngyng to the cherche, and the morowe-masse boythe Spaneards and Englysmen syngyng.

The xxx day of November the Kyng('s) grace and ys [lords] rod to Westmynster abbay to masse, for the Spaneards [sung], and ther mett ym at the cort gate a C. He-Alman [High Almaines] in hosse and dobeletes of whyt and red, and yelow welvet cotes [trimmed], with yelow sarsenet, and yelow velvet capes and fethers . . . coler, and drumes and flutes in the sam coler, and with gylt [halbards], and C. in yolow hosse, dobelets of welvett, and jerkens of [leather] gardyd with cremesun velvett and whyt, fether yelow and red; and thos be Spaneards; and a C. in yelow gownes of velvett with [blank] And the sam nyght my lord cardenall cam to the courte, and whent to the chapell with the Kyng, and ther *Te Deum* songe.[18]

The ij day of Desember dyd com to Powlles all prestes and clarkes with ther copes and crosses, and all the craftes in ther leverey, and my lord mayre and the altherman, agaynst my lord cardenall('s) commyng; and at the bysshopes of London plase my lord chansseler and all the bysshopes tarehyng for my lord cardenall commyng, that was at ix of the cloke, for he landyd at Beynard Castell; and ther my lord mayre reseyvyd him, and browgth ym to the Powllse, and so my lord chanseler and my lord cardenall and all the byshopes whent up in-to the quer with ther meyturs; and at x of the cloke the Kyng('s) grace cam to Powlles to her mase with iiij C. of gaard, on C. Engyls, on C. He-Almen, on C.

17. The Windsor Herald recorded the same event. "The 18 of Octobre, beinge the day of St. Luke, the Kinge rode from his pallace of Whitehall to Paules Church in the forenoone, and there heard masse, which was sunge by the Spaniards of his owne quier." Charles Wriothesley, *A Chronicle of England,* ed. W. D. Hamilton, II (Camden Society, n.s., XX, 1877), 123.

18. Following a High Mass of the Order of the Golden Fleece, whose patron saint's day it was, and a two-hour sermon, the Chancellor, empowered by the papal Legate, absolved the congregation "and admitted them once more into the fold of Holy Mother Church and obedience to the Pope." The Ambassador to the King of the Romans estimated over 15,000 persons were present. See *C.S.P., Span.,* XIII, 122; also A. P. Stanley, *Historical Memorials of Westminster Abbey* (6th ed.; 1886), pp. 399–400. This entry and the following one describe events connected with Cardinal Pole's arrival and first week in England; see *C.S.P., Span.,* XIII, 118–22. According to Count G. T. Langosco da Stroppiana, in a letter to the Bishop of Arras dated December 3, "The crowd, both in the church and in the streets, was enormous and displayed great joy and piety, begging the Cardinal for his blessing."

Spaneards, on C. of Swechenars [Switzers], and mony lords and knyghtes, and hard masse. Boyth the quen('s) chapell and the kynges and Powlles quer song.[19]

The viij day of Desember, the wyche was the Conception of owre blessed lady the Vyrgyn, was a goodly prossessyon at the Save [Savoy] be the Spaneards, the prest carehyng the sacrement ryally be-twyne ys hands, and on deacon carehyng a senser sensyng, and anodur the ale-water stoke [holy-water stock], and a nombur of frers and prestes syngyng, [and every] man and woman, and knyghts and gentylmen, bayryng a gren tapur bornyng, and viij trumpeters blohyng; and when they had don plahyng, and then begane the sagbottes plahyng; and when they had don theyr was on that cared ij drumes on ys bake, and on cam after playng; and, so don, they whent a-bowt the Sawve with-in; and a wyll after playing a-gayn, and so came in syngyng, and so after they whent to masse, wher the bedes w . . . (*unfinished*).[20]

The viij day of June [1556] was a goodly pressessyon at Whyt-hall by the Spaneards; the hall hangyd with ryche cloth, and at the [screen] in the halle was a auter mad, and hangyd rychely with [a canopy], and with grett baseins clen gylt and candyll-stykes; and in the [court] at iiij corners was mad iiij godly auters hangyd with clothe of gold, and evere auter with canepes in brodere; and [in the] court mad a pressession way with a C. yonge okes sett in the grond and of evere syd sett ard [hard, i.e., close] to the wall with gren boughs; and then cam the pressessyon out of the chapell syngyng and playing of the regalles; and after the sacrament borne, and over ytt the rychest canepe that the Quen had, with vj stayffes borne by vj goodly men, and a-bowt the sacrement a C. torchys burnyng, and sum of whytt wax; and at ever auter [was ringing] and senst with swett odurs, and all the kyng['s] garde with [partizans] gyltt, and after to messe in the chapell, and song by the Spaneardes.[21]

19. John Stowe, *The Summarie of Englishe Chronicles* (1567), fols. 178r and 178v, states that on this occasion "the byshop of Winchester beinge lord chancelor of England made a sermon, declaryng how this realme was agayne restored to the church of Rome."

20. The Hospital of the Savoy, suppressed under Edward VI, was "new founded, erected, corporated, and endowed with lands by Queen Mary." John Stowe, *A Survey of London* (1603; Everyman ed., 1956), p. 397.

21. Processions of this sort were instituted during the last weeks of Mary's supposed pregnancy. See, e.g., Wriothesley's *Chronicle*, p. 136: "This moneth [July 1556] the Bishop of London and other the Queenes Commissioners caused a new order to be made for processions, viz.: That everie Munday, Weddnesday, and Fridaye, weekelye, the children schollers in everie parishe should goe in procession afore the crosse, with the schole-master followinge them; and mens apprentices followinge the crosse, then the priests and clerks, and after the parishioners. And that everie of the sayde dayes one of everie howse at the least to goe in procession upon payne of xii d."

With these entries, Machyn provides evidence that Spanish musicians were heard in important public places. It is hardly surprising to learn that they sang at the funerals of Spanish nobles who died while attending their Prince in London; not only Philip but also some of his companions, e.g., the dukes of Alba and Medinaceli, brought household musicians with them. Noteworthy is the singing of Mass by three choirs, the Queen's, the King's, and that of Paul's. Many of the most active musicians of the period were in the English choirs, e.g., Thomas Tallis, John Shepherd, Richard Edwards, William Hunnis, all gentlemen of the Chapel Royal, and Richard Bowyer, master of the children of the Queen's Chapel; the children of St. Paul's were almost certainly in the charge of Sebastian Westcott, the successor to John Redford.[22] There is, of course, no hint of what the three choirs sang, whether plainsong or part-music, nor of whether they performed together or separately, though the latter is more likely.

Although Machyn's information encourages us to assume that English musicians, especially those attached to the Court, the Abbey, and St. Paul's were able to hear music of Spain performed by some of the best musicians of that country, it does not provide much additional support for the assertions, frequently made, that through this encounter the Spaniards exerted an important influence on the development of English music or, contrariwise, that English musicians influenced the Spaniards. Specifically, it has been asserted of Antonio de Cabezón, despite our knowing only that he was physically present in England during this period, that in the months between July 1554 and September 1555 he taught the English—or vice versa—the art of writing variations. That he spent a good part of the time in bed, suffering, as did many in Philip's entourage, the effects of a change in climate, has yet to be proposed, though it would be as easy to prove as those things said to have been accomplished by or upon him. Indeed, were I mischief bent, I might suggest that a need to recuperate from an English sojourn prompted Cabezón's request, made shortly after he left England for the Continent in the small

22. See A. Brown, "Three Notes on Sebastian Westcott," *Modern Language Review,* XLIV (1949), 229–32.

company of retainers Philip took with him to the Lowlands, for a year's leave of absence to visit Spain.

To insist, as some have, that the art of writing variations was learned or even influenced in any measurable way by either the Spaniards or the English in 1554–1555 is to ignore the facts. Every aspect of variation technique found in the works of Cabezón, and of the Englishmen whose music he might have heard, is to be found at an earlier date in Italian, German, Spanish, and English sources. In other words, 1554–1555 is late in the history of variation writing.[23] Moreover, what remains of instrumental music from the sixteenth century and earlier is but a fragment; and that fragment is more often representative of the pedagogical than of the artistic side. For example, we know that the Spanish and English nobles danced together a good deal during the year Philip was in England, yet not one identifiable scrap of the music the minstrels played remains; from what we know of dance musicians, no group—unless it be church organists—makes less use than they of scores, or greater use of variation technique to expand music to fill the amount of time available.

It has also been asserted that Cabezón's playing may have influenced, perhaps significantly, the keyboard style of Tallis, who was about fifty years old at the time; that it may have been the other way about, the forty-four-year-old Spaniard having learned new tricks from the Englishman; and that it may have been the young, presumably impressionable Byrd who fell under the foreigner's spell. To sustain any one of these claims requires proof based on style analysis; but how are we to discover the 1554–1555 keyboard style of the three men? Some of Cabezón's music was printed in 1557, the rest in 1578; none of it can be dated more precisely.[24] Only two of

23. We might as well credit Arnolt Schlick with the first cantus firmus variation cycle merely because a manuscript of the eight *Gaude Dein genitrix* variations composed for the coronation of Charles V at Aachen in 1520 happens to have been preserved. The pieces have been edited by M. S. Kastner, *Hommage à l'Empereur Charles-Quint* (Barcelona, 1954).

24. Moreover, Cabezón's music was first written down by the amanuensis a blind composer required; then translated from pitched into tablature notation; then printed, first by an editor known to have had few scruples about altering his texts; later by keyboard-playing relatives, with a large cash investment in the publication, working in a period of great editorial and performing license, whose attitude towards the musical remains of a composer twelve years dead is only to be guessed at.

Tallis's surviving keyboard pieces, both *Felix namque* settings in the Fitzwilliam Virginal Book, can be dated, the one 1562, the other 1564; assuming these to be dates of composition, the value of the two works for the comparison proposed is vitiated by the lack of comparable pieces dated before the time of Cabezón's arrival in England. As for Byrd, we have not a single piece of keyboard music that can be dated with any certainty before September 11, 1591, the *terminus ad quem* of those John Baldwin copied into *My Ladye Nevells Booke.* How, then, are we to discover the music the three men might have played for one another at Tallis' house in Greenwich one late October afternoon, the time the young Byrd stayed on after his organ lesson for an unexpected master class?

Of musical facts that might be construed to connect Cabezón with England, and vice versa, we have an equivocal two. His posthumously printed *Obras de Música* contains a simple arrangement of Philip van Wilder's *Je file quant Dieu me donne de quoi.* Nothing proves that he learned the most popular song of Henry VIII's favorite musician during a stay in England; indeed, Cabezón, or his editor, credits the original to Adrian "Villarte." One might as well inquire where Le Roy and Ballard found their copy of the piece for the 1572 *Mellanges.*[25]

The other musical fact is that the *Pavana Italiana* on which Cabezón composed a few variations became in England a popular dance tune, ballad tune, and variation theme under the title *The Spanish Pavan.*[26] For those who prefer conjecture to history, the travels of this theme are as easy to follow as V to I. The conjectural sequence might run something like this: Didn't Blitheman hear Cabezón play the *Pavana Italiana* on a number of occasions? And wasn't Bull, who wrote a set of *Spanish Pavan* variations, Blitheman's

25. Wilder's original, together with the Gosse chanson of which it is a parody, is printed by H. M. Brown, *Theatrical Chansons of the Fifteenth and Early Sixteenth Centuries* (1963), pp. 99–105; see also Brown's note on both pieces in his *Music in the French Secular Theater, 1400–1550* (1963), p. 236. To the sources for Wilder's piece there cited, the following English ones can be added: British Museum Add. MS. 4900, fol. 62 (for lute); Add. 31390, fol. 51 (*a* 5, without text); Christ Church MSS. 984–88, No. 82 (attributed to Parsons); Aberystwyth, National Library of Wales, Brogyntyn MS. 27, p. 14 (for lute); Nottingham University Library, the Willoughby Lute MS., fols. 91′–92′ (for keyboard); the Lord Braye MS., now in the library of Mr. James M. Osborn (for lute).

26. Diana Poulton, "Notes on the Spanish Pavan," *Lute Society Journal,* III (1961), 5–16, includes a generous list of literary references and sources for the music.

pupil? And didn't Bull teach the tune to Sweelinck, who then invited Scheidt to join him in composing a set of variations on the *Pavana Hispanica?* Of course, it might just as well have been one of Philip's musicians who made the tune popular with the English by playing it so often during the dance sessions of 1554–1555—though this would require us to explain why there are no literary references to the *Spanish Pavan* and no English sources for the music dating before the 1580's, some thirty years after Philip's visit. Perhaps it wasn't the Spaniards after all, but a whistling Dutch sailor, one with ample opportunity to learn a Spanish tune at home, who brought it to English ears.[27]

27. The Lord Braye MS., compiled probably in the 1560's and now in Mr. Osborn's library, includes a piece entitled *The Base of Spayne;* the "Base" proves to be the *Baxa de contrapunto* with which Luys de Narváez's *Delphín de Música* of 1538 concludes. The unknown compiler may have obtained his copy of the piece direct from one of the guitarists whom, it is easy enough to guess, some of Philip's grandees had brought with them; or we might guess that he made his mangled translation of the piece from vihuela into French lute tablature from a copy, or a copy of a copy, of the print which he had obtained in much the same way he obtained copies of two Francesco da Milano recercars found elsewhere in the MS. It is easier to trace the Narváez fantasia, No. 10 of the *Delphín,* with which the Willoughby lute MS. opens, since it is there identified as *Fantaci de morlaye* and came, probably directly, from a copy of Guillaume Morlaye's *Premier livre . . . de leut* (1552), fols. 5′–6, where the piece is printed without the composer's name. Earlier, in both 1546 editions of his *Des chansons reduictz en tabulature de luc, livre deuxieme,* sig. b2′, Phalèse had reprinted the same fantasia, also without the composer's name.

Among the guiterne pieces in the Osborn MS. is one called *Quando claro, quando claro,* a set of variations on the well-known *romance* formula *Conde Claros.* A different set of variations on the same theme is in the Willoughby lute MS., fols. 38–39′; in the Cambridge University Library lute MS. Dd. 5.78.3, fols. 73′-74; and in the lute MS. in Archbishop Marsh's Library, Dublin, Z3.2.13, pp. 232–33. (According to J. Ward, *The Lives of the Professors of Gresham College* [1740], p. 203, there was a piece, probably a set of variations, entitled *Quando claro,* by John Bull in one of the Messaus manuscripts formerly in Dr. Pepusch's library and now believed lost.) Rather than explain the presence in English manuscripts of these variations on a Spanish theme by bringing in a Cabezón-ex-machina, we ought to note that: at Rome in 1538, Francisco Salinas heard Francesco da Milano improvise on the *Conde Claros* tenor; in 1552 Phalèse reprinted a selection of Valderrábano's *Conde Claros* diferencias in an arrangement for two lutes in his *Hortus Musarum,* fols. 102¹–03; in 1552–1553 Morlaye included five sets of *Conteclare* variations, 4 for guiterne, 1 for cistre, in the Granjon-Fez and at prints described by Daniel Heartz in *Musical Quarterly,* XLVI (1960), 448–67; in 1564 Jean d'Estrée, *Quart livre de danceries,* fol. 17, published "La basse Gaillarde," which begins with *Conde Claros* and continues with other well-known bass patterns; the dance was reprinted by Phalèse and Bellère in 1571. Obviously, this *Bergamasca*-in-hemiola Spanish recitation formula was in the mid-century air—put there, one must assume, by Spaniards. It is as impossible to prove that the compiler of the Osborn MS. got his *Quando claro, quando claro* variations from one of Philip's musicians or from a lost French guiterne print as it is to prove that he found the theme in the same book that provided him with a copy of Narváez's *Baxa de contrapunto* and then composed his own variations of it.

What, then, remains of the artistic results of Philip's English visits? Perhaps no more than the beginnings of a friendship between de Monte and the young Byrd, memorialized in an exchange of Psalm-verse settings in 1583 and 1584, the evidence for which occurs in John Alcock's eighteenth-century annotations to his scorings of the two motets.

24 / Nature and Function of the Sequence in Bruckner's Symphonies

ERIC WERNER
Hebrew Union College, New York

I

SEQUENTIAL devices are familiar to every musician, and it is easy to define them. Every strict sequence is a configuration of at least two different individual tones, or of a harmonic progression that goes up or down the scale either stepwise or in a series of disjunct intervals that have the same numerical designation from one statement to another. This scale may be either diatonic or chromatic. Though a musician might describe the sequence in still another way, the above definition will serve. It is noteworthy, however, that great theoreticians evaluate or analyze the concept of the sequence in many varying ways. Thus Fétis views it as a device to suspend the tonality for the length of the sequence, and also as a means of protracting the final cadence.[1] He is fully aware of its fundamentally symmetrical nature and therefore opposes sharply as "une cause de perturbation" any slightest deviation from the original "model motif," its chordal and rhythmic arrangement.

August Halm, confining himself to the purely harmonic aspects of the sequence, does not touch on the question of tonality and its temporary suspension. Instead, he sees in the sequence chiefly a device offering "that satisfaction which every logical continuation provides, a kind of feeling of security . . . This satisfaction, . . . this triumph of logic and analogy over the proper function of harmonic texture can, if used to an extreme, produce the opposite effect: in

1. J. F. Fétis, *Traité complet . . . de l'Harmonie* (Paris, 1844), pp. 26–30, 81–83, 253 f.

such cases the sequence causes ennui and boredom; we consider it, in those cases, a composer's undue indulgence in a mechanical device contrary to artistic principles."[2]

Neither Halm nor Fétis considers purely melodic sequences, nor does Schoenberg. For the latter the sequence is a legitimate means of avoiding literal repetition and therefore beneficial to the composer, if used sparingly, for it "guarantees continuity and coherence."[3] In a later work, *Structural Functions of Harmony*, Schoenberg pays much more attention to the sequence than in his classical *Harmonielehre*, but does not essentially deviate from his original point of view. Of recent theoreticians, it seems that only Bence Szabolcsi has fully recognized the importance of pure melodic sequences and evaluated their style-shaping significance in music history.[4] All musical scholars agree on the bad effect of deviations from the model. Schoenberg pays some attention to the value of sequential patterns for modulations and variations, and his work may be seen as an expansion and corollary of Fétis's observation about the suspension of tonality.

Thus the theoreticians offer no categorization of the various types of sequence, nor do they seriously consider the importance of variation within the sequential framework, again with the exception of Schoenberg. Yet it is exactly this element that is most characteristic of Bruckner's sequences. We must therefore examine the device of the sequence *de novo* and a little more closely. In so doing, we shall encounter a few complicating elements that warrant a wider interpretation of the concept of sequence.

It will be useful to distinguish between diatonic and chromatic sequences, their nature depending upon the scale in which the statements take place. In the diatonic system it is necessary, in turn, to distinguish between a tonal and a real sequence as these were under-

2. August Halm, *Harmonielehre* (Leipzig, 1912), pp. 68–70.

3. A. Schoenberg, *Harmonielehre* (3d ed.; Vienna, 1922), pp. 148, 338. It is astonishing that so profound a theoretician as Schenker should pay so little attention to the sequence. Perhaps the reason for his strange silence lies in his desire to explain all musical events through the concept of "auskomponierte Stufen" (secondary dominants, etc.). This insistence leads him occasionally to grotesque misinterpretations, as, for example, of Beethoven's Piano Concerto in G, in *Musikalische Theorien und Phantasien*, I (Stuttgart-Berlin, 1906), p. 334, No. 124.

4. Bence Szabolcsi, *Bausteine zu einer Geschichte der Melodie* (Budapest, 1959). Not quite so extensive is the analysis of sequence in R. Erickson's *The Structure of Music*, pp. 48 ff, which deals exclusively with melodic sequence.

stood during the seventeenth and eighteenth centuries. Chromatic sequences appear to reach their first peak in Bach's keyboard music. Moreover, there occur mixed sequences, especially in the works of Wagner and of those after him, preponderantly in modulatory passages. We shall in the following pages take cognizance of the rhythmic, the melodic, and the harmonic components of the sequence. When all three are varied at the same time, the basic idea of the sequence is all but destroyed; hence we shall first consider variations of one or of two components, while one or two remain fixed. In addition, we shall consider one special type: sequences over a pedal point. A brief tabulation of the types yield this disposition:

A. "Strict Sequences" (with fixed rhythmic and melodic pattern)
(1) Tonal
(2) Real and chromatic

B. "Varied Sequences" (one or two of the components varied)
(3) Mixed (tonal and real)
(4) "Free" (changes in rhythm or harmonic structure)
(5) Over a pedal point

In No. (5) the pedal point counteracts or neutralizes the principle of "suspended tonality," establishing a kind of tonal anchorage in the bass. We shall now illustrate the five types with appropriate musical examples, which begin on the next page. Each is discussed in a paragraph preceded by the example number.

(1) The model motif consists of an upbeat and the eight following sixteenth-notes. It is easy to see that in this part of the sequence the intervals of the model do not preserve their exact size, but change with the form of the diatonic D minor scale.

(2) Here the sequences (on the same model) do adhere to the exact size of the intervals of the model, this being made possible by the form of the chromatic scale.

(3) In this example of a slightly "mixed" sequence, the rhythmic and melodic patterns remain fixed; the harmonic progression of the model is V^6—VI^6_5—IV^4_3; it undergoes a slight change in the sequence. In bar 5 we encounter a G-flat triad in root position where a 6 chord was expected; in bar 8 there is a triad where the model calls for a $^4_3$ chord. These irregularities are caused by the composer's reluctance to repeat the F in the bass during measures 5 and 6.

EX. 1. Beginning of Kyrie of *Requiem* (K. 626)—Mozart.

EX. 2. Extract from Kyrie of *Requiem* (K. 626)—Mozart.

EX. 3. Extract from Scherzo of *Quartet*, Op. 80—Mendelssohn.

EX. 4a. Extract from Act III, Scene 4 of *Die Meistersinger von Nürnberg*—Wagner.

EX. 4b. Beginning of Scherzo of *Quartet*, Op. 127—Beethoven.

EX. 4c. Extract from Scherzo of *Quartet,* Op. 127—Beethoven.

EX. 5a. Extract from Act II of *Carmen*—Bizet.

EX. 5b. Extract from "Der Abschied" of *Das Lied von der Erde*—Mahler.

(4a) Here the rhythmic deviation from the model is clearly recognizable.

(4b and c) In the two passages from the Scherzo of Beethoven's Quartet, Op. 127, we find a fundamentally strict sequence (rhythm and melody are fixed), which by added counterpoints in imitation and inversion is so loosened that its structure is veiled, if not concealed. Many lesser talents have tried to becloud their poverty of ideas by similar devices, but they have usually failed: either the sequence becomes threadbare, or the passage loses coherence.

(5a) In this exquisite example the pedal point establishes a very strong feeling of tonality, although the harmonic component of the sequence is treated quite freely (through the introduction of secondary dominants). The inherent rhythm, the fixed melodic contour, and the pedal point, however, invalidate the suspension of tonality, although sharp frictions occur (E-sharp against E-natural in measure 6 of the example).

(5b) In the example from Mahler's *Das Lied von der Erde*, only the melodic contour of the model has been retained, while harmony and rhythm undergo free variation over two pedals. In passages like this we reach the point where we must ask ourselves if such variation of *all three* components still permits the use of the term "sequence." This is basically a semantic question; the disciples of Schoenberg will insist on the sequential character of such passages, whereas other theoreticians may be inclined to see in them the terminal line of the sequence. But our example would still belong to the proper domain of the sequence if we adhered to our definition, since only two out of the three variables have been affected. Apparently no sharp line of demarcation can be drawn between the different specimens of "varied sequences," since every small deviation (in rhythm or harmony or melodic line) produces a different kind, thus eluding a generalization in musical terms.

Since we hope to find a system of description that will encompass all sequences without neglecting their variances, we must establish a vantage point from which a comprehensive view is possible. This is offered by drawing an analogy with geometry, with the help of which we shall be able to define not only all sequences as a class, but also each of the categories within it.

Every sequential passage can be described as a linear transformation (of intervals and/or rhythm). Hence we may state:

a) Every "strict" sequence, tonal or real, where neither the harmonic nor the rhythmic or melodic pattern undergoes a variation, is, geometrically speaking, a congruent translation.[5] This translation

5. Its equation reads: if X_n, Y_n, X_{n+1}, Y_{n+1} are the coordinates of the model's characteristic interval; i.e., if

$$\begin{vmatrix} X_n, X_{n+1} \\ Y_n, Y_{n+1} \end{vmatrix} \quad \text{then} \quad \begin{vmatrix} X_{n+2} = X_{n+1} + C_l \\ Y_{n+2} = Y_{n+1} + C_h \end{vmatrix}$$

where C_l (the length of the shift) and C_h (the height of the shift) relate to the original position.

originates by moving the original model in regular intervals up or down the scale. It may be compared to an ornament on a frieze.

b) A "mixed" sequence, combining elements of the tonal and real treatment of the model, is likewise a translation, albeit not a congruent one. The equation of the model must make allowance for the degree of freedom by an additional constant.[6]

A brief remark must suffice to elucidate the intrinsically *symmetrical* character of the sequence. Again it was Fétis who first recognized this property, and, so far as I know, no other theorist has again investigated this attribute, one common to all sequences. All mathematical symmetry is the result either of translation, of reflection, of rotating a basic figure, or of a combination of two or three of these operations. A strict sequence may be represented simply by parallel or vectorial shifts of a musical configuration, e.g.,

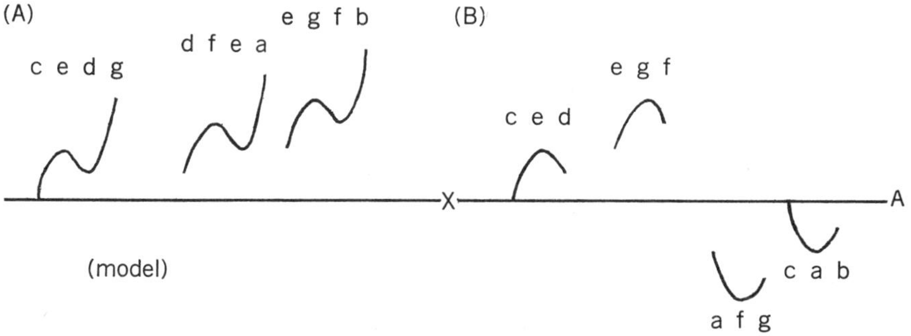

In (A) we have a simple translation, in (B) a translation plus reflection; the axis of symmetry is the line XA.

Most conspicuously, *double* translations in a real sequence are also interestingly symmetrical. I shall mention just one fine example: Mozart, Quartet in G major, K. 387, second movement (Menuetto) measures 13–17.

So long as only tonal or strictly chromatic sequences are used, their scalar quality remains clearly discernible. In nineteenth-century harmony the mediants assumed a far greater importance than ever before, with the result that now sequences, too, were built upon *any*

6. In the "mixed" sequences the intervallic variation occurring in the translations of the model may accumulate to a whole tone plus or minus. This maximum variation V satisfies the inequality $-1 \leq V \leq +1$. Varied sequences may be mathematically described by the introduction of weighted coordinates, whereby the number of measures per model-unit remains invariant.

interval-relation whatsoever—with often striking effects, as, for example, in Schubert's *Auf dem Flusse* to the words "ob's unter seiner Rinde wohl auch so reissend schwillt."

In the following pages we shall apply our categorization to a scrutiny of Bruckner's sequences.

II

Bruckner was already in his lifetime called a "Sequenzenreiter," and, if one disregards the pejorative connotation of the term, it must be admitted that the observation was correct. If we compare the number of sequences (reckoned per hundred measures) in the music of the eighteenth and nineteenth centuries with the percentage in Bruckner's music, we find only two other composers who used sequential patterns with similar gusto: Schumann and Wagner. It will be our task to examine the different and often variegated functions of Bruckner's sequences.

Simon Sechter was Bruckner's teacher and mentor for many years. In view of this, one might expect to find some emphasis on the sequence or a new conception of it in Sechter's theoretical writings. Yet a search there for any extensive remarks on the sequence will be in vain. In his usual dull and arid way, Sechter explains the sequence *modo ordinario*—i.e., he remains strictly in the tonal realm, disregarding chromatic-real patterns altogether. He condescends to supply one relevant footnote: "The chromatic progression by semitones is not fitting, if the composer aspires to decorum and dignity; it is suitable, however, if he wishes to express sorrow or humility."[7]

Nor will the study of Bruckner's own lectures on harmony prove more fruitful for our purpose. Two fully edited notebooks by his own students are at our disposal: C. Speiser's notes, critically edited by A. Orel, and E. Schwanzara's notebook, edited by himself. Except for the discussion of elementary chains of diatonic sequences, neither contains any explanations of, or any remarks on, the structural principles or the functions of sequences in free composition.[8] Nor

7. Simon Sechter, *Die Grundsätze der musikalischen Komposition* (Leipzig, 1854), III, 61. See also, in Vol. II, p. 240, the paragraph on Tonreihen.

8. Alfred Orel's *Ein Harmoniekolleg bei Bruckner* (Berlin-Vienna-Zurich, 1940), p. 6, contains the following calumny of his erstwhile teacher, the late Professor Guido Adler: "G. Adler, the Jewish lecturer, deliberately tried to cause Bruckner inconveniences . . ." That Adler championed Bruckner's work is a fact carefully suppressed by Orel.

may we expect to find that Bruckner was familiar with Fétis's treatises or with the profound studies of Moritz Hauptmann—at least his lectures do not indicate any such knowledge of contemporary theoretical writings. Thus there remains for us only a careful scrutiny and analysis of Bruckner's symphonic work, but for our purposes this is sufficient.

Even a cursory glance through his symphonies, beginning with the Fourth, yields a rather unexpected result: the ratio of the number of sequences to the number of measures per movement is fairly constant; it varies between 6 percent and 13 percent for the slow movements, and from 8 percent to 11 percent for the first and last Allegros. Upon second thought, this is perhaps not so astonishing in itself, in view of the fundamentally uniform structure of Bruckner's symphonies. Yet, if this regularity is a consequence of tectonic principles, another relation is independent of them: in twelve symphonic movements the numerical relation between strict (i.e., tonal or real) sequences and varied ones (mixed or free) remains also relatively constant. There are normally two and a half to three times as many strict sequences as there are mixed or free ones.[9] Such regularity must have causes deeper than uniformity of structure can produce. We must ask ourselves at what points Bruckner usually places his sequences; also, what direction they take and what function they assume.

In which way and through what means do Bruckner's expositions differ from those of the Viennese School as a whole? In order to answer this question fully, we should have to canvass all the major elements of the composer's symphonic style. Here we shall limit ourselves to the study of three characteristic form-elements of his expositions, and shall pursue our quest by examining the sequences pertaining to them:

(1) The tonality as it evolves in the exposition;

(2) The group of initial themes;

9. A fairly reliable statistical approximation yields the following equation:

$$\Sigma S \sim \frac{8S_s}{12} \pm \frac{1S_s}{12} + \frac{4S_v}{12} \mp \frac{1S_v}{12}$$

in which ΣS is the sum of all sequences, S_s the number of strict, and S_v the number of varied sequences.

(3) The technique of continuous development and thematic climax (*Fortspinnungs- und Steigerungstechnik*).

(1): The idea of the nascent theme, as first conceived in the opening movement of Beethoven's Ninth Symphony, impressed Bruckner profoundly, as we know from his conversations and still more from his works.[10] Out of an unordered mass of vague chords there emerges the tonality, in which the group of initial themes takes form. Examples of this *modus operandi* are frequent in Bruckner's symphonies; to mention only the most significant, we may refer to the opening passages of Symphonies II:1; IV:4; V:1; VIII:4; and IX:1. One might refer to these erratically preluding passages as "pre-tonal" or at least "pre-thematic" portions, patterned after the introduction of Beethoven's Ninth Symphony. In all five we encounter sequences; particularly impressive are the sequential "terraces" of the Finale of the Eighth Symphony, where the model itself encompasses sixteen measures, and the chain of sequences that dominates the opening of the Fifth Symphony. Although both passages are "pre-thematic," they are later integrated into the whole of the thematic development. Such initial sequences have two opposite functions: to conceal—or, at least, to delay—the entrance of the main tonality or theme; and conversely to establish, when they are connected with a pedal point, a safe anchorage of tonic or dominant.

(2): Sequences occur as intrinsic parts of first-theme groups, e.g., in IV:2; IV:3; V:1; V:2; VI:2; VI:3; VII:3; VIII:2; VIII:3; and IX:1. This is a relatively long list, and by no means an exhaustive one. Bruckner's practice here differs from that of classic style: in the thirty-seven movements of Beethoven's nine symphonies there are only ten opening themes that contain sequential passages; in the last nine symphonies of Mozart, with thirty-three movements, there are only seven initial themes with sequences; whereas among the last six symphonies of Bruckner (IV–IX), with twenty-three movements, there are ten sequential themes at the opening of movements. In percentages this means that 21.2 percent of Mozart's opening themes are sequential, 27 percent of Beethoven's, and 43.5 percent of

10. Hans Redlich, *Bruckner and Mahler* (London, 1955), pp. 52, 55 ff; August Halm, *Die Symphonie Bruckners* (2d ed.; Munich, 1923), pp. 58 ff; also Friedrich Blume in *Die Musik in Geschichte und Gegenwart*, II, cols. 371 and 372.

Bruckner's. Bruckner has more than twice as many sequential opening themes as Mozart and many more than Beethoven. Only first themes of movements have been considered. A cursory glance into the other thematic groups yields a still higher percentage for Bruckner in comparison with the Vienna classics. As an explanation of this fact, we cannot content ourselves solely with the emergence of an apparently "different style." It is true that Bruckner's invention was affected by Wagner's thematic structure on the one hand, and by the Austrian church-composers of the eighteenth and early nineteenth centuries on the other. Wagner uses sequential devices often in his themes and leading motifs. To mention only a few characteristic examples, these appear in *Tannhäuser* (Overture, Elisabeth's Prayer); in *Tristan* (the Love Duet and "Liebestod," the strange passage after the "traurige Weise," Act III, Tristan's entrance in Act I, Scene 5, and most dramatically in Act II, "Da Tristan mich verriet" and "Das Wunderreich der Nacht"); and in *Die Meistersinger* (the first theme of the Prelude, the Preislied, Beckmesser's Serenade and song at the contest). We emphasize again that these are examples of sequences in the first appearance of themes only, not in their continuation.[11] The Austrian church-composers, too, were rather fond of sequential themes, and we shall mention here only two examples, although the stream of sequential themes flows continuously from Adlgasser to Beethoven. The long chromatic sequence in Mozart's *Requiem Mass*, beginning with "Oro supplex et acclinis," has become famous; but no less impressive is the passage from the Credo of Beethoven's Mass in C: "Deum de Deo, lumen de lumine," etc. With all these works Bruckner was familiar as a matter of course. Thus, if we search for models of his sequential themes, the older Austrian church-music and Wagner's operas must be thought of *pari passu*.

(3): By far the most important function of Bruckner's sequences lies in the technique of continuous development (*Fortspinnungstechnik*). There the sequence performs services in connection with:

(a) expansion or delay of cadences;

11. The only comprehensive and at the same time definitive chapter on Wagner's sequence-technique is found in Ernst Kurth's admirable *Die Krise der romantischen Harmonik in Wagners 'Tristan'* (Berlin, 1920), Sec. 5, Ch. 2, pp. 302–334.

(b) harmonic crescendo and decrescendo (climax and anti-climax);

(c) modulation (loosening of tonality);

(d) the building of thematically coherent groups;

(e) the delimitation of sonata-sections (exposition, end of development section, end of recapitulation, coda, stretto, etc.);

(f) emphasis on individual motifs not previously highlighted.

We shall best understand Bruckner's technique of continuation if we compare it with the continuation techniques of Mozart, Beethoven, and Brahms. In Mozart's mature works the thematic *Fortspinnung* is achieved by varied repetition, or by secondary dominants, interspersed with brief sequential passages, deceptive cadences, and modulations, as, for example, in the first movement of the Quartet in D minor, K. 421. For the "middle" Beethoven, though rarely the "late" one, two devices are characteristic: the "developing variation" ("entwickelnde Variation"; the term was coined by Schoenberg)[12] and the principle of fragmentation or breaking up of thematic material into ever smaller units. Both kinds of continuation make ample use of short sequences, even at the statement of the principal themes: for example, in the "Waldstein" Sonata, first movement (shift from C to B-flat), the "Appassionata" (shift from F minor to G-flat), or the Quartet in F minor, Op. 95, first movement, measures 6 and 7 (shift from F minor to G-flat). For the developing variation and the secondary dominants there are innumerable instances in Beethoven's work, e.g., Sonata "Les Adieux," Op. 81a, first movement. In the *allegro* section of that movement we encounter sequences in the opening statement of the first theme and later on in the development. The Coda opens with a chain of sequences, based upon the dominants of the first and second steps of E-flat major. Yet neither in Mozart's nor in Beethoven's secular music has the sequence a clearly architectonic function: it delays the cadence, it links various thematic complexes, it helps in modulation, it serves as a means of continuation. Its function is further varied somewhat in Mozart's church music, where, owing to its archaizing trend, the sequence occurs more frequently than in his secular music, and where it occasionally serves an architectonic

12. Arnold Schoenberg, *Style and Idea* (New York, 1950), pp. 185 ff.

purpose, especially in closing off one part of a Mass from the next. Sequences are almost always on hand when especially solemn ideas are to be stressed.[13]

Brahms, while not avoiding sequences altogether, is much more circumspect in their use. In thirty major works of his, with more than one hundred and ten movements, only twenty-four primary themes contain actual sequences, although many more play around sequence-like transformations of a motif; and Brahms' *Fortspinnungs-technik* rests upon developing variation, secondary dominants, very subtle rhythmic shifts, and the device of interversion (a sort of permutation of the tones of a given motif: if it is first stated as a-b-c-d-e, it may reappear in the order b-a-e-d-c or in any other order of permutation). Such interversions are frequent in Brahms' larger works and occur sometimes together with sequences, as, for example, in the first movement of the Violin Concerto, measures 49–64.[14] With great care, however, Brahms avoids strict sequences in the subsequent solo. In his compositions generally, he often approaches permutative transformations of a melodic motif. An exception is the first movement of his Fourth Symphony, in which the first theme is a long-drawn-out sequence with extended variations. His late works show a distinct preference for tonal over real (chromatic) sequences, for example in the Clarinet Quintet. Perhaps his return to a more rigid treatment was a reaction against the misuse of the chromatic sequence by the radical followers of Wagner in the Neudeutsche Schule. Schoenberg criticized these composers, fashionable around the turn of the century, with the blunt words: "It was the Brahmsian school which at that time fought violently against the sequences of the Neudeutsche Schule. Their attitude was based upon the opposite viewpoint that unvaried repetition is cheap. And, in fact, to many composers sequences were a technique to make a short story long. . . ."[15]

13. E.g., in the Kyrie fugue, and at "libera eas de ore leonis," or "Ne absorbeat eas tartarus," or the shattering "Rex tremendae majestatis" of the *Requiem;* but also in many choral movements of Mozart's vespers and litanies.

14. On the rare occasions when Brahms makes use of sequences, as in the second theme of the first movement, he takes pains to disguise the strict pattern by changing the accompaniment here by means of a pizzicato motif in the lower strings; but this could perhaps be alternatively regarded as the variation of one component.

15. Schoenberg, *Style and Idea,* p. 188. In his compositions Schoenberg liked to conceal his sequences by varying one or two of their elements; Berg and Webern

III

It was for their bewitching dramatic power that Wagner's sequences first impressed Bruckner. His sequence technique started with Wagnerian patterns, but in his later works he left them far behind. In his earlier dramatic works. Wagner employed all sorts of sequences, but beginning with *Tristan* the mixed sequences came to prevail—that is, sequences that are neither tonal nor real and still do not vary any of the three components in earnest. We shall here attempt a definition of the mixed sequence without trying to circumscribe its functions precisely. A mixed sequence contains both diatonic and chromatic elements; the latter come into being through the sequential treatment of secondary steps, which momentarily assume the functions of tonics. To make clearer what this intricate device is, we shall juxtapose a model that is first treated by Mahler in a tonal manner, with its later treatment in a mixed manner.

EX. 6a. Extract from movt. 6 of *Symphony, No. 3*—Mahler.

EX. 6b. Extract from movt. 6 of *Symphony, No. 3*—Mahler.

In spite of the chromaticism in the middle parts, Example 6a, as already stated, is strict. It yields, in conventional analytical terms, the following:

occasionally preferred the simple, lapidary repetition of a motif to its sequential treatment. The "mathematized" style of ultramodern music, in which one might expect to find new ideas of sequential patterns, avoids them altogether (probably for fear of appearing trivial), thus eliminating an important element in musical coherence. This last-named principle, hitherto considered a necessary condition in musical esthetics, has been dropped entirely by the *avant-garde*.

1.	I ${}^{8}_{\natural 5}{}^{\natural 7}_{\sharp 5}$ II^{6} IV	II ${}^{\natural 5}_{\natural 3}{}^{\sharp 5}_{\sharp 3}$ III^{6} V	III ${}^{8}_{\natural 5}{}^{\natural 7}_{\sharp 5}$ IV^{6} VI	IV ${}^{\natural 7}_{\natural 5}{}^{-}_{\sharp 5}$ V${}^{6}_{\flat}$ ♮VII
	D G	E A	F♯ B	G C

In Example 6b, Mahler uses secondary steps in addition to chromaticism:

2.	I $^{-\sharp 5}$ II^{6} IV	II ${}^{\natural 5}_{\natural 3}{}^{\sharp 5}_{\sharp 3}$ III^{6} V$^{\sharp 5}$	III $\natural 5\ \sharp 5$ IV${}^{6}_{\flat}$ ♭VI	IV ${}^{\natural 7}_{\natural 5}{}^{-}_{\sharp 5}$ V${}^{6}_{\flat}$ ♮VII
			=F: II^{6} IV	=C: V ${}^{\natural 7}_{\natural 5}{}^{-}_{\sharp 5}$ VI^{6} I

This example has been chosen in order to show the essential deviation that occurs in the third measure of Example 6b, while elsewhere harmony, rhythm, and melodic contour remain unchanged. Similar examples may be found in Beethoven, Quartet Op. 127, Scherzo, first theme; Brahms, Violin Concerto, first movement, coda, solo-violin part; Mendelssohn, Quartet in F minor, Op. 80, Scherzo, main theme. In *Die Meistersinger*, some of the most famous passages grow out of mixed sequences, e.g., the entire development of the Flieder monologue of Hans Sachs, with the culmination at "Lenzes Gebot, die süsse Not,"[16] upon the (secondary) dominant of the second step of F major. Although Bruckner borrowed a great many of Wagner's sequential devices, he, at least in his last three symphonies, by far transcended them. Wherein and to what extent did Bruckner differ from his demigod, Wagner?

1) Wagner rarely varies the rhythm of his original model; Bruckner is considerably more free in this respect (for example, in the Sixth Symphony, the slow movement, before *Grave;* in the Eighth Symphony, the Trio of the Scherzo).

2) Sequences over pedal points do occur in Wagner's operas, but they never attain the structural function of closing large complexes, as they do in Bruckner's works, where the end of the exposition or the beginning of the coda is almost invariably initiated by a sequence on a pedal point. The great symphonic sequence that follows the chorale in *Die Meistersinger,* Act I, Scene 1, corresponds to Bruckner's patterns.

3) In the last three symphonies, Bruckner applies sequential

16. Cf. Guido Adler's penetrating remarks about Wagner's sequences, in his *Vorlesungen über Richard Wagner* (2d ed.; Munich, 1923), pp. 247 ff.

treatment to entire thematic blocks of considerable length; e.g., in the finale of the Eighth Symphony, where at the very opening secondary dominants and subdominants appear within the model theme. Here the "breathless" kind of Wagnerian sequence (as it occurs in the climactic passages of the Liebestod or at the end of Act I of *Die Meistersinger*) is abandoned in favor of broad sequential treatment of entire thematic complexes.

In all of symphonic work, few traits are more characteristic of their composer than these sequences of Bruckner's, particularly those over a pedal point. He was often criticized for this trait, it is true—but not fairly or intelligently, even by his own disciples.[17]

It is not difficult to ascertain the structural value of these massive devices. Whereas in general a sequence serves to suspend tonality for a short time, or to loosen its gravitational and cadential pull, especially in chromatic passages and modulations, Bruckner's sequences over a pedal point produce the opposite result: after a modulatory passage they set up a new tonality and, so to speak, provide it with anchorage. This is the reason for the pedal points at the end of an exposition or at the beginning of a coda. When a sequence over a pedal is coupled with augmentation or imitation, Bruckner aspires to the ideal of thematic integration.

Processes of rhythmic transformation such as augmentation, diminution, or other changes in time-value, were not frequently applied in symphonic or chamber music after the time of Bach. The great exception to this rule is found in Beethoven's last five quartets, which make use of all kinds of such transformations in contrapuntal style—for example, in the Fugue in the Quartet in C-sharp minor, where the sequential element is restricted to the melodic component of the first and second violins, whereas the other parts move in one great "developing variation." The sequences of the mature Bruckner move in much the same general manner. If we distinguish between the melodic, harmonic, and rhythmic components of a sequence—a somewhat mechanistic procedure, but it must suffice for the purpose of this paper—we find that Bruckner went far in varying the harmonic and melodic components. It was Mahler who extended the

17. Cf. Heinrich Schenker, *Musikalische Theorien und Phantasien,* I (Stuttgart and Berlin, 1906) 422 *n* 1: "It may be useful to observe even bad . . . pedal points such as those that occur like a *deus ex machina* in Bruckner's symphonies."

rhythmic frontiers to the borderline of free variation; a passage such as our Example 5b, in which the model motif is

subjected to varying intervals, harmonies, and rhythms, presages even greater complexity in variational sequences. Such sequences were developed by Berg and especially by Schoenberg. Operating from entirely different premises, Max Reger, too, shows similar structures of freely developing sequences, especially in his great works for the organ.

From these brief analytical remarks, we may draw certain historical conclusions. Bruckner combined elements of Austrian church music of the eighteenth and nineteenth centuries with the technique, but not with the function, of Wagner's sequences; to the resulting combination he added his own characteristic devices, such as sequences over a pedal point, sectional grouping, the presentation of entire thematic blocks in sequence, etc., and in the process he varied both the melodic and the harmonic components, especially in his mixed sequences. In these he used the idiom of the late Beethoven, and through it opened the way toward a loosening of tonality over wide passages, such as we find in Mahler's later works, in which all components of the sequence are subjected to alteration. Retrospective though Bruckner often appears—or, as was sometimes argued, even anachronistic—he emerges, at least in his sequential technique, as a most important link in the chain of symphonic composers from Haydn through Schubert, Beethoven, Wagner, Mahler, and Schoenberg. Thus Dika Newlin's statement that "in Bruckner [we find] the chief link between the Viennese classicists and their modern counterparts" is fully justified.[18] And Schoenberg's claim to rightful membership in this mainstream of tradition is legitimate and historically correct.

18. Dika Newlin, *Bruckner, Mahler, Schoenberg* (New York, 1947), p. 102.

25 / The Publications of Dragan Plamenac

THOR E. WOOD
The New York Public Library

EDITIONS OF MUSIC

OCKEGHEM, JOHANNES

Sämtliche Werke, Vol. 1 (Messen I–VIII). Leipzig: Breitkopf & Härtel (Deutsche Musikgesellschaft), 1927. 37, 125 pp. (Publikationen älterer Musik, Jg. 1, T. 2.)

Collected Works, Vol. 1 (Masses I–VIII). Second, corrected edition. New York: American Musicological Society (general agent: Galaxy Music Corporation), 1959. (American Musicological Society. Studies and Documents, No. 3.)

——— Vol. 2 (Masses and Mass Sections IX–XVI). New York: Columbia University Press (published for the American Musicological Society), 1947. 40, 116 pp. (American Musicological Society. Studies and Documents, No. 1.)

——— Vol. 2. Second, corrected edition. New York, 1966. 46, 116 pp.

LUKAČIĆ, IVAN

Odabrani moteti (duhovni koncerti) iz djela "Sacrae cantiones" (1620). Concerts spirituels choisis. Obradio i s historijsko-kritičkim uvodom izdao Dr. Dragan Plamenac. Zagreb: Izdanja Hrvatskog Glazbenog Zavoda, [c1935]. 16, 53 pp.

Eleven motets selected from Lukačić's *Sacrae cantiones.* pp. 3–12: Predgovor; pp. 13–14: Introduction; pp. 14–15: Zur Einführung (pp. 13–15 are summaries in French and German.)

Keyboard Music of the Middle Ages Era in Faenza, Biblioteca comunale, Codex 117. (American Institute of Musicology. Corpus mensurabilis musicae.) [in preparation.]

STUDIES AND ARTICLES

"O godišnjici smrti Césara Francka (9. novembra 1916.)," *Savremenik* (Zagreb), Vol. 11 (1916), pp. 330–33.

"Vatroslav Lisinski," *Književni Jug* (Zagreb), No. 4–5 (1919), pp. 129–45.
In Cyrillic print.

"Razvitak novih nastojanja u francuskoj muzici," *Savremenik,* Vol. [16], No. 4 (1921), pp. 228–31.
Footnote to title: "Uvodno slovo, izrečeno na klavirskoj večeri moderne francuske muzike dne 16. januara 1922."

"La chanson de L'homme armé et MS. VI. E. 40 de la Bibl. Nationale de Naples." Résumé published in *Annales de la Fédération archéologique et historique de Belgique, Congrès jubilaire.* Bruges, 1925, pp. 229–30.

"Johannes Ockeghem als Motetten- und Chansonkomponist." (Unpublished Ph.D. dissertation.) Wien, 1925.

"O starijoj muzici," *Savremenik,* Vol. 20, No. 11 (November 1927), pp. 465–72.
Note following title: "Slovo izrečeno na Radio-stanici u Zagrebu, oktobra 1927, kao uvod u dvije večeri stare klavirske muzike."

"Autour d'Ockeghem," *La Revue musicale* (Paris), Vol. 9, No. 4 (February 1928), pp. [26]–47.

"O stogodišnjici smrti Franza Schuberta, 1828–1928. Predavano 19. XI. 1928. u Hrvatskom Glazbenom Zavodu," *Hrvatska revija* (Zagreb), Vol. 2, No. 1 ([January] 1929), pp. [35]–44.

"Zur 'L'homme armé'–Frage," *Zeitschrift für Musikwissenschaft,* Vol. 11, No. 6 (March 1929), pp. 376–83.

"O tristogodišnjici tvorca francuske opere, Jean-Baptiste Lully (29.11. 1632–22.3.1687)," *Hrvatska revija,* Vol. 6, No. 1 ([January] 1933), pp. [42]–46.

"XII. festival Internacionalnog društva za savremenu muziku (S.I.M.C.) u Firenci (2–7 Aprila 1934)," *Zvuk* (Belgrade), Vol. 2, Nos. 7, 8 (May, June-July 1934), pp. 274–80, 355–60.

"En marge de Florence," *La Revue musicale,* No. 147 (June 1934), pp. 62–64.

"Nepoznat hrvatski muzičar ranoga baroka: Ivan Lukačić i njegovi moteti," *Obzor* (Zagreb),Vol. 75, No. 293 (1934).

"O hrvatskoj muzici u vrijeme renesanse," *Hrvatska revija,* Vol. 9, No. 3 (March 1936), pp. [145]–150.
Note on p. 150: "Uvodna riječ u koncert . . . održan u Hrv. Glazbenom Zavodu dne 19. XII. 1935."

"Uz napjeve Forkove zbirke," transcription of old Croatian folk-tunes and concluding editorial notes published as part of a study by Dr. Franjo Fancev, "Hrvatska dobrovol ja u popijevkama, zdravicama i napitnicama prošlih vjekova," *Zbornik za narodni život i običaje Južnih Slavena* (Yugoslav Academy of Sciences and Arts, Zagreb), Vol. 31, No. 1 (1937), pp. 90–98, 166–68.

"Toma Cecchini, kapelnik stolnih crkava u Splitu i Hvaru u prvoj polovini XVII stoljeća," *Rad Jugoslavenske Akademije Znanosti i Umjetnosti* (Zagreb), Vol. 262 (1938), pp. 77–125.

"Music of the 16th and 17th centuries in Dalmatia," *Papers Read at the International Congress of Musicology, Held at New York, September 11th to 16th, 1939.* New York: Music Educators' National Conference (published for the American Musicological Society), [c1944]. pp. 21–51. Also printed, in condensed form but with some additions, as "Music in the Adriatic coastal areas of the Southern Slavs" (q.v., 1954).

"An unknown violin tablature of the early 17th century," *Papers of the American Musicological Society, 1941* (1946), pp. 144–57.

"New light on the last years of Carl Philipp Emanuel Bach," *The Musical Quarterly,* Vol. 35, No. 4 (October 1949), pp. 565–87.

"A postscript to volume II of the *Collected Works* of Johannes Ockeghem," *Journal of the American Musicological Society,* Vol. 3, No. 1 (Spring 1950), pp. 33–40.

"Keyboard music of the 14th century in Codex Faenza 117," *Journal of the American Musicological Society,* Vol. 4, No. 3 (Fall 1951), pp. [179]–201.

"A reconstruction of the French chansonnier in the Biblioteca Colombina, Seville," *The Musical Quarterly,* Vol. 37, No. 4 (October 1951), pp. 501–42; Vol. 38, No. 1 (January 1952), pp. 85–117; Vol. 38, No. 2 (April 1952), pp. 245–77.
For Curt Sachs on his 70th birthday; read in part at the annual meeting of American Musicological Society, Washington, D. C., 1950.

"Deux pièces de la renaissance tirées de fonds florentins," *Revue belge de musicologie,* Vol. 6, No. 1 (January-March 1952), pp. 12–23.

"New light on Codex Faenza 117," [*International Musicological Society*] *Fifth Congress, Utrecht, 3–7 July 1952, Report.* Amsterdam: G. Alsbach, 1953, pp. 310–[326].

"An unknown composition by Dufay?" *The Musical Quarterly,* Vol. 40, No. 2 (April 1954), pp. 190–200.
Errata note published in Vol. 40, No. 3 (July 1954), p. 494.
Also published as "Une composition inconnue de Dufay?" *Revue belge de musicologie,* Vol. 8, No. 2–4 (1954), pp. 75–83; dedicated to Charles van den Borren on his 80th birthday.

"Music in the Adriatic coastal areas of the Southern Slavs," in Gustave Reese, *Music in the Renaissance.* New York: Norton, 1954; rev. ed. 1959, pp. 757–62.
This is a condensation, but with some additions, of the paper, "Music of the 16th and 17th centuries in Dalmatia."

"The 'second' chansonnier of the Biblioteca Riccardiana (Codex 2356)," *Annales musicologiques,* Vol. 2 (1954), pp. [105]–187.

"Another Paduan fragment of Trecento music," *Journal of the American Musicological Society,* Vol. 8, No. 3 (Fall 1955), pp. 165–81.

"A 'Second Copenhagen Chansonnier.'" Paper read at the Annual Meeting of the American Musicological Society, Urbana, Ill., December 28, 1956. Unpublished.

"A postscript to 'The "second" chansonnier of the Biblioteca Riccardiana'," *Annales musicologiques,* Vol. 4 (1956), pp. [261]–265.

"German polyphonic lieder of the 15th century in a little-known manuscript." Résumé published in [*International Musicological Society*] *Bericht über den siebenten Internationalen Musikwissenschaftlichen Kongress, Köln 1958.* Kassel: Bärenreiter, 1959, pp. 214–15.

"*Excerpta Colombiniana:* Items of musical interest in Fernando Colón's 'Regestrum,'" *Miscelánea en homenaje a Monseñor Higinio Anglés.* Barcelona: Consejo Superior de Investigaciones Científicas, 1958–1961. Vol. 2, pp. [663]–687.

"Browsing through a little-known manuscript (Prague, Strahov Monastery, D.G.IV.47)," *Journal of the American Musicological Society,* Vol. 13, No. 1–3 (1960), pp. 102–11.
Written in honor of Otto Kinkeldey's 80th birthday.

"Faenza, Codex 117," *Die Musik in Geschichte und Gegenwart,* Vol. 3, col. 1709–14.

"Lukačić, Ivan," *Die Musik in Geschichte und Gegenwart,* Vol. 8, col. 1296–97.

"Ockeghem, Johannes," *Die Musik in Geschichte und Gegenwart,* Vol. 9, col. 1825–38.

"Facsimile Reproduction of the Manuscripts Sevilla 5–I–43 & Paris N.A.Fr. 4379 (Pt. 1), with an Introduction." Brooklyn: Institute of Mediaeval Music [1962]. 99 pp. (Publications of Mediaeval Musical Manuscripts, No. 8.)

"Music libraries in Eastern Europe: a visit in the summer of 1961," *Music Library Association Notes,* 2nd series, Vol. 19, No. 2–4 (March, June, September 1962), pp. 217–34, 411–20, 584–98.

"A note on the rearrangement of Faenza Codex 117," *Journal of the American Musicological Society,* Vol. 17, No. 1 (Spring 1964), pp. [78]–81.

A further communication is in Vol. 17, No. 2 (Summer 1964), p. 233.

"Faventina," in Albert van der Linden, ed., *Liber Amicorum Charles van den Borren.* Anvers: Lloyd Anversois, 1964, pp. 145–64.
For van den Borren's 90th birthday.

"The two-part quodlibets in the Seville chansonnier," in Gustave Reese, ed., *The Commonwealth of Music.* New York: Free Press, [c.1965], pp. 163–[181].
Memorial volume in honor of Curt Sachs.

"The recently discovered complete copy of A. Antico's *Frottole Intabulate* (1517)," in Jan La Rue, ed., *Aspects of Medieval and Renaissance Music.* New York: Norton, 1966, pp. 683–703.
Volume in honor of Gustave Reese.

"Tragom Ivana Lukačića i nekih njegovih suvremenika," *Rad Jugoslavenske Akademije Znanosti i Umjetnosti* (Zagreb), Odjel za muzičku umjetnost, Knjiga II [in press].

REVIEWS

O. Fortunat Pintarić, Kompozicije za klavir (1927)—*Ferdo Livadić, Dva scherza* (1932), éditions critiques par Svetislav Stančić. *Revue de musicologie,* nouvelle série No. 47, Vol. 17 (August 1933), pp. 173–76.
A brief summary appeared as "Kompozicije za klavir Fortunata Pintarića i Ferda Livadića (Kritičko izdanje Svetislava Stančića)," *Zvuk* (Belgrade), Vol. 2, No. 3 (January 1934), pp. 119–20.

"O novom izdanju sabranih djela M. Musorgskoga." *Zvuk,* Vol. 2, No. 1 (November 1933), pp. 26–29.

La música en la corte de los Reyes Católicos, Vol. I, *Polifonia religiosa,* por Higinio Anglés. Consejo Superior de Investigaciones Científicas, Madrid, 1941. *The Musical Quarterly,* Vol. 34, No. 2 (April 1948), pp. 289–93.

Monumenta polyphoniae liturgicae Sanctae Ecclesiae Romanae, Series I, Tomus I, fasciculus IV–X, ed. R. D. Laurence Feininger, Rome, 1948. *Music Library Association Notes,* 2d series, Vol. 6, No. 3 (June 1949), pp. 484–85.

Francisco Correa de Arauxo, Libro de tientos y discursos de musica practica, y theorica de organo intitulado Facultad organica (1626), Vol. I, transcripción y estudio por Santiago Kastner. Monumentos de la música española, VI, Instituto Español de Musicología, Barcelona, 1948. *The Musical Quarterly,* Vol. 36, No. 2 (April 1950) pp. 311–14.

Documenta polyphoniae liturgicae S. Ecclesiae Romanae. Serie I, No. 3, G. Dufay: Et in terra "ad modum tubae." No. 4, G. Dufay: Missa de Sanctissima Trinitate. No. 5, G. Binchois: Missa de angelis. *Monumenta liturgiae polychoralis S. Ecclesiae Romanae.* Psalmodia cum sex choris. No. 1, Orazio Benevoli: Psalmus Dixit Dominus XXIV vocum. Rome, 1949–1950. *Music Library Association Notes,* 2d series, Vol. 7, No. 4 (September 1950), pp. 622–24.

Catalogue critique et descriptif des imprimés de la musique des XVIe et XVIIe siècles conservés à la Bibliothèque de l'Université Royale d'Upsala, Tome II and III, by Åke Davidsson, Upsala, 1951. *The Musical Quarterly,* Vol. 38, No. 2 (April 1952), pp. 327–33.

Bibliografia della musica strumentale italiana stampata in Italia fino al 1700 [by] Claudio Sartori, con prefazione di Alfred Einstein. Biblioteca di bibliografia italiana, XXIII, Firenze, 1952. *Music Library Association Notes,* 2d series, Vol. 10, No. 4 (September 1953), pp. 616–19.

Documenta polyphoniae liturgicae S. Ecclesiae Romanae. Serie I, No. 8, John Dunstable: Gloria e Credo. Jesu Christe Fili Dei vivi; No. 9, Leonel Power (?): Missa super Fuit homo missus; Serie IV, No. 1, Standley (?): Quae est ista; Serie I, No. 11, Johannes Franchoys (?): Gloria e Credo; Serie IB (a 6 voci), No. 1, Pierre de la Rue: Missa Ave Sanctissima; ed. Laurence Feininger, Rome, 1950–1952. *Music Library Association Notes,* 2d series, Vol. 10, No. 4 (September 1953), pp. 666–67.

Annales musicologiques: Moyen-âge et renaissance. Tome I. Publications de la Société de musique d'autrefois. Direction G. Thibault . . . , Paris, 1953. *Music Library Association Notes,* 2d series, Vol. 11, No. 2 (March 1954), pp. 301–03.

François Lesure, compiler: Anthologie de la chanson parisienne au XVIe siècle, réunie par François Lesure, avec la collaboration de N. Bridgman, I. Cazeaux, M. Levin, K. J. Levy, et D. P. Walker, Monaco, 1953. *Music Library Association Notes,* 2d series, Vol. 11, No. 3 (June 1954), pp. 431–33.

Catalogue critique et descriptif des imprimés de musique des XVIe et XVIIe siècles conservés dans les bibliothèques suédoises; Catalogue critique et descriptif des ouvrages théoriques sur la musique imprimés au XVIe et au XVIIe siècles et conservés dans les bibliothèques suédoises, by Åke Davidsson, Upsala, 1952, 1953. *The Musical Quarterly,* Vol. 41, No. 1 (January 1955), pp. 107–09.

Niederländische und italienische Musiker der Grazer Hofkapelle Karls II, 1564-1590. Bearbeitet von Hellmut Federhofer; Literarhistorische Bemerkungen und Textrevision von Robert John. *Denkmäler der Tonkunst in Oesterreich,* Bd. 90, Wien, 1954. *Music Library Association Notes,* 2d series, Vol. 13, No. 3 (June 1956), pp. 520–21.

Der Squarcialupi-Codex Pal. 87 der Biblioteca Laurenziana zu Florenz: Zwei- und dreistimmige italienische Lieder, Ballate, Madrigali und Cacce des vierzehnten Jahrhunderts, herausgegeben von Johannes Wolf, Lippstadt, 1955. *The Musical Quarterly,* Vol. 42, No. 4 (October 1956), pp. 539–43.

Walter Senn: Musik und Theater am Hof zu Innsbruck: Geschichte der Hofkapelle vom 15. Jahrhundert bis zu deren Auflösung im Jahre 1748, unter Verwertung von Vorarbeiten Lambert Streiters, Innsbruck, 1954. *Erasmus,* Vol. 11, No. 3–4 (February 1958), cols. 106–08.

Dizionario degli editori musicali italiani: Tipografi, incisori, librai-editori, di Claudio Sartori. Biblioteca di bibliografia italiana, XXXII, Firenze, 1958. *Music Library Association Notes,* 2d series, Vol. 16, No. 2 (March 1959), pp. 242–43.

Catalogo dei manoscritti musicali della Biblioteca nazionale di Firenze, [by] Bianca Becherini, Kassel, 1959. *Music Library Association Notes,* 2d series, Vol. 18, No. 3 (June 1961), pp. 423–24.

Capellae Sixtinae Codices: musicis notis instructi sive manu scripti sive praelo excussi, recensuit Josephus M. Llorens. Studi e Testi, 202, Città del Vaticano, 1960. *Music Library Association Notes,* 2d series, Vol. 19, No. 2 (March 1962), pp. 251–52.

Pierre Attaingnant: transcription of chansons for keyboard, ed. Albert Seay. Corpus mensurabilis musicae, 20, [Rome], 1961. *Music Library Association Notes,* 2d series, Vol. 21, No. 4 (Fall 1964), pp. 604–05.

MUSICAL COMPOSITIONS

Dvije stare dubrovačke pjesme za mješoviti zbor bez pratnje. Zagreb, 1915.

Trois poèmes de Ch. Baudelaire, chant et piano. Zagreb, 1915.

Pjesma od Kananskog veselja. (Song of the Feast at Cana, on a Yugoslav folk tune, for women's chorus & piano [or orchestra]), 1918. Reproduced from manuscript, New York, 1945.
Performed (including New York, 1945 and 1946) but not published.

All other compositions (for orchestra, chamber music, voice, and piano), some performed but not published, were destroyed during World War II.